Expression

JAMES CARNEY
& BRENDA COLLINS

Published by
Forum Publications Ltd.
Unit 2 Hillview Campus
Eurobusiness Park
Little Island, Cork

Tel: (021) 4232268
Fax: (01) 6335347
info@forum-publications.com
www.forum-publications.com

Edited by:
Brenda Collins, Brian Forristal and Billy Ramsell

Design and Layout:
Faye Keegan
www.fayekeegandesign.com

ISBN: 978-1-906565-23-7

Extract from 'The Gecko' by Dan Purdue, by kind permission of the author
Extract from The Man of the World' by Frank O'Connor by kind permission of Knopf
Extract from 'White Socks and Weirdos' by Sophie Hampton by kind permission of the author
Extract from *Gilead* by Marilynne Robinson appears by kind permission of Farrar, Strauss & Giroux
Extract from 'The Bankrupt Man' by John Updike appears by kind permission of Random House
Extract from *Super-Cannes* by J.G. Ballard appears by kind permission of Flamingo
Extract from *On the Road* by Jack Kerouac appears by kind permission of Penguin
Extract from 'Goodbye to All That' by Joan Didion appears by kind permission of Farrar, Strauss & Giroux
Extract from *Notes from a Big Country* by Bill Bryson appears by kind permission of Black Swan

Despite their very best efforts, in the case of some copyright material, the publishers
have not been able to contact the copyright holders, but will be glad to make the
appropriate arrangements with them as soon as they make contact.

FORUM PUBLICATIONS

Contents

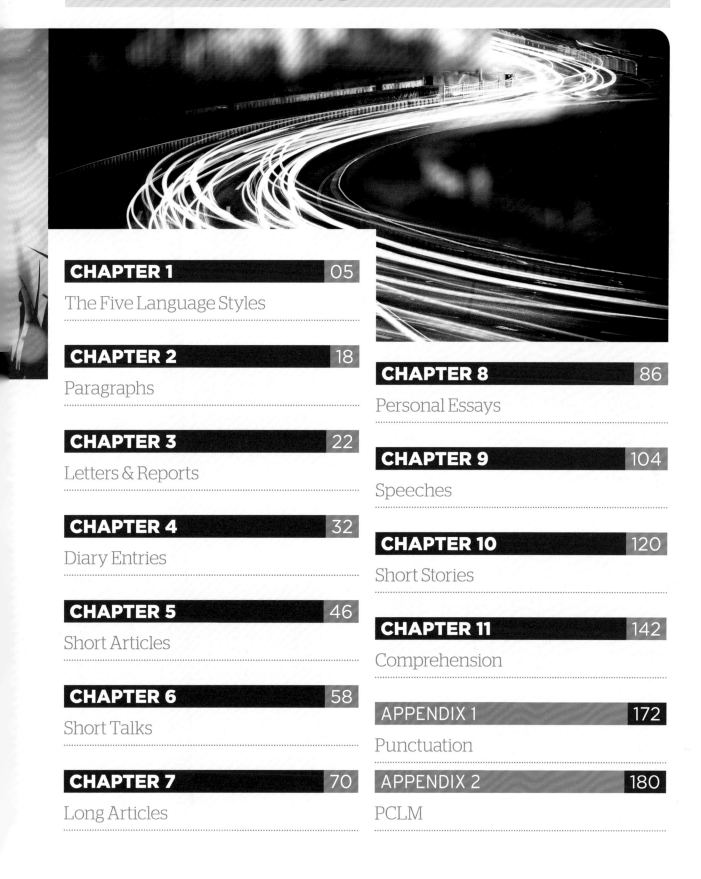

Chapter 1:
Language Styles

Introduction

THE LEAVING CERT FOCUSES ON FIVE DIFFERENT WAYS OF USING LANGUAGE. THESE ARE KNOWN AS THE FIVE LANGUAGE STYLES.

- The language of information, which we use to give information.

- The language of argument, which we use to make an argument.

- The language of persuasion, which we use to persuade people that a particular point of view is correct.

- The language of narration, which we use to tell a story.

- The aesthetic use of language, which involves using language in a way that is artistically pleasing.

Certain genres or types of writing are associated with certain language styles. For example, news reports tend to use the language of information a lot, while advertisements tend to use the language of persuasion.

It is important to note, however, that many pieces of writing use more than one language style. For example, a short story might use the language of narration and the aesthetic use of language. A magazine article might mix the language of persuasion and the language of argument.

The Language of Information

Not surprisingly, we use the language of information when we want to give the reader information. An informative piece of writing should focus on presenting the relevant information in a clear, concise and objective manner. A good piece of informative writing will emphasise the facts rather than the writer's own opinions.

≫ EXAMPLE 1

The following brief description of Venice taken from an encyclopaedia is a good example of informative writing.

Venice, Italian Venezia, city, major seaport, and capital of both the provincia (province) of Venezia and the regione (region) of Veneto, northern Italy. An island city, it was once the centre of a maritime republic. It was the greatest seaport in late medieval Europe and the continent's commercial and cultural link with Asia. Venice is unique environmentally, architecturally, and historically, and in its days as a republic the city was styled la serenissima ('the most serene' or 'sublime'). It remains a major Italian port in the northern Adriatic Sea and is one of the world's oldest tourist and cultural centres.

This paragraph satisfies all the basic criteria for a good piece of informative writing:

- **It is economical.** Despite the fact that there are many book-length guides to Venice, this short passage still manages to convey many important details about the city.
- **It is straightforward.** There is nothing in the piece that is likely to confuse the reader or leave them questioning what it means.
- **It is objective.** The writer does not tell us what he thinks personally about the city, nor does he recount his own personal experiences.

≫ EXAMPLE 2

The following description of the fashion industry is another good example of informative language:

The fashion industry is a multibillion-dollar global enterprise devoted to the business of making and selling clothes. Some observers distinguish between the fashion industry (which makes 'high fashion') and the apparel industry (which makes ordinary clothes or 'mass fashion'), but by the 1970s the boundaries between them had blurred. Fashion is best defined simply as the style or styles of clothing and accessories worn at any given time by groups of people. There may appear to be differences between the expensive designer fashions shown on the catwalks of Paris or New York and the mass-produced sportswear and street styles sold in malls and markets around the world. However, the fashion industry encompasses the design, manufacturing, distribution, marketing, retailing, advertising, and promotion of all types of apparel (men's, women's, and children's) from the most rarefied and expensive haute couture (literally, 'high sewing') and designer fashions to ordinary everyday clothing – from couture ball gowns to Juicy Couture-brand sweatpants. Sometimes the broader term 'fashion industries' is used to refer to myriad industries and services that employ millions of people internationally.

- **It's economical.** You could write volumes about the fashion industry, discussing who the influential designers were and what styles were popular at different times, but this extract focuses only on the essential facts and on clearly defining what the industry entails.
- **It is straightforward.** This piece does not delve into needlessly complex or non-essential information. Instead, it distils the most essential information into a single paragraph. When we have finished reading the piece we come away with a clearer understanding of what the fashion industry is about.
- **It is objective.** Many people have strong feelings about the fashion industry. Some love it while others loathe it. However, the writer of this piece does not give his personal take on the industry.

» EXAMPLE 3

Directions to The O2

Travelling to The O2 couldn't be easier. We are situated in the heart of Dublin's docklands which is well served by public transport. Bus, Rail and DART services all leave you within 20 minutes' walk of the venue and the Luas Red Line leaves you right at The O2's doorstep. It therefore makes sense to use public transport, ensuring you arrive on time and leaving you nothing else to do but enjoy your visit.

The Red Line operates from Tallaght station right into the city centre and all the way through to The O2, its last stop. There are extra trams on show nights to cater for the large numbers that use the service on their journey home.

Dublin Bus offers a high frequency, accessible and easy to use service from all over Dublin to within a 20-minute walk of the Venue. The 151 route operates every 10 minutes during rush hour and will leave you on Castleforbes Rd, the closest stop to the Venue, only two minutes' walk away. The last bus departs Castleforbes Road at 23.15pm Mon - Sat.

Again, this is a good example of informative language:

- **It is focused and relevant.** The writer just gives us information on how to get to and from The O2 arena.
- **It is clear and concise.** When we read the text we quickly understand the different options available to us should we wish to get to the venue. We do not have to navigate long, complicated sentences, nor do we have to wade through lengthy passages of irrelevant text to get the information that we need. We are simply told how, when and where to catch the buses and trams that serve The O2.
- **It is objective.** The writer just gives us the facts and does not tell us what he or she thinks about the quality of the venue or what he or she thinks about the latest act performing there, nor does he or she say what his or her preferred method of transport is.

The Language of Argument

The language of argument is used when a writer wants to convince us that some particular point of view is true. A good piece of argumentative writing will appeal to the reader's power of reasoning rather than to our feelings and emotions. It will attempt to make claims that anyone, regardless of their personal background or experience, will recognise as being true.

Consider this article from *The Economist*, which looks to convince us that it is the demand for oil and not the supply of oil that is set to decline.

» EXAMPLE 1

The Future of Oil: The world's thirst for oil could be nearing a peak. That is bad news for producers, excellent for everyone else.

The Economist

THE dawn of the oil age was fairly recent. Although the stuff was used to waterproof boats in the Middle East 6,000 years ago, extracting it in earnest began only in 1859 after an oil strike in Pennsylvania. The first barrels of crude fetched $18 (around $450 at today's prices). It was used to make kerosene, the main fuel for artificial lighting after overfishing led to a shortage of whale blubber. Other liquids produced in the refining process, too unstable or smoky for lamplight, were burned or dumped. But the unwanted petrol and diesel did not go to waste for long, thanks to the development of the internal-combustion engine a few years later.

Since then demand for oil has, with a couple of blips in the 1970s and 1980s, risen steadily alongside ever-increasing travel by car, plane and ship. Three-fifths of it ends up in fuel tanks. With billions of Chinese and Indians growing richer and itching to get behind the wheel of a car, the big oil companies, the International Energy Agency (IEA) and America's Energy Information Administration all predict that demand will keep on rising. One of the oil giants, Britain's BP, reckons it will grow from 89m b/d now to 104m b/d by 2030.

We believe that they are wrong, and that oil is close to a peak. This is not the 'peak oil' widely discussed several years ago, when several theorists, who have since gone strangely quiet, reckoned that supply would flatten and then fall. We believe that demand, not supply, could decline. In the rich world oil demand has already peaked: it has fallen since 2005. Even allowing for all those new drivers in Beijing and Delhi, two revolutions in technology will dampen the world's thirst for the black stuff. Not surprisingly, the oil 'supermajors' and the IEA disagree. They point out that most of the emerging world has a long way to go before it owns as many cars, or drives as many miles per head, as America.

But it would be foolish to extrapolate from the rich world's past to booming Asia's future. The sort of environmental policies that are reducing the thirst for fuel in Europe and America by imposing ever-tougher fuel-efficiency standards on vehicles are also being adopted in the emerging economies. China recently introduced its own set of fuel-economy measures. If, as a result of its determination to reduce its dependence on imported oil, the regime imposes policies designed to 'leapfrog' the country's transport system to hybrids, oil demand will come under even more pressure.

There are several reasons why this is a good piece of argumentative writing. The writer makes a point and then backs it up by reference to facts. He tries to convince us that he is right by arranging these facts into a logical, coherent argument. He avoids emotive language and 'real life' examples that tug on our heartstrings. The writer appeals to our reason, not to our hearts.

» EXAMPLE 2

The following article by Robert Lustig in *The Guardian* on the regulation of fructose used in processed foods is another example of good argumentative writing.

Fructose: the poison index

A ruling on fructose boosts the powerful sugar industry, either by incompetence or collusion, but is based on pseudoscience

The concept of glycaemic index is simple. This is how high your blood glucose rises after ingesting 50 grams of carbohydrate in any specific food, which is a measure of a food's generation of an insulin response, and is used as a way of showing a food's potential for weight gain. Glycaemic index is a proxy for how high your insulin level will rise, which determines whether that blood glucose will get shunted to fat cells for storage. Low-glycaemic-index diets promote blood sugar stability and are associated with weight loss. But the EFSA has missed the point. Glycaemic index is not the issue.

Glycaemic load is where it's at. This takes into account how much of a given food one must eat to obtain 50 grams of carbohydrate. The perfect example is carrots. Carrots have a high glycaemic index – if you consume 50 grams of carbohydrate in carrots, your blood sugar will rise pretty high. But you would have to eat 1.3lbs – 600 grams – of carrots to get 50 grams of carbohydrate. Highly unlikely. Any high-glycaemic-index food can become a low-glycaemic-load food if it's eaten with its inherent fibre. That means 'real food'. But fructose is made in a lab. It's anything but 'real'.

Yes, fructose has a low glycaemic index of 19, because it doesn't increase blood glucose. It's fructose, for goodness sake. It increases blood fructose, which is way worse. Fructose causes seven times as much cell damage as does glucose, because it binds to cellular proteins seven times faster; and it releases 100 times the number of oxygen radicals (such as hydrogen peroxide, which kills everything in sight). Indeed, a 20oz soda results in a serum fructose concentration of six micromolar, enough to do major arterial and pancreatic damage. Glycaemic index is a canard; and fructose makes it so. Because fructose's poisonous effects have nothing to do with glycaemic index; they are beyond glycaemic index.

The food industry is fond of referring to a 1999 study showing that liver fat generation from oral fructose occurs at a very low rate (less than 5%). And that's true, if you're thin, insulin sensitive, fasting (and therefore glycogen-depleted), and given just fructose alone (which is poorly absorbed). Conversely, if you're obese, insulin resistant, well fed, and getting both fructose and glucose together (like a sizable percentage of the population), then fructose gets converted to fat at a much higher rate, approximating 30%. In other words, the toxicity of fructose depends on context.

The industry points to meta-analyses of controlled isocaloric 'fructose for glucose' exchange studies that demonstrate no effect from fructose on weight gain or other morbidities. Perhaps one reason for this is because crystalline fructose is incompletely absorbed. When that happens, residual fructose in the gastrointestinal system causes pain, bloating, and diarrhoea: ask any child the morning after Halloween in between trips to the bathroom relieving his diarrhoea. Furthermore, those meta-analyses where fructose was supplied in excess do show weight gain, high levels of lipids in the blood, and insulin resistance. The dose determines the poison.

The EFSA has boosted the position of the sugar industry, either through incompetence or collusion. But it is clear that this recommendation is scientifically bogus. Nutritional policy should be based on science – not pseudoscience, as we have seen over the past 30 years.

Again, this is a good example of argumentative language. The writer uses facts to back up his claims, citing reports and experts throughout the article. He does not resort to emotive language, nor does he let his own personal feelings cloud his judgement. Instead, he builds his argument around objective fact, looking to sway the reader with reason rather than emotion.

The Language of Persuasion

We use the language of persuasion when we want to persuade someone that a certain point of view is correct. In this regard it is somewhat similar to the language of argument. However, there is one important difference. Whereas the language of argument appeals to a person's reason, the language of persuasion appeals to his or her emotions. In this regard, it is important to realise that the language of persuasion is a lot 'dirtier' than the language of argument. Unlike logical argumentation, where an argument will stand or fall on its merits, the language of persuasion will often appeal to personal prejudices and beliefs that have no real bearing on the truth of the claims being made.

» EXAMPLE 1

Stop Making Superhero Movies

Charlie Brooker, *The Guardian*

Kick-Ass, that was a good one. *Iron Man*, fair enough. But now we don't need any more superhero films. Especially not pretentious ones. There's a new Dark Knight film out this year. Calling Batman 'the Dark Knight' is like calling Papa Smurf 'the Blue Patriarch': you're not fooling anyone. It's a children's story about a billionaire who dresses up as a bat to punch criminals on the nose. No normal adult can possibly relate to that, which makes his story inherently boring, unless you're a child, in which case you can enjoy the bits where he rides his super-bike around with his cape flapping behind him like a prat. The scenes where some improbable clown-like supervillain delivers a quasi-philosophical speech are even worse, incidentally.

This piece is a good example of persuasive writing. The writer appeals to our hearts rather than our heads, telling us that 'No normal adult can possibly relate to that' and that you would have to be a 'child' to enjoy certain aspects of the movie under discussion. The extract is full of the writer's own opinions and feelings about the movies and short on objective facts. In place of logic and carefully reasoned argument the author uses wit and humour to convince us that recent 'superhero' movies are juvenile and ridiculous.

» EXAMPLE 2

The following is an extract from an article looking to persuade us that an artist's personal life ought to have no bearing on how we perceive his or her work.

The idea of 'ethical art' is nonsense.

We have to separate art from life

Rachel Cooke, *The Observer*

We have to give it up, this weird inability of ours to separate art and life. It makes fools of us. People were after Ted Hughes for years – the old misogynist, the monster, the wife killer – and then, in 1998, he published *Birthday Letters* and they had to eat their words. All that love and pain and regret. 'Drawing calmed you,' he wrote, and suddenly they had it from his side. But it also robs us, if we give in to it, of so much that is good and beautiful. When Andrew Motion published his biography of Philip Larkin in 1993, and we learned of his casual racism, and the way he behaved with women, they all lined up to have a go at him: Lisa Jardine, Tom Paulin, Alan Bennett. Jardine said, somewhat gleefully: 'We don't tend to teach Larkin much now in my department of English. The Little Englandism he celebrates sits uneasily within our revised curriculum.' I remember feeling enraged by this. For one thing, Larkin doesn't celebrate anything terribly much – he's not that kind of poet (and when he does, it's mostly love). For another, I could not get over the idea that someone would deny their students the pleasure of discovering Larkin's poetry – so clear, so plangent, so intensely beautiful – because they didn't agree with his politics. It felt criminal to me.

- You will notice how the style of the piece is a little more forceful than that of the argumentative pieces in the previous section. The piece begins with an aggressive call for us to 'give it up' before specifying what it is we ought to cease doing.

- The writer does not always make claims that can be supported with objective facts. She generalises, suggesting that there is a collective inability to separate art and life, saying that it is a 'weird inability of ours' and that it 'makes fools of us'. This is a clever device, as it immediately involves and implicates us in the issue at hand.

- The writer also includes her own personal feelings in the piece, telling us that she felt 'enraged', that she 'could not get over the idea' and that it 'felt criminal to me'. Such emotive language would be out of place in a more formal piece of argumentative writing, but works effectively here to persuade us that the author is correct in her point of view.

The Language of Narration

We use the language of narration when we want to tell a story. Remember a story can also be referred to as a narrative.

» EXAMPLE 1

This extract from John Steinbeck's *The Pearl* is a good example of fictional narrative writing:

The sun was warming the brush house, breaking through its crevices in long streaks. And one of the streaks fell on the hanging box where Coyotito lay, and on the ropes that held it.

It was a tiny movement that drew their eyes to the hanging box. Kino and Juana froze in their positions. Down the rope that hung the baby's box from the roof support a scorpion moved slowly. His stinging tail was straight out behind him, but he could whip it up in a flash of time.

Kino's breath whistled in his nostrils and he opened his mouth to stop it. And then the startled look was gone from him and the rigidity from his body. In his mind a new song had come, the Song of Evil, the music of the enemy, of any foe of the family, a savage, secret, dangerous melody, and, underneath, the Song of the Family cried plaintively.

The scorpion moved delicately down the rope toward the box. Under her breath Juana repeated an ancient magic to guard against such evil, and on top of that she muttered a Hail Mary between clenched teeth. But Kino was in motion. His body glided quietly across the room, noiselessly and smoothly. His hands were in front of him, palms down, and his eyes were on the scorpion. Beneath it in the hanging box Coyotito laughed and reached up his hand towards it. It sensed danger when Kino was almost within reach of it. It stopped, and its tail rose up over its back in little jerks and the curved thorn on the tail's end glistened.

Kino stood perfectly still. He could hear Juana whispering the old magic again, and he could hear the evil music of the enemy. He could not move until the scorpion moved, and it felt for the source of the death that was coming to it. Kino's hand went forward very slowly, very smoothly. The thorned tail jerked upright. And at that moment the laughing Coyotito shook the rope and the scorpion fell.

Kino's hand leaped to catch it, but it fell past his fingers, fell on the baby's shoulder, landed and struck. Then, snarling, Kino had it, had it in his fingers, rubbing it to a paste in his hands. He threw it down and beat it into the earth floor with his fist, and Coyotito screamed with pain in his box. But Kino beat and stamped the enemy until it was only a fragment and a moist place in the dirt. His teeth were bared and fury flared in his eyes and the Song of the Enemy roared in his ears.

But Juana had the baby in her arms now. She found the puncture with redness starting from it already. She put her lips down over the puncture and sucked hard and spat and sucked again while Coyotito screamed.

» EXAMPLE 2

The following extract from the *Memoirs of Sherlock Holmes* by Sir Arthur Conan Doyle provides us with another fine example of narrative writing:

Again and much louder came the rat-tat-tat. We all gazed expectantly at the closed door. Glancing at Holmes, I saw his face turn rigid, and he leaned forward in intense excitement. Then suddenly came a low guggling, gargling sound, and a brisk drumming upon woodwork. Holmes sprang frantically across the room and pushed at the door. It was fastened on the inner side. Following his example, we threw ourselves upon it with all our weight. One hinge snapped, then the other, and down came the door with a crash. Rushing over it, we found ourselves in the inner room. It was empty.

But it was only for a moment that we were at fault. At one corner, the corner nearest the room which we had left, there was a second door. Holmes sprang to it and pulled it open. A coat and waistcoat were lying on the floor, and from a hook behind the door, with his own braces round his neck, was hanging the managing director of the Franco-Midland Hardware Company. His knees were drawn up, his head hung at a dreadful angle to his body, and the clatter of his heels against the door made the noise which had broken in upon our conversation. In an instant I had caught him round the waist, and held him up while Holmes and Pycroft untied the elastic bands which had disappeared between the livid creases of skin. Then we carried him into the other room, where he lay with a clay-colored face, puffing his purple lips in and out with every breath – a dreadful wreck of all that he had been but five minutes before.

» EXAMPLE 3

It is important to note that the language of information is also used when describing events that actually happened. The following extract is from a report filed by the BBC journalist John Simpson shortly after the convoy of US Special Forces and Kurdish fighters with whom he was travelling came under attack from an American warplane.

The officer in charge of the American Special Forces saw an Iraqi tank in the plain about a mile away from us, and it was I think firing in our direction – and he called in an air strike to deal with the tank.

I saw two F15 American planes circling quite low overhead and I had a bad feeling about it, because they seemed to be closer to us than they were to the tank.

As I was looking at them - this must sound extraordinary but I assure you it is true – I saw the bomb coming out of one of the planes, and I saw it as it came down beside me.

It was painted white and red. It crashed into the ground about 10 or 12 metres from where I was standing.

It took the lower legs off Kamaran, our translator, I got shrapnel in parts of my body. I would have got a chunk of shrapnel in my spine had I not been wearing a flak jacket, and it was buried deep in the Kevlar when I checked it.

Our producer had a piece of shrapnel an inch long taken out of his foot. But apart from that and ruptured eardrums which is painful but not serious, and a few punctures from shrapnel, the rest of us were all right.

But our translator was killed and he was a fine man.

I think what probably happened was that there was a burned out Iraqi tank at the crossroads and I suspect that either the pilots got the navigational details wrong, which is possible, but I think it is probably more likely one of them saw the burned out Iraqi tank, assumed that was what was to be hit – and dropped the bomb.

The planes circled round I shouted out at the American Special Forces 'Tell them to go away – tell them it's us – don't let them drop another bomb.'

These are well-written pieces of narrative writing, but it is important to remember that the language of narration does not just feature in novels, short stories and history books. We use it all the time in everyday life: when we tell jokes, share a piece of gossip or describe a night out to a friend.

The Aesthetic Use of Language

We can also use language in a way that is creative and original. We can attempt to bring out the strangeness and beauty of words, and create something that is artistically pleasing. This is known as the aesthetic use of language. We often associate the aesthetic use of language with short stories, but it can also occur in non-fiction writing. The following are just a few of the ways in which language can be used aesthetically.

RHYTHM

Sometimes writing can create an artistically pleasing effect through the rhythm of its words. This is evident at the beginning of Dylan Thomas's *Under Milk Wood* where the author describes a small Welsh town at night. The repetitive, rolling rhythm produces an almost hypnotic effect upon the reader:

> It is spring, moonless night in the small town, starless and bible-black, the cobblestreets silent and the hunched, courters'-and-rabbits' wood limping invisible down to the sloeblack, slow, black, crowblack, fishingboatbobbing sea. The houses are blind as moles (though moles see fine to-night in the snouting, velvet dingles) or blind as Captain Cat there in the muffled middle by the pump and the town clock, the shops in mourning, the Welfare Hall in widows' weeds. And all the people of the lulled and dumbfound town are sleeping now.

A similar effect is created in the opening page of Laurence Durrell's *The Black Book*:

> The slither of rain along the roof. It bubbles in along the chinks of the windows. It boils among the rock pools. Today, at dawn (for we could not sleep because of the thunder), the girl put on the gramophone in the gloom, and the competition of Bach strings, resinous and cordial as only gut and wood can be, climbed out along the murky panes. While the sea pushed up its shafts and coils under the house, we lay there in bed, dark as any dungeon, and mourned the loss of the Mediterranean. Lost, all lost; the fruiting of green figs, apricots. Lost the grapes, black, yellow, and dusky. Even the ones like pale nipples, delicately freckled and melodious, are forgotten in this morning, where our one reality is the Levantine wind, musty with the smell of Arabia, stirring the bay into a muddy bath. This is the winter of our discontent.

Non-fiction works can also use rhythm to produce an artistically pleasing effect. We see this in the following passage taken from Elie Wiesel's *Night*, a work based on his experiences as a prisoner in concentration camps during the Second World War. The repetition of the phrase 'Never shall I forget' lends the piece a harsh, monotonous rhythm appropriate to the horrific experiences being described:

> Never shall I forget that night, the first night in camp, that has turned / my life into one long night, seven times cursed and seven times sealed. / Never shall I forget that smoke. / Never shall I forget the little faces of the children, whose bodies / I saw turned into wreaths of smoke beneath a silent blue sky. / Never shall I forget those flames which consumed my faith forever. Never shall I forget that nocturnal silence which deprived me, / for all eternity, of the desire to live. / Never shall I forget those moments which murdered my God / and my soul and turned my dreams to dust. / Never shall I forget these things, even if I am condemned / to live as long as God Himself. / Never.

DESCRIPTIVE WRITING

Writers can also create a pleasing aesthetic effect by describing something in a fresh, vivid and original way.

The opening paragraphs of Charles Dickens' *Dombey and Son* provide us with a fine example of descriptive writing:

> Dombey sat in the corner of the darkened room in the great arm-chair by the bedside, and Son lay tucked up warm in a little basket bedstead, carefully disposed on a low settee immediately in front of the fire and close to it, as if his constitution were analogous to that of a muffin, and it was essential to toast him brown while he was very new.
>
> Dombey was about eight-and-forty years of age. Son about eight-and-forty minutes. Dombey was rather bald, rather red, and though a handsome well-made man, too stern and pompous in appearance to be prepossessing. Son was very bald, and very red, and though (of course) an undeniably fine infant, somewhat crushed and spotty in his general effect, as yet. On the brow of Dombey, Time and his brother Care had set some marks, as on a tree that was to come down in good time – remorseless twins they are for striding through their human forests, notching as they go – while the countenance of Son was crossed with a thousand little creases, which the same deceitful Time would take delight in smoothing out and wearing away with the flat part of his scythe, as a preparation of the surface for his deeper operations.

There are many wonderful descriptive passages to be found in F. Scott Fitzgerald's *The Great Gatsby*.

Here the narrator describes the area in which he has just rented a house:

> It was a matter of chance that I should have rented a house in one of the strangest communities in North America. It was on that slender riotous island which extends itself due east of New York — and where there are, among other natural curiosities, two unusual formations of land. Twenty miles from the city a pair of enormous eggs, identical in contour and separated only by a courtesy bay, jut out into the most domesticated body of salt water in the Western hemisphere, the great wet barnyard of Long Island Sound. They are not perfect ovals — like the egg in the Columbus story, they are both crushed flat at the contact end — but their physical resemblance must be a source of perpetual confusion to the gulls that fly overhead. To the wingless a more arresting phenomenon is their dissimilarity in every particular except shape and size.

METAPHOR AND SIMILE

An aesthetically pleasing effect can also be created through the inventive use of metaphor and simile. The use of a good metaphor or simile can bring something vividly to life in the mind of the reader:

In *London Fields*, for example, Martin Amis compares the plumes of cigarette smoke in a snooker club to the ghosts of referees.

In *The Big Sleep*, Raymond Chandler describes a balding man as follows:

> 'A few locks of dry white hair clung to his scalp, like wild flowers fighting for life on a bare rock'.

In *The Handmaid's Tale*, Margaret Atwood uses a memorable simile to describe the ravages of time:

> 'Time has not stood still. It has washed over me, washed me away, as if I'm nothing more than a woman of sand, left by a careless child too near the water.'

Sir Arthur Conan Doyle uses the following simile to describe the awkward appearance of a lady in *The Adventure of the Three Gables*:

> 'She entered with ungainly struggle like some huge awkward chicken, torn, squawking, out of its coop.'

The following simile is taken from Vladimir Nabokov's *Lolita*:

> 'Elderly American ladies leaning on their canes listed toward me like towers of Pisa.'

Language Style Exercises:

1. Read the following how-to excerpt and comment on why you think it is (or isn't) an effective use of the language of information:

Using iTunes, you can add music to your iTunes library from your audio CD collection in a few easy steps.

- Open iTunes and insert an audio CD into your computer's CD or DVD drive.

- If your computer is connected to the Internet, iTunes will automatically look up information for the CD such as song name, album and artist. This feature will work with most commercially produced audio CDs.

- A dialog appears asking if you would like to import the CD. To import all songs from the CD into your iTunes library, simply click Yes. If you don't want to import all songs from the CD, click No, uncheck the checkbox next to the songs you don't want to import, and then click the 'Import CD' button in the lower-right corner of the iTunes window.

- iTunes will show the progress of the import for each song selected.

2. Below is an excerpt from an article that appeared in *The Independent* newspaper in the UK. It is written by journalist and author Robert Fisk and describes Fisk's own perilous experiences as a war correspondent. What style or styles of language does Fisk employ in this extract? Do you think it's effective? Explain your answer.

In Beirut in the late 1980s, when journalists were being abducted almost by the week, I adopted the Fisk method of staying free. Drive fast. And never, ever let them grab you. The one time they tried – a beaten up old car in Madame Curie Street, guns waved from the window – I was by immense good fortune recalling an interview I'd conducted that very morning with a Lebanese man who had been kidnapped. That was the moment their car tried to drive me off the road. So I pretended to slow down, then accelerated past them, crashed the front of their car and sped off through the streets. It took me several minutes before I realised they didn't know the area as well as I did. But I was sure I had been wounded. There was a film of moisture all over me. It was my own perspiration.

3. How would you describe the language and writing style used in the following extract from Barbara Kingsolver's novel *The Poisonwood Bible*?

The trees are columns of slick, brindled bark like muscular animals overgrown beyond all reason. Every space is filled with life: delicate, poisonous frogs war-painted like skeletons, clutched in copulation, secreting their precious eggs onto dripping leaves. Vines strangling their own kin in the everlasting wrestle for sunlight. The breathing of monkeys. A glide of snake belly on branch. A single-file army of ants biting a mammoth tree into uniform grains and hauling it down to the dark for their ravenous queen. And, in reply, a choir of seedlings arching their necks out of rotted tree stumps, sucking life out of death. This forest eats itself and lives forever.

4. In your opinion, is this piece from a Scientific American article on climate change a successful piece of argumentative writing? Explain your answer.

This year also brought some milestones. Arctic sea-ice cover retreated to a record low in September. As with unusually warming temperatures, the record sea-ice retreat did not come out of the blue. In recent years, the sea-ice cover has fallen below the average extent for 1979 to 2000, and, likewise, the first decade of this century was the warmest decade ever recorded in all continents of the globe, according to the World Meteorological Organization. Scientists who study sea ice have blamed a combination of natural fluctuations and human-caused warming for the increased loss of ice, although some differ as to how much humans have contributed, Claire Parkinson, a senior scientist who studies climate at NASA's Goddard Space Flight Center, said in September.

5. Would you agree that the following paragraph – take from an article *The Daily Mail* – represents a good piece of persuasive writing? Give reasons for your answer.

A keen British bird watcher has been trampled to death by an elephant in an Indian forest he has been visiting for years. Colin Manvell, 68, from Havant, Hampshire, suffered fatal injuries when the large elephant knocked him to the ground with its trunk and then stomped on him in the Masinagudi forest in Tamil Nadu, southern India. Bleeding profusely from his severe injuries, Mr Manvell was rushed to a local hospital – but there was no doctor on duty to treat him. His desperate helpers then had to drive him to a medical facility in Cuddalore city, more than 14 miles away, but he died on the way.

6. Would you agree that the following paragraph satisfies all the basic criteria for a good piece of informative writing? Give three reasons for your answer.

The Moon is Earth's only natural satellite. The average centre-to-centre distance from the Earth to the Moon is 384,403 kilometres (km) – about 30 times the diameter of the Earth. The Moon's diameter is 3,474 km, a little more than a quarter that of the Earth. This means that the Moon's volume is about two per cent that of Earth and the pull of gravity at its surface about 17 per cent that of the Earth. The Moon makes a complete orbit around the Earth every 27.3 days.

7. Read the following extract from James Joyce's short story 'The Dead'. Explain why this is a good example of aesthetic language.

A few light taps upon the pane made him turn to the window. It had begun to snow again. He watched sleepily the flakes, silver and dark, falling obliquely against the lamplight. The time had come for him to set out on his journey westward. Yes, the newspapers were right: snow was general all over Ireland. It was falling on every part of the dark central plain, on the treeless hills, falling softly upon the Bog of Allen and, farther westward, softly falling into the dark mutinous Shannon waves. It was falling, too, upon every part of the lonely churchyard on the hill where Michael Furey lay buried. It lay thickly drifted on the crooked crosses and headstones, on the spears of the little gate, on the barren thorns. His soul swooned slowly as he heard the snow falling faintly through the universe and faintly falling, like the descent of their last end, upon all the living and the dead.

8. Below is an extract from an *Empire Magazine* review of the 2012 movie, *Avengers Assembles*. In your opinion, what makes this a persuasive piece of writing?

Whedon has taken the various threads of the Marvel universe and weaved an impressive tapestry filled with action, humour, charm and heart. There was always the danger that this could become The Tony Stark Hour, but Whedon is canny enough to realise that he's got a well-balanced cast, and everyone shoulders their respective portion of the storyline with ease. It's not really surprising coming from the man who handled a large, charismatic set of characters in the undervalued movie *Serenity*, and it's even more satisfying to see him pull off the same trick twice. Chris Evans' Captain America is the conflicted hero, adrift in a world he doesn't quite truly comprehend. Chris Hemsworth's Thor is still full of his Asgardian swagger, but even he manages to find a way to fit in with everyone else when truly called upon, while working out more of his sibling issues. Mark Ruffalo is a superb Bruce Banner, bringing a subtlety and sweetness to the role that counterpoints well with the rage-fuelled big, green roaring machine. And, of course, there is ol' Shellhead. Robert Downey Jr's trademark dry wit and easy magnetism is on full display, and there's a real joy to Stark's comic undercutting of the more OTT elements. The leads are handed some cracking interplay, bolstered by set-pieces that combine both the comedy and the drama.

9. Read the following extract from an opinion piece from Harvard University's student newspaper, *The Crimson*, and comment on what you think is effective or not effective about it.

Internet generation, we need to talk. This National Security Agency problem is your problem. These recent NSA leaks are your leaks. Think about it. Who uses digital communications the most? Who visits the most websites? Who texts the most, chats the most, and tweets the most? It's not your parents, and it's definitely not your grandparents. No, the answer is inarguably you. You do those things; you rely on them; you live through them. You are the internet community; sorry older folks, but you're just the guests (though you shouldn't put up with this either). So for God's sake my fellow Millennials, wake up! You've grown up with the internet, developed alongside it, and stored a significant amount of your lives on it. And now you know that they, the NSA, are collecting your stuff, your information – not rightfully theirs, but rightfully yours. If any generation should be most offended and threatened by this massive privacy breach, it should thus be your own.

10. The paragraph below is an extract from an article by Edward McClelland that featured in the current affairs website Salon.com. Do you think it satisfies the criteria for an effective piece of persuasive and argumentative writing? Give reasons for your answer.

Not long ago, I was in Flint, Michigan, to meet with its new congressman, Dan Kildee. No American city has suffered more during the Age of Deregulation than Flint. In 1978, Flint had 80,000 automaking jobs, and the highest per capita income in the nation. Today, it has 6,000 automaking jobs, and the highest murder rate in the English-speaking world. Instead of Corvettes and speedboats, the yards are filled with mean dogs, 'This Property Protected by Smith & Wesson' signs, and weeds. So far, Kildee's biggest achievement has been securing federal funding to tear down 2,000 abandoned houses. In Flint, where the average home sale price is $15,000, eliminating blight increases property values. Having seen the consequences of government indifference, Kildee wants to return to the days of government activism. As county treasurer, he founded a public land bank that helped revive downtown Flint by purchasing and renovating a hotel that had sat empty since 1973.

Chapter 2:
Paragraphs

What is a paragraph?

A PARAGRAPH IS A COLLECTION OF
SENTENCES THAT RELATE
TO THE SAME IDEA.

- The subject or topic of a paragraph is often stated in
  the first sentence, which is called a 'topic' sentence.

- The remaining sentences develop this idea and are
  known as 'body' sentences.

- The paragraph is unified, with all the sentences
  contributing to create a single idea.

- A paragraph is complete when the idea the writer
  wants to express is brought clearly into focus.

When you write for the Leaving Cert it is vital that you
use paragraphs correctly.

Topic sentences and body sentences

The sentence containing a paragraph's central idea is known as its topic sentence.

In order to come up with an effective topic sentence, you must be clear in your own mind about what you want your paragraph to convey. Here are examples of effective topic sentences:

- Too many film-makers are sacrificing plot and characters – the cornerstones of a good story – in favour of high-octane action and slick special effects.
- We must believe ourselves to be invincible to say that we inhale poisonous smoke into our lungs or turn the ignition in the car when our heads are swimming with drink.
- As a nation, we lead highly sedentary lives and the long-term effects are fast becoming clear.

The topic sentence should usually be the first sentence in your paragraph. The remainder of a paragraph consists of what are known as 'body' sentences. These serve the topic sentence by supporting or developing the idea it expresses. The following paragraphs are good examples of how this works:

» EXAMPLE 1

While many might count Gandhi or Mandela among their heroes, it is the fluffy-haired physicist, Albert Einstein, whom I count among mine. Einstein's pioneering work changed the course of scientific research and has had a massive impact on humanity. And if this weren't enough, he was also an incredibly compassionate and moral person. He was a staunch defender of human rights and contributed greatly to the civil rights movement in the US at a time of heightened racial tension. He advocated for co-operative and peaceful solutions to conflict in Israel and Palestine as well as warning governments of the dangers of developing nuclear weapons using his E=mc2 research.

» EXAMPLE 2

Few things are capable of affecting us more than alcohol. Just like the influence of the moon on the tides, the command drink has on us is both profound and predictable. Every weekend, scores of us pour onto the streets at night and what follows for many hours after, with the aid of alcohol, is a picture of human stupidity. It seems that no-one is immune. Our A&Es are choked with men and women of all ages who have fallen victim to its unpleasant side effects – drink-driving tragedies, violent brawls and alcohol-related illness. It is an ugly, embarrassing scene and no amount of bravado or cheer can alter this fact.

Sometimes, however, it may be more natural for the topic sentence to be the second or third sentence. In the following examples, the topic sentence is the third sentence:

» EXAMPLE 3

I can remember the stiff feel of the shoes around my feet and the smell of the crisp pages of my new books. I can still feel the anxiety zinging around my stomach as my dad walked me through those imposing gates. **My first day of school may have been 14 years ago now, but it has yet to leave my memory.** It is something that I remember with particular clarity every September, when I pass the primary school and see the new junior infants waddling into classrooms and wailing for their parents.

» EXAMPLE 4

Maybe it's the sensation of sand sliding across your feet. Or maybe it's the promise of a good night's sleep after a day spent breathing in the salty sea air. **Whatever the key to its allure, I am an avid fan of the beach.** I've spent my whole life waking up and falling asleep to the swish of the waves on the shore. I've left a million footprints in the sand and skimmed a thousand stones across the water. To sit on top of a dune and watch the sun set late on a summer evening is, for me and many others, a little slice of heaven.

As a rule of thumb, however, it is best to have the topic sentence as the first sentence in the paragraph.

How long should a paragraph be?

Your paragraphs should be as long as they need to be but not a sentence longer. Each paragraph should be concerned with one central idea. When you've said all you wish to communicate regarding that idea it's time to move on and begin your next paragraph.

There is, therefore, no 'correct' length for a paragraph, no rule that says paragraphs should be seven, eight or ten sentences in length. Again and again students make the mistake of writing paragraphs that go on and on. They continue droning about the paragraph's topic long after they've exhausted everything meaningful they have to say about it. Or they write endless paragraphs that 'mash up' many different ideas in a way that's confusing and irritating for the reader. The best way to avoid such mistakes is to plan your composition carefully.

How do I start a new paragraph?

There are two ways to start a new paragraph. You can indent its first line:

In my opinion, schools need to seriously consider starting up classes in coding and programming. All we are hearing in newspapers and reports is how we need to invest in the 'smart economy' to fix the country. The experts are telling us that the IT industry is booming and Ireland has, indeed, attracted top technology companies to its shores. And yet, bizarrely, there is also a shortage in the number of people with these IT skills. Many people, we are told, are not 'technically literate' and this prevents them from getting any of the thousands of IT jobs that are available in Ireland. This seems absurd when so many people, both young and old, are forced to emigrate to earn a living.

Is it right that our education system offers slightly arcane subjects such as Classical Studies and Japanese at Leaving Cert level and yet does not offer courses in coding, programing, graphic design, or even ECD? Should we be offering strictly academic subjects like religion, art history or Latin and yet ignore subjects for which there is a strong demand? With all due respect to the linguistic whiz kids out there, perhaps the languages we should be focusing on now are C++, JavaScript and Ruby?

Alternatively you can skip a line:

In my opinion, schools need to seriously consider starting up classes in coding and programming. All we are hearing in newspapers and reports is how we need to invest in the 'smart economy' to fix the country. The experts are telling us that the IT industry is booming and Ireland has, indeed, attracted top technology companies to its shores. And yet, bizarrely, there is also a shortage in the number of people with these IT skills. Many people, we are told, are not 'technically literate' and this prevents them from getting any of the thousands of IT jobs that are available in Ireland. This seems absurd when so many people, both young and old, are forced to emigrate to earn a living.

Is it right that our education system offers slightly arcane subjects such as Classical Studies and Japanese at Leaving Cert level and yet does not offer courses in coding, programing, graphic design, or even ECDL? Should we be offering strictly academic subjects like religion, art history or Latin and yet ignore subjects for which there is a strong demand? With all due respect to the linguistic whiz kids out there, perhaps the languages we should be focusing on now are C++, JavaScript and Ruby?

Whichever of these paragraph styles you use is entirely up to yourself, but it is important that you are consistent. If you start using an indented style, use the indented style throughout your essay, and the same applies for the skipped-line style.

Exercises

1. What is the function of a 'topic' sentence in a paragraph?

2. What are 'body' sentences'? How do these relate to 'topic' sentences?

3. Arrange the following sentences so that they form a coherent paragraph:

This is a lot for a five-year-old to deal with, but it all goes to hell in a basket when mom or dad announce that they're leaving and you have to survive the day without them.

The uniforms are uncomfortable.

Those new faces and names inspire intense shyness and social anxiety.

Few things in life traumatise a child more than his or her first day at school.

Everything about it is new and overwhelming.

4. Arrange the following sentences so that they form a coherent paragraph:

Every paragraph brings you deeper into the minds of characters who can go on to feel like your best friend or your worst nightmare.

When you turn the first page you embark on a thrilling adventure, and when you finally close the last one, you mourn its ending and are left hungry for more.

Nothing is more satisfying than delving into a great book.

You simply cannot have the same love affair with a movie or television series that you can have with a good novel.

5. Arrange the following sentences so that they form a coherent paragraph:

But here's the truth: they once had to start at the same rung of the ladder as you.

We don't always feel like pulling on those shorts and runners and heading out into the cold.

Physical fitness is a challenging but worthwhile pursuit.

The prospect becomes even less appealing when you know that you'll have to puff and pant and sweat for an hour or so.

And those lithe athletes you see swanning effortlessly around don't make you feel any better about yourself.

6. Arrange the following sentences so that they form a coherent paragraph:

He possesses all of the qualities of a great anti-hero. His vigilante activities are fuelled primarily out of a desire for revenge. He is not always idealistic or courageous. Batman is one of the finest anti-heroes to grace the pages of a comic book. His intent is not to comfort the people of Gotham City with his crusade, more to terrify its villains – often with brute force and morally dubious tactics. This is what makes him so compelling.

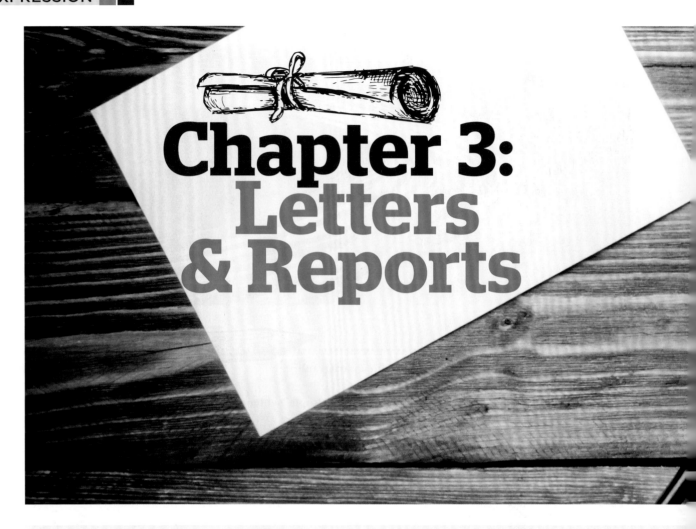

Chapter 3: Letters & Reports

Introduction

STUDENTS ARE OFTEN ASKED TO WRITE LETTERS IN THE LEAVING CERT EXAM. TYPICALLY YOU WILL BE ASKED TO WRITE TO SOMEONE YOU DON'T KNOW PERSONALLY, RATHER THAN TO AN ACQUAINTANCE OR A FRIEND.

Sometimes you will be asked to write to an individual person, for example a celebrity, a famous musician or a sports star. Sometimes what you write will be intended for the letters page of a magazine.

Often letters require you to **make a case** of one kind or another.

• Letters to publications, for instance, typically require you to take a stand on a matter of public interest.

• If you are asked to write about a general topic such as youth culture or your hopes for the future it is best to adopt a definite stance on the topic which you develop throughout the letter.

• A letter inviting a celebrity to your locality also requires you to make a case. You have to argue or suggest why your school or club is worthy of such a visit.

• Even fan letters require you to take a stance of sorts. In praising the celebrity's work you should state clearly why it impresses you so much and offer arguments and evidence to support such praise.

In past exams students were asked to write a letter arguing about the smoking ban, proposing a particular photograph for an award or making a case for themselves as a ghost writer for a celebrity autobiography.

STRUCTURE

Your **opening paragraph** will state who you are and why you are writing. This is also where you should state clearly your point of view on the topic in question. For example, you might state that the smoking ban is an unfair restriction on individual rights or that today's youth culture is shallow and destructive.

Two or three **body paragraphs** will then develop the letter's topic. Each body paragraph should make a point that backs up the point of view presented in your opening. Here you find yourself using phrasing identified with the language of persuasion and the language of argument.

In a **final short paragraph** you might briefly restate your case in a sentence or two. You should also thank the recipient for taking the time to read your letter and, if necessary, express the hope that you will hear from them soon. For example, a letter to a celebrity might conclude: 'In short, I firmly believe that if you decide to visit St Cuthbert's you will not be disappointed. Thank you for your consideration and I look forward to hearing from you soon.'

PLAN IN ADVANCE

With letters, as with all compositions, it is important to plan in advance. Your letter will consist of four or five paragraphs. Take time to jot down what each paragraph will be about before you commence work on the letter itself. Having such a plan in front of you as you compose will prove invaluable.

HAVE PURPOSE AND FOCUS

As you compose, always remain conscious of your letter's purpose. Again and again students are penalised for drifting off topic. If you have been asked to invite Lionel Messi to your school, remember to actually invite him. Such a letter should suggest to Messi different reasons why he might consider visiting your school. You shouldn't go on at length about how great a footballer Messi is or describe his 20 greatest goals. Again, advance planning should ensure you stay focused on the letter's purpose.

CONTROL YOUR TONE AND REGISTER

Remember that almost always you will be writing to someone you don't know personally. This is not a text message or an email to a friend. The tone of the letter should be friendly but formal. Casual and slang terms should be avoided, for instance. Reading the samples that follow will give you a sense of what is required here. There are many marks to be won for maintaining a consistent register throughout.

KEEP YOUR RECIPIENT IN MIND

Always remember that you are writing to someone. Keep the recipient in mind at all times. All too often students begin with a paragraph clearly addressed to their recipient but follow it up with paragraphs that seem to have no recipient in mind. Remember that every line in your letter should be intended for your recipient.

REMEMBER THE LETTER FORMAT

There are marks to be gained from reproducing the conventions of the letter format, which is something that is very easy to do but is all too often neglected by students. Your letter should have the following features:

- Your address
- Your recipient's address
- A salutation (Dear Somebody)
- A sign-off (Yours sincerely)

Walk Thru 1

Write a letter to a sports star inviting them to make an appearance at your local club.

PLANNING

I'm going to jot down some key words **quickly.** These will help me to thrash out the basic content of the letter.

Local GAA club end of season. Player awards. Medals. Club renovation. People inspired by this player's performance. Past problems with injury. Return to form. MoTM game in final. Presence will delight younger players.

Five paragraphs will suffice for this letter. I will plan it out first by writing down what each paragraph should focus on.

1: Introduce myself – name, where I'm writing from. Why I'm writing.

2: Congratulations on recent victory. Great performance. Award deserved.

3: Young players here inspired by you.

4: Doing up club facilities – your presence likely to help fundraising efforts.

5: Summary and wrap up.

WRITING

I know there are marks for reproducing the conventions of the letter genre. Therefore, I will begin by including the address from which I am writing, the recipient's address and an opening salutation. I'll also remember to conclude the letter with an appropriate sign-off.

Geraldine Molloy,
Glenview GAA Club,
The Old Road,
Glenview,
Co. Wexford

Mr O'Riada,
The Glen,
Longford Town,
Co. Longford
11/10/2014

Dear Mr O'Riada,

My name is Geraldine Molloy and I'm the junior PRO for Glenview GAA club in Wexford. The club will be hosting a medal ceremony in a fortnight's time at the Glenview Park Hotel and we would love it if you could present the Player of the Year awards to the winning candidates in our senior and intermediates sides.

I've included all of the essentials in my opening paragraph – I've introduced myself and explained straight away my reasons for contacting the player. I look back at my plan and remind myself of what I intended to talk about in the next three paragraphs: offer my congratulations to him; tell him that our own players would be delighted to see him at the ceremony; inform him that we are renovating the facilities and his presence would make a big difference to fundraising efforts.

Your team's recent victory in the All-Ireland Hurling Final was most impressive – particularly considering your injury setbacks. It was a thrilling game for the neutral spectator and your man-of-the-match award was richly deserved. Many congratulations to you.

Your performance on the day has clearly motivated our young players to strive for success at a local level with Glenview and we are reaping the benefits with plenty of success in the league and championship.

We hope to renovate our facilities over the coming months and your presence at the ceremony will help to raise awareness about the upgrade and, hopefully, improve our funding.

Okay, I've done what I set out to do in my plan. Now I need to write my concluding paragraph. I need to ask him if he can RSVP to the invite and remind him again of the positive impact his presence would have. I must remember to finish with the correct sign-off.

Please let me know if you would be willing to attend – I know the players, children and club administrators would love to meet you and that it would encourage everyone to kick on with their outstanding efforts to improve the set-up here.

Yours sincerely,

Geraldine Molloy

Walk Thru 2

Imagine you have seen the above image of drought in a newspaper and have been inspired to take action. Write a letter to a local politician, informing her/him of your efforts.

PLANNING

I am going to look at the image and jot down some key words **quickly**. These will help me to thrash out the basic content of the composition.

> Describe picture briefly. Drought, poverty. Inspired to take action. TD. Charity. Raising money. Awareness among public and politicians. All students to take part. Aim to raise €???? and bring struggles into focus. Details of walk – X miles long, date, route/location.

In the Leaving Cert five paragraphs will usually suffice for a letter.

1: Introduce myself – name, where I'm writing from. Why I'm writing.

2: About the image – how it inspired us to take action.

3: Goals. Reach target funds for charity organisation and bring issue to public attention.

4: Details of the walk – where we're going, when we're going, who is participating.

5: Summarise, wrap up, sign off.

WRITING

I am aware that letters have specific conventions and rules, so I will begin with my own address, the recipient's address, the date and an opening salutation. I will also remember to conclude the letter with an appropriate sign-off.

Paul Murphy,

St Brendan's Secondary School,

Newbridge,

Co. Kildare

Cllr Mary Hughes,

Newbridge Town Council,

Newbridge,

Co. Kildare

30/03/14

Dear Ms Hughes,

My name is Paul Murphy and I am a sixth-year student in St Brendan's Secondary School. We are organising a sponsored walk to raise money for families in drought-stricken regions of India and we would really appreciate your help in making the public aware of this crisis.

As set out in my plan, I've included the formal conventions of a letter (addresses, salutation, etc.) and I've also stated the most important things in the opening paragraph (who I am, why I am writing). I know from my plan what I want to outline in the next three paragraphs: the picture that motivated us, our fundraising goals and details about the walk. As in the majority of letter questions in the Leaving Cert, I am addressing somebody I don't know, so I will write in a formal but polite tone.

We recently saw some harrowing newspaper photographs that showed the devastation the drought has caused. One particular picture shows two young children walking barefoot across the arid land to get some water – most of which is not safe enough to drink anyway. This tragic image inspired us to take action.

We have two goals. Our primary aim is to raise €1,000 for the Red Cross Drought Crisis fund, which sends vital medical care to children and families suffering most because of the drought. Our secondary objective is to raise awareness of this crisis among local government, businesses and members of the community.

Weather permitting, all students and teachers from St Brendan's will be going on an eight-mile sponsored walk on 14 April. Some students will be making extra efforts to raise funds by jogging the route or wearing costumes.

Now I want to conclude the letter by emphasising how the recipient could help us achieve our goal and what the fundraising could do for the people in need.

We hope you can help us to bring news of this tragic event to all in our community. I believe that, together, we can make a huge difference in the lives of those who are suffering as a result of the disaster.

Yours sincerely,

Paul Murphy

Exercises

1. What information should you usually provide in your opening paragraph?

2. How might the salutation in a letter to an organisation, institution or group differ to that intended for an individual?

3. Rearrange the following sentences to form a properly structured paragraph:

We recently upgraded our training facilities and hope to officially reopen the club next month. Dear Mr O'Brien, I am writing to you from St Enda's Hockey Club in Waterford. The success of the Irish hockey team in recent years has boosted our numbers noticeably and it would do wonders for our dedicated members if you could attend the reopening ceremony. Our generous sponsors and local politicians will be present at the event as will players of all levels and ages.

4. Complete a paragraph based on the following sentence:

Dear Ms. Rowling, I am writing to you on behalf of the Clondalkin Library book club.

5. Write the opening paragraph of a letter to a well-known Irish athlete asking him or her if she/he could visit Crumlin Children's Hospital with the latest trophy/medal.

6. Write a closing paragraph that begins with the following sentence:

Congratulations again on your recent Emmy.

7. Write a letter of thanks to a local business person who sponsored a charity cycle you completed recently.

8. An article has appeared in a national magazine criticising today's youth culture as being destructive, lazy and shallow. Write a letter to the magazine outlining your own views on the topic.

9. Write a letter to a celebrity that you admire in which you urge them to write their autobiography. Outline why you think it is important for them to tell their story.

10. You are running for student union president in your college. Write a letter to your fellow students asking for their support in the upcoming student union elections.

Marked Example 1:

Write a letter to a newspaper explaining why you think your home town should be considered for this year's Best Small Town award.

Tom Murphy,

Main St,

Baile na mBruach,

Co Clare

20/07/13

Editor,

Irish Observer,

Observer House,

Harcourt Street,

Dublin 2

Madam,

My name is Tom Murphy and I am a student at the local gaelscoil here in my hometown of Baile na mBruach. I would like to propose that Baile na mBruach be considered for Ireland's Best Small Town 2013 award.

Despite its small population of just over 2,000, there is plenty to see and do in this vibrant town. We are blessed to live on the outskirts of one of Ireland's best-kept secrets: Baile na mBruach Park – an official National Heritage site. This 700-acre forest is a great spot for hikers and it surrounds a lake where locals and tourists can enjoy a variety of water activities including boating, kayaking, swimming and fishing.

There is great community spirit in Baile na mBruach. Residents of all ages are heavily involved in the annual Tidy Towns competition. These efforts keep our town in good nick and culminated in Baile na mBruach winning the overall Tidy Towns competition two years ago.

Baile na mBruach is blessed with excellent infrastructure and amenities, such as an hourly shuttle bus to the nearest train station and some award-winning restaurants and bars. These ensure that the town maintains a lively social scene and a thriving tourism industry.

For these reasons – and many more – I respectfully seek your publication's backing for Baile na mBruach as the Best Small Town in Ireland 2013.

Yours etc.,

Tom Murphy.

Comments:

» Clarity of purpose:

Is it relevant? Yes. The student has been asked to write to a newspaper to explain why his home town should be given a particular award. He clearly understands what the task asks of him – he addresses a formal letter to a newspaper and includes all of the relevant customs a letter requires. In doing so, he demonstrates an understanding of the questions as well as of the genre and format.

Is it focused from start to finish? Yes. He methodically describes the various qualities of his home town and emphasises that these are features that make them worthy of the award.

» Coherence of delivery:

He states his beliefs from the outset and convincingly explains the town's merits in every paragraph.

He demonstrates that he is in control of tone and register throughout the letter. He does not switch from one authorial voice to another.

Does the student manage his ideas? Yes. Each paragraph is constructed around one strong topic – e.g. outdoor activities, the Tidy Towns accolades, local amenities – and these justify the writer's call for the town to win the prize.

Does the student sequence his topics carefully? Yes. He does not rush through it. Instead, he progresses steadily through his points in a coherent and logical fashion. He concludes by repeating his opening request that his home to be awarded the Best Small Town in Ireland prize.

» Efficiency of language use:

This student demonstrates a wide range of vocabulary ('lively social scene and a thriving tourism industry') and employs sentences of different lengths to create a clear but engaging piece of writing. The paragraphs are formatted correctly. They are not too long or too short and the breaks occur only when he has finished dealing with one concept.

» Mechanics:

The student's spelling, punctuation and grammar are sound.

Marked Example 2:

Write a letter to your favourite author inviting them to visit your school.

Sarah Ryan,

25 Main Street,

Wexford Town,

Co. Wexford

28/03/2013

Dear Mr Tolfer,

My name is Sarah Ryan and I'm writing to you on behalf of my transition year classmates. As part of our TY portfolio, we have put together an anthology of our own creative material and hope to launch it in April when the school year comes to a close. It would be really excellent if you could attend the launch and say a few words.

We all love your young adult series of books and were really delighted with the most recent instalment, which has been a frequent topic of our tweets and classroom conversation. A number of the students have been inspired by your books and are now considering careers in English and writing.

Our anthology contains a selection of creative writing from 15 students and includes samples of poetry, short stories and theatre scripts (some of which were even staged at the Christmas play to much laughter and fanfare).

We have not yet finalised the launch date. If you think you might like to meet some of your biggest fans and perhaps some of the country's future best-selling authors, we would be happy to schedule the launch around your own timetable.

I have enclosed a copy of the anthology, in case you want to read it. Please let us know before 10 April if you will be able to attend the launch.

Yours sincerely,

Sarah Ryan

Comments:

» **Clarity of purpose:**

This student's composition is relevant because it addresses the question effectively. She has been asked to write to her favourite author and invite him/her to her school and she does so.

She understands what the question is asking and is aware of the conventions of the letter form – she includes proper style of address and employs a formal salutation. In this way, she proves that she has read the question and is comfortable with the genre and format.

The composition is focused from start to finish. She does not ramble on at length about the author's works. She does not make any comparisons between the students' writing and the author's writing. The recipient of this letter can be in no doubt as to the purpose of the letter.

» **Coherence of delivery:**

She is clear from the very beginning of the letter why she is writing. She states who she is, where she is from and why she is writing to the author. Every paragraph thereafter is centred on this key information.

She displays a consistent tone – one that is friendly but not too familiar or conversational.

This student has managed her ideas well. She devotes one paragraph to one subject and does not muddy the waters by drifting off-topic.

She sequences her topics well. She expresses her message in a measured way – she does not let it all out in one go and then run out of steam at a later stage. There is a pleasing regularity to her delivery and conclusion, which makes the letter quite comprehensible.

» **Efficiency of language use:**

This student demonstrates competent vocabulary (e.g. 'finalise', 'schedule', 'anthology', etc.). She has picked one paragraph style and stuck with it throughout.

» **Mechanics:**

She demonstrates a solid grip on the mechanics of the English language, with correct spelling, punctuation and grammar.

Past Exam Questions:

1 (2004): My Kind of Work. Write a letter to one of the people from the collection of visual images in this text, indicating what appeals and/or does not appeal to you about the work which that person does.

2 (2005): Write a letter to a photographic magazine in which you propose one of the four images for the award 'Best War Photograph of the Year'.

3 (2006): Write a letter to a famous writer or celebrity or sports personality of your choice offering your services as a ghost writer for a future book. In your letter you should outline the reasons why you believe you would make a successful ghost writer for your chosen author.

4 (2007): Imagine you have a friend in another country which is considering the introduction of a ban on smoking in public places. Write a letter to your friend advising him/her either to support or not to support the proposed ban. In giving your advice you may wish to draw on the recent experience of the smoking ban in Ireland.

5 (2008): Write a letter to Jon Savage responding to this extract from his book and giving your own views on today's teenage culture.

6 (2009): '...photography's unique ability to freeze time...'
Imagine your art teacher is compiling a photographic exhibition to reflect the lives of young people today. She has asked students to suggest images they would like included. Write a letter to your art teacher proposing five images that you believe should be included and give reasons for your decision in each case.

7 (2010): 'So I want to end as I began, with a vision of two futures ...'
Write a letter (dated June 2010), intended to be read by future generations, in which you express your hopes for planet Earth in the year 2050.

8 (2012): Write a letter to Margaret Laurence, in response to Text 1, commenting on what you find interesting in the extract, and telling her about your home place and its impact on you.

Chapter 4: Diary Entries

Introduction

SOMETIMES YOU WILL BE ASKED TO WRITE A SERIES OF DIARY ENTRIES BASED ON A GIVEN COMPREHENSION TEXT. YOU'LL BE ASKED TO SELECT A CHARACTER FROM THE TEXT AND WRITE FROM THEIR POINT OF VIEW.

- Identify the correct character in the text and understand what it is that they have seen and done.

- You may wish to underline or highlight important passages relating to that character.

- Take a moment to imagine yourself as that character.

- Consider what they have witnessed and how they might react to these events.

- Because this is a diary, you must write in the first person: 'I did this…', 'I saw that…'

Remember, you will usually be asked to write a series of short entries rather than a single long entry. It is important that each entry is headed with the appropriate date. If it is not clear what time of year it is, just use your imagination and make something up.

PLAN IN ADVANCE

Though the diary entry is a question that favours creativity, advance planning is still essential. Before you commence work, make sure you fully grasp whose point of view you are writing from. Understand what kind of person they are, what they have seen and their likely reactions. Don't start writing straightaway.

Be clear about how many diary entries you have been asked to write. Usually you are asked to write more than one, so it is important that you sequence them logically and sequentially.

Jot down briefly what you wish to express in each entry and the order in which you wish to express it.

USE YOUR IMAGINATION

The diary entry rewards creativity and imagination.
- You are required to 'get inside the head' of another person, often a fictional person. Your writing should reflect the character's personality.
- Because you are writing from a particular person's point of view you will have to come up with words and phrases that your subject might actually use.
- You must also try to capture the detail and atmosphere of the world the character lives in.

This is a question suitable for those comfortable with creative writing and imaginative thinking.

TONE AND REGISTER

There are no hard-and-fast rules regarding tone in diary entries. Some diarists use a serious, formal tone, even when describing their most intimate thoughts and experiences. Most diarists, however, tend to write in what might be described as an informal and chatty fashion.

Be conscious of who you are pretending to be and choose the tone appropriate to that person. For example, if you are pretending to be a government official, you might write in a serious or formal tone. If you are writing from the point of view of a teenage girl you might adopt a more chatty or informal register. As always, consistency is the watch-word. Once you adopt a particular tone, you should stick to it throughout.

SPELLING AND GRAMMAR

You might notice that in the real world diarists sometimes ignore the rules of grammar, spelling and punctuation. However, in the context of the Leaving Cert, you are well advised to adhere to these rules unless there is a very good reason not to.

Walk Thru 1

Read the following extract from George Eliot's *Adam Bede*. Imagine you are the character Hetty. Write two diary entries – one describing your thoughts and reflections on the events described in the text, and another in which you describe the day of the dance.

Hetty blushed a deep rose-colour when Captain Donnithorne entered the dairy and spoke to her; but it was not at all a distressed blush, for it was inwreathed with smiles and dimples, and with sparkles from under long, curled, dark eyelashes; and while her aunt was discoursing to him about the limited amount of milk that was to be spared for butter and cheese so long as the calves were not all weaned, and a large quantity but inferior quality of milk yielded by the shorthorn, which had been bought on experiment, together with other matters which must be interesting to a young gentleman who would one day be a landlord, Hetty tossed and patted her pound of butter with quite a self-possessed, coquettish air, slyly conscious that no turn of her head was lost.

There are various orders of beauty, causing men to make fools of themselves in various styles, from the desperate to the sheepish; but there is one order of beauty which seems made to turn the heads not only of men, but of all intelligent mammals, even of women. It is a beauty like that of kittens, or very small downy ducks making gentle rippling noises with their soft bills, or babies just beginning to toddle and to engage in conscious mischief – a beauty with which you can never be angry, but that you feel ready to crush for inability to comprehend the state of mind into which it throws you. Hetty Sorrel's was that sort of beauty.

"I hope you will be ready for a great holiday on the thirtieth of July, Mrs Poyser," said Captain Donnithorne, when he had sufficiently admired the dairy and given several improvised opinions on Swede turnips and shorthorns. "You know what is to happen then, and I shall expect you to be one of the guests who come earliest and leave latest. Will you promise me your hand for two dances, Miss Hetty? If I don't get your promise now, I know I shall hardly have a chance, for all the smart young farmers will take care to secure you."

Hetty smiled and blushed, but before she could answer, Mrs Poyser interposed, scandalized at the mere suggestion that the young squire could be excluded by any meaner partners.

"Indeed, sir, you are very kind to take that notice of her. And I'm sure, whenever you're pleased to dance with her, she'll be proud and thankful, if she stood still all the rest o' th' evening."

"Oh no, no, that would be too cruel to all the other young fellows who can dance. But you will promise me two dances, won't you?" the captain continued, determined to make Hetty look at him and speak to him.

Hetty dropped the prettiest little curtsy, and stole a half-shy, half-coquettish glance at him as she said, "Yes, thank you, sir."

"And you must bring all your children, you know, Mrs Poyser; your little Totty, as well as the boys. I want all the youngest children on the estate to be there – all those who will be fine young men and women when I'm a bald old fellow."

"Oh dear, sir, that 'ull be a long time first," said Mrs. Poyser, quite overcome at the young squire's speaking so lightly of himself, and thinking how her husband would be interested in hearing her recount this remarkable specimen of high-born humour. The captain was thought to be "very full of his jokes," and was a great favourite throughout the estate on account of his free manners. Every tenant was quite sure things would be different when the reins got into his hands – there was to be a millennial abundance of new gates, allowances of lime, and returns of ten per cent.

"But where is Totty to-day?" he said. "I want to see her."

"Where is the little un, Hetty?" said Mrs Poyser. "She came in here not long ago."

"I don't know. She went into the brewhouse to Nancy, I think."

The proud mother, unable to resist the temptation to show her Totty, passed at once into the back kitchen, in search of her, not, however, without misgivings lest something should have happened to render her person and attire unfit for presentation.

"And do you carry the butter to market when you've made it?" said the Captain to Hetty, meanwhile.

"Oh no, sir; not when it's so heavy. I'm not strong enough to carry it. Alick takes it on horseback."

"No, I'm sure your pretty arms were never meant for such heavy weights. But you go out a walk sometimes these pleasant evenings, don't you? Why don't you have a walk in the Chase sometimes, now it's so green and pleasant? I hardly ever see you anywhere except at home and at church."

"Aunt doesn't like me to go a-walking only when I'm going somewhere," said Hetty. "But I go through the Chase sometimes."

"And don't you ever go to see Mrs. Best, the housekeeper? I think I saw you once in the housekeeper's room."

"It isn't Mrs Best, it's Mrs Pomfret, the lady's maid, as I go to see. She's teaching me tent-stitch and the lace-mending. I'm going to tea with her to-morrow afternoon."

The reason why there had been space for this tete-a-tete can only be known by looking into the back kitchen, where Totty had been discovered rubbing a stray blue-bag against her nose, and in the same moment allowing some liberal indigo drops to fall on her afternoon pinafore. But now she appeared holding her mother's hand—the end of her round nose rather shiny from a recent and hurried application of soap and water.

"Here she is!" said the captain, lifting her up and setting her on the low stone shelf. "Here's Totty! By the by, what's her other name? She wasn't christened Totty."

"Oh, sir, we call her sadly out of her name. Charlotte's her christened name. It's a name i' Mr Poyser's family: his grandmother was named Charlotte. But we began with calling her Lotty, and now it's got to Totty. To be sure it's more like a name for a dog than a Christian child."

"Totty's a capital name. Why, she looks like a Totty. Has she got a pocket on?" said the captain, feeling in his own waistcoat pockets.

Totty immediately with great gravity lifted up her frock, and showed a tiny pink pocket at present in a state of collapse.

"It dot notin' in it," she said, as she looked down at it very earnestly.

"No! What a pity! Such a pretty pocket. Well, I think I've got some things in mine that will make a pretty jingle in it. Yes! I declare I've got five little round silver things, and hear what a pretty noise they make in Totty's pink pocket." Here he shook the pocket with the five sixpences in it, and Totty showed her teeth and wrinkled her nose in great glee; but, divining that there was nothing more to be got by staying, she jumped off the shelf and ran away to jingle her pocket in the hearing of Nancy, while her mother called after her, "Oh for shame, you naughty gell! Not to thank the captain for what he's given you I'm sure, sir, it's very kind of you; but she's spoiled shameful; her father won't have her said nay in anything, and there's no managing her. It's being the youngest, and th' only gell."

"Oh, she's a funny little fatty; I wouldn't have her different. But I must be going now, for I suppose the rector is waiting for me."

With a "good-bye," a bright glance, and a bow to Hetty Arthur left the dairy.

PLANNING

I have been asked to imagine that I am Hetty and to write two diary entries. In order to understand Hetty better, I'll re-read the text and underline the things that strike me as important insights into the character.

I will now take a moment to imagine myself as Hetty and quickly jot down a few key words and sentences to get some ideas going.

> Story set in an older era – lots of things to consider here incl dress, etiquette, lifestyle, etc. Hetty swooning girlie girl. Captain swarthy and handsome. Dance equals courtship, potentially something more serious. Reflect on events as told in the story, invent for the second. Getting ready for the dance. Dress. Gossip. Excitement about seeing Captain Donnithorne.

FIRST ENTRY	Captain Donnithorne visited the dairy today. Emphasise his dashing appearance, his patience with Mrs Poyser, how he is liked by the other tenants and workers on the farm, his conversation with Hetty about the dance and how she blushed around him.
SECOND ENTRY	Just about to go to the dance. Describe getting dolled up for the dance on the 30th. Mrs Poyser helping Hetty into a gown, pinning up hair. Reflecting on the deeper meaning of the dance. Noting her aunt's attempt to steer her away from Donnithorne.

The question has asked me to reflect, as Hetty Sorrel, on Captain Donnithorne's visit to the farm, and to imagine Hetty's thoughts on the day of the dance. I know from my plan that I want the focus of the first entry to be about illustrating Hetty's idealised picture of the Captain and how he gracefully handled Mrs Poyser's ramblings about the farm. It's important for me to remind myself of the key components of a good diary entry. I need to include a date or dates.

25 July, 1801

Dear diary, I was labouring through another day in Auntie Poyser's dairy when who should come in only our landlord, Captain Arthur Donnithorne. He really is an exceedingly handsome fellow – very kind and charming too. Everybody on the farm is looking forward to the day his father bestows the estate on him. 'I suspect the young Captain will do things differently,' Mrs Pomfret said one day to Mrs Best. They say he's 'self-effacing', not pompous like old Mr Donnithorne. He was so patient, listening to Auntie go on and on about butter and cheese and turnips and shorthorns. I'm sure a gallant man like him has no interest in the workings of the farm when he's got soldiers to command and wars to fight.

And then, if you can believe it, he asked me to the dance next week. I near couldn't look at him when he started talking to me. One glimpse of those broad shoulders, the square brow and those pensive, blue eyes set my heart a-flutter. I was too embarrassed. 'Will you promise me your hand for two dances?' he asked me. He said if he didn't ask now he'd have no chance at the dance because all the 'smart young farmers' would be sure to 'secure me'. I hardly think so, but it was kind of him to say. He wouldn't leave until I promised. I could barely even think about tossing the butter after he'd gone.

Now I must write the second entry.

This requires more imagination because it deals with events after those described in the extract. I know from my plan that I want Hetty to elaborate on the process of getting organised for the dance – her dress, her makeup. She'll also have to express her feelings of anticipation and excitement at the prospect of meeting this handsome solider again.

30 July, 1801

I can't stay on too long, diary. The dance is tonight, and Captain Donnithorne has sent a carriage to bring me and Totty and Auntie Poyser to the hall. Auntie helped me to put on a beautiful blue gown. She was a bit severe lacing up the corset – I hate wearing it, truth be told, but she insisted. I could hardly breathe in it by the time she was done. She lent me a muslin shawl to wear over the dress and had me powder my face and pin up my hair. 'Unruly', she called it: 'Here. We must put manners on that unruly hair of yours. Can't have you dancing with Captain Arthur Donnithorne looking like you just staggered in from the dairy.'

She told me if I played my cards right I could find myself a husband. The whole town is going to the dance and many eligible bachelors are going to attend – not just Captain Donnithorne, she made a point of saying to me. She clearly doesn't count him among potential suitors. He's a wealthy man, she told me, soon to inherit his father's estate. I know what she was trying to say: Arthur Donnithorne won't marry a girl like you, Hetty Sorrel. She thinks he just wants to have his fun before he marries a girl his own class. Well, she's wrong. I've seen heads turn when I walk down the town and they'll turn tonight at the dance as well. I'd best go – the carriage is outside and Auntie and Totty are waiting for me.

More anon. H.

Walk Thru 2

Read the following short story, 'The Gecko', by Dan Purdue. Imagine you are Gary. Consider what happened to you on your first few nights of adventuring in the guise of The Gecko. Write a series of diary entries describing what occurs.

One night in September, up late and drunk, Gary bought three CDs and something described as a 'Superhero Franchise' on eBay. The following morning he hunched over fizzing Alka-Seltzer and inspected his purchases. Two of the CDs were albums he hadn't heard before; the third was just a replacement for one Janice took with her when she left. He wasn't sure what to make of the superhero thing. The description was vague and the underexposed, out-of-focus photo didn't help at all. The seller had zero feedback. Perhaps it was just some comic books and an action figure or two. Gary didn't particularly want any superhero gear; he wasn't a collector—although he did have a few *Marvel* and *DC Comics* adaptations on DVD. He hoped he'd be able to sell whatever he'd bought for a profit. He shrugged, shut down the computer, and headed to the local shop to buy Wotsits and a Cornetto.

A couple of days later, Gary opened the front door to a postman bearing three Jiffy bags and something like a pizza box, only deeper. He took the delivery, put on one of his new CDs and inspected the package. It was lighter than he expected, and it didn't make any noise when he shook it. He couldn't find a return address, or decipher the smudged postmark. It had clearly been wrapped with great care, though, with dead-straight strips of brown packing tape and obsessively neat corners. He slit the tape with the edge of a key and lifted the lid.

Inside, folded into a perfect square, lay what turned out to be a one-piece bodysuit in mottled greys and greens, with a sort of dark-brown diamond pattern printed over the top that made it look a little like it was covered in scales. As Gary lifted it from the box, a card with a picture of a puppy fell from the folded suit. Inside that, *Birthday Greetings* had been scored out and replaced with precise strokes of a blue biro:

Hi, thanks for agreeing to become The Gecko! Good luck with your new life as a vigilante!!! All the best, Scott. P.S. Sorry about the card, it's all I could find.

Gary put the card and suit to one side and rechecked the box, but there was nothing else there. He couldn't remember anything about a costume in the item description. In what way did that count as a franchise? And who'd ever heard of 'The Gecko'? It felt horribly like he'd wasted twenty-five pounds, plus postage and packaging. He logged into eBay to recheck the details. The seller's account had been deleted.

The suit seemed way too small, more like a child's size, but an investigative tug on one of the legs revealed it was remarkably stretchy. It felt tough, though, and there didn't appear to be any seams to worry about. Gary took the suit into the bedroom, spending a while looking at it, stretching it this way and that, and holding it against himself in front of the mirror. He tried to resist the irrational but growing urge to put it on.

It had gloves, feet and a hood with a kind of eye-mask all built in. Gary hunted for but couldn't find a zip, poppers, Velcro strips, or any other means of getting into the suit. The only way in appeared to be the hole where the bottom half of his face would go – assuming he managed to squeeze his decidedly unchildlike frame into the rest of the suit.

Gary stripped down to his underpants and sat on the edge of the bed. He poked first one foot then the other in through the hole in the suit's neck. As he pulled the material up over his calves, he batted away mental images of sausages being manufactured, fatty meat straining inside a tight skin. Gary wasn't badly overweight, but nobody would ever accuse him of having a 'physique'. Already the sweat was beading on his forehead, just from the effort of squeezing his legs into the suit.

He stood up and managed to work the suit up to waist level. The first arm went in okay, but the second one required him to all but dislocate his shoulder to line his hand up with the sleeve, which had by this point disappeared behind his back. He got it, eventually, and as the suit slipped over his shoulders, closing around his neck, he thought he might pass out. It hugged his chest so tightly he could barely breathe. The urge to tear it off again was immense. He sat back down on the bed, feeling trapped and dizzy, closed his eyes, and put his head between his knees for a while.

When the room stopped spinning, he got to his feet. He took a deep breath and pulled the hood over his head. It felt like a vice clamped around his skull, and Gary panicked that it would crush his brain. He imagined his corpse being found, weeks later, dressed in what the police, his parents, and – worst of all – Janice, would surely assume was some kind of fetish outfit. But then, as he tugged the eye mask into place, he felt a shift, a change that seemed to come from both the suit itself and a deep place somewhere inside him. The costume was no longer crushing the life out of him; it was supporting him, perhaps even protecting him. He felt compact, focussed, aware of his edges. Stood before the mirror, Gary first looked in horror at the way it clung to every lump and bulge, then – as he turned first one way, then the other – he couldn't help thinking his body looked more toned, more alive than ever before.

He found the suit enabled him to stick to any surface. First, he tentatively climbed the bedroom wall, and then crawled across the ceiling on his hands and knees. After that, he explored the house, going from room to room without touching the floor. As a finale, from standing on the ceiling of the living room, he performed an upside-down somersault, which proved so disorientating he had to climb down and lie on the sofa for an hour.

When it got dark, Gary stood at the window, watching the lights of the city and thinking about the card that had come with the costume. A vigilante, he thought. That must be a joke, right? Nobody really did that. Did they? Yet, standing there in the suit, with the night stretching out before him, he felt fate pushing him in a new direction. He wasn't sure it was a direction he wanted to take. Fighting crime sounded quite... confrontational, after all - and he'd never been very good at that kind of thing. Still, the gecko suit worked, the capabilities it offered were exciting, and Janice had always complained that he never took enough interest in the community. So he decided he would go out, test the suit, and see how things turned out. Gary threw on a long coat, turned up the collar and pulled a baseball cap low on his head.

'Well, criminal scum,' he mumbled, pulling the door closed behind him. 'Prepare to meet... The Gecko.' It sounded a lot better in his head than it did out loud.

PLANNING

It's important to remind myself of the key components of a good diary entry. I need to include a date or dates. I know I have to write from The Gecko's point of view. I'll re-read the text and highlight the passages that reveal Gary/The Gecko's personality. After all, it is his attitudes and reactions that I need to capture.

I'll quickly jot down a few key words and sentences – this will help me to generate some ideas and assemble an interesting composition.

Gary is an anti-hero. Hungover slob. Not obviously heroic. Funny edge to this story. Doesn't know what he's doing. Pining for his ex. Neither interested nor equipped to fight crime. Goes out to save the goodies and jail the baddies – where is the crime? Police well able. Sense of anti-climax. Stuck with petty criminals. Makes lots of mistakes, like accidentally damaging property. Meets Janice again some time later. Not as interested in her. Tackling bigger crime now.

FIRST ENTRY	Sitting in an ordinary café, noting the lack of crime, how his attempts to observe were frowned upon by the public.
SECOND ENTRY	Tales of minor vigilante successes – preventing houses from being burgled, but also accidentally destroying valuables. Still reliant on human invention – not a self-sufficient superhero.
THIRD ENTRY	Bumping into Janice. She's interested but The Gecko is not – he's too busy stopping guys who have stolen a car for a joyride.

WRITING

Okay, I know from my plan that I want to make this a humorous and quirky series of diary entries. The Gary in the text seemed a bit hapless, so that's something I want to take advantage of. I want to write a funny, unexpected scene in the first entry – something not associated with superheroes and action. I've got almost free rein to be as creative as I like with this. The more into the character I can get, the better.

5 April, 2012. Dear diary.
No. That's not manly enough. I'll start again.
Gecko's log, stardate 5-4-2012

I thought it best to record my new-found experiences of fighting crime as 'The Gecko'. Well, I went out a few hours ago to seek out a damsel-in-distress somewhere or an elderly shop-owner besieged by thugs. Turns out the police have a lot of that sorted already (who knew?).

And, in fact, my standing there on a street corner watching the world go safely by attracted the curiosity of two police officers and a guy by the name of Derek, who worked for a charity aimed at ending homelessness.

After an hour of this, I started to get a bit bored and nippy, so I called into a WH Smith shop, bought a coffee, a Danish pastry and a pen and pad to write this journal entry in. I think the best way to deal with this lack of obvious crime is to Google geckos and find out what's in store for me. They eat insects, don't they? I'm sure Janice would just *love* to see me do that. Vindictive cow. God I miss her.

Okay, the first of the series of entries is done. I'm happy enough with what I've done. I'll take a quick look back at my plan to see what the next entry should be about and then get stuck in.

Gecko's log, stardate 19-4-2012

I'm getting the hang of this vigilante thing. I started out small – thwarting miscreant teenagers from nicking cans of Dutch Gold and that sort of thing. They're very enterprising, I must say. But it seemed like there were better ways I could use my time as The Gecko. So I staked out the worst areas for theft and stopped *three* B-and-Es (that's code for breaking-and-entering, according to *Law & Order* – I'm trying to swot up on the crime-fighting speak).

Of course, in the process of foiling these blokes, they simply dropped and smashed most of the laptops/ HD tellies/family crystal they were trying to make off with. So, in that sense, it was a little counterproductive. But I've taken to dragging the thieves back into the houses/apartments and tying them up with tree-ties that I bought down the local B&Q and then calling the police on them. It's always an awkward moment when they ask who's calling.

I'm now down to the last entry. I want to show that Gary has improved as 'The Gecko' and that it's changing his attitude and his personal life. I see from the grid that I wanted him to encounter his ex, Janice. He's not really pining for her as much anymore and he's starting to tackle bigger crimes.

Gecko's log. Stardate. ~~3-5-2012 4-5-2012~~
Well. Whatever. It's May.

Bumped into Janice tonight. She was surprised and weirdly cheerful when she saw me. At one point I even thought I saw her blush. It's probably the suit. It does wonders for my four-pack. She was asking me how I was and was saying something about how we should grab dinner sometime or something. I don't know. I was too distracted by the sight of three guys breaking into a car in an unattended car-park up the road. She kept peering over her shoulder to see what I was looking at. Basically, I had to cut the conversation short.

As I ran up the street towards the car-park, she told me to give her a call. Initially I was quite pleased by that, but it sort of occurred to me as I clung to the roof of the speeding car that it was actually Janice who dumped me, not the other way around. And, like, was I even happy when I was with her? I'm kind of busy these days anyhow. For someone whose main form of exercise involved repeatedly lifting cans to my mouth, I'm really starting to enjoy the physical challenges of being The Gecko. Those guys' faces when I crawled out onto the windscreen – priceless. It was even covered on page 2 of the *Gazette*. I'm starting to think that was the best twenty quid I've ever spent in a drunken stupor.

Marked Example

Read the following extract from *The Man of the World* by Frank O'Connor. Write three or four diary entries by Jimmy in which he describes his experience of Larry's visit to his house.

When I was a kid there were no such things as holidays for me and my likes, and I have no feeling of grievance about it because, in the way of kids, I simply invented them, which was much more satisfactory. One year, my summer holiday was a couple of nights I spent at the house of a friend called Jimmy Leary, who lived at the other side of the road from us. His parents sometimes went away for a couple of days to visit a sick relative in Bantry, and he was given permission to have a friend in to keep him company. I took my holiday with the greatest seriousness, insisted on the loan of Father's old travelling bag and dragged it myself down our lane past the neighbours standing at their doors.

'Are you off somewhere, Larry?' asked one.

'Yes, Mrs Rooney,' I said with great pride. 'Off for my holidays to the Learys.'

'Wisha, aren't you very lucky?' she said with amusement.

'Lucky' seemed an absurd description of my good fortune. The Learys' house was a big one with a high flight of steps up to the front door, which was always kept shut. They had a piano in the front room, a pair of binoculars on a table near the window, and a toilet on the stairs that seemed to me to be the last word in elegance and immodesty. We brought the binoculars up to the bedroom with us. From the window you could see the whole road up and down, from the quarry at its foot with the tiny houses perched on top of it to the open fields at the other end, where the last gas-lamp rose against the sky.

Each morning I was up with the first light, leaning out the window in my nightshirt and watching through the glasses all the mysterious figures you never saw from our lane: policemen, railwaymen, and farmers on their way to market.

I admired Jimmy almost as much as I admired his house, and for much the same reasons. He was a year older than I, was well-mannered and well-dressed, and would not associate with most of the kids on the road at all. He had a way when any of them joined us of resting against a wall with his hands in his trouser pockets and listening to them with a sort of well-bred smile, a knowing smile, that seemed to me the height of elegance. And it was not that he was a softy, because he was an excellent boxer and wrestler and could easily have held his own with them any time, but he did not wish to. He was superior to them. He was – there is only one word that still describes it for me – sophisticated.

I attributed his sophistication to the piano, the binoculars, and the indoor john, and felt that if only I had the same advantages I could have been sophisticated, too. I knew I wasn't, because I was always being deceived by the world of appearances. I would take a sudden violent liking to some boy, and when I went to his house my admiration would spread to his parents and sisters, and I would think how wonderful it must be to have such a home; but when I told Jimmy he would smile in that knowing way of his and say quietly: 'I believe they had the bailiffs in a few weeks ago,' and, even though I didn't know what bailiffs were, bang would go the whole world of appearances, and I would realise that once again I had been deceived.

It was the same with fellows and girls. Seeing some bigger chap we knew walking out with a girl for the first time, Jimmy would say casually: 'He'd better mind himself: that one is dynamite.' And, even though I knew as little of girls who were dynamite as I did of bailiffs, his tone would be sufficient to indicate that I had been taken in by sweet voices and broad-brimmed hats, gaslight and evening smells from gardens.

Forty years later I can still measure the extent of my obsession, for, though my own handwriting is almost illegible, I sometimes find myself scribbling idly on a pad in a small, stiff, perfectly legible hand that I recognise with amusement as a reasonably good forgery of Jimmy's. My admiration still lies there somewhere, a fossil in my memory, but Jimmy's knowing smile is something I have never managed to acquire.

We were in by seven bright because we got mass in the morning and we decided because the night sky was so clear we'd bring the binoculars up to my room and look out over all of Cork. We legged it up to my room – Larry, in more of a sprinting mood, beat me – and we sat at the biggest window. The sun was just setting. Lighting the whole area orange. We could see the whole road up and down. The quarry was in view and at the end of it the tiny perked houses. Up at the top were open fields. You could see the gas lamps being turned on and they glowed softly against the sky. Larry just stared, seemingly astonished that his own neighbourhood could be so beautiful.

Friday 5th of May

Mam and Dad went away this weekend. Aunty May's sick again. Jesus if that woman comes down with any more illnesses she'll have no defences left in her. Larry's coming over at five to keep me company till they come home on Monday. Larry and I don't really know how to cook so Mam left us with a chicken. I think we'll probably make sandwiches.

Friday 5th of May (evening)

Oh my God, I can't believe Larry brought his bear with him. You know at ten you think you'd be alright for a few nights without house comforts. Larry's after bringing his trusty travel suitcase. I don't know what he put in it for his holidays this time but it took the two of us to pull it up the high flight of steps. We step one foot into the house and Larry just stares at the piano. I finally get him to move down the hall and he starts laughing at the toilet. I never really understood what was so funny.

It finally reached eight o'clock, we were both so exhausted from playing cowboys and Indians we both nearly died in the bed as soon as we laid our heads down.

Saturday 6th of May

Larry was up at the crack of dawn peering through the binoculars watching everyone on their way to the market. The usual crowd you'd never really see on Larry's street, farmers, policemen and railwaymen. After some breakfast we headed outside and rested against Crary's wall as the sun began to heat up. Some of the lads from Larry's lane came up chatting to us. When they were done talking about insubordinate, futile little matters we finally go to split into two teams for soccer. We stuck Larry in Goal cause he always had this problem of touching the ball with his hands which in a way is very useful.

Comments:

» Clarity of Purpose

The student has clearly read and understood the question. The student has been asked to write a series of diary entries describing Larry's visit from Jimmy's point of view. Everything she writes is relevant to, and focused on, the events described in the Frank O'Connor's story. Her diary entries deal with Larry's visit only. She shows that she understands what a diary entry should be, and reproduces the conventions of the genre.

» Coherence of Delivery

The student uses a register appropriate to the task and maintains it throughout the diary. She successfully manages to write as though she were Jimmy. The student displays a high level of creativity in her convincing and coherent portrayal of Larry's visit.

» Efficiency of Language Use

This piece features some vibrant and lively use of language, which effectively conjures up a fictional world. The vocabulary is good and the sentence patterns are varied enough not to bore the reader. The diary entries make good use of paragraphs, with each paragraph focusing on different aspects of Larry's visit.

» Accuracy of Mechanics

There are several places where this piece departs from conventional grammar and syntax. However, this is excusable given the fact that the student is writing from Jimmy's point of view. In fact, these irregularities enhance our enjoyment of the piece. The spelling is accurate throughout.

Exercises

1. Read the following extract from 'The Diamond as Big as the Ritz' by F. Scott Fitzgerald. Imagine you are John T. Unger. Write two diary entries, one detailing your experience of leaving Hades and arriving at St Midas's, and another reflecting on your impression of, and interaction with, Percy Washington.

John T. Unger came from a family that had been well known in Hades – a small town on the Mississippi River – for several generations.

John's father had held the amateur golf championship through many a heated contest; Mrs Unger was known "from hot-box to hot-bed", as the local phrase went, for her political addresses; and young John T. Unger, who had just turned sixteen, had danced all the latest dances from New York before he put on long trousers. And now, for a certain time, he was to be away from home. That respect for a New England education which is the bane of all provincial places, which drains them yearly of their most promising young men, had seized upon his parents. Nothing would suit them but that he should go to St Midas' School near Boston – Hades was too small to hold their darling and gifted son.

Now in Hades – as you know if you ever have been there – the names of the more fashionable preparatory schools and colleges mean very little. The inhabitants have been so long out of the world that, though they make a show of keeping up to date in dress and manners and literature, they depend to a great extent on hearsay, and a function that in Hades would be considered elaborate would doubtless be hailed by a Chicago beef-princess as "perhaps a little tacky".

John T. Unger was on the eve of departure. Mrs Unger, with maternal fatuity, packed his trunks full of linen suits and electric fans, and Mr Unger presented his son with an asbestos pocket-book stuffed with money.

"Remember, you are always welcome here," he said. "You can be sure boy, that we'll keep the home fires burning."

"I know," answered John huskily.

"Don't forget who you are and where you come from," continued his father proudly, "and you can do nothing to harm you. You are an Unger – from Hades."

So the old man and the young shook hands and John walked away with tears streaming from his eyes. Ten minutes later he had passed outside the city limits, and he stopped to glance back for the last time. Over the gates the old-fashioned Victorian motto seemed strangely attractive to him. His father had tried time and time again to have it changed to something with a little more push and verve about it, such as "Hades – Your Opportunity", or else a plain "Welcome" sign set over a hearty handshake pricked out in electric lights. The old motto was a little depressing, Mr Unger had thought – but now....

So John took his look and then set his face resolutely toward his destination. And, as he turned away, the lights of Hades against the sky seemed full of a warm and passionate beauty.

St Midas' School is half an hour from Boston in a Rolls-Pierce motorcar. The actual distance will never be known, for no one, except John T. Unger, had ever arrived there save in a Rolls-Pierce and probably no one ever will again. St Midas' is the most expensive and the most exclusive boys' preparatory school in the world.

John's first two years there passed pleasantly. The fathers of all the boys were money-kings and John spent his summers visiting at fashionable resorts. While he was very fond of all the boys he visited, their fathers struck him as being much of a piece, and in his boyish way he often wondered at their exceeding sameness. When he told them where his home was they would ask jovially, "Pretty hot down there?" and John would muster a faint smile and answer, "It certainly is." His response would have been heartier had they not all made this joke – at best varying it with, "Is it hot enough for you down there?" which he hated just as much.

In the middle of his second year at school, a quiet, handsome boy named Percy Washington had been put in John's form. The newcomer was pleasant in his manner and exceedingly well dressed even for St Midas', but for some reason he kept aloof from the other boys. The only person with whom he was intimate was John T. Unger, but even to John he was entirely uncommunicative concerning his home or his family. That he was wealthy went without saying, but beyond a few such deductions John knew little of his friend, so it promised rich confectionery for his curiosity when Percy invited him to spend the summer at his home "in the West". He accepted, without hesitation.

It was only when they were in the train that Percy became, for the first time, rather communicative. One day while they were eating lunch in the dining-car and discussing the imperfect characters of several of the boys at school, Percy suddenly changed his tone and made an abrupt remark.

"My father," he said, "is by far the richest man in the world."

"Oh," said John, politely. He could think of no answer to make to this confidence. He considered "That's very nice," but it sounded hollow and was on the point of saying, "Really?" but refrained since it would seem to question Percy's statement. And such an astounding statement could scarcely be questioned.

"By far the richest," repeated Percy.

"I was reading in the World *Almanac*," began John, "that there was one man in America with an income of over five million a year and four men with incomes of over three million a year, and–"

"Oh, they're nothing." Percy's mouth was a half-moon of scorn. "Catchpenny capitalists, financial small-fry, petty merchants and money-lenders. My father could buy them out and not know he'd done it."

"But how does he –"

"Why haven't they put down *his* income tax? Because he doesn't pay any. At least he pays a little one – but he doesn't pay any on his *real* income."

"He must be very rich," said John simply. "I'm glad. I like very rich people.

"The richer a fella is, the better I like him." There was a look of passionate frankness upon his dark face. "I visited the Schnlitzer-Murphys last Easter. Vivian Schnlitzer-Murphy had rubies as big as hen's eggs, and sapphires that were like globes with lights inside them –"

"I love jewels," agreed Percy enthusiastically. "Of course I wouldn't want any one at school to know about it, but I've got quite a collection myself, I used to collect them instead of stamps."

"And diamonds," continued John eagerly. "The Schnlitzer-Murphys had diamonds as big as walnuts –"

"That's nothing." Percy had leaned forward and dropped his voice to a low whisper. "That's nothing at all. My father has a diamond bigger than the Ritz-Carlton Hotel."

2. Read the following short story entitled 'White Socks and Weirdos' by Sophie Hampton. Based on your reading of the extract, write three diary entries from the point of view of Lorraine Abbot in which you detail her encounters with the narrator.

My face goes the colour of Mum's lipstick. I know what the colour feels like because when Lorraine makes my cheeks hot and my heart B-BOOM, B-BOOM, I go to the girls' toilets: two plums in the mirror.

'Tights are for spastics,' says popular Lorraine in knee-high white socks and patent shoes. On Monday, her eighth birthday, she was the first girl in my class to walk to school on her own. She showed off about it All Day Long. On Tuesday she came into the classroom at twenty to ten, with puffy frog eyes and her mum; big boys on bikes had chased her and she had run back home and cried. The Witches had crowded round and made stupid noises. By afternoon register, the big boys had turned into men wearing balaclavas.

'I'm allowed to choose my own clothes,' Lorraine says. She flicks back her long hair cut straight at the ends. 'Skip with us.' She pushes me into the middle of the Witches.

Ooh, ahh, I lost my bra. I left my knickers in my boyfriend's car! they chant as the skipping rope twirls faster and faster under my feet. I know they're going to trip me up so I hope they do it soon; the waistband on my tights has lost its grippiness and the tights will slither down my skinny legs, sticky-out knee bits round my ankles.

The girls jerk the rope and when I fall everybody laughs. I graze my palms: red scratches, grey dust, yellow gunk.

'Why don't you ever invite anyone to tea?' asks Lorraine. 'Is it because you live in a gippo caravan?'

I don't invite anyone for tea because our flat is embarrassing. Nobody I know lives anywhere like me, in a block in King's Cross where people throw rubbish into the yard from their windows at night and the corridor walls are stained yellow with wee. Lorraine and the Witches live in the new estate on the edge of the park.

Other things are embarrassing too. Last Christmas, Mum made leaflets about being vegetarian: Meat is Murder she wrote and No Blood on my Hands. Nathan, my brother, and I drew pigs and cows and splodges of red paint on the sheets of paper. Mum took the leaflets, and us, round all the local butchers and all the local butchers told her to fuck off. She was brave: butchers are scary what with their stained-brown aprons and sharp knives. Their shops smelt like the taste when I nibble my nails after I've been on the rusty swings in the rec.

43

On Saturday mornings, when everyone else in my class watches Multi-Coloured Swap Shop, Mum and I take the washing to the launderette in black plastic sacks. I worry that the bags will split and our jumble sale clothes will spill onto the pavement. I have to carry my sack with both hands so I can't pull up my tights or scratch the eczema on the insides of my knees.

'Weirdo, don't ignore me. I said why don't you invite anyone to tea?' Lorraine gives me a dark and narrow look.

B-BOOM, B-BOOM. I want to slot two pence pieces into her eyes, push them into her brain. Who'd be the spaz then? She dangles the skipping rope from the middle and the handles knock together: click, click, click, click. She swings the rope and the handles whizz round in a blur, like a spinning top. When she flicks the skipping rope into my tummy, quick and hard, I bend over a bit. A sound pushes out. Like an animal.

The milk I drank at playtime bubbles into my mouth and I spit it into the sink. I turn on the tap, whoooosh, and close my eyes and shoot Lorraine Abbot through the head.

'Come on, Mummy,' I say, walking as fast as I can. Mum's clogs clip-clop on the pavement. Once we turn the corner I slow down.

'What did you have for lunch?' asks Mum.

'Nothing,' I say. 'Wasn't hungry.' I start to cry. Mum holds my hand and the graze stings. I tell her some of what happened in the playground and why I was too scared to eat.

She digs some rice cakes out of her bag. 'I'm going to speak to Miss Harvey after the holidays. Lorraine Abbot is a bully.'

'No! You can't. Lorraine'll kill me.'

'You'll kill yourself if you don't eat.'

'I could take packed lunches. Children who take packed lunches eat in a different room. Please, Mum.'

'Okay. It will be easier for you to be vegetarian. Have another rice cake.'

'Yes?'

I take a breath of warm air, full of the clean smell of washing. 'Please will you buy me some white socks for school?'

'Why?'

'Because all the other girls wear white socks.'

'No.'

'Why not?'

'Because it's not about what the other girls wear. It's hard to keep socks white and hot washes are bad for the environment. Anyway, you've got plenty of tights.'

I want to curl up in a washing machine and go round and round.

'But Mummy ...'

'No.'

My chin drops onto my chest. My blue shoes are sprinkled with soap powder. Like stars.

Past Exam Questions:

1 (2005): 'On Saturday afternoons Margaret Ann would go to the market to buy the meat for Sunday.' Write three diary entries that Margaret Ann might have written over a series of Saturday evenings. Your writing should relate to her experience as described in the passage.

2 (2006): Imagine that, in an attempt to control his feelings, the boy writes into his diary an account of the incident and his reactions to it. Write his diary entry.

3 (2008): Write two diary entries: one written by Alexander, recalling his encounter with Eva in Tompkins Square Park and the second by Zach, giving his thoughts on hearing that Eva has purchased the violin.

4 (2011): Imagine you are Sarah, the young girl in Text 3 above. Based on your reading of this extract, write two diary entries, one shortly before and one shortly after your journey to Dublin.

Introduction

SHORT ARTICLES ARE SIMILAR TO TALKS AND LETTERS IN THAT THEY
TYPICALLY REQUIRE YOU TO MAKE A CASE OF ONE KIND OR ANOTHER.

In one past exam students were asked to make a case opposing or supporting a school trip. In another
they were asked to make a case for a particular Irish town as a must-see tourist attraction.

Sometimes you will be specifically asked to write an opinion piece or persuasive article. In such cases it's
vital that you actually do have an opinion on the topic and express it at the beginning of your article.
For example, if you're writing about the benefits of sport don't ramble on for five paragraphs about last
night's match. Take a stance and express it early.

Sometimes the question can be phrased in a more general manner. You might be asked, for instance, to write an introductory article for a book about ordinary people. Even with such a general question it is often best to take a definite stance which you develop throughout the article. You might make the case, for instance, that the everyday heroism of ordinary people is underrated in this age of celebrity.

PLAN IN ADVANCE

With short articles, as with all compositions, it is important to plan in advance before you begin to write. Your short article should contain four or five paragraphs. Take the time to jot down what each paragraph will be about before you start writing.

MANAGE YOUR PARAGRAPHS

In short articles you are generally trying to make a case. Sometimes, you might want to state this point plainly in your opening paragraph. We see this in the following opening to an article entitled 'Modern music has little merit'.

> The standard of popular music is in decline. The artists who now top our charts are, in the main, talentless, shallow creatures whose careers are short-lived – here today and gladly forgotten tomorrow. There is no depth to what they have to say, the lyrics that they spout depressingly devoid of genuine sentiment and meaning. They are part of an industry that is all about profit, an industry in which the artist and the music that he or she creates is disposable, a sound that is briefly heard and signifies nothing.

It is also possible to begin your article with an 'impact' paragraph that grabs the audience's attention before stating your point clearly in the second paragraph. The 'impact' paragraph might often focus on a shocking statistic, real-life story or dramatic event that brings your point vividly to life. For example:

> The Beatles, Joan Baez, the Rolling Stones, Elvis Presley, Led Zepplin, Bob Dylan, Eric Clapton, Aretha Franklin. These are the giants of the music world. Their rise to prominence began decades ago and their music and lyrics continue to reverberate melodiously across the sound-waves long after they have shuffled off this mortal coil. Their talent is a precious guiding light in this dark age of music. Look at today's crew of talentless pretenders. How many of those will still be loved and revered by our children and grandchildren? Pop music is dying a slow and tuneless death.

In each of the two or three body paragraphs you should focus on a single topic. Each paragraph should support the point you make at the beginning of the article. In the body paragraphs of your article, you can use facts and statistics to appeal to your audience's intellect. You can also use real-life stories and emotional language to appeal to their hearts. Every single paragraph should be geared towards one thing: convincing the audience that your point of view is correct.

The closing paragraph should briefly summarise the main points of the article before concluding with a snappy, memorable phrase. It can also be very effective to conclude your article with a rhetorical question that will linger in the audience's mind.

HAVE PURPOSE AND FOCUS

As you compose, always remain conscious of your article's purpose. Every paragraph should be geared towards advancing your stance or point of view. Remember you will be penalised if you ramble or drift off topic. Advance planning will prevent this. Keep your plan open in front of you as you compose.

TONE AND REGISTER

The tone of your article will vary depending on the topic and the article's intended readership. An article for a school website about the need for longer lunch breaks, for example, might be written in a light-hearted tone. An article for a national newspaper about the issue of unemployment will, however, require a more serious or formal tone to be adopted. What is important to remember is that, once you adopt a given tone, be it serious or light-hearted, stick to it throughout the article. Reading the samples that follow will give you a sense of what is required here.

Walk Thru 1

Write a short article entitled 'Why we should lower the voting age to 16'.

PLANNING

My first task is to establish a point of view. I see that the title of the article has done this for me. I know what case I have got to make here. I must give clear reasons why we should lower the voting age.

Now I'm going to structure my article. Five paragraphs will be enough for a short article like this one.

1: The first paragraph, the introduction, will clearly state my point of view.

2: The second paragraph will deal with the many legal entitlements that 16-year-olds already possess.

3: The third paragraph will argue that young people, contrary to popular belief, have a real interest in politics.

4: My fourth paragraph will deal with the fact that young people are often the ones most affected by political decisions.

5: In my final concluding paragraph I am going to try to sum up my position in a snappy and memorable way.

WRITING

I will start with my introduction. This will be a relatively short paragraph and will engage with the topic and state clearly my point of view:

In Ireland, 16-year-olds are granted quite a number of adult privileges and responsibilities. However, they are not permitted to vote. Withholding this right from our youths is unfair, especially when we consider that by many legal and financial definitions 16-year-olds are already considered adult.

I see from my plan that my first body paragraph will deal with the fact that 16-year-olds already have numerous legal entitlements. I will start the paragraph with a short topic sentence, a sentence declaring what the paragraph is going to be about:

16-year-olds have many legal entitlements.

Every other sentence in this paragraph is going to relate to or expand on this topic sentence. If I find myself writing something that does not relate directly to this topic sentence I know I've gone wrong.

To complete this paragraph I am going to back up my topic sentence with some relevant facts about these entitlements. I am going to mention their entitlement to work, to drive, to travel unaccompanied and to possess a firearm:

They are legally entitled to work a 40-hour week – and subject to all of the lovely taxes and charges associated with it, including PAYE, PRSI, and the Universal Social Charge. Provided they hold a valid licence, a 16-year-old can legally drive mopeds, work vehicles (i.e. tractors) and certain types of motorcycles. They can travel abroad unaccompanied, be held criminally responsible and charged for illegal activities. They can open a bank account. They can even apply for a licence to own a firearm! These all sound mature and adult to me. And yet they cannot vote. Is this fair?

Note how every sentence I have written relates to my topic sentence. I don't wander off the point by talking about my favourite computer game or social networking activities.

Note how I concluded with a question that challenges the reader. This is an effective device when we are looking to persuade someone of our point of view.

I see that my next paragraph is going to examine the notion that young people are not interested in politics. Once again I start off with the simple topic sentence – 'Let no one say that teens are simply not interested in politics' – immediately arguing that this is untrue. Then I am going to write a number of sentences that relate to this topic sentence. I'm going to make sure that nothing I write strays from this topic.

Let no one say that teens are simply not interested in politics. Those who argue against giving youths a vote because they think 16-year-olds pay no attention to political discourse, wouldn't take it seriously and are not able make informed decisions about it, are being unreasonable and hypocritical. Secondary school students in this country are obliged to study CSPE up to Junior Cert level. They are forced to learn about the country's political and electoral system.

Again I will round the paragraph off by challenging the reader to see the unfairness in denying 16-year-olds the right to vote:

And yet they are denied the right to vote. Is this fair?

My final body paragraph will deal with the fact that young people are often the ones most affected by political decisions. Again, I will begin with a clear topic sentence and back this up with relevant facts supporting my argument:

Children and teenagers are often the ones who experience the impact of political decisions ahead of everyone else. If there are cutbacks in education, they will bear the brunt of that – not politicians. If there is a change to the curriculum, they are the ones who test it out. And, indeed, if things are not changed when they clearly need to be changed, they are the ones who will suffer most without it. And yet they have no say in who should have the privilege of making these decisions. Is this fair?

In my conclusion I want to briefly summarise the argument I have made in the article.

The answer is no, it's not fair. When so much expectation and responsibility is placed on the average Irish 16-year-old, it seems illogical not to also give them the right to vote.

I would like to conclude my article with a powerful and memorable message. I will link the voting restrictions placed on 16-year-olds with the fact that society once denied women the right to vote.

You have to wonder why so many politicians are against it. Do they fear the changes the young people of this country could bring about? Once upon a time, society didn't allow women to vote. We look back on those restrictions now and we can't believe how insulting and unfair they were. Some day – hopefully some day soon – we will look back on the same voting restrictions we once placed on 16 and 17-year-olds, and we will think the same thing: insulting and unfair.

Note how the conclusion is short and does not ramble on and on repeating the points made in the article. Note also how the conclusion is tied into the point of view established at the start of the article.

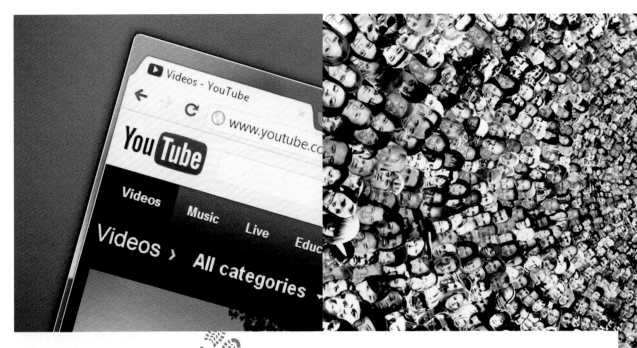

Walk Thru 2

Write a short article entitled 'Playing the fame game'.

PLANNING

I must first establish a point of view: I believe that the culture of celebrity is unhealthy and has a malign impact on society.

This is a short article. Five paragraphs should suffice.

1: In the first paragraph, the introduction, I will state clearly my point of view that society, young people in particular, are obsessed with fame.

2: In the second paragraph, I will talk about the popularity of celebrity photo magazines, which publish intrusive pictures of celebrities' personal lives

3: In the third paragraph, I will point to the growth of celebrity television shows, packed with B-list celebrities who are famous for being famous.

4: In the fourth paragraph I will examine how the celebrity culture is leading many people to seek their own exposure through YouTube, vines, Instagram selfies, Facebook and Twitter.

5: In the fifth and final paragraph I will wrap up by concluding with a strong point that draws together the previous topics.

WRITING

Now I must write my introduction. I will state my point of view straight away. This decides the direction of the entire essay.

> The culture of celebrity has grown to become a monstrous vehicle of desperation, hysteria and obsession. Society – young people in particular – has an infatuation with fame. We have an intense craving for information about and insights into the lives of actors, musicians and TV personalities, and it is driving us all to seek out our own fame. This might not seem like a big deal, but the impact of what Lady Gaga herself called 'the fame monster' is really damaging.

My plan says that the second paragraph should be about magazines that are full of pictures of celebrities.

> This is a terribly unhealthy trend. We are all familiar with those trashy magazines that decorate the shelves of our newsagents. They are printed in garish colours and grainy photographs of second-rate celebrities doing totally unimportant things (like going to the beach, or getting out of a car) are splashed all over the covers, as if it was breaking news. Most of them aren't even justifiably famous. They are simply famous for being famous and not because they are exceptionally talented. These photos are designed to do one of two things: To put ordinary people up on a pedestal above the rest of us, to be adored and worshipped; or to expose all their flaws in order to shame them.

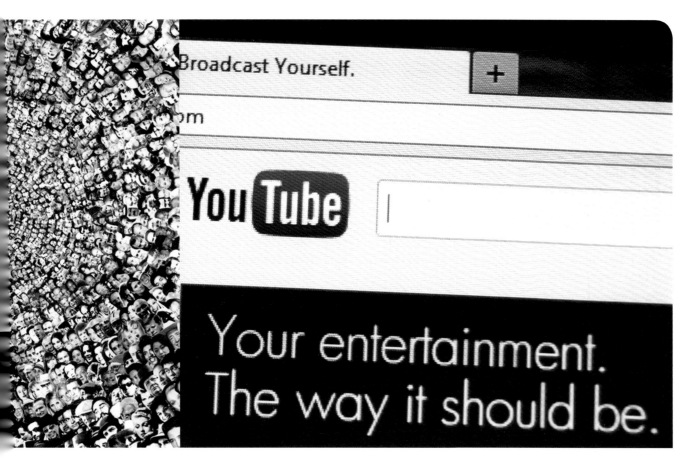

The next paragraph, according to my plan, should be about the rise of the celebrity television shows.

Fifteen years ago, nobody ever heard of reality television and the only talent show worth gossiping about was Eurovision. Now, there's almost nothing else to watch except this rubbish. From 'X-Factor', to 'I'm A Celebrity, Get Me Out of Here', 'Strictly Come Dancing' and 'America's/Britain's Got Talent', there is an endless supply of low-grade celebrity programmes filling our television channels. They're almost exclusively populated by B-list celebrities who are trying to resurrect their careers, or ordinary people who are desperate for the limelight. They make a profit by broadcasting the auditions of the most talentless people – again, just so that viewers can point and laugh at them – and even the winners disappear into obscurity after a year or two, only to be replaced by other would-be starlets.

This is leading more and more of us to seek out our own fame. We pose for ridiculous 'selfies' on Instagram, broadcast our every opinion, thought and emotion on the likes of Facebook and Twitter, and churn out 15-second 'Vines' of our reactions and 'fails'. Even the name YouTube points to the growing pomp of today's celebrity-obsessed culture. It sells a message. Make a video about you, broadcast you to the world. But this is a very risky idea. We are literally putting our lives into other people's hands. Playing the fame game is leading people to do some stupid things and exposes them to needless criticism and abuse.

Now I want to wrap up. I want to make a powerful point that shows how unhealthy, silly and negative the celebrity culture is, and how we should save our admiration for people who really make a difference.

This poisonous celebrity culture is bringing out the worst in us. The more we revere people in the world around us, the worse we start to feel about ourselves. It tricks us into building our sense of self-worth on the approval of strangers we never meet. We want people to be impressed by us. We try so hard to replicate these celebrities, to get on television, to go viral, to be liked, shared, followed, retweeted, admired. Loved. Fame is like a desert mirage – something we thirst for, something that looks good from afar but that ultimately doesn't exist. We should save our adoration for those who truly make a positive impact on the world and on ourselves.

Exercises

1. **When writing an opinion piece or persuasive article, what must you always do? You might begin your article with an 'impact' paragraph. What might such a paragraph consist of?**

2. **What should you aim to achieve in your closing paragraph?**

3. **The following is the topic sentence of a paragraph in a short article on the benefits of travel. Read it carefully and then complete the paragraph:**

It cannot be denied that travel broadens the mind.

4. **The following is the topic sentence of a paragraph in a short article about the Irish diet. Read it carefully and then complete the paragraph:**

When compared with many of our European neighbours, the Irish diet seems dull and uninspired.

5. **Rearrange the following five sentences so that they create a properly structured paragraph:**

Bus and train routes are being cut, fares are going up and transport projects are being jettisoned in favour of building new roads.

We are consigning ourselves to endless traffic problems and our environment to an ugly, polluted fate. Looking at public transport, it's clear that the government does not intend to reduce our greenhouse gas emissions.

With policies like these in place, we have no hope of meeting our targets and will be fined by the EU.

Despite a growing body of evidence to suggest there is an appetite among the people to use public rather than private transport, our politicians have made it more difficult and costly than ever to do so.

6. **Rearrange the following sentences so that they form a properly structured paragraph:**

The fights – called The Hunger Games – are held every year and are designed to both entertain the nation and as well as punish districts that rebelled in an earlier civil war.

The Hunger Games is a movie based on a series of science fiction books by Suzanne Collins.

In this kill-or-be-killed world, Katniss and her friend, Peeta, must deal with life-threatening challenges and troubling moral decisions.

Katniss is forced to represent her district in a series of televised gladiatorial-style fights. It follows the story of teenage heroine Katniss Everdeen from District 12.

7. **The following paragraph was written for a serious national newspaper. Read it and then comment on whether or not the tone and language is appropriate.**

Nuclear power is just a bad idea and if we introduce it to Ireland it will go down as the biggest screw-up in our history. The stakes are way too high. The Yanks messed up with Three Mile Island, the Soviets with Chernobyl and the Japanese with Fukushima. If you put a nuclear plant in Paddy's hands, you can be sure the grass isn't the only thing that'll have a green hue.

8. **Complete this opening paragraph to an article of young people and politics:**

For many young people, politics is something that older people engage with. It is a tedious affair, populated with uninspiring individuals who have nothing to say to the youth of modern Ireland.

9. **Imagine you have been asked to write a short article about famine in the Sudan region. Work in pairs and write two different opening paragraphs. Make one an impact paragraph and the other a more standard, fact-based opening paragraph.**

10. Complete the following plan for a short article about violent video games:

STANCE: It is harmless entertainment.		
PARA	**SUBJECT MATTER**	**TOPIC SENTENCE**
1	Establish point of view	The idea that violent video games lead to the perpetration of violent acts is plainly ridiculous.
2	Personal experience	I have been playing video games for many years.
3		
4		
5		

11. Complete the following plan for a short article about the state funding of the arts:

STANCE: Keep it, don't cut it.		
PARA	**SUBJECT MATTER**	**TOPIC SENTENCE**
1		
2	Benefits to economy	Irish films and television programmes have won much global praise recently.
3		
4		
5	Conclusion	Arts are the soul of the country and contribute hugely to our society.

12. Use the following grid to plan a short article about the effects of money on sport:

STANCE: Professional games are more concerned with sponsorship deals and advertising than sportsmanship.		
PARA	**SUBJECT MATTER**	**TOPIC SENTENCE**
1		
2	Soccer – player transfer fees, e.g. Cristiano Ronaldo, Gareth Bale	Is any player really worth £100 million?
3	Ticket prices	Going to support your local GAA or rugby team is more expensive than it has ever been.
4		
5		

13. Use the following grid to plan a short article on nuclear power:

STANCE: Ireland needs nuclear power to cater for our growing energy demands.		
PARA	**SUBJECT MATTER**	**TOPIC SENTENCE**
1	Electricity use increasing	Between 42' televisions and electric cars, we use more electricity now than ever before.
2	Fossil fuels costly, finite and bad for the environment	We cannot rely on oil, coal and gas forever, and there are several reasons why.
3		
4		
5		

Commentary 1:

Write an article for your school website, explaining to your fellow students why you believe the school should or should not continue to use uniforms.

Acknowledges the readers her article is aimed at.

Takes a point of view early on.
Strong topic sentence and topic paragraph.

At the risk of being lynched by my fellow students, I would like to sound a word of caution against the recent movement to retire our school uniform. Every year, September kicks off with kids groaning about having to put on their uniforms and parents having to buy them. Uniforms are an easy target for criticism but in this article I would like to address the complaints of both students and parents and prove that uniforms are not the evil we think they are.

I disagree with the popular theory that uniforms are nothing more than a money-making scheme for certain businesses. Although uniforms have historically been very expensive, I believe this has changed a lot. Schools around the country now permit students to purchase cheaper alternatives from shops like Aldi, Dunnes, Lidl and Tesco. These generic uniforms are usually a fraction of the cost of the 'official' school attire but are no different thanks to stitch-on or iron-on school crests.

It's easy for us to forget that uniforms have a practical function. Those drab jumpers, shirts, trousers and skirts are designed to last. The sacks of heavy books that rest on your shoulders and back, the constant bustling and shuffling up and down stairs, around corridors, the mucking around with friends, pulling items on and off for PE or in warm weather – I think you'll agree that the school environment subjects clothes to a lot of wear and tear. If you think your fashionable Nike sweatshirt or Roxy hoodie is going to outlast the frumpy but durable uniform in these conditions, you're wrong. When you add it all up at the end of the school year, a uniform is still a lot cheaper than maintaining civilian fineries!

Evocative and persuasive language ('busting and shuffling').

Uniforms offer some important social benefits too – as much as you might dislike that frumpy, chafing jumper, nobody's ever really going to judge you for it. Fashion competition is not a possibility where uniforms are mandatory. Nobody can be mocked, rated or teased about their choice of clothes when students of all colour, creed and class wear the same thing. Uniforms level the social playing field and promote a sense of togetherness. When we wear our uniforms, we tacitly become part of something larger than ourselves – a sort of local academic community.

Shows empathy – that can win people over to her point of view. Says 'we', which reminds us that she is a young person writing for a young readership.

So, before we throw out the humble uniform we should really take the time to think it through fully. Do we want to swap the annual costs of a jumper, shirt, tie and pants for the annual costs of an entire wardrobe? Do we want to face catwalk competition on top of everything else you already have to deal with at school? I'm not sure about you, but I certainly don't.

Good conclusion that summarises her points concisely and efficiently. Use of rhetorical questions creates impact.

Comments:

» Clarity of purpose:

She has been asked to write a short article explaining why she thinks the school should or should not continue to use uniforms and has done so. This is proof that she has read, understood and answered the question. The importance of this cannot be overstated.

The composition is focused from start to finish. She has been asked to pick a side, to make a case, and she has done this. She does not indulge in any irrelevant discussion about clothing or fashion.

The student makes her point of view obvious from the opening and she stays on message throughout the article. She chooses early on to argue for keeping uniforms and she sticks to that task.

She does not address an audience or an individual recipient, as one might in a letter or speech. In this way she illustrates her familiarity with the genre and format.

» Coherence of delivery:

She uses a consistent tone in her composition. The piece is brimming with author's personal enthusiasm and belief. And yet her arguments are objective and logical.

She deploys her arguments in a sensible way, which shows she has the skill to rein in and master her ideas. Each paragraph is crafted around one topic, which in turn is used to strengthen her overall argument.

She orders her topics well, ensuring that she has something new and relevant to say at each stage of the article. She does not repeat or recycle her points. This makes it a very strong piece of writing.

» Efficiency of language use:

This student employs some good vocabulary and phrases. E.g.: 'At the risk of being lynched', 'Retire the uniform', 'Bustling and shuffling'.

She has done well not to repeat the use of simpler words like 'clothes' and 'uniforms' in an article about clothes and uniforms. Instead she brings in alternatives such as 'civilian fineries' and 'attire' to ensure the piece remains fresh and interesting.

» Mechanics:

This student obviously understands the ins and outs of spelling, punctuation and grammar.

Commentary 2:

Write a short article about whether or not you think video games are to blame for anti-social behaviour.

States point of view early on.

'pen this article' – clever technique proves he understands genre.

'What a load of nonsense!' – reaffirms his opinion, ensures article remains focused.

Addresses readership. Good topic sentence.

Doesn't allow himself to get distracted by tempting but unnecessary details about the games.

Good structure – is managing his ideas and paragraphs well.

Strong conclusion – captures his stance in three well-written sentences.

Something happened recently that forced me take action and defend the much-criticised world of gaming. I was warned by my doctor that I'm developing something he called 'gamer's thumb'. He told me the bones in my thumbs were becoming pronounced because I was spending 'excessive amounts of time' punching buttons on my Xbox controller. My mother or father almost certainly put him up to this. There is just no way he could've known how much time I spend playing video games or even what console I use. His comment just reeked of 'parent'. I didn't say anything at the time, but his remarks inspired me to pen this article to clear the name of gaming and gamers everywhere.

Gaming is my hobby, it's something I'm passionate about and, like a lot of gamers these days, I'm tired of people slagging and criticising my pastime. Video games have been accused of a lot of social crimes. People like to say that they are responsible for promoting violence, that they glorify criminal behaviour and are generally a mindless form of entertainment. To make matters worse, gamers like myself are then portrayed as brainless layabouts who sit drooling in front of computer or television screens all day. What a load of nonsense!

Readers, I want to address and dispel these myths once and for all. First, the violence myth. I can understand the notion people have that by playing out violent scenarios in a game I might, in some subconscious way, be given a message that it's okay to do this in real life. Fair enough, but if you're going to take that approach then you should do it across the board. Have you noticed that nobody seems to have the same attitude towards any other form of entertainment? In for a penny in for a pound, as my Ma likes to say. If we're going to accuse video games of sending the wrong message, then we should also probably be concerned about the kid who laughs when the Jenga tower falls over. And don't even get me started on Cluedo! People who play video games deserve more credit than they are currently getting. They have enough sense to know that gun violence (as an example) is a serious crime with serious consequences. A few hours playing 'Medal of Honour' or 'Hitman' isn't going to flick some hidden switch in youngsters' heads and send them into a killing frenzy.

Secondly, I want to look at the notion people have that gaming is somehow a mind-numbing activity. There have been buckets of research to show that when you play a game your brain works overtime. It makes sense if you think about it – when you play you are constantly making assessments and strategising ahead of time. Games invite you to interact, to take control. Very often the action is built on smart storylines with multiple outcomes – books and movies are two dimensional by comparison! You go to the cinema, you watch the pretty pictures. It's all over after two hours. Or maybe you read a book over the course of a fortnight. All you can do is absorb the story. You can't influence the outcome. Gaming, by contrast, is great for improving decision-making and encouraging you to pause for a moment and consider how your actions may impact your progress later on.

All in all, I think gaming has got an unfair rap. It gets all the blame for society's problems and none of the credit for making kids sit up and actually think about what they're doing. I don't advocate displays of unnecessary violence in video games, but we're fooling ourselves if we think that this is somehow encouraging youths into crime any more than television, film or literature.

Comments:

» Clarity of purpose:

The question asks the student to make a case either for or against the idea that video games have a negative impact on society and he has done just this. His article gets full marks for being relevant to the task.

He writes that he was 'inspired to pen this article' and he later directly addresses his readers, which shows that he understands the genre.

» Coherence of delivery:

The student has ensured that the article is centred on the subject matter throughout. He doesn't get distracted and talk in excessive detail about any particular games or what he liked about them. In fact, there are very few specific references. His argument is correctly geared towards video games as a whole and how they do and don't affect us.

He takes a stance early on: 'Something happened recently that forced me take action and defend the much-criticised world of gaming.'

He maintains a constant tone throughout, using a relaxed but convincing style to make his point – this would help to win people over to his way of thinking. His piece makes good use of both the language of persuasion and the language of argument.

He has put great thought into planning his ideas and getting them down on paper in a controlled fashion. Each paragraph deals with one strong topic and together they strengthen the case he makes, from the introductory paragraph right through to the end.

» Efficiency of language use:

The student has used a lively and interesting writing style and this serves to engage and amuse the reader. For example: 'His comment just reeked of 'parent'' and 'If we're going to accuse video games of sending the wrong message, then we should also probably be concerned about the kid who laughs when the Jenga tower falls over. And don't even get me started on Cluedo!'

Note, too, how he varies the length of his sentences: 'Maybe you read a book over the course of a fortnight. All you can do is absorb the story. You can't influence the outcome. Gaming, by contrast, is great for improving decision-making and encouraging you to pause for a moment and consider how your actions may impact your progress later on.'

» Mechanics:

The student's grammar, spelling and punctuation are all good.

Past Exam Questions:

1 (2008): Students in your school have been invited to contribute articles to the school website on issues relevant to young people. This week's issue is 'We are what we wear'. Write an article for the website expressing your views on the topic.

2 (2011): Places one has never visited often hold a certain mystery or fascination. Write a feature article for a travel magazine about a place you have never been to but would like to visit. In your article explain what you find fascinating about this place and why you would like to go there.

3 (2012): Your school's Student Council is currently discussing the issue of school outings, educational trips, theatre visits, etc. Write a persuasive article for your school website supporting or opposing such events.

4 (2013): Write an opinion piece, for inclusion in a series of newspaper articles entitled: Must-see Attractions for Tourists, in which you identify one place or public building in Ireland that, in your opinion, tourists should visit and explain your choice.

5 (2013): Your class has decided to produce a book about 'un-heroic' or ordinary people as a fundraiser for a local charity. Write the text for the introduction to this book, in which you explain the purpose of the book and why your class thinks it is important to celebrate ordinary people.

Chapter 6:
Short Talks

Introduction

SHORT TALKS OR PRESENTATIONS ARE A COMMON FEATURE OF PAPER 1. SHORT TALKS TYPICALLY REQUIRE YOU TO MAKE A CASE OF ONE KIND OR ANOTHER.

Sometimes you have to write a piece specifically resembling a speech in a debate. For example, students in the past were asked to persuade a group of parents that teenagers should be trusted to make their own decisions.

Sometimes the question can be phrased in a more general manner. For example, you might be asked to talk about the benefits of reading or the role of technology in young people's lives. In such cases, it is often best to take a definite stance which you develop throughout the talk. You might argue, for instance, that reading is greatly overrated as a pastime or that technology makes young people feel miserable and isolated.

PLAN IN ADVANCE
With short talks, as with all compositions, it is important to plan in advance. Your short talk will consist of four or five paragraphs. Take the time to jot down what each paragraph will be about before you commence work on the talk itself. It is difficult to overstate the importance of such advance planning.

MANAGE YOUR PARAGRAPHS

As we noted above, in short talks you are generally trying to make a case. Sometimes, you might want to state this point plainly in your **opening paragraph**. We see this in the following opening to a talk entitled 'Changing our lives to save our planet'.

Good evening Ladies and Gentlemen,

Man's impact on the environment over the course of the last century has been devastating. With unbridled consumption, economic growth, materialism, insensitive development and booming population growth, we have all but destroyed this great and beautiful planet. We have now come to a grave juncture, Ladies and Gentlemen, and the time for idle talk has passed. It is time for each of us to take responsibility for our actions and to change our lifestyles so that the environment can be saved. We are not helpless in this matter: there are many things we can start to do today that will help.

It is also possible to begin your talk with an 'impact' paragraph that grabs the audience's attention before stating your point clearly in the second paragraph. The 'impact' paragraph might often focus on a shocking statistic, real-life story or dramatic event that brings your point vividly to life. Check out the following example:

Ladies and Gentlemen, over 40 per cent of all tropical forests have been destroyed, and another acre is lost each second. The annual catch in 13 of the world's 15 major fishing zones has declined and in four of those – three in the Atlantic and one in the Pacific oceans – the catch has shrunk by a startling 30 per cent. One-half of our nation's lakes and one-third of our rivers are too polluted to be completely safe for swimming or fishing. Millions of pounds of toxic chemicals – like lead, mercury and pesticides – pour into our waterways each year, contaminating wildlife, seafood and drinking water. I am here today to tell you what we can do to save our dying planet ...

Each of the two or three **body paragraphs** should focus on a single topic. Each paragraph should support the case you introduce at the beginning of the talk. In the body paragraphs of your talk you can use facts and statistics to appeal to your audience's heads. You can also use real-life stories and emotional language to appeal to their hearts. Every single paragraph should be geared towards one thing: convincing the audience that your point of view is correct.

The **closing paragraph** should briefly summarise the main points of the talk before concluding with a snappy, memorable phrase. It can also be very effective to conclude your talk with a question that will linger in the audience's mind.

HAVE PURPOSE AND FOCUS

As you compose, always remain conscious of your talk's purpose. Every paragraph should be geared toward advancing your stance or point of view. Remember you will be penalised if you ramble or drift off topic. Advance planning will help no end in this regard. Jot down your plan and keep it in front of you as you compose.

KEEP YOUR AUDIENCE IN MIND

You will be required to address a specific audience and this must be kept in mind as you write. For example, you might be asked to address your fellow students at an assembly or the members of your local council.

Always keep this audience to the forefront of your mind. All too often students begin with a paragraph clearly addressed to the audience in question but follow it up with paragraphs that seem to lose focus on this listenership.

A good way to maintain this focus is to address the audience directly at intervals during the talk. For example you might say 'As students in this difficult modern world all of us understand...' or 'As

councillors and politicians you will be more than aware of this issue...'

TONE AND REGISTER

The tone of your short talk will vary according to the audience you're addressing. A talk given to your school's parents' council, for instance, should adopt a formal and serious tone. A talk given to your fellow classmates might be more light-hearted. However, slang terms and overly casual language should be used sparingly or not at all. Once you adopt a given tone, be it serious or light-hearted, stick to it throughout the talk. Consistency will win you marks. Reading the samples that follow will give you a sense of what is required here.

REMEMBER THE FORMAT

There are marks to be gained from reproducing the conventions of the short-talk format. These are very simple:
• An opening salutation ('Ladies and Gentlemen' or 'My Fellow Students');
• A closing sign-off in which you thank the audience for their time and attention.

Walk Thru 1

You have been asked to give a short talk to your fellow students in which you respond to the statement 'Adolescents never had it so good'.

PLANNING

First I'm going to decide what my point of view is. I'm going to declare that teenage life is much easier now than it was for our parents, grandparents and perhaps even our older siblings. This is one of the most important steps in the whole process. I have decided on a point of view. Everything in my answer will now relate to this point of view.

Now I'm going to structure my essay. I'm going to write five paragraphs.

1: The first paragraph, the introduction, will clearly state my point of view.

2: The second paragraph will deal with how recent technological advances have greatly improved our lives.

3: The third paragraph will discuss the travel opportunities now available.

4: My fourth paragraph will deal with the freedom and entertainment afforded to teens.

5: In the final paragraph I will sum up my argument in a snappy fashion.

WRITING

My introduction: the first one or two sentences will simply state the point of view I came up with in the planning stage:

> I am here to propose that today's teenagers have never had it so easy. None of you gathered here today could dispute the fact that teenage life is much easier now than it was for our parents, grandparents and perhaps even our older siblings.

I am now going to flesh this out in a few more sentences:

> Change and progress is occurring at a rapid pace. In our six years in secondary school, we have enjoyed more positive change in how we learn, interact and are entertained than previous generations experienced over six decades.

In just a few short sentences I have already engaged with the topic and established a point of view. I am aware that this is a speech and a sense of audience is important. For that reason I have used phrases like 'None of you gathered here…' and 'In our six years

in secondary school'. Phrases like this make it clear that I am speaking to a live audience composed of my fellow students.

I am going to conclude this paragraph with a flourish that further reinforces this sense of audience. The language I am using here is relaxed and playful, suitable for an audience my own age:

> I can see how pleased you all are with that statement. Who doesn't relish being told that their life is an easy ride? Please, hear me out before you hurl those rotten tomatoes at the podium.

I see from my plan that my first body paragraph will deal with how technological advances have made our lives easier. I'm going to start the paragraph with a strong topic sentence:

> Technological advances have changed our lives for the better, in ways that no one could have predicted.

Every other sentence in this paragraph is going to relate to or expand on this topic sentence. If I find myself writing something that does not relate directly to this topic sentence I know I've gone wrong. To complete this paragraph I am going to back up my topic sentence with some relevant facts about technology. I am going to mention social media, entertainment and education:

> Tools like Facebook and Twitter have brought us closer than ever, making it easy to stay in contact with friends and family. With Skype and Viber we can even stay close to people who are living in foreign lands. The internet has opened up a whole world of entertainment, with millions of songs, books and movies waiting to be downloaded at the click of a button. But it's not all fun and games. Technology helps education too. Sites like Wikipedia place vast mountains of information at our disposal, making essays and research projects easier than ever before.

Note how every sentence I have written relates to my topic sentence. I don't wander off the point by talking about my favourite computer game or social networking activities.

These days, we are blessed with buckets of free time to enjoy. There are endless concerts and festivals that we can attend. There is a constant stream of high-octane films in our cinemas (not to mention online). In the past, many teenagers spent their summers helping out on the family farm or working part-time jobs and contributing their earnings to the upkeep of house and family. Between school and hard labour, they had very little free time and were lucky if they could enjoy the odd trad dance at the local hall.

Now I am going to write the conclusion. The idea here is to sum up what I have said in the talk without repeating myself too much. I am going to restate my case but I will express it differently to the opening paragraph:

When you step back and think about it, it seems obvious that adolescents are faring much better today than they did in the past.

Now I am going to add two or three more sentences that flesh out this point.

Adolescence will always present us with challenges – that will never change. But with the technology, the opportunities and the luxuries that are available to us now, we are in a much better position to fulfil our own potential and get the most out of life.

Note how the conclusion is short and does not ramble on and on repeating the points made in the talk.

If you've got a poetic streak, it can be impressive to finish with a flourish. This might involve using a memorable phrase, a quote from a famous writer or some poetic sentence of your own.

Things are much brighter for adolescents now than they were in the past and this is no accident. We are reaping the fruits of our parents' labour and can expect to repay the debt to future generations. It's up to us to recognise what we have and make the most of it so that we can ensure an equally bright future for tomorrow's youths.

I see that my next paragraph is going to deal with travel. Once again I start off with a simple topic sentence:

In the past 15 years, travel has become more accessible than ever to Irish adolescents.

As in previous paragraphs, I am going to write a number of sentences that relate to this topic sentence. As always, I'm going to make sure that nothing I write strays away from this topic.

Once upon a time, holidays to sunny climes like France, Spain, Portugal and Italy were a luxury that only the wealthiest jet-setters in society could afford. Now, however, travelling abroad is thought of as more of an important milestone than as a privilege or luxury. Very often, once exam season finishes, gaggles of teenagers head off inter-railing around Europe, enjoy fun-filled sun holidays together or go on J1 visas to the US. By the time many of us reach adulthood, we will have been on countless flights to exotic locations around the globe. In the past, teenagers could only dream of embarking on such adventures.

Note again how every sentence I have written relates to my topic sentence. The remainder of the final body paragraph will follow the same format outlined above.

Walk Thru 2

You have been asked to give a short talk entitled 'Where is our civic pride?'

PLANNING

First, I have to decide what point of view I'm going to take. I'm going to highlight some of the problems in the town and community that demonstrate a lack of civic pride and how this came about. This is one of the most important steps in the process as it will determine the direction of the essay.

This is a short talk, so five good paragraphs are enough.

1: The first paragraph, the introduction, will declare my point of view.

2: In the second paragraph, I will highlight problems in the town due to vandalism.

3: In the third paragraph, I will talk about the growing problem of litter in the community.

4: In the fourth paragraph I will describe the problem of gangs of people loitering around in isolated areas, intimidating others.

5: In the final paragraph, I will conclude by summing up the impact these problems are having and encourage people to work together to resolve them.

WRITING

Because I'm writing a talk, I first must address my audience – this is an important convention of this genre. I will address them at the end and once or twice throughout the talk.

Ladies and gentlemen, friends:

Thank you for letting me speak. Tonight, I would like to talk to you about civic pride and some of the problems that this town is facing. First, I think I speak for everyone when I say that we all think of this town as a great place in which to live – the people here are warm and welcoming and this friendliness has attracted a lot of visitors and new residents in recent years. But lately a few issues have been taking the joy out of living here, and I believe a lack of civic pride in the community has a lot to do with it.

Okay, my introduction is done. I've achieved my objective – I've stated my point of view clearly and I'm now set up to launch the rest of my argument. I see from my plan that the next paragraph should be about vandalism in the town.

Vandalism has become a serious problem here – and it is only getting worse. A large number of buildings have, of late, been badly graffiti'd with derogatory slurs and sketches. Elsewhere, the glass on the bus shelter was smashed and replaced only to be smashed again. I'm sure you'll agree this is very frustrating because so many people here rely on the bus for work and school. Nobody likes to wait for the bus in the wind and rain, and nobody wants to tip-toe around a pool of shattered glass on the ground and seat. This is not acceptable.

Okay, that's the second paragraph done. I quickly look at my plan again. I see that I want to address a litter problem now. I will directly address my audience again.

Friends, litter is also becoming a major issue. Why people choose to dump their cigarette butts on the ground right next to a perfectly good cigarette tray and rubbish bin, I don't know. But there's nothing more off-putting than seeing a scattering of them on the ground along with patches of chewing gum. It seems childish and spiteful to deliberately ignore the bins and facilities that are put in place to prevent just such problems. Every morning when I walk to school, I see that our footpaths, greenery and flower baskets are peppered with wrappers, plastic bottles, drink cans and fast-food cartons. Again, I think this is a needless problem and it really makes the town look terrible.

We have fabulous parks and amenities that are very attractive for young families and stay-at-home parents, but a number of people have complained recently about gangs loitering in these areas, usually drinking and smoking. That's not what these facilities were intended for and it is very frustrating for parents and elderly people who want to use the park for play and recreation. In addition, many of them have remarked that they feel intimidated by it, particularly if they are shouted or jeered at.

Now I must wrap up this short talk by highlighting what effect these things have on the community and town as a whole, and why we should try to fix it. I will speak directly to my audience one last time.

Ladies and gentlemen, it's very easy for a town to look and feel completely run-down – spray-painted walls and doors, shattered glass and rubbish can turn both residents and visitors off. It damages local business as well as the morale in our schools and the wider community. We need to reaffirm our sense of civic pride and regenerate the area. A small effort from us all will go a long way to restoring this town to its former glory.

Exercises

1. **Name one thing you are required to do in a short talk.**

2. **Describe in your own words two ways to begin a short talk.**

3. **What is the role of body paragraphs in the short talk?**

4. **Name one effective way of keeping your audience in mind as you write your short talk.**

5. **The following is the topic sentence of a paragraph in a short talk. Read it carefully and then complete the paragraph:**

There are so many ways in which young people today are more fortunate than those at any other time in history.

6. **The following is the topic sentence of a paragraph in a short talk. Read it carefully and then complete the paragraph:**

It can't be denied that the school we attend has many fine facilities.

7. **Rearrange the following five sentences so that they create a properly structured paragraph:**

Yes, those critics have a point when they try to tell us that we are just machines, that we desire nothing else in life other than food, sleep and work. Maybe they are right – I suppose William Shakespeare didn't have any positive influence on the world at all. They are only the frivolous things that make us people and not just living, breathing bodies. Ladies and gentlemen, in recent years I have heard too many people criticise the arts and call them insignificant and trivial. We don't need music, books, theatre, television, film, photography, sculptures, paintings, design or architecture, do we? And I guess Banksy's famous graffiti murals haven't given a voice to the millions of people who feel tyrannised by the world's corporate and military elite.

8. **Rearrange the following sentences so that they form a properly structured paragraph:**

In France and Spain – which are surely the two most popular holiday destinations in Europe – huge numbers of people have learned English and will accommodate English-speakers, despite being in their own country. I have noticed, ladies and gentlemen, that whenever I go abroad on family holidays many of the locals speak English and yet none of the tourists speak the native language. In my opinion, this is an extraordinary display of arrogance and laziness. And yet, most of us cannot even manage to muster up enough words to ask for directions.

9. **Identify what is wrong with the following paragraph:**

Good afternoon ladies and gentlemen. Today I would like to propose that we increase the legal age for purchasing and consuming alcohol to 21. At the moment, you can apply for a driver's licence at age 17 but the number of road deaths we see in this country every year suggests that many young drivers do not fully grasp the risks of getting behind the wheel and therefore do not drive responsibly. We should therefore widen the gap between the gap between the legal driving age and the legal drinking age to ensure that young drivers go through an obligatory 'bedding in' period during which they can experience first-hand the skills and mature attitude needed to drive safely.

10. **Complete this opening paragraph in a talk on the benefits of sport to society:**

Ladies and Gentlemen, fellow students, I am here today to talk to you about the many benefits that sport brings to society.

11. **Imagine you have been asked to write a short talk about the life of the modern teenager. Working in pairs, write two different opening paragraphs. Try to make one an impact paragraph and the other a more standard fact-based opening.**

12. Complete the following plan for a short talk about littering:

PARA	SUBJECT MATTER	TOPIC SENTENCE
STANCE: Littering - it's a national disgrace.		
1	Establish my point of view	Fellow students, I am here today to discuss the problem of littering in Ireland.
2	Tarnishes our beautiful country	This is a beautiful country that we live in.
3		
4		
5	Conclusion	Let's take pride in our country and put a stop to this disgraceful behaviour.

Now write your short talk.

13. Complete the following plan for a short talk on school uniforms:

PARA	SUBJECT MATTER	TOPIC SENTENCE
STANCE: School Uniforms - they are a good thing.		
1		
2	Ensure no competition between students	
3		
4	Practical and comfortable	
5		

Now write your short talk.

14. Use the following grid to plan a short talk about piracy and the illegal downloading of media. When you have completed your grid write the text of the talk:

PARA	SUBJECT MATTER	TOPIC SENTENCE
STANCE: Piracy and illegal streaming/downloading of media.		
1		
2		
3		
4		
5		

15. Use the following grid to plan a short talk about the merits of having a transition year. When you have completed the grid, write the text of the talk:

PARA	SUBJECT MATTER	TOPIC SENTENCE
STANCE: The merits of Transition Year.		
1		
2		
3		
4		
5		

Commentary 1:

Write a short talk to be delivered to your school's parents' association on the subject of bullying and suggest some ways to stop it.

Acknowledges her audience.

States her objectives early on.

Offers a personal anecdote – this makes listeners sit up and take notice, and proves she has personal insight into the situation.

Strong idea and good topic sentence.

Controls her ideas well. Paragraphs structured properly and focused on one strong topic.

Eloquent and moving conclusion.

Good evening ladies and gentlemen. First of all, I wanted to say thanks to everyone for coming and for letting me speak. My name is Clíona and I'm a sixth-year student here. I wanted to share my experiences of bullying with you and discuss some ideas about what we can do to stop it happening.

I myself was bullied before I came to this school. I was taunted by a particular cohort in my previous school and it really affected me. I can take some good-natured jokes as well as the next person, but what I was experiencing was calculating, nasty and habitual. It was happening in class, between classes, after class and online. Eventually it started to take its toll. I got very down about it and started self-harming. I was able to confide in one close friend though, and she encouraged me to tell my parents and teachers who gave me lots of support. Crucially, what didn't change much was the bullying. In my opinion, efforts to deal with bullying have failed because they were too black and white and did not invite students to participate.

We need to develop a sort of social immune system among the students that prevents bullying behaviour from getting a foothold. We can't just regulate bullying out of existence. I propose writing up a kind of social pact that is sent out to every student with the annual booklists. This document – to be read and signed by both students and their parents – should invite families to actively contribute to a culture that promotes respect and rejects all forms of bullying.

I also think that it would be a good idea to display 'Safebook' anti-cyberbullying posters around the school – particularly where students are more likely to socialise and engage with one another, such as in the canteen, locker area, gym hall and restrooms. This is a free poster developed by an Irish media company and promotes easy ways of staying safe online. If students are reminded of this regularly, it will help to reduce the nasty online tormenting that is now affecting thousands of students up and down the country.

I believe that an energetic and well-rounded approach involving students, parents and teachers will make a noticeable difference to the atmosphere in this school and cut out cases of bullying. It will help to make student life a lot more manageable for the countless other teenagers who will pass through these halls in future. I hope this gives you food for thought and maybe a bit of comfort too for anyone whose own kids are struggling with bullying. Thanks for listening.

Comments:

» Clarity of purpose:

The student has clearly grasped that she has been asked to do two things: discuss the nature of bullying and also how it might be stopped. The talk she has written is geared towards this twin purpose.

The composition is also focused from start to finish. She discusses nothing else other than bullying. She doesn't venture into unnecessary or irrelevant detail.

She informally addresses an audience or assembly ('I want to say thanks to everyone for coming and for letting me speak'). This is a great way to show that she is aware of the genre and of the format of the composition she has been asked to write.

» Coherence of delivery:

She uses a consistent and appropriate tone in her composition, remaining serious but positive throughout.

She manages her ideas well. She writes about distinct topics in her body paragraphs and sets them down in a methodical and logical way (personal experience, solution A, solution B).

» Efficiency of language use:

This student demonstrates a wide range of vocabulary and seems quite articulate. Her language is varied and interesting enough to maintain the audience's interest (e.g. 'This document…should invite families to **actively contribute to a culture that promotes respect** and rejects all forms bullying').

» Mechanics:

This student obviously understands the essential rules of spelling, punctuation and grammar.

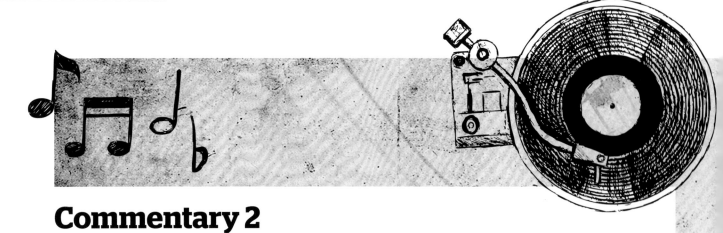

Commentary 2

Write a short radio talk in which you discuss the importance of music in your life.

Good evening listeners and welcome to The Music Show. In our first quarter tonight, we're going to discuss the importance of music in our personal lives. Someone once said that 'without music, life would be a mistake', and I wholeheartedly concur with this sentiment. From soothing the crying child to rousing the masses, music is a tool of expression unmatched in its power and versatility. For me, music is essential. It's my morning coffee, my evening relaxant, my oxygen. It's what gets me through my day.

She uses her opening paragraph to introduce the subject matter and establish a point of view.

She demonstrates an awareness of her audience by referring to them in the opening sentence.

School can be stressful sometimes, but music helps me deal with it. I rush around packed corridors from one class to another, frantically scribbling down notes and definitions and explanations in my copybook. I find myself sometimes frowning at concepts on the whiteboard or standing in a daze as a teacher barks at me. When I walk out those gates at 3:30, I can panic a little wondering how to handle it all. And then I take out my earphones. As I walk home I'll listen to Simon & Garfunkel's 'Bridge Over Troubled Water' or Bell X1's 'Bad Skin Day'. And by the time I get home, I feel a bit better about things.

This is well-written paragraph. It opens with a clear topic sentence and expands on her idea in the sentences that follow.

Naturally, there are plenty of days when I feel I need a bit of a kick; days when I need to be pushed not less, but more. Music is great then too. What better to inject a bit of life into you than Kanye West's beat-heavy numbers 'Stronger' or 'No Church In The Wild'? Or maybe the epic strings of Clint Mansell's instrumental colossus 'Lux Aeterna'? If I'm losing focus or simply not motivated enough, music will shake me out of it.

The student continues to maintain focus. She has not drifted off topic. She has also maintained the same light-hearted tone that she used in the first two paragraphs.

Sometimes, of course, I just need to put things into perspective. I need to be able to burst the school bubble and recognise that, as important as school is, there's a whole world out there waiting for me and that test that I failed last week isn't going to make or break me. What could better help me to step back from the insular school environment and get my priorities in order than John Lennon's famous song 'Imagine'? When he sings that line 'Imagine all the people/ Living for today/', I find myself reasoning that school is just a doorway to a massive, vibrant world, and that all I need to do is be patient and wait for it to open.

Again the student commences her paragraph with a clear topic sentence and ensures that the rest of the paragraph relates to this.

I really don't think we appreciate how much we rely on music or how important it is in our everyday lives. For me, it's not just something I idly bop along to, but often a powerful resource that helps me to take life on and live it to its full potential. I hope that you too get the same joy and inspiration from music. Thank you for listening and good night.

She reiterates her point of view, wraps the talk up and thanks her listeners.

Comments:

» Clarity of purpose:

The subject matter of this student's composition is relevant to the task. She has been asked to write about the impact music has on her life and this forms the entire basis of her short talk.

The student makes her case at the start of the talk and remains focused on this throughout the composition.

She demonstrates that she understands the conventions of the genre by greeting imagined listeners and welcoming them to the show.

» Coherence of delivery:

The student ensures that the tone and register of the composition are consistent throughout.

She has controlled and deployed her ideas effectively by ensuring each paragraph is dedicated to distinct topics that are, in turn, used to back up her overriding concept or message (i.e. music is important to me, let me now show you why).

» Efficiency of language:

She exhibits comfort with English and her vocabulary helps to paint a clear and vivid picture of the sometimes hectic nature of school life ('I rush around packed corridors from one class to another, frantically scribbling down notes and definitions and explanations').

She refers to a number of songs in the composition to make her point and in this respect she describes well the qualities that make these songs appealing to her.

The student's sentences are lively, interesting and engaging. She maintains a rhythmic quality by mixing long sentences with short ones.

» Mechanics:

This student displays a good understanding of grammar, punctuation and spelling.

Past Exam Questions:

1 (2004): You have been asked to give a short talk to a group of students who are about to start first year in your school. Write out the text of the talk you would give.

2 (2006): Imagine your local radio station is producing a series of programmes entitled 'Changing Times', in which teenagers are asked to give their views on the changes they welcome in the world around them. You have been invited to contribute. Write out the text of the presentation you would make

3 (2009): 'You're old enough, I reckon, to make your own decisions.'
Write a short speech in which you attempt to persuade a group of parents that older teenagers should be trusted to make their own decisions.

4 (2010): 'books are forbidden…' Write the text for a short radio talk where you explain the importance of books in your life and in today's world.

5 (2011): Write a talk, to be delivered to your School Book Club, on the enduring appeal of the mysterious in books, films, etc. You might refer to some of the following aspects of the mystery genre in your answer: setting, tension, suspense, dialogue, characterisation, atmosphere, music, special effects, etc.

Chapter 7:
Long Articles

Introduction

THERE ARE THREE MAIN QUESTIONS YOU SHOULD ASK BEFORE YOU COMMENCE WORK ON A MAGAZINE OR NEWSPAPER ARTICLE:

- What **type of article** am I writing? Is it a discursive piece, a narrative piece or an opinion piece?

- What is my **audience** or **readership**? Am I writing for a school magazine, a popular magazine or a newspaper?

- Should my **tone** and **register** be serious or light-hearted?

TYPES OF ARTICLE

There are several different types of newspaper and magazine article for you to consider:

- You might choose to write a **personal article**. This closely resembles a personal essay and contains both a narrative and reflective element. For example, you might write an article about the difficulties of adolescent life in which you describe the problems that you faced and reflect on how they made you feel.

- You might choose to write an **opinion piece**. This usually requires you to take a definite stance on the issue at hand, which you support using argumentative and persuasive language. For example, you might write an article about the difficulties of adolescent life in which you argue that the recent focus on adolescent stress is completely over the top and that in fact teenage life has never been easier.

- You might choose to write an **opinion piece with a personal component**. For example, you might write an opinion piece about the difficulties of adolescent life in which you discuss your own experiences.

In 2012 students were asked to write a feature article for a newspaper or magazine on the role played by memory and the past in our lives. Here you could choose to write a personal article in which you describe your childhood memories and discuss what they mean to you. However, you could also choose to write an opinion piece. For instance, you might argue that the commemoration of old wars and battles glorifies violence.

In 2011 students were asked to write an article for a serious newspaper or magazine on the twin issues of discrimination and tolerance. Here you could write a straightforward opinion piece, where you take a clear stance on these issues supported by the language of argument and persuasion. Alternatively, you could choose to write a personal essay in which you describe and reflect on your own experiences of discrimination and tolerance. But in either case it is important that you adopt a formal tone appropriate to a serious newspaper or magazine.

In 2009 students were asked to write an article for a school magazine about their experience of education over the last number of years. At first glance, this lends itself to a personal article in which you describe and reflect on the good and bad times you experienced over the last five or six years. However, you could also write an opinion piece in which you argue for a complete overhaul of the Irish education system using your own experience as evidence.

AUDIENCE OR READERSHIP

Articles that display a strong sense of audience will also be rewarded. It is vital, therefore, that you keep your readership in mind. Before you launch into your article ask yourself, who am I writing for?

Sometimes you'll be asked to write for a **school magazine** or for a magazine **aimed at young people.** Here your writing should be aimed at your own peer group. This is your generation. You can and should appeal to a shared set of experiences and values:

> I'm sure everyone reading this can remember their first day at this school. We huddled together in the yard, chattering nervously. We were so small that lifting our school bags felt like an Olympic sport. We smelled of new uniforms and fresh paper. Our shirts were buttoned all the way to the top and our ties were prim and proper. Oh, how things have changed...

Sometimes you'll be asked to write for a **popular magazine** or for a **newspaper.** In these instances you're writing for a more general readership. Imagine an audience of adults. These are people who, by and large, won't share your particular outlook and life-experiences. Here the above example is rewritten for a more general readership:

Starting secondary school is a daunting experience for a lot of young teenagers, so don't be surprised if your child finds the transition difficult to manage. They must navigate a very different environment. In primary school, kids sit in the same seat and beside the same people. They deal with the same room, the same classmates and the same teacher for the whole year. However, when they start secondary school, they must adjust quickly to timetables, to dealing with distinct classes, subjects and faces, not to mention more challenging learning material. They must absorb new social rules and learn to take greater responsibility for their education.

TONE AND REGISTER

Sometimes you'll be told to write a serious piece, sometimes a light-hearted and entertaining one, and sometimes you'll be specifically asked to choose between the two. For example, a question on the 2008 exam reads as follows: 'Write a magazine article (serious and/or light-hearted) in which you give advice to adults on how to help teenagers cope with the 'storm and stress' of adolescence'.

However, there are also occasions when the question contains no reference to tone. In such instances it's up to you to decide if you're going to be serious or light-hearted. A seemingly light-hearted title (for example 'Children's Games') can be dealt with using a serious tone. The opposite is also true. Even serious issues like depression can be dealt with using flair, wit and humour.

The crucial issue, as always, is consistency. Once you decide on a particular tone it's best to stick to it throughout your article. The Leaving Cert rewards articles that manage to establish and maintain a given tone rather than those that drift from one tone to another.

It can be tempting when writing for school and popular magazines to adopt a light-hearted tone, to create something funny, breezy and entertaining. There's a similar temptation to always be serious when writing for a newspaper.

However this is not compulsory. It's perfectly acceptable to write something funny for a newspaper and something serious for a school or popular magazine.

Unless, of course, the question specifically requires you to be light-hearted or serious in your approach.

PLAN IN ADVANCE

With articles, as with all compositions, it is important to plan in advance. Your article will consist of about eight paragraphs. So take the time to sketch out what each will contain rather than simply 'diving in' to the article proper.

Walk Thru 1

Write an opinion piece for a popular magazine claiming that travelling abroad is overrated.

PLANNING

The first thing to decide on is what approach I'm going to take and then stay with it for the duration of the essay.

It's an opinion piece, so I'm going to focus on just one of side of the argument. I'm going to stick to one side of the argument and state that travel abroad is overrated.

I want to write this composition in a relatively informal tone that's laced with some sharp humour. This will work to engage the reader and invite them to see things from my point of view.

I am aware that I am dealing with the large and general readership of a popular magazine, so I won't make any references to my fellow students or anything like that.

I'll jot down some key words **quickly** – these will help spark ideas that will form the content of my essay:

> Passports lost. Airports busy, chaotic, queuing for the security checkpoint. Can't carry liquids. Metal detector. Flights delayed because of weather/strikes/volcanic ash cloud. No music during take-off/landing. Sea sickness on the boat. Long journeys. Luggage. Waiting around. Boredom. Not speaking French/Spanish etc. Home is easier. Come and go when you like. No delays etc. More comfort. Same language. Still lots to do but no hassle.

I am now going to get it straight in my head what each paragraph is going to be about. The grid will be my roadmap and I can refer to if I feel I'm getting lost or drawing a blank later on.

1: Intro. State my point of view. We didn't always travel. Bit of a fad. Travelling abroad is lots of hassle.

2: Frustration of travelling abroad: Passports missing. Panic.

3: Frustration: airport security.

4: Frustration: flight delayed, waiting around at the airport.

5: Frustration: Air travel is v. restrictive – no phones, music, etc. Boats long and sometimes unpleasant.

6: No such problem when holidaying at home.

7: No delays because of fog or volcanic ash at home. No weight restrictions. Listen to music, text away.

8: No worrying about how to speak the language.

9: Conclusion. Emphasise original point. Neatly summarise arguments and focus on what's to enjoy at home.

WRITING

I want to say that travelling abroad, though fashionable today, was not always the standard and can actually be fraught with difficulties. This message must be the driving force behind the rest of my essay.

Heading off to far-flung locations is all the rage now. For a long time in Ireland, there was only one reason people got on a boat or a plane and that was to emigrate for a long time. Now, however, we believe that holidays are only holidays if you go abroad. Maybe it's sun stroke, but in my opinion people really fool themselves into thinking travelling abroad is better than it really is. Just look at the trials of travelling abroad.

The intro is done and I've set myself up to tackle the body of the essay. I see from my plan that I want to talk humorously about how we end up in a panic looking for essential travel documents like passports.

In general, if you want to visit another country you need an important but elusive document called a passport. Passports are tricky creatures. They do not want to be found. They get stowed safely in a folder or drawer somewhere in your house and disappear completely from your memory, sending intrepid travellers everywhere into cold sweats the night before they are due to depart. Boarding passes are not much better in that regard.

Now I want to talk about the joys of airport security.

It's after this that the fun really begins though. If you're flying, then airport security is a real treat. It is only when you are about to load your carry-on luggage onto the conveyor belt that you remember the rule about carrying liquids on board. In a panic, you hastily throw the lot out. You pass through the metal detector and the alarm goes off – naturally. After removing several articles of clothing and being groped by the security guard, you realise it was those pesky one-cent coins the whole time and are waved through, humiliated.

The next two paragraphs will follow a similar pattern and emphasise different aspects of the same message: 'travelling abroad is a hassle and here's why'.

Having arrived at the airport two hours in advance, your flight is delayed – probably fog obscures the runway, or the French go on strike, or a volcano in Iceland erupts and grounds every plane in the northern hemisphere (you know how it is). You're hanging around the airport terminal for a few hours, tired and cranky, with nothing but those expensive plastic airport 'sandwiches' to sustain you. You try to find the silver lining and reason with yourself that you can at least spend the next few hours brushing up on the language that you don't actually speak but will need to use on a daily basis over the coming fortnight. What a great way to start your holiday...

The journey, too, can be very monotonous. Are you travelling by plane? If you are, then you, like me, love that you can't even listen to music during take-off and landing. And that thrilling safety demo at the start of every flight. Who doesn't love taking yet another class in learning about what to do should you plummet to your death? The aircraft might fall out of the sky, but don't worry, the little light and whistle on the inflatable life jacket will come to your rescue. Perhaps you're taking the car across the pond by ferry. You don't have to put up with as much hassle there. Just a 14-hour journey to your destination and a bit of sea-sickness. That's all. Yes, travelling abroad. Good times.

In the following paragraphs I'm going to focus more on the comfort and convenience of travelling around at home instead. A rhetorical question will add a bit of impact and maintain my reader's attention.

So what if, instead of going abroad, we stayed grounded for our holidays? How much easier would it be? We wouldn't have to deal with any of the inconveniences mentioned above. If you travel at home you don't need to bring your passport, which means you won't have to tear the house apart trying to find out where you put it the last time. There's no need to check-in online or print off boarding passes. There's no need to hang around baggage carousels either.

Happily, you won't need to arrive at the airport or ferry port a few hours in advance. In Ireland, it's unlikely that fog or natural disasters in foreign countries will delay your departure. You can pack as little or as much as you like – nobody will stop you if you're carrying half a litre of water or shampoo in your bag. There's no awkwardness associated with the metal detectors and security guards. You can just hop in the car or a bus or a train and go. Turn on the radio or listen to your iPod whenever you like. There's no safety protocol to go through – just be sure to fasten your seatbelt and enjoy the ride.

When you reach your destination, you won't need to reach for a dictionary or phrasebook to communicate with anyone or to read anything. There's no need to worry about the rules of grammar or pronunciation – this is always a major headache for me! When I travel at home, everybody speaks my language. With a 'staycation' you too can enjoy the comforts and conveniences of home with all the refreshing adventure of going overseas.

Okay, great. I've written my intro, I've written my body paragraphs. I've made my point and I haven't strayed from my main message. The hard part is over, now I just need to tie it up neatly in my conclusion. Job done.

For me, travelling abroad is overrated. There are so many terms and conditions, so much preparation and so much that can go wrong. However, we can cut out many of these painful inconveniences simply by choosing to explore the hidden world on our own doorstep. Come rain, hail or shine, there's always tonnes to do and enjoy here – kayaking, cycling, swimming, camping. You can socialise and make friends with new people. You can even watch television in the evenings without subtitles or bad dubbing. When you really think about it, it's hard to see the appeal of travelling abroad at all.

Walk Thru 2

Write a long article, serious or light-hearted, about the importance of friendship.

PLANNING

My first task is to choose what type of article I am going to write. I am going to go for an opinion piece with a personal component. I am going to make the case that friendships are vital to maintaining a healthy and happy life and I will refer to my own experiences to back-up my argument.

I am going to write in an informal and light-hearted tone and will stick to this throughout.

As I have not been asked to write for a specific audience, I will decide that the article is intended for a popular magazine. I am not going to assume that the readers share the values and experiences of my own peer group.

I will now decide what each of my paragraphs is going to be about.

1: The the first paragraph, the introduction, I will come right out and state my point of view, that friendship is one of life's great blessings.

2: In the second paragraph, I will describe a specific friendship that I struck up with someone when I was much younger – what we did in our time, the hijinks we got up to.

3: In the third paragraph I want to reflect on these events – about how I realise, looking back, that the fun and games of friendship are a really crucial part of growing up.

4: In the fourth paragraph I want to talk about how we drifted apart a lot because we went to different schools and didn't bother to stay in touch.

5: In the fifth paragraph, I want to reflect on how this impacted on me.

6: In the sixth paragraph, I will describe how we bumped into each other again at a music festival.

7: In the seventh paragraph, I will reflect on how it was as though nothing had changed and how helpful it's been to have rekindled this friendship in the run-up to the exams.

8: In the final paragraph, I will conclude by stating that friendships offer an important outlet during challenging times and that, even if we drift apart, we should make an effort hold on to them.

WRITING

Remember, the introduction is where I will state my point of view – in one or two sentences I will lay out the message that I want to put across. I will base my intro on the idea that I jotted down in my plan:

When we look back on our childhood and adolescence, usually what stands out most in our memories is the people we shared that time with. Friendships enrich and animate otherwise unremarkable life experiences, and yet we often take a cavalier attitude when it comes to maintaining our friendships.

I am going to complete this introduction by expanding on this point a little more:

When it comes to friendships, we can veer from one extreme to another, texting and 'Facebooking' and hanging out every day for a year or two, and then just dropping all communication without a thought. This is something we could easily live to regret. A good friendship is like gold dust – rare and worth holding on to.

Now I am going to write my body paragraphs. I am going to make my case by relaying the personal story of one of my own friendships:

This is precisely what happened to me with one of my close friends, Dara – my partner in crime since the halcyon days of lollipop sticks and plasticine. We were friends from a young age in primary school, having swapped pencil parers and erasers during a particularly testing bout of addition and subtraction in senior infants. We were thick as thieves from then on. We progressed to first year in secondary school, hatching pranks so successful that they are now part of student lore – like the time we 'accidentally' dropped a box or two of detergent into the school fountain and flooded it with a floral-scented tower of foam. Or that time when, after we finished the Junior Cert, we covered all the walls of three classrooms with multi-coloured Post-its. And we proudly served detention together for those pranks too!

In the above paragraph I have given an amusing story of how we became friends as kids and the fun things we got up to when we moved on to secondary school. In the next body paragraph I will go on to reflect on why our friendship was really important to me.

I never gave our friendship much thought beyond the fits of hysterical laughter it gave me, but I realise in hindsight how important it was to me. This bit of comic relief really helped me to put some of the harder parts of school life – like exams and run-ins with bullies – into perspective. I knew if I ever needed to talk to Dara about something, I could. Although I was unaware of it at the time, our friendship helped me to figure a lot of stuff out.

In my next body paragraph I will describe how our friendship changed after Junior Cert, how we drifted apart a little bit.

We drifted apart a lot after the Junior Cert. My mom changed job and we had to move, so I enrolled in a new school. I was gutted by this turn of events, but the new school was good too and I got on with things. School is basically the same principle no matter where you go – you have to deal with the same curriculum and generally the same social scene. I was so busy figuring out the new places and faces that I didn't have as much time to stay in touch with Dara. The friendship was shelved and gathered dust.

I've now successfully described the beginnings of this good friendship and how we drifted apart a bit.

The Leaving Cert cycle came fast and furious from fifth year onwards. A lot of it is daunting but there's so much to take on and do that you don't actually have the opportunity to panic. You just have to put your shoulder to the wheel and hope the results come your way. Fifth year was a stressful enough time. With calculus, poetry, irregular verbs, chemistry experiments and still-life sketches, I was totally swamped. I wasn't socialising much, wasn't talking to people much and the laughs were few and far between. Eventually, I began to feel a bit burnt out.

Now, looking again at my original plan, I can see that I want to describe how we bumped into each other again. I build the paragraph around a topic sentence that gets the action of this paragraph going for me.

After fifth year, I cobbled enough money together from a part-time job to go to Electric Picnic. I was slogging through the rain with a few friends and trying unsuccessfully to pitch my tent when who sloshed through the muck right up to me? Dara. We hadn't really spoken in about two years but that seemed to have little impact on our friendship. Fuelled by an endless supply of dodgy festival food, we waded for three days through the mud to the mosh pits. We've been in touch regularly since then and it's been the usual barrel of laughs.

Again, I want to reflect on this and comment on how this new turn of events in our long friendship has had a positive impact and proves the importance of good friends in your life. I need to make sure I don't stray away from the point in this paragraph. I know from my plan that it's got to centre on how friendship soothes exam stress.

It's not quite fountain foam this time around, but our rekindled friendship has really made all the difference in sixth year. Even with all of the exam hype and CAO dilemmas, having Dara and my other friends around has made it all much easier to manage. Even though we hadn't spoken in a long time, we found it easy to pick up where we left off – for me, this is a sign of true friendship, but it was pure coincidence that we got talking again and this has taught me not to take my mates for granted and let good friendships fall to the wayside when life gets hectic.

Great. That was the last body paragraph. Now all I have to do is wrap it up by drawing all the ideas together to reach a strong conclusion that reflects the opening point of view.

My experience has given me a valuable lesson in the importance of a good friends and solid friendships. I think we are a little too prone to taking people for granted. Maybe we assume, with the prevalence of social media, that we don't really have to make the same effort to keep our friendships going, but I think this is a mistake. No platform is going to substitute the friendships built up by interacting with people, no matter if it involves just going to the cinema or painstakingly wallpapering a few classrooms with tiny Post-it notes (probably not a good idea, in the long run). The friends you make in childhood and adolescence have a huge influence on the person you become later in life and we should value them more.

Exercises

1. What three fundamental factors should you take into consideration before you start working on your article?

2. When should you not adopt a light-hearted tone in your article?

3. Complete a paragraph based on the following sentence:

My own experience of cyclists – those sanctimonious eco-terrorists – has not exactly endeared them to me over the years.

4. Rearrange the sentences below to form a properly structured paragraph:

It is absurd that one student who excels in languages but scrapes by in science and math could get a place on an engineering course while another student, who is gifted at science and math, misses out because he failed Irish.

The focus on points scoring is destroying our education system and turning thousands of talented students off the rewards of learning.

It's high time that we reformed the Leaving Cert.

This is the academic equivalent of disqualifying tennis ace Roger Federer from competing at Wimbledon because he couldn't explain the rules of cricket.

5. Complete the paragraph that begins with the following topic sentence:

Few inventions have changed the course of human life more than the Internet.

6. Comment on the tone used in the following paragraph. Can you identify what's wrong?

It gets pretty irritating for us students to be talked about at length in the media by parents, teachers and politicians, and yet never get the opportunity to contribute to the conversation ourselves. We're the ones who must face the bullying and the social media gymnastics and the binge drinking hangovers. But how often do the teachers or the parents or the politicians really try to engage with us about these issues? They are much happier to talk down at us or set up a task force to produce a report. A review of the literature suggests that adolescents respond better to inclusivity and engagement, but key stakeholders in both the domestic and educational milieu have repeatedly failed to approach issues in this way.

7. You have been asked to write an opinion piece for a serious newspaper about motor insurance prices for young drivers. Complete the following plan and then write the article:

STANCE: Companies unfairly regard all young drivers as dangerous and favour older drivers.		
PARA	SUBJECT MATTER	TOPIC SENTENCE
1	Compare two drivers, identical except for age.	Mary (25) and Paul (35) both drive 2002 VW Polos, but Mary pays three times as much as Paul for car insurance.
2	Older drivers' knowledge of the rules of the road is never tested.	The driver theory test was not introduced until 2001.
3		
4		
5		
6		
7		
8		

8. You have been asked to write an article for a popular magazine about the lack of imagination and originality in modern cinema. Complete the following plan and then write the article:

PARA	SUBJECT MATTER	TOPIC SENTENCE
STANCE: Modern films lack imagination and originality. More sequels, adaptations and spin-offs than ever before.		
1	Well known film adaptations	What do *Harry Potter* and *Lord of the Rings* have in common?
2	Sequels	
3		
4		
5		
6		
7		
8		

9. You have been asked to write an article for a school magazine about how PE and sport are neglected in schools. Complete the following plan and then write the article:

PARA	SUBJECT MATTER	TOPIC SENTENCE
STANCE: PE and sport neglected in schools. PE should be tested at Junior and Leaving Cert.		
1	PE is necessary today	
2		
3		
4		
5		
6		
7		
8	Long lasting benefits of PE	

10. You have been asked to write an opinion piece for a national newspaper in which you argue that technology isn't all it's cracked up to be. Use the following grid to plan your piece and then write the article:

PARA	SUBJECT MATTER	TOPIC SENTENCE
STANCE: Technology isn't all it's cracked up to be.		
1		
2		
3		
4		
5		
6		
7		
8		

Commentary 1:

Write an article to highlight either the positive or negative contribution of fashion to the world.

Persuasive intro. Takes a definite stance and puts forward an impassioned statement of the writer's personal beliefs.

Good use of topic sentences to establish focus of this body paragraph.

Uses language of persuasion to appeal to our emotions: 'starved female models', 'It doesn't take a rocket scientist'.

Refers to her readership – reminds us that she knows it's an article.

Good structure – spends two paragraphs discussing the impact of fashion on consumers and then two paragraphs discussing the impact of fashion on its workers.

Fashion is one of the most exalted art forms in the world. Although it is centred on the concept of beautiful design, the truth is far uglier. The fashion industry is represented by a clutch of powerful and wealthy individuals who seem to ignore the industry's moral crimes. From models to designers, the celebrity status of names like Naomi Campbell, Kate Moss, Louis Vuitton and Ralph Lauren signifies the enormous influence that fashion exerts on society. More is the pity, then, that such influence is not put to better use. Instead, what we see is an industry guilty of exploitation and superficiality.

Fashion often quietly endorses some incredibly damaging definitions of beauty. When starved female models stride down runways to flaunt the latest fashions, the industry sends a message that only the most beautiful women can wear the most beautiful clothes – and all these women are thin. It doesn't take a rocket scientist to notice that the huge rise in eating disorders seems to be tied to the growing hype surrounding fashion and fame. The desire among girls and young women to be thin hasn't just emerged from the ether – it's promoted on the pages of magazines everywhere. The industry actively discriminates against curvier women and has been found to change models' appearances using sophisticated software like Photoshop.

It's not only women who are judged in this way. Many young men are also under pressure to achieve an unrealistically athletic appearance. Clothing and footwear is often promoted by professional sports stars like David Beckham who spend their lives reaching peak levels of human fitness. All of this influences what young people expect not only of themselves, but also of each other. The result is that young people everywhere are pushing themselves to unhealthy extremes.

Unfortunately, readers, the industry's questionable behaviour extends far beyond this. Fashion supports modern-day slavery by taking advantage of young workers in some of the poorest countries in the world. Very often, children and teenagers are forced to work long hours in so-called sweatshops across India and Asia. They are paid almost nothing for long gruelling shifts in factories where our fancy runners and brand-name hoodies are made. Many of them have no rights. Their poverty is used against them and they live in fear that if they demand better pay, they will lose their jobs.

Pay is not the only problem these workers face. The majority of them work in terrible conditions. A number of high-profile stories highlighted the kind of unsafe conditions they are forced to operate in. A clothing factory in India, which supplied Primark (that's Penney's to you and me) burnt down. Another collapsed. No doubt these things happen all the time and we never hear about them. Fashion happily puts people's lives are at risk to produce the clothing that the rest of buy every day of the week.

You would think that such cold cost-cutting would at least make clothes more affordable for the rest of us, but this doesn't appear to be the case. It is likely that those pricey runners, jerseys, T-shirts and jeans are all made at a very low cost in some poor and distant nation. And when I say 'low cost', I mean *pennies*. And yet by the time the products make it to the shops, the price has mysteriously sky-rocketed. So where is the money going? The workers aren't getting it. The consumers aren't *saving* it. It's probably being pocketed by a small number of people at the top of the ladder.

Rhetorical question makes it more personal, invites the reader to engage with her.

However, there is plenty we can do to change this. People power is everything in the fashion industry. By voicing your dissatisfaction with these greedy practices, you will force the fashion industry to change. Without you and me, they cannot exist. It's easy to dismiss this idea – you're probably thinking 'I am just one person, I can't change the industry'. But we need only change ourselves. We can boycott businesses, petition companies online, picket outside shops to make others more aware. And above all, we can change how we shop. A bit of Googling will almost certainly offer some insights as to which companies are more ethically-minded, and those are the ones that deserve our custom.

Here the writer employs a conversational tone, e.g. 'A bit of Googling'. By referring to 'you' and 'we', she involves the reader, invites them to be part of a solution – highly effective technique.

The fashion industry needs to wake up to the reality that it is doing more harm than good. Its creative merit has been overshadowed by the greedy corporations behind the brands. Right now, fashion is only adding to an unfair world where the rich get richer and the poor are getting poorer. As if that wasn't bad enough, it's also telling talented youths all over the globe that they should aspire to a harmful and narrow-minded concept of beauty. It's up to the ordinary people to take a stand and force this fickle industry to change.

Comments:

» Clarity of purpose:

The core message of the composition is relevant to the question asked.

The writer has set out to write an opinion piece and has achieved this, using persuasive and sometimes emotive language to convince the reader of her point of view.

She remains focused from beginning to end and ensures that every paragraph highlights the industry's moral failures.

» Coherence of delivery:

The student maintains a serious tone throughout the article.

Every idea she discusses is relevant to the larger task and is set down in sensible order.

» Efficiency of language use:

This student has managed to write a powerful and convincing piece, helped in no small part by her skilful use of language. She uses some clever and catchy phrases (e.g. 'Although centred on beautiful design, the truth is far uglier').

Her range of vocabulary is impressive and makes the composition a highly engaging read (e.g. 'A **clutch** of powerful and wealthy individuals', '**gruelling** shifts in factories', 'Fashion often quietly **endorses** some incredibly **damaging definitions of beauty**').

» Mechanics:

Again, as seen in other compositions, this student is comfortable with the technical side of the language, displaying excellent spelling, grammar and punctuation.

Commentary 2:

Write an article for a popular magazine in which you describe what makes you happy.

It's different strokes for different folks, as the saying goes, and while many people today seem to be driven by material wealth and the latest gadgetry, happiness, for me, lies in the small things. The novelty of a shiny new phone or toy is temporary and what makes me happy now is not stuff, but the events, people and seasons that last in my memory for years.

I'm a huge Christmas fan. I know it's not for everyone – some people just don't celebrate it and others can find it depressing – but nothing fills me with more joy than the coloured lights that adorn streets and windows throughout the month of December. I love the sweet-scented pines of the Christmas tree. I love untangling the Christmas lights and trying to figure out which dud bulb is stopping the set from working. I love wrapping the presents – even the awkward biscuit tins or lamp shades that my parents hate doing. I love slaving over the Christmas baking and cooking. I love the cheesy movies that are played on the television channels every year. I love the bumper Christmas edition of the *RTÉ Guide*. I love the bucks fizz on Christmas day, not to mention the turkey, ham and pudding. I love opening the presents and singing the carols. Every bauble, every shred of old tinsel, the holly wreaths and sprigs of mistletoe – these are special to me.

It's not simply that I like these 'things'. It's that I love what they represent. They are all part of this time of year when everyone in the family comes home. Work and school are both set aside for a week. Everyone is together and enjoying the time off. Everyone is relaxing, telling stories and having a laugh. We sit down and eat together in good spirits and we pose for unflattering photographs. The sights, smells and sounds of Christmas put an immovable grin on my face for most of December and half of January.

Equally delightful is the scent of cut grass. Come April and May, the grass-cutting season kicks off in earnest. It's like a domino effect: one trendy soul dusts off the lawn-mower and pretty soon everyone starts to do it. Within a week it seems like the air around the entire country is perfumed with the fresh, tangy fragrance of finely-chopped grass.

This scent brings out my inner child. It is the smell of possibility, the end of school and homework. It evokes thoughts of long summer evenings and sometimes even bright sunny days. For me it also signifies casting off the bleak winter months. The smell of cut grass lingering in the air wakes me up. I could be imagining it, but it makes me feel as though I have more energy and optimism. It reignites my sense of excitement and hope. It marks the end of one school year and all of the hard work that year entailed. It gives me a sense of satisfaction and relief that I came through all the equations and irregular verbs unscathed. Just like Christmas, this, too, is something that makes me happy.

I don't want to give the impression that my sense of happiness and contentment is centred on two isolated seasonal events. There is plenty between Christmas and summer to keep me going. A lot of the time it's the little things that bring me joy. Let's be honest, few things in life are more thrilling than finding money in the pocket of a pair of jeans you haven't worn in a few weeks. It doesn't matter how much or how little. When you pull those bad boys on and suddenly discover a crinkled up five, 10 or 20 euro note in the back pocket, you are practically overwhelmed with an unexpected surge of happiness. It feels almost as good as that glorious moment when you peel your eyes open to get up and get dressed for school or work and then realise that it is, in fact, a Saturday and you can go back to sleep.

Good reflective paragraph.

The personal tone is maintained here.

Summarises earlier points and wraps up in a coherent way.

It's not any one tangible thing that makes me happy. It's the everyday things, the little things. It's feeling yourself drift off to sleep or remembering that it's the weekend and you can have a lie-in. It's getting stuck into a really good book. It's the anticipation of the summer holidays or finishing the year with a feast of pudding and bubbly. It's the joy of finding something you lost (or sometimes losing things you don't want anymore). This is what happiness is for me.

Comments:

» Clarity of purpose:

The student has written a highly relevant article. She stays on-topic throughout, talking about a number of different things, all of which contribute to her happiness.

She set out to write a more personal article as opposed to an opinion piece, and she does so, focusing effectively on her own thoughts, feelings and experiences throughout.

» Coherence of delivery

Her objective is to show what makes her happy and each body paragraph in this composition is dedicated to illustrating this.

She successfully maintains a light-hearted tone throughout.

Her essay is well structured. She has distributed her ideas in a clear and intelligible fashion, dealing with them one at a time. For example, she describes what she likes about Christmas and

then she reflects on why those things make her happy. Then she goes on to describe the scent of cut grass and reflects on why she likes it so much.

She controls the content of her paragraphs well. In general, she does not write too much on one topic and too little on another. The composition is well balanced as a result.

» Efficiency of language use:

The student makes good use of lively and vivid language. She writes, for example, about 'shreds of tinsel', 'sprigs of mistletoe' and Christmas lights that 'adorn' streets. She mentions 'bleak winter months' and provides an evocative description of the 'fresh, tangy fragrance of finely-chopped grass'. This is a good example of sophisticated (but not convoluted) vocabulary.

» Mechanics:

This student shows a sound knowledge of spelling and punctuation.

Past Exam Questions:

1 (2008): '...advised adults to treat adolescents with sympathy, appreciation and respect...' (TEXT 1)
Write a magazine article (serious and/or light-hearted) in which you give advice to adults on how to help teenagers cope with the 'storm and stress' of adolescence.

2 (2008): 'I was happy...' (TEXT 2) Write an article for a school magazine in which you explore aspects of life that make you happy.

3 (2009): '...a living classroom...' (TEXT 1) Write an article (serious and/or light-hearted) for a school magazine about your experience of education over the last number of years.

4 (2009): '...a good deal of humming and ha-ing...' (TEXT 2) Write an opinion piece for a popular magazine entitled 'Indecision – my own and other people's'.

5 (2009): '...a respected figure.' (TEXT 2) Write a newspaper article on some of today's respected public figures, exploring the qualities that make them worthy of respect.

6 (2010): 'You're a new neighbour, aren't you?' (TEXT 3) Write an article (serious and/or light-hearted) for a popular magazine on being a good neighbour.

7 (2011): '...a thin girl...flips the key-guard of her phone and scrolls her texts.' (TEXT 3) Write an article for a popular magazine in which you outline your views about the impact of technology on the lives of young people.

8 (2011): 'I don't discriminate...' (TEXT 1) Write an article for a serious newspaper or magazine on the twin issues of discrimination and tolerance.

9 (2012): '... all the time in the world...' (TEXT 3) Write a light-hearted and entertaining article, intended for publication in a magazine aimed at young people, in response to the phrase, '...all the time in the world'.

10 (2012): 'Memory is a ghost train too.' (TEXT 3) Write a feature article for a newspaper or magazine on the role played by memory and the past in our lives.

11 (2013): Write a feature article for a popular magazine in which you discuss the competing attractions of both urban and rural lifestyles.

pter 8:
al Essays

Introduction

A PERSONAL ESSAY REQUIRES YOU TO MEDITATE OR REFLECT ON A GIVEN TOPIC.

You are required to look into yourself and discover your thoughts, your ideas, responses and emotions about the topic at hand. The challenge, of course, is to express these in a readable and engaging manner.

As you might expect, the topics involved here are largely personal in nature. In past exams students have been asked to write about daydreams, a place they considered beautiful, the 'marvels of today's world', and on how they express themselves through their clothes.

Remember the personal essay is personal. You must give something of yourself. You should not be afraid to expose yourself, to reveal something of your inner life, of your thoughts, feelings and emotions.

WHAT DOES A PERSONAL ESSAY CONSIST OF?

Personal essays usually consist of two different components: there is a **narrative/descriptive** element and a **reflective/meditative** element. In the narrative/descriptive paragraphs you'll be telling stories or describing things, usually in a very personal way. For example, here's a narrative passage from a personal essay about music:

> My father always had a great love of music. Every weekend I would awake to the sound of the records he would play. There was a great variety to the music he loved. Depending on his mood, the music of choice might be Beethoven's thunderous *Fifth Symphony*, The Beatle's *Sergeant Pepper's Lonely Heart Club Band*, or the mellow sound of Miles Davis's *Kind of Blue*. These would be played at considerable volume and my father would march to the beat of the music or wave his hands in passionate response to the crescendos and rousing choruses. He also loved to perform. As far back as I can remember, whenever there was a cause for celebration, the guitar would make an appearance. Christmases, birthdays, weddings and anniversaries would not be complete without the singing of songs, and everybody had to get involved.

Here's a descriptive passage from an essay about place:

> Gorse bushes grew close to where I lived. There were acres of land of dense and prickly gorse through which we would tunnel. We established a maze of paths that would wind and weave through the gorse, arriving sometimes at a clearing or sometimes at no particular destination at all. In the summer the gorse would become dry and the needles would blanket the ground. It would take no more than a single, careless match to set the whole area alight. In a matter of minutes the bushes would be engulfed in a thundering fire. And when the flames were gone the whole place was suddenly transformed into a blackened wasteland and the charred branches would smudge your clothes and the scent of the burnt gorse would linger long in your nostrils.

The meditative/reflective passages can be trickier to get right. You have described something – it could be a place, a situation a story or memory – now it is time to express your thoughts and feelings about what you have described. However, the trick is to do this in a structured and organised manner. For example, the following is a **reflective passage** from the essay on music:

I guess the most important lesson I learnt from my father about music was to enjoy it. Music was not something I was forced to learn. My father exposed us to many varieties of music but he let us form our own responses and develop our own passions. We saw the pleasure that he derived from it and that inspired us. In time we would develop our own tastes and discover our own sounds. But since my childhood I've always considered music as something joyous and celebratory. I saw how it united people, how a babble of voices would suddenly come together in a chorus of song. This is something glorious to behold.

Here's a **reflective passage** from the essay on place:

Will any of the places we visit as adults hold the same magic and wonder as those we visited in childhood? When we were young a field of gorse offered the possibility of play, of escape and adventure. When we entered such a place as this it was as if we were entering another world. There was a real sense of fun and possibility and, of course, danger. I suppose when you get older you cannot be so carefree. Your mind is occupied with a hundred plans and worries and there is just no space for the imagination that a child brings to the places he or she visits.

HOW SHOULD I STRUCTURE THE PERSONAL ESSAY?

There are two broad approaches to structuring the personal essay:

- Begin with three or four narrative/descriptive paragraphs. Follow this with three or four paragraphs of reflection.
- Alternate between narrative/descriptive and reflective, switching from one type of paragraph to the other as you move through the essay. This can be more demanding but it can also be more effective.

The key thing is always to plan your essay in advance. Work out how many paragraphs of description/narration you are going to have and jot down what each one is going to be about. Similarly work out how many reflective paragraphs you are going to have and the thoughts that each one will contain. As always, jot down the order of your paragraphs before you commence writing. This will give your essay the focus and drive that it requires.

HOW SHOULD I OPEN AND CLOSE THE PERSONAL ESSAY?

It can often be effective to open with a **narrative/descriptive** paragraph. See for example the following opening paragraph on music:

Shakespeare said that music is 'the food of love' and, for me, no band understood this better than The Beatles. Their famous number 'Hey Jude' is, in my experience, one of the greatest feel-good love songs of all time. The sweet melody and simple, driving rhythm imbue the seven-minute track with the distinctive warm qualities that ultimately make it an inspiring piece of music. The band's rousing chorus of 'nah, nah, nahs' builds to a hair-raising crescendo that fills me with a powerful sense of hope and courage.

However, **reflective openings** can be equally effective:

Does music play a fundamental role in everybody's life? I just can't imagine living without it. It was what sets me up for the day and helps me to sleep at night. It helps me cope with the stresses and pains of life and enhances the times of joy and celebration. There is nothing else like it. How poor life would be without it, how mundane and trivial. What would a party be without the beats and rhythms that get us dancing and singing? What would Christmas be without the tinkling of bells and the chorus of carols? Would a life without music be worth living?

Similarly, both narrative/descriptive paragraphs and reflective paragraphs can give your essay an effective closure.

Example of **narrative/descriptive closure**:

From the rhythmic thrum of hip-hop to the intricacies of classical movements, music has become as vital to me as the air I breathe. It doesn't matter if I pound the pavements to the beat of a crunching U2 song or meditate to the gentle melody of Beethoven's 'Moonlight Sonata', I am certain that, without music, my life would be drab and bleak.

Example of **reflective closure**:

I sometimes wonder how different my life would be if had never heard a particular song or been introduced to a particular band, such is the profound impact that music has had on me. It is the compass that guides me safely through the highs and lows of life and I feel lucky to have discovered and been exposed to so many great musicians and composers down through the years.

WHAT TONE OR REGISTER SHOULD I ADOPT?

In the personal essay you should express yourself and write from the heart. You should use the words, phrases and expressions that come naturally to you. If you practise writing personal essays and composition pieces in general you will find your personal style and writing voice.

If your natural style is plain spoken, so be it. Don't feel that you have to employ elaborate sentence structures and fancy words to impress the examiner. But if such an intricate style is your thing, go for it. It's worth pointing out, though, that slang terms and overly casual language are best avoided in the Leaving Cert.

Writing a speech or an article can be like putting on a mask. You adopt a particular stance or opinion and attempt to convince your audience that it is true even though you might not necessarily hold this opinion yourself. There is an element of debate-club showmanship here. It is best to avoid this when it comes to the personal essay. If there is a personal essay question on the exam paper about music and you have no strong feelings about music, don't just try to make something up. Your lack of sincerity will almost certainly come through and cost you marks. Choose a different question instead.

WHAT SHOULD I AVOID DOING?

In the personal essay you are not necessarily trying to make a case. For example, you might be writing about Carna in County Galway, describing how it is your favourite place in the world. In such an essay you are not trying to convince your reader that they too ought to believe Carna is an outstanding location. You're not trying to sell Carna to the reader using the language of argument and persuasion. Instead, you are writing about what the place means to you.

It is also important that your essay doesn't become an overly informative piece. It's fine to devote a couple of paragraphs to describing Carna for your reader, but then you have to get personal. You're not writing an entry in a travel guide or for Wikipedia. Don't go on paragraph after paragraph about Carna's history, geography and industry. Your goal is not to leave your reader better informed but to leave them with a better sense of your outlook on the subject at hand.

Walk Thru 1

Write a personal essay reflecting on some of your favourite childhood memories.

PLANNING

I'll jot down some key words quickly – these will help spark ideas that will form the content of my essay:

> Going on trips to West Cork with brother and father. Summer time. Blue skies. Winding roads. Mountains. Trees. Long journeys in the car. Music in the car. Stopping for ice cream or picnics. Walking through the forest. Talking, laughing, photographs, sleeping in the car on the way back. Looking back now. Enjoying it. No technology, no distractions. A proper day out.

STRUCTURE THE ESSAY

This is a long composition, so eight paragraphs will suffice. I am going to alternate between narrative and reflective paragraphs.

I'll take some time to quickly write down what I would like to discuss in each paragraph.

The following table is the blueprint that I can refer to as I write.

1: Describe: Lots of good memories, but loved trips to Gougane Barra with dad and brother.

2: Describe: Summers, sitting in front of the TV. Dad hunting us out. The journey down, ice-cream, weather.

3: Describe: Arriving, walking, photographs.

4: Describe: Finishing, getting in the car, going back, asleep in the car.

5: Reflect: We have a beautiful country – we should appreciate and explore it more.

6: Reflect: It's important to get away from technology and spend quality time with others.

7: Reflect: I'm grateful my Dad spent that time with us. A good memory is priceless and that affects my outlook now.

8: Reflect: Glad he dragged us away from the TV. Important time together. Will someday do same with my own kids.

When I cast my mind back to my childhood, I can recall a lot of joyful occasions – Christmases, birthdays, Hallowe'ens – but few are more important than my memories of going to Gougane Barra with my Dad and my brother. In my personal experience, there aren't many places in Ireland that offer the kind of raw beauty that West Cork does. My dad always liked driving down there and taking in a walk around Gougane, and my memories of these trips are some of the most precious souvenirs of my childhood.

I have completed my opening paragraph by referring to a specific childhood memory. I see from my plan that I want to spend the next few paragraphs describing the details of these trips.

I'm sure he thought it would be a lovely surprise treat for me and my siblings. He'd be off work in the summer and used to lament the two of us passing the sultry days in front of the television. We'd be slumped on the couch in front of the box, our eyes almost glazing over when he'd march in and announce mysteriously: 'Right, hop into the car. We're going for a spin.' We'd set off under blue skies with a cool breeze pouring in through the open windows and his old-timer music playing on CD. As we drove farther from the city, the wide roads would shrink around us and take a meandering path through the rugged country. A sacred ritual of these trips was to stop for a snack in Inchigeela – usually an Iceberger or a cold can of Coke and a packet of Taytos between us. We always knew we were getting close to our destination when we saw tufts of grass sprouting up in the middle of the quiet roads.

Eventually, after spending more than an hour driving into the Cork countryside, we'd finally pull into the car park just outside the Gougane Barra woods. We'd scramble out of the humid car. Then we'd set off together, swatting away midges and hiking high into the hills while my dad kept us occupied by quizzing us on the capital cities of distant countries. We used always grumble when he stood us stiffly beside each other and then knelt down to take a few photographs. 'It's for posterity,' he used to say – as if we understood this term.

Our energy would be well spent at the end of the trip. We'd fall into the car and doze off, freckled from the sun and wrecked tired from long walks in the fresh country air. My dad, of course, was delighted by this predictable outcome. With me and my siblings conked out, he'd be free to listen to the long-haired rockers of his hippie youth without being teased or troubled by the rest of us. Getting us to go to bed on time later that night was also much more manageable. You don't have the same energy to protest 'bedtime' when you've walked the socks off yourself in the sun.

Okay, I've described these memories in good detail. Now I want to reflect on them a little bit more and tease out why I like them so much and how the trips impacted on me.

Looking back on it now, I realise those spontaneous day-trips gave me an appreciation of three things. The first is the beauty of our own country. I'd be the first person to complain about home and rant on about how other places have beautiful beaches and actual sunshine. But when I stop and think about it, we have a lot of gems in Ireland too. Gougane is a fairly picturesque spot. I can still see in my mind's eye the endless expanse of tall pine trees, the quaint old monastery and the dance of sunlight on the lake. You just won't find that kind of lush and peaceful landscape on the Costa Del Whatever. And there are hundreds of places just as beautiful all over Ireland, from Oughterard in Galway to the Giant's Causeway in Antrim. We're really spoilt. I now have a pretty long bucket list of places in Ireland that I want to see and I intend on ticking them all off before I finish college.

The second thing I learned to appreciate is the importance of getting away from the trappings of modern life. We kicked up fair stink about being dragged away from our beloved Pokémon or Spiderman cartoons at the time. But it was the right thing to do. Down there, we had no smartphones or Nintendo DSs or anything like that to keep us entertained. We passed the time talking and laughing and telling stories, and those are the things that live on in my memory. Even though I am partial to the odd game of Candy Crush on Facebook, what I look forward to most is enjoying shared experiences with my friends and family – the craic, the banter, the photographs. I know first-hand now that no toy or gadget or television programme could replace that.

Finally, I'm truly grateful that my Dad made the effort to take us on those trips. Of course, I didn't really understand it at the time, but now I'm aware of both the desire he had and effort he made to spend time with us. When I look back, I can't help but grin at the fun we had. We talk about them at dinners and family get-togethers and laugh at some of the mishaps we experienced on the many trips (like running out of petrol or getting drenched by sudden downpours). I sometimes find myself digging around cupboards, drawers and shoeboxes to look at those grainy photos of me and my siblings squinting at the camera. Though we gave out about it at the time, I'm really glad he insisted on taking them. The trips were a gift to us and the memories they left me with are worth more than gold to me now. The gift of a good memory is priceless. It's like bottled happiness – something you can taste and enjoy whenever life leaves you thirsty. This is something I always bear in mind when a friend or sibling comes to me just looking to talk or hang out. I remind myself that it costs me nothing to be giving of my time and myself, and the rewards are long-lasting and immeasurable.

I will reflect a little more in my closing paragraph and wrap it up.

All these years later, I can still smell the sweetness of the air. I can still remember scratching the fly bites. I can still laugh at some joke or funny story he told us. I'm grateful that he pulled us away from the telly and brought us out to the wild beauty of West Cork to spend time with us. I know if I ever have kids of my own when I'm older, I'll want to do the same for them.

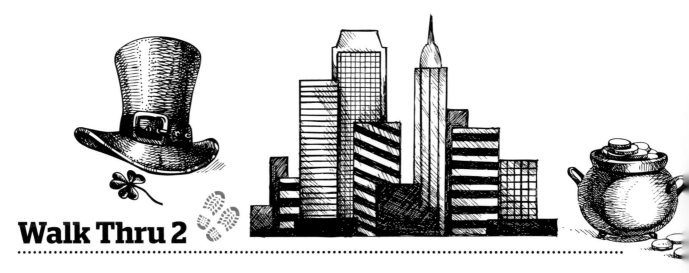

Walk Thru 2

Write a personal essay in which you discuss what being Irish means to you.

PLANNING

Personal essays are different from a lot of other types of composition in that they don't require me to put forward a particular point of view and sway the reader.

This is about my own thoughts, opinions and feelings on the subject.

I should describe a situation or event and then reflect on it in an organised way. I do not necessarily have to adopt a particular tone or elaborate style of language – it's more about using the writing and speaking voice that comes most naturally to me.

I'll jot down some key words **quickly** – these will help spark ideas that will form the content of my essay:

> Recent holiday to America. Very different sense of Irishness there. Specific. Paddy Irish. Pubs. Shamrocks. Leprechauns. Harps. The tricolour flag. Old trad music. Irish dancing. Aran jumpers. Sport – GAA is unique. Amateur players, representing their home county. Heineken Cup successes. Katie Taylor. Sense of pride. Irish food – simple, taste of home. Relationships with Irish language: most people dislike it, can't see the point of it. Until they're abroad and want pass remarks.

I'll take some time to quickly write down the ideas I would like to discuss in each paragraph.

The following table is the blueprint that I can refer to as I write.

1: Intro. Recent holiday abroad – concepts of Irishness.

2: Describe: Our sports. The excitement of GAA season – from Senior intercounty, all the way down to Junior C club level. Think of the Heineken Cup hysteria, or Katie Taylor in the Excel Arena during the Olympics.

3: Reflect: Our national pride emerges in sport. It is how we commemorate and celebrate where we're from, our sense of home, and allows us to express our identity to the world.

4: Describe: Irish food and eating habits – Tayto butties, our love of black pudding, beef and guinness stews.

5: Reflect: We appreciate simply things, home-cooking. Good food over fancy cuisine.

6: Describe: Talk about the Irish language. How we hate learning it at home. The trial of learning the verbs and deciphering the pronunciation. The aural and oral exams.

7: Reflect: And yet we love using it abroad.

8: Wrap up and conclusion.

I went on a trip to the US recently and visited New York and Boston. These cities are hotspots of second and third-generation Irish people – there are a lot of O'Sullivans, O'Learys, O'-this-and-that. We found the people there incredibly friendly and some were eager to talk about Ireland and their own Irish heritage when they heard our accents. We Irish have a tendency to be very self-deprecating, but when you step outside the motherland, you never forget your pride in being Irish. It's easy to forget, to take it for granted, but I believe that our culture and our ways are, indeed, unique.

In this introduction, I've described a holiday to America and the way that many people of Irish descent have a very specific idea of Ireland. This sets me up to describe some of the things that define for me what it means to be Irish. I take a look at my plan and see that in the next six paragraphs I want to describe and reflect on things that make me Irish – sport, food and our native language.

You can spot the Irish abroad. It's usually the local GAA jersey that gives it away. The distinctive colours and designs, not to mention the unusal brands that nobody else would recognise, are like a secret code that can only be understood by other Irish people. Supermacs, Carroll's, Arnott's, Enfer. These are our tribal tattoos. Sport is a strong part of who I am and, I think, of who we all are. Come rain or shine, our summers fizzle with hysteria about club and intercounty championship competitions. Even if it's nothing more than a local Junior 'A' game, you know there'll be small crowd tearing their hair out as they watch from the sidelines. They would be screaming at the referee for not spotting something or talking about how John's or Mary's season was going. This passion and excitement defines my summers in Ireland – the banter at training, the old man and his dog cheering you on from the edge of the pitch and the craic in the clubhouse after winning a championship match.

I know from my plan that I should now reflect on this subject.

I think sport is a key part of being Irish because it is how we express our patriotism and celebrate our identity. Ireland is a small nation, so I feel immense pride when I see ordinary people – locals, so to speak – stepping out and competing with others in the most prestigious sporting competitions. I cried myself silly when Katie Taylor competed in the Olympics. I wasn't much better when Rob Heffernan crossed the finishing line in the World Championships. It was all too much for me when Munster lifted the Heineken Cup in 2006 and Leinster in 2009. And don't even get me started on the cricket team. When I see those men and women saluting the crowds, hoisting up flags, grabbing their jerseys with their fists and singing the anthem, I feel a deep sense of what

it means to be Irish. They represent their town, county, province and country with so much heart. We love being the underdog, we love being David taking on Goliath. I think surprising people is what it also means to be Irish.

Next up are two paragraphs on Irish food.

Irish food is another curious experience. Our cuisine is not world famous, but sometimes I feel like it should be! Let's face it, a Tayto buttie is an absolute delicacy. I feel genuinely excited when I spill some of those cheese and onion bad boys on to a slice of buttered bread and fold the whole lot in half. It's no exaggeration to say that this is an exquisite 'foodie' experience. And what about a few rashers, sausages and black pudding on a dark winter's evening? Or your mam's Sunday roast? Sometimes, after a long day, I desire nothing more than a bit of tea and toast. A few cream crackers with a bit of Kerrygold always goes down well, and some 'fancy' chocolate Kimberlys if you've been good.

Our culinary inclinations are... Distinctive, to say the least (some might say bizarre, but they just don't get it). For me, this is a defining part of being Irish. It's part of the reason that Irish pubs are found everywhere around the world. When we're abroad, we tend to crave the tastes of home – real Irish butter, teabags, Jacob's biscuits, crisps, Galtee rashers and so on. These are all much sought-after by the Irish living abroad. There's a simplicity to the food that reminds me of attitudes in Ireland. There's no pretence, no airs and graces. There's no paté or caviar. It's not complicated for the sake of it, it's just the simple things done well and it's something that we're proud of.

However, over and above these things, I don't think anything captures what being Irish means to me better than my own confusing relationship with our mother tongue. It's a mystery. I have spent years trying and failing miserably to crack the grammar, spelling and pronunciation. All the vocab and tenses disappear from my brain at crucial times, like during a test. But I have noticed a strange phenomenon: I develop a mysterious fluency in Irish when I'm abroad and in the presence of a bit of talent. All of a sudden the words will come rushing back when I need to pass remarks about someone sitting nearby. I feel strongly that if I could just sit the oral exam on a sunny beach in Portugal, all would be well.

Again, however, this particular example brings me back to the idea that we Irish sometimes need to fly the nest to understand and appreciate what it means to be Irish.

Now I want to write my conclusion and finish the essay.

My holiday to the US made me realise that there's a lot more to being Irish than shamrocks and leprechauns. It's seeing the local jerseys crop up around the world. It's our fanatical love of our national games. It's our tendency to loath our language at home and yet love it when we're abroad. It's reading the death notices and obsessively watching the weather forecast. It's the everyday things.

Exercises

1. **What is the one essential thing that you are required to do when writing a personal essay?**

2. **Personal essays usually consist of two different components. What are they?**

3. **How does writing a personal essay differ from writing a speech or an article?**

4. **Describe in your own words the two different approaches you might take when structuring a personal essay.**

5. **Consider the following list:**
   - The last sporting event you attended.
   - The last book you read that made an impact on you.
   - The last video game you became really absorbed in.
   - The last concert you really enjoyed attending.
   - The last movie that you rated highly.
   - The last song or album you downloaded.

   Pick three of these items. In each case, write one paragraph describing your experience of the object or the event in question. Then write a more reflective paragraph describing your emotional reaction to that experience.

6. **Imagine you have been asked to write a personal essay about what freedom means to you.**
   Using the grid below, plan the essay that you intend to write.

PARA	NARRATIVE OR MEDITATIVE	SUBJECT MATTER
1		
2		
3		
4		
5		
6		
7		
8		

7. **Imagine you have been asked to write a personal essay about the marvels of today's world. Use the grid provided below to plan your essay.**

TOPIC: The Marvels of the Modern World.		
PARA	**NARRATIVE OR MEDITATIVE**	**SUBJECT MATTER**
1		
2		
3		
4		
5		
6		
7		
8		

8. **Imagine you have been asked to write a personal essay about your favourite place in the world. Using the grids below, come up with two different plans for this essay. Firstly, plan to write four descriptive paragraphs followed by four meditative paragraphs. Your second plan should alternate between narrative paragraphs and meditative paragraphs.**

TOPIC: My Favourite Place in the World.		
PARA	**NARRATIVE OR MEDITATIVE**	**SUBJECT MATTER**
1		
2		
3		
4		
5		
6		
7		
8		

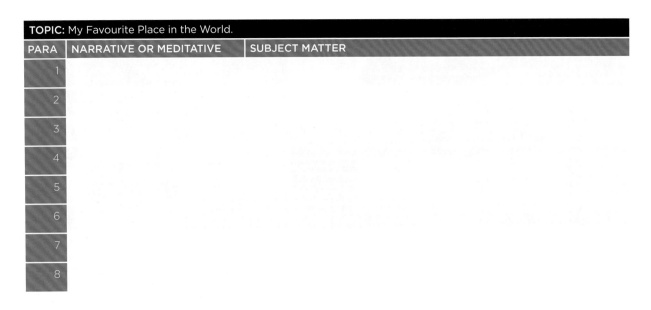

TOPIC: My Favourite Place in the World.		
PARA	**NARRATIVE OR MEDITATIVE**	**SUBJECT MATTER**
1		
2		
3		
4		
5		
6		
7		
8		

9. Imagine you have been asked to write a personal essay about your experience of the dramatic arts, i.e. comedies, musicals, plays and concerts etc. You can write about your experience as a performer and/or an audience member. Using the grids below, come up with two different plans for this essay. Firstly, plan to open and close your essay with narrative paragraphs. In your second plan, open and close with reflective paragraphs.

TOPIC: My Experience of the Dramatic Arts.		
PARA	**NARRATIVE OR MEDITATIVE**	**SUBJECT MATTER**
1		
2		
3		
4		
5		
6		
7		
8		

TOPIC: My Experience of the Dramatic Arts.		
PARA	**NARRATIVE OR MEDITATIVE**	**SUBJECT MATTER**
1		
2		
3		
4		
5		
6		
7		
8		

10. Using the grid below, plan a personal essay on your earliest childhood memories.

TOPIC: My Earliest Childhood Memories.		
PARA	**NARRATIVE OR MEDITATIVE**	**SUBJECT MATTER**
1		
2		
3		
4		
5		
6		
7		
8		

11. Using the grid provided below, plan a personal essay about your experience of friendship and what it has meant to you over the years.

TOPIC: My Experience of Friendship.		
PARA	**NARRATIVE OR MEDITATIVE**	**SUBJECT MATTER**
1		
2		
3		
4		
5		
6		
7		
8		

12. Pick one of the grids above and use them as the basis for a personal essay.

13. Write a personal essay about life's pressures and life's promises. Remember to plan your essay carefully first.

14. Write a personal essay about your daydreams, hopes and fantasies.

15. 'A change is as good as a rest, but in its own way can also be terrifying'. Write a personal essay about your own positive and/or negative experiences of change.

Commentary 1:

Write a personal essay on why I love sport.

Offers personal belief early on.

Student speaks in emotive terms.

Describes childhood, growing up with GAA.

Includes lots of personal experiences.

Good topic sentence for this reflective paragraph.

Referring to a 'you' is a natural of speaking and writing for this student – this style works well for personal essays.

Self-deprecating humour gives us a sense of who the student is.

Sometimes, when people hear the word 'sport', they can equate it with the ultra-competitive type of person who has a burning desire to win at all costs. When I think of the word 'sport', I think about lifelong friendships, fun, arguing with my brother over football socks and long car journeys to matches. I feel very lucky because I have been involved in some sort of sport my entire life and I can safely say that, even if you have no interest in it at first, eventually it succeeds in drawing you in.

I grew up next to the local GAA club. I am still not sure if my father built the family home there because of the scenic location or because it was a stone's throw away from the pitch. For the first 18 years of my life I never used the road to get to the football pitch. Instead, I simply jumped over the barbed-wire fence in our garden into the GAA grounds. My father was secretary of the GAA Club for 21 years and so I found myself spending a lot of time on the pitch. Football and hurling were all we knew growing up. As kids, we had to help line the pitch, put the flags out for big games and sell match programmes. At that age, the most thrilling job you could have was keeping the score of a game on the scoreboard. If you were lucky enough to be bestowed with this privilege, you knew you had hit the big time! Of course, it was a high-pressure and ruthless job and the honour was quickly withdrawn if you ever put up the wrong score. You always knew your time was up if you got a phone call while keeping the score during a match.

The GAA definitely played a significant role in my life. I realise now that there is more to sport than just playing it. To be involved so deeply in something requires a lot of sacrifice. When I was younger, my football training might have ended at seven o'clock, but my father would've been training the older teams until nine. At that age, only hunger and midges could drive us away from that football pitch. Even when you left your football gear in the garage, sport still managed to follow you in the front door. I think back now about all the hours my father spent on the phone organising matches and referees. Like any sport, GAA teaches you commitment and instils in you a good work ethic. People put in many hours of thankless work because they love the sport not because they are being paid to do it – the GAA is, after all, a volunteer-run organisation.

I have been playing football since I was seven years old. I remember my first training session being the one of the toughest of my life. A tedious task for a child at their first training session is trying to master the pickup. To a six or seven-year-old it just doesn't make any sense to put your foot under the ball in order to lift it off the ground. But it is the sense of satisfaction you get when you finally learn, however, that makes it all the sweeter. Of course like any sport, playing GAA means you will get injured at least once in your playing career. Even after all the broken bones and torn muscles, my worst injury was a concussion and stitches to my face back in 2007. I'd love to tell you that I suffered these wounds in the heat of battle, bravely defending the goal, but the embarrassing truth is that my own teammate ran into me as we both went for the ball. I still maintain that I called for it first. When I tell this story, some people will ask me why I don't just give up. I always answer: 'What else would I be doing?'

If I'd never played football I would have missed out on so much. I wouldn't have made the friends that I did – and those are the people I am still friends with today. There is a strong bond between players on a team. You celebrate together, you suffer losses together and you suffer through those tough pre-season training sessions together. Like any team sport, football or hurling can't be won by one player and as the old saying goes there is no 'I' in team. Our trainer always says that a team learns more by losing than by winning. The wheel is always turning in sport – particularly the GAA, where great teams are built not on big-budget signings, but on hard work on cold winter evenings and early Sunday mornings. This gives hope to a team that has lost five games in a row and is part of the reason I love sport. Your team could be on top one year and the next year you could be out in the first round. The unpredictability adds a bit of excitement to life.

Nice colloquial phrase ('the wheel is always turning').

Sport is so important in my life that most of my heroes are athletes. To me, sports people exemplify the discipline and drive you need to succeed and that's what makes them great role models. Roger Federer, for example, is deemed the most successful tennis player of all time because he has won 17 grand slam titles. But I admire more than just his ability to win a game; it is the manner in which he conducts himself off the court as well. He is a great representative for the game of tennis because he is humble in victory but also gracious in defeat. He does not make excuses when he is beaten by a better player and he still shows a burning desire to keep playing even though he is now 32 years of age. Another role model of mine growing up was hurling legend Diarmuid 'The Rock' O'Sullivan. I still remember the first time I saw him play in 2002, in Thurles. He was a sub for the Cork footballers that day and was due to play for the hurlers against Tipperary straight after. He was one of the best full-backs that ever played and was, as they say in GAA circles, 'teak tough'. His athleticism was mind-boggling, but so too was his passion for and commitment to the game.

Solid reflective paragraph for the conclusion.

For most people, sport is just a hobby. It won't pay the bills or put food on the table but people still love it and they love it for all of the reasons outlined above – and more besides. For me, it's a privilege to be so heavily involved in something I love so much – regardless of whether or not that means training with my friends a couple of nights a week or selling programmes at matches. The pitch still needs to be lined and the flags still have to be put out and – who knows? – maybe someday I will win back the chance to change the scoreboard again! Either way, my affection and respect for sport will long continue.

Comments:

›› Clarity of purpose

The student has been asked to write a personal piece explaining why sport is important to her. She has addressed this subject, ensuring that her essay is relevant.

She demonstrates an awareness of the genre – she writes in first person (I, me, etc.), giving her piece a personal feel throughout.

She remains focused on the central subject from start to finish and avoids going into unnecessary and irrelevant detail about her family, her hometown or the successes and failures of the local football team.

›› Coherence of delivery

The student's tone is consistent. She adopts a conversational tone throughout the piece, one that gives her essay an appropriately personal feel.

Her topics are appropriately sequenced, moving logically from one subject to the next. She discusses her early childhood experiences playing Gaelic football and how she grew up immersed in the sport. Then she goes on to talk about the friendships she developed from being involved with the team for so many years. After that she mentions her sporting idols.

›› Efficiency of language

The student demonstrates a good grip on the English language – for example, her sentence patterns are varied enough to avoid being monotonous. The essay also features some lively and interesting phrases. For example, she uses the phrase 'teak tough' to describe the resilience of Diarmuid O'Sullivan. Elsewhere, she refers to the exciting 'unpredictability' of sport and the admirable 'athleticism' of some sports stars.

›› Mechanics

This student's spelling, punctuation and grammar are of a high standard.

Commentary 2:

Write a personal essay describing and reflecting on your experiences of the world of theatre, be it as a participant or an audience member.

'I remember it well' – opens essay with a personal memory.

I remember it well. The year was 1998. Christmas. Our school was stage the annual retelling of the Nativity Story. I was a shepherd – and a convincing one at that. My costume comprised a picnic rug knotted about my shoulders and a towel tied around forehead. I used my granda's walking stick for a staff and taped cotton wool to my face for a subtle beard. Timmy Nolan and Jessica McCarthy were my bleating sheep. Me and the wise kings gathered around Mike O'Shea and Alison Connolly, who were draped in massive bed-sheets for the roles of Joseph and Mary. Our production received rapturous applause from the rows of misty-eyed mothers, fathers, aunts and uncles.

Humorous story, describes lots of personal detail.

Great sense of the student's personality.

Good reflective paragraph. Discusses what she loved about early theatre experiences.

It was my first involvement in theatre and – aside from a few cameos later in life – my last. I retired from the acting limelight having been hounded by the paparazzi (my parents) for photographs after my performance as 'Second Shepherd'. But my brush with fame left me with an abiding love of all things theatre. I went on to appreciate more sophisticated plays, such as *Cinderella, Snow White, Jack and the Beanstalk* and other panto classics. As a kid (and secretly as a teenager), I found the interplay between the actors and the audience hugely enjoyable. Pointing out lurking villains and participating in the 'oh-no-he's-not, oh-yes-he-is' rigmarole was the epitome of entertainment. For me, the joy of panto melodrama just could not be bettered.

Again, a descriptive paragraph. Describes the set and costumes in vivid detail.

More recently, I went to see *The Lion King* in the Grand Canal Theatre and I must admit I was blown away by the innovation and creativity that went into creating the scenes and costumes. The fanfare of the first scene at Pride Rock was pretty spectacular. I just thought the colour, the dance and the earthy African music thumping out from the orchestra in the pit below the stage was wonderful. The audience – myself included – broke into thunderous applause after this breath-taking opening and that set the tone for the rest of the performance.

Reflecting on her experiences here. Develops her ideas.

This is what I really love about theatre. No production is ever the same and, in fact, no performance is ever the same. The story is the only thing that stays the same, but it's also only one part of a much bigger artistic package. I believe that a story told on stage is a living thing and it can change according to the creative energy of both the players and the spectators. Television and film is very different in that sense. The director can shoot and reshoot a scene dozens of times until he or she gets exactly what they want in terms of the look, tone and feel of the scene. The result is that what you or I see in the final cut is sometimes so perfect that it can seem a bit sterile.

Explains why she appreciates theatre more than others.

Not so long ago I went to see *The Beauty Queen of Leenane* in the opera house. I didn't really know what it was about and it seemed like it was intended for an older audience, so I wasn't sure I'd enjoy it or 'get' it. It was a howl from start to finish. It was written by Martin McDonagh, who also wrote the famous dark comedy movies, *In Bruges* and *Seven Psychopaths*. The play was just as entertaining as those movies and, in many ways, being so physically close to the actors as they brought the characters to life made it even more memorable than any movie could ever be.

Insightful comment.

It was this play, in particular, that made me realise what I appreciate most about theatre: it's all about dialogue. Things move quickly through conversation. So much can happen in one sentence – the plot can take a vital twist, the relationship between the characters can change dramatically. I think it's this liveliness that has has kept me going back to watch different plays every year. Talking and performing is how people traditionally told stories and passed on a country's myths and history to new generations. It's better than the written word in that sense. I think we're hardwired to respond to theatre – I certainly am anyway.

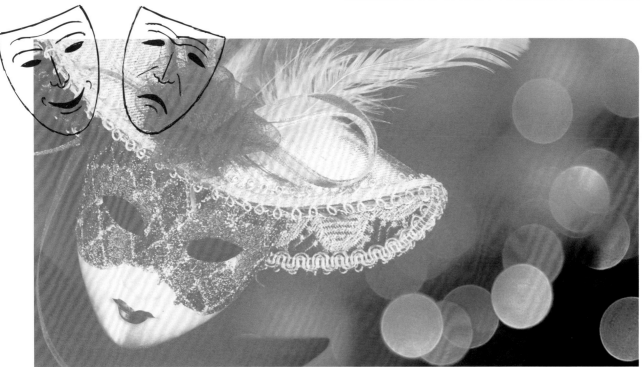

Again, a genuine personal response.

A drama is supposed to be lived and acted, not just read. In my opinion, this actually ruins a play. I won't lie, I was bored to tears by *Romeo and Juliet* when I studied it for my Junior Cert. Reading those lines every day for a term was about as exciting as watching paint dry. But then I went and saw a student production. What a difference! All of a sudden I felt for the characters and understood the tragedy of their ill-fated romance. Why? Because instead of simply reading the lines, I was hearing them, watching them being played out. I found I was better able to understand the play as it was brought to life than by just reading and analysing the script and stage directions.

As far as I'm concerned, theatre is a superior art form. I think people don't take it as seriously as film and television because it doesn't generate millions of euros at the box office like a blockbuster movie does. I think it gets a bit neglected because of this, which is unfair because it's a unique way of telling stories.

Comments:

» Clarity of purpose:

The student has been asked to write a personal essay describing and reflecting on her relationship with theatre. She succeeds – the content of the essay is relevant to the task from start to finish. Every paragraph deals with her personal experiences of theatre, both as a participant and spectator, and also deals with her reasons for loving theatre.

» Coherence of delivery:

The student maintains a consistent tone throughout. The essay is quite personal and sometimes light-hearted, notably in the opening paragraph.

She arranges her ideas in a way that is easy to follow. For example, she describes the Nativity play and then reflects on it; she describes *The Lion King* and then reflects on it. Each paragraph contains plenty of ideas and references that are arranged in a logical manner.

» Efficiency of language:

The student uses some lively and interesting language. For example, the mothers etc are 'misty eyed', there are 'lurking villains' and we are 'hardwired' to respond to theatre.

She mixes short and long sentences to great effect, e.g. 'This is what I really love about theatre. No production is ever the same and, in fact, no performance is ever the same.'

» Mechanics:

The mechanics of this essay are fine. There are no major issues with spelling, punctuation, syntax or grammar.

Past Exam Questions

1 (2008): 'I have a beautiful view…' (TEXT 3) Write a personal essay in which you describe a place that you consider beautiful.

2 (2009): '…the dreamtime of my own imaginings.' (TEXT 2) Write a personal essay on the topic of daydreams.

3 (2010): '… it was terrific theatre …' (TEXT 1) Write a personal essay about your experience (as performer and/or audience member) of the dramatic arts: plays, musicals, concerts, comedy, etc.

4 (2010): … a certain freedom …' (TEXT 1) Write a personal essay about your understanding of freedom and why you think it is important.

5 (2011): My favourite T-shirt…' (TEXT 1) Write a personal essay about your clothes, what they mean to you and what they say about you.

6 (2012): 'Yet the outside world had its continuing marvels…' (TEXT 1) Write a personal essay on what you consider to be the marvels of today's world.

7 (2013): '…the storyteller's connection to his audience.' (TEXT 1) Write a personal essay in which you explore the storytelling evident in music and song and its impact on you as a listener.

8 (2013): In TEXT 3, Belinda McKeon refers to the tension between the everyday treadmill and the gilded promises of Grand Central Station. Write a personal essay about the tension you find between the everyday treadmill and the gilded promises of life.

Chapter 9: Speeches

Introduction

SPEECHES TYPICALLY REQUIRE YOU TO MAKE A CASE OF ONE KIND OR ANOTHER.

Sometimes you will be explicitly asked to write a persuasive argumentative speech. For instance, in past exams students were asked to argue for or against the importance of national culture or to write a persuasive speech about technology's benefits.

Sometimes the question can take a more general form. In past exams students were asked to write a speech encouraging the audience to be optimistic about the future or to speak about how appearances can be deceptive. Even in such general cases it is best to adopt a definite stance which you develop throughout the speech.

PLAN IN ADVANCE

With speeches, as with all compositions, it is important to plan in advance. Your speech will consist of about eight paragraphs. As always, take the time to sketch out what each paragraph will contain before you commence work on the speech itself. It's often beneficial to jot down a version of each paragraph's topic sentence along with a few other notes and reminders. This will keep you cool, calm and collected as the clock ticks down.

OPENING PARAGRAPHS

In speeches, as in short talks, you are generally trying to make a convincing case of one kind or another. This is often stated plainly in the opening paragraph. The following opening, to a speech entitled 'Changing our lives to save our planet', illustrates this:

> Ladies and gentlemen, in the past number of years we have heard so many depressing doomsday stories about the environment that repairing the damage can sometimes seem like an impossible task. Tonight I want to show you that this is not the case, and that, with a little patience and a few small changes, we can shape this planet in a positive way.

It is also possible to begin your speech with an 'impact' paragraph that grabs the audience's attention. You will then go on to state your case clearly and explicitly in the second paragraph. Sometimes such 'impact' paragraphs invoke a shocking statistic:

> The eco-sceptics would like to fool us into thinking that our effect on the environment is negligible, but this is not so. There are approximately 27 oil spills every day, each one spilling poisonous chemicals into the sea and killing delicate marine life. There are so many disposable chopsticks used in China that nearly four million trees are destroyed every year to meet the demand. The thing is, if we all agree to make a few minor changes in our everyday lives, we could reverse a lot of this damage.

Sometimes an impact paragraph will make use of an arresting anecdote or story:

> I wish I could tell you, ladies and gentlemen, that nature is resilient, that she can endure the pollutants and toxins and destruction that we inflict on her. But my own experience is that she is struggling. The family farm has been flooded three out of the past five summers. And just two months ago, my father opened up six beehives – each one housing about 20,000 bees – only to find that they were all dead.

Sometimes an impact paragraph hits us with a poetic or memorable phrase:

> It is said that a journey of a thousand miles must begin with a single step, and I believe that our path to environmental recovery is no different: we must all start with just one step.

Sometimes an impact paragraph will grab the audience's attention by asking them a direct question:

> When it comes to the environment, there are two kinds of people: there are the people who are aware of the seriousness of the situation and who are inspired to live a more sustainable life and to campaign for sustainable policies. And there are people who are in denial of the problem, who think they cannot make any difference and who are happy to let their children to clean up a mess that others have made. The question that everyone must ask himself is this: what kind of person are you?

BODY AND CLOSING PARAGRAPHS

Each of the speech's **body paragraphs** should focus on a single topic. It's essential that each body paragraph supports your central case. The language of persuasion and the language of argument will feature heavily here. You will deploy facts and figures to convince your audience of the validity of your case. But you will also use emotional language to tug on their heartstrings, to appeal to their biases, prejudices and opinions.

Remember, every paragraph should be geared toward advancing your argument or point of view. The plan you jotted down should be front and centre at all times. One of the surest ways to lose marks is to drift away from your speech's central theme.

A speech's **closing paragraph** often contains a brief summary of its main points before concluding with a memorable flourish. However, such a dry summary isn't essential. It's also possible for your closing paragraph to be rousing, moving and perhaps even a little inspiring. Repetition can often be effective in creating a memorable conclusion:

> Securing our environment is the most important investment humanity can make today because without clean air, clean water, rich forests and thriving wildlife, we literally do not have a future. If we pedal instead of drive, if we shut down instead of sleep, if we recycle instead of dump, then we can have some hope of rescuing our children and grandchildren from the mistakes of the past.

This is a good opportunity to use aesthetic language. If you have a knack for poetic or dramatic phrasing you should use it to conclude your speech with a rhetorical bang:

> Don't allow yourself to be fooled, ladies and gentlemen, by the corporate bigwigs who would tell you that climate change is not happening and that the movement is populated by tree-hugging hippies. If we cannot take this matter seriously then perhaps we deserve the bleak consequences of our collective apathy. We don't have the luxury of being complacent. So, do you want to be part of the solution, or part of the problem? Thank you.

It can also be very effective to conclude your speech with questions that will linger in the audience's mind:

> A lot of people like to finish talks with a question-and-answer session, but today I want to put some questions to you. Is it asking too much to recycle? Is it asking too much to buy food that's grown in Ireland? Is it asking too for us much for us to get the bus, walk or cycle even one day a week? Or are we just lazy? We have to be honest when we answer these questions because it's small adjustments like these that will determine the future of the world.

REMEMBER YOU'RE WRITING FOR AN AUDIENCE

Remember at all times that you're writing a speech designed to be read aloud before an audience. This is not an article intended to be read silently by the reader of a magazine.

A good way to maintain such focus is to address the audience directly every now and then. For example you might start a sentence 'Ladies and gentlemen' or 'Fellow classmates'.

> Good evening esteemed guests and fellow classmates. Tonight, we are here to celebrate the best and brightest in this school. I'm sure you will all agree with me when I say that it has been a long and challenging year. While some of the demands of the past few months have been very trying, I think that the collective drive and the sense of solidarity among this group has been genuinely inspirational.
>
> Ladies and gentlemen, welcome to the Young Sportsperson of the Year Award. These awards recognise the sporting achievements of those under the age of 18 and this year we are particularly blessed. The athletes among us tonight are ambitious and disciplined in their pursuits, but also humble and generous in character – in short, they are models of sportsmanship.

However, don't do this too often or it can start to sound a bit ridiculous. Every other paragraph should suffice.

TONE AND REGISTER

The tone of your speech will vary according to the audience you're addressing.

- Sometimes you'll be asked to address a group of adults, for example members of your school's parents' council or of a government body. In these cases you should adopt a formal and serious tone. A touch of humour is acceptable. However, slang terms and overly casual language should be avoided.

- A speech intended for your fellow classmates might be more light-hearted. Again slang terms and overly casual language should be used sparingly or not at all.

- Sometimes no audience is specified. In such instances it's advisable to use a generally formal tone throughout.

Once you adopt a given tone, be it serious or light-hearted, stick to it throughout the speech. Consistency will win you marks. Reading the samples that follow will give you a sense of what is required here

REMEMBER THE FORMAT

As with the short talk there are marks to be gained for simply reproducing the conventions of the speech format. These are very straightforward:

- An opening salutation ('Ladies and Gentlemen' or 'My Fellow Students').

- A closing sign-off in which you thank the audience for their time and attention.

Walk Thru 1

Write a speech to be delivered to your classmates on the following topic: Nostalgia: a dangerous habit?

PLANNING

I want to make a case that glorifying the past can sometimes make us unhappy about the present and disheartened about the future.

I will state my point of view from the beginning and emphasise it in every paragraph of the speech.

The question does not specify what tone I should use, so I must make that decision and be consistent. I am making a speech to my classmates. I don't want to preach to them or bore them, so I'm going to use a slightly playful tone to get across a more serious message.

I'll jot down some key words **quickly** – these will help spark ideas that will form the content of my essay:

> Penny sweet shops popping up everywhere. Old cartoons and ads. Reminiscing about the weather – summers used to be better and sunnier. Simpler toys and games. Memory just playing tricks. Life wasn't better in the past, but our outlook on life was. Glorifying the past often leads to disillusionment with the future.

I am aware that I am writing a speech. I will lose easy marks if I don't follow the obvious speech-writing conventions.

So, I will **address my audience** at the beginning, once or twice throughout the body of the speech, and acknowledge them again at the end.

I'll spend a few minutes planning by putting my ideas-per-paragraph on paper first.

The table below is the blueprint that I can refer to as I construct my essay. By relying on this, I can steer myself through the composition quickly and coherently.

1: Intro. Our love of the past, our tendency to return to it.

2: Nostalgia for penny sweets.

3: Nostalgia for cartoons.

4: Nostalgia for old games vs new games.

5: Nostalgia for summer, weather in childhood.

6: Correct memory and present.

7: Wrap up and conclusions.

WRITING

My fellow students, today I want to talk to you about the perils of glorifying the past. As we drift closer to the end of our time in secondary school, we are likely to look back on our years of shuffling down these narrow corridors with a wistful smile. For all the homework and the tests, the fighting and detention, there is a good chance that both you and I will fall victim to nostalgia. It's a good thing to be able to review the past and say with satisfaction that it was good, that it was worth the effort. But sometimes glorifying the past is unhelpful.

Great. My introduction is done. I know from my plan that I want to use the first few body paragraphs to talk about the specifics of what we pine for from childhood and how that pining can affect our outlook on the future.

Have you noticed those penny sweet shops opening up around the country? I'm sure you've called into Mr Simms or Auntie Nellie's. I certainly have. Many's the hard-earned euro I've frittered away in there just to delight in the sugary flavours of my youth. Nothing brings you back to the glory days of your childhood quite like grinding down on a few black jacks or drooling over a slab of Highland Toffee. Those were the days. Not like now, we sigh. Now all we can focus on is how dreary life seems in comparison with our youth.

Our YouTube history is packed with mash-ups of cartoons and television programmes from the 80s and 90s. None of the sweetness-and-light nonsense like *Dora the Explorer* or *Barney and Friends*, we scoff. *Bosco*. Now that was a good show. *Transformers*. *Batman the Animated Series*. Kids nowadays are too protected. I wish things could be like they used to be, we say – as if life now is boring and flat. Our love affair with the past is starting to kill our optimism for the future.

Many of us believe that our childhood was in some way uncorrupted. We were the last generation to enjoy a 'pure and wholesome' youth. We laugh at kids now and tell them we had no Xboxes. No smartphones. Skipping ropes and footballs, we boast. Not like today's kids, who plonk in front of the big screen playing Sim City or Medal of Honour. Kerbs, hide-and-seek, tip-the-can, red rover – we knew how to have a good time. We spent whole days playing 'keepie uppies'. But does that mean we were better kids or does it just mean we were simpler kids? Very often, when we glorify yesterday we end up criticising today. The romantic past is making us bitter about the present.

I take a quick look back at my plan. I see that my next paragraph is going to be about memories of childhood summers past.

I recently found myself wondering if I hadn't spent my childhood summers in another country. My memory is of fine sunny days, chalky blue skies and grass-stained kneecaps. This account really doesn't tally with my more adult experiences of summer in Ireland – Biblical rains and horizons so gloomy with cloud that we could do nothing more than grumble about the impending downpour. I know that global warming is a more pressing concern now than it was 20 years ago, but I doubt that it's impacted on our local weather patterns this much already. What's more likely is that I just didn't focus on the weather when I was a kid. I didn't care if it rained or not. I played and had fun regardless of what was brewing over my head. Why don't I do that now? Why, my fellow students, don't we all do that now?

Again, I glance back at my trusty plan. I want to start talking about how we should learn to be more grateful for today and more hopeful for the future.

Friends, it's great that we can look back and appreciate our childhood contentment, but I think the extent to which we glorify the past ultimately does nothing but make us sour about the present and the future. Kids play the same games, just in a different way. The long summer evenings still echo with the bounce of footballs and sliotars, the snap of skipping ropes. Schoolyards are not populated by console-playing zombie kids. There are still masses of children chasing one another around and running to 'den' for safety. The weather is just as unpredictable now as it was when we were in primary school – a heat wave one month, a flood the next, that's just Ireland.

Okay, I've said all I can say. Now I need to sum it all up in the conclusion and perhaps finish with a memorable quote.

We would be wise to stop basking in the glorious past we remember and start looking forward to a truly bright future. Life was not rosier then and it is not any gloomier now. The world has not changed for the worse. *We* have changed and how we look at things is entirely our choice. As Winston Churchill once said: 'If we open a quarrel between past and present, we shall find that we have lost the future.'

Thank you.

Walk Thru 2

Write a speech to be delivered to your fellow students on the value of volunteering in modern society.

PLANNING

The purpose of a speech is to make a powerful case. I want to persuade my audience of the many benefits of volunteering and how modern life may be negatively affecting the culture of volunteering.

I will state my opinion in the introductory paragraph and then go about proving it in the body paragraphs. Some illustrative facts and statistics will help to make an impact and inspire them.

No tone has been specified. However, just because I am addressing my fellow students does not mean I have to be light-hearted. I think that it will be easier for me to tackle this topic in a serious tone, so that is what I will go for. The most important thing is to adopt a particular tone and stick with it throughout.

If I simply follow the standard conventions of writing a speech, I will automatically be awarded some marks. I will open by addressing my audience and will acknowledge them occasionally throughout.

I'll jot down some key words quickly – these will help spark ideas that will form the content of my essay:

Irish known for volunteering, for generosity to causes. Missions. Suas. SVP. Irish Red Cross. Irish Cancer Society – Daffodil Day. Charity fundraisers. Donating millions in aid for natural disasters abroad. Community. GAA. Less caring in boom years, more sceptical. Wealth makes us less inclined to help.

First I will spend a couple of minutes on planning the speech out by getting my ideas for each paragraph down on paper.

1: Intro. Stats – Irish recently found to be among the most charitable people.

2: Focus on forms of volunteering: GAA.

3: Focus on forms of volunteering: SVP.

4: Focus on forms of volunteering: Daffodil Day.

5: Focus on changing attitudes over the boom years.

6: Focus on why we should keep volunteering – some benefits for recipients.

7: Focus on why we should keep volunteering – some benefits for the volunteers.

8: Wrap up and conclusion.

WRITING

Good afternoon classmates.

I recently found out that Irish people are among the most charitable in the world. A 2012 study ranked us number two in the world for donating money to charity, volunteering time to good causes and in our willingness to help strangers. I think this is an extraordinary achievement. We haven't had an easy ride in the past few years with the recession and our own national hardship is what makes this news all the more heartening. With this in mind, I want to talk to you today about our history of volunteering and why we should make every effort to maintain this admirable custom.

My introduction is done – I have included good factual information for impact and have opened the door to talk about volunteering in Ireland. I see from my plan that I want to spend three body paragraphs detailing some well-known volunteer organisations or charitable events.

The GAA is a great example of this. It is a huge part of the fabric of our communities. When we think of Gaelic games we usually think of the colour and thunderous applause of the All Ireland Championship on television. Looking at the polished team performances on television can almost make you forget that the sports are built on an enormous network of volunteers in towns and villages across Ireland. From the locals who cut the grass, to the mothers and fathers who drive kids to training sessions, not to mention the players and supporters who pack bags at supermarkets in order to raise funds for improving a club's facilities – everyone gets involved and our national games are thriving because of this strong volunteer spirit. It generates neighbourly goodwill and inspires people from all quarters of the country to work toward something greater than themselves.

It doesn't stop with community games, of course. Our volunteering efforts meet some of the most pressing challenges of modern life. The Saint Vincent de Paul Society has been active in Ireland (and the world) for many decades, with members volunteering their time to collect spare change and redistribute much-needed money and food to the most impoverished people in society. These acts of kindness make a massive impact on the lives of people who rely on the SVP and are a tribute to the unquenchable goodwill of this nation of volunteers.

Equally encouraging is the annual sight of cheerful volunteers rattling buckets and selling bunches of bright yellow flowers on Daffodil Day to raise money for the Irish Cancer Society. So many people are affected by cancer and this organisation provides an invaluable service to them. The efforts of thousands of ordinary Irish people on Daffodil Day ensure that vital services and research are kept going. It really is a testament to the power of volunteering and to the generosity of the Irish people.

Great. I'm half way there. Looking back at my plan, I can see that the next step is to devote two paragraphs to talking about changing attitudes to volunteering and charity and why we shouldn't let our volunteer spirit die.

Lately, however, I feel we have changed our attitude to volunteering. I think our commitment to it has faded in the past 10 years or so. The Celtic Tiger years, although long gone by now, flooded Ireland with money and I think as a nation we forgot what it meant to really help others. Wealth buried our memory of the poverty that our parents and grandparents struggled with. I believe we were stripped of some of the empathy and compassion that spurred us on to help others for so many decades. It's important that we claim back the values that made us shine in the world.

Friends, we need to remind ourselves why we volunteer. Perhaps it's a cliché, but the phrase 'in giving you receive' sums up the best part of volunteering. Everybody wins. Everybody gains. Those who rely on the work and kindness of volunteers gain essential funds, services and support. People who volunteer with educational charities can help disadvantaged children in foreign countries who otherwise would not have the chance to go to school and learn. Doctors, nurses and dentists can volunteer their life-saving skills to the Red Cross or Doctors Without Borders. Construction workers can help to rebuild towns and cities that have been destroyed.

And then there's you and me – the volunteers. What do we get from this? Well, often overlooked is the opportunity to develop skills and experience that will stand to you for the rest of your life – and it'll shine on your CV too! Volunteering is a great way to meet new people and make friends, to expand your social circle and learn from them. Finally, there is that warm glow you feel when you realise that the time and energy you volunteered has made a positive difference to someone else's life. What more could you want?

I must now write my conclusion.

My fellow students, the value of volunteering cannot be overstated. Volunteering gives each one of us the chance to make a big difference to other people's lives – it doesn't matter if that means packing bags to get a few pennies for a favourite charity or travelling the globe to personally help out in a natural disaster. In 2012 we were the second most charitable nation in the world. What's to stop us from being number one for 2013? Thank you.

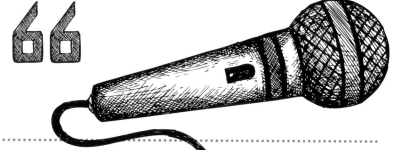

Exercises

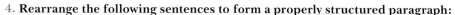

1. Describe two different ways of opening a speech.

2. How do you determine which tone you should adopt in your speech?

3. Mention one thing that makes a speech different to an article, report or other written work.

4. Rearrange the following sentences to form a properly structured paragraph:
However, a huge body of research has now emerged that shows that gaming is actually an excellent form of exercise for your brain. This form of entertainment has often been written off as nothing more than a mindless waste of time. Fellow students, today I would like to talk to you about gaming. Studies show that it improves creativity, decision-making and visual perception Critics of the gaming space often refused to see anything other than graphic depictions of violence which, they claimed, encouraged disturbing behaviour among players.

5. You have been asked to write a speech, which will be delivered to an audience that will include the Taoiseach and other dignitaries, in which you nominate someone as Person of the Year. Write the opening paragraph of this speech.

6. Rearrange the following sentences to form a proper paragraph:
Thank you. Tonight, ladies and gentlemen, we've learned some little known facts about heroes and inventors whose long paths to success were often littered with rejection. I would like to leave you now with the following quote from the great John F Kennedy: 'Only those who dare to fail greatly can ever achieve greatly.' Their glittering achievements were pulled from the darkest pit of disappointment and remind us that our ambition is only as strong as our perseverance and ability to see past our errors and mistakes.

7. You've been asked to write a speech about the dangers of the internet. Write two opening paragraphs for such a speech, one in which you clearly state your position and one 'impact' opening.

8. Complete the following plan for a speech entitled: 'Racism is a real problem in modern Ireland'.

STANCE: We must all work to stamp it out.		
PARA	**SUBJECT MATTER**	**TOPIC SENTENCE**
1	Diversity in Ireland.	'Friends, teachers, parents, Ireland has experienced a huge amount of immigration in the past 10 years.'
2		
3		
4		
5		
6		
7		
8		

9. Complete the following plan for a speech entitled: 'Rescuing the future from climate change'.

PARA	SUBJECT MATTER	TOPIC SENTENCE
STANCE: Wealthy nations must lead by example.		
1		
2	The cost of prosperity	Since the industrial age, westernised countries have auctioned off the environment in exchange for more and more economic success.
3		
4		
5		
6		
7		
8	Don't leave it to future generations to clean up our mess.	If we don't change how we live now, future generations may not live at all.

10. Complete the following plan for a speech about Irish being a compulsory subject at Second Level:

PARA	SUBJECT MATTER	TOPIC SENTENCE
STANCE: The subject should be optional for Leaving Certificate.		
1		
2		
3		
4		
5		
6		
7		
8		

11. Use the following grid to plan a speech entitled: Irish life is being destroyed by American culture.

STANCE:		
PARA	**SUBJECT MATTER**	**TOPIC SENTENCE**
1		
2		
3		
4		
5		
6		
7		
8		

12. Use the following grid to plan a speech entitled: Young people today are spending too much time staring at screens:

STANCE:		
PARA	**SUBJECT MATTER**	**TOPIC SENTENCE**
1		
2		
3		
4		
5		
6		
7		
8		

13. Select any one of the grids that you have completed above and write the complete speech.

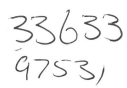

Commentary 1:

You have been asked to deliver a speech to your local community in which you argue that sport should be part of everyone's daily life.

Addresses audience – shows understanding of genre.

Convincingly illustrates how much we love to watch sport.

Persuasive sentence regarding couch-potato lifestyle.

Refers again to the audience. Uses positive verbs for desirable qualities of a healthy life ('improves', 'boosts'), and negative verbs for unwanted health problems ('slashes').

Good topic sentence. Student moving clearly and methodically from one point to the next.

Again, reminds us that she knows it's a speech she's writing by addressing an audience.

Good evening ladies gentlemen,

Tonight I would like to speak to you about sport and why we should strive to make it part of our daily lives. In this country we have a great passion for sport. We tune in by the millions to huge sporting events. We are glued to our television sets for all manner of major games and matches. There's the European Cup and the Six Nations in rugby. For soccer there's the Premier League and the Champions League. Wimbledon is broadcast *as gaeilge* on TG4. And, of course, we still fanatically follow hurling and football. Despite all this, we don't actually play much sport.

I believe that sport is the best way to incorporate an exercise regime into their daily routine and everyone should make the effort to get involved in whatever sport tickles their fancy. Lots of children, teenagers and adults wear the jerseys of their favourite sports team, but far fewer actually play the sport they like to watch. With today's sedentary lifestyles, it's simply not enough to be a spectator. There is a wealth of research showing that we are not active enough and will be burdened with serious health problems in later life if we do not exercise. We have a penchant for making excuses about why we can't exercise – 'I'm too tired', 'I don't have the time', 'It's boring' – but we can't really afford to indulge this tendency anymore.

Ladies and gentlemen, if we really considered the myriad benefits that sport offers we would realise very quickly that exercise is really a gift that keeps on giving. Let me start with the obvious one. The physical gains are almost endless. Aside from toning up and staying in shape, developing good fitness is a proven way to simply feel good. It improves the condition of your skin, boosts your immune system, improves your quality of sleep and increases your energy. As if that weren't incentive enough, exercise slashes your risk of developing serious diseases later in life (including heart disease, all manner of cancers, and diabetes).

Often overlooked are the psychological benefits. Sport and exercise are great for washing stress out of your system. By getting your heart rate up, your lungs heaving and working up a sweat, you will cancel out a lot of the nasty side effects of stress. Exercise engages your brain like nothing else. Most sport requires you to focus on a set of constantly changing factors and this gives your mind a break from the worry and stress that builds up throughout the working day. No matter what sport you get involved in, I can guarantee that you will come away from your sporting session feeling energised and upbeat.

Of course, there are plenty of social benefits. Few sports are played in isolation. It doesn't matter if you play tennis, a team sport or just go jogging or swimming with a friend, you will soon find yourself really appreciating the banter, the laughs and sometimes even the tears that emerge when you exercise with others. You will bond with your team or your training partner by sharing your troubles and your joy. The fun and the memories will lure you back every time and you will make friends for life.

And, ladies and gentlemen, sport instils in us some of life's most important values. It teaches us how to work with others and how to challenge ourselves. It teaches us that trying and failing is better than not trying at all. Through sport we learn that success is attained not simply by the talents we inherit or through luck, but by hard work and an ability to persevere no matter how many times we fail. It generates a sense of civic pride and benefits communities by keeping millions of people all over the world on the straight and narrow. Are you familiar with the saying that the devil makes work for idle hands? Well, sport is really one of the best ways to stop yourself from becoming idle. The research shows that young people are less likely to engage in antisocial and criminal behaviour if they regularly participate in sport or organised exercise.

Breaks up the composition with some humorous phrases.

Upbeat conclusion. Clever turn of phrase: plenty reasons to exercise, therefore no excuses not to.

'But,' I hear you all say, 'It's, like, hard.' I won't lie to you, it's not always easy starting out. Rome wasn't built in a day and neither is fitness. The first step towards getting off the couch is to remind yourself of the positives. Attitude is half the battle and, as a society, we have some terrible misconceptions of exercise. We think of it as a form of punishment and, yes, if you haven't exercised in some time then getting back on the saddle can be daunting and physically demanding, but we were designed to be active. Go at your own pace – no matter how slow, no matter how little – and build it up slowly in manageable steps.

There are plenty of reasons for us to make sport part of our daily lives and plenty of ways to do it. This, ladies and gentlemen, means that there are no excuses not to! It doesn't matter if it's basketball or swimming or hillwalking. It also doesn't matter if you're simply rusty or a complete rookie. Just get out there and do it – I promise you, you won't look back.

Comments:

» Clarity of purpose:

Is it relevant? Yes. The question asks students to write a speech to an unspecified audience about why they should make sport part of their daily routine. The student has clearly understood the question.

Does the student demonstrate an awareness and understanding of the genre? Yes. She has included a formal salutation at the beginning (ladies and gentlemen) and she addresses the audience three times throughout the body of the speech.

Is it focused from start to finish? Yes. She identifies and explores rigorously the benefits of sport and why we should participate. She reiterates this message again and again in the speech.

» Coherence of delivery:

She states her objective and belief at the beginning and illustrates it effectively in every paragraph.

Does the student control tone and register? Yes. The register and tone of the speech are consistent throughout – the student adopts a serious tone and sticks to it. Each paragraph is constructed around one strong topic – such as the social benefits of sport, or the physical benefits of sport – and these serve to reinforce the core message outlined in the opening. She does not deviate from this message.

The student sequences her topics carefully. Each paragraph deals with one topic and it is well thought through.

» Efficiency of language:

The student demonstrates a wide vocabulary and varies sentence length to create a clear but engaging piece of writing. The paragraphs are formatted correctly and consistently. They are not too long or too short and the breaks occur only when she has finished dealing with one concept.

» Mechanics:

The student clearly has good spelling, punctuation and grammar.

Commentary 2:

Write a speech to your classmates and teachers on Social Networking: a force for good or evil?

Good afternoon. I would like to begin today by welcoming you all, especially my fellow students and teachers. I am here to talk to you about the positives of social networking. Before we begin, I invite you all to check in and tag yourselves on your fancy iPhones and smartphones – imagine how envious your friends will feel knowing you're sitting here, listening to this riveting speech! In today's society there is no escaping social media and networking sites. Recently they've got a bit of a bad rap as breeding grounds for bullying and other forms of abuse. Some of these criticisms are warranted but complaining about them endlessly is a futile exercise. Social networking is here to stay and pointing the finger at organisations like Twitter, Facebook or Ask.fm instead of getting to the core of a human problem will not solve anything.

Social networking helps us to keep treasured friendships going. I want you all to take a good look at the people around you. Next year, some of the people sitting beside you could be emigrating to US or Australia, some may end up going to college a hundred miles away and others will be working a 40-hour week. It's inevitable that you will lose touch with some, but those nearest and dearest to you can stay in touch thanks to Facebook and Twitter. I, for one, want to be able to see what my cousin in New Zealand did last Saturday night – even if nobody else does – and I'm grateful for these free services. In the past, such dramatic changes in circumstance spelled heartbreak for many people, but not for us. We are lucky to have such a facility at our fingertips and yet all we can do is criticise it.

The power of social networking does not stop at opening up communication with your friends. It's also a powerful tool of protest. Not everybody has the confidence to express their opinions or ideas in a public platform. Social networks have given a voice to people who lacked the courage or ability to speak up for themselves. Did you feel hard done by in the budget? Did a business ignore your consumer rights? Get on Facebook. Share your grievances. Tweet about it. Be your own publisher, your own news outlet. You will find that others have experienced similar problems and they will share your troubles. Word will travel and change will happen.

Businesses, too, can benefit hugely from social networking. These are tough times for a lot of companies so it's a no-brainer to make use of the likes of Facebook to promote your business and connect with all of your customers. It costs customers nothing to 'like' a page and it costs a business nothing to create one. From small companies to massive multinationals, businesses everywhere make positive use of social networks to help their customers, advertise their products or events. Budding entrepreneurs can promote their fledgling companies to thousands of people at no cost and can even use social networks to sell their products online. Businesses can also connect with other business and source the right staff using the professional social network LinkedIn. These tools are greasing the wheels of the global economy and yet so many people rush to complain about them!

Ladies and gentlemen, modern life rushes by at the speed of light and the result is that society is more fragmented than ever before. We are constantly racing from one thing to another and trying to get more done in less time. This hectic lifestyle means that people suffer far more stress and anxiety and feel more isolated. They find it harder to find the time to meet up and socialise with others. Of course, online social networking can't replace the benefits of talking and laughing with another person, but it can offer the busiest workers and students a chance to meet new people – and remind them to stay in touch with old friends too. For the meek and the shy, social networks are an easier and more comfortable way to manage these important social engagements – and they can cut out the hassle of having to go to a pub or club and suffer through awkward conversations.

Clever technique.

Humour breaks the ice.

Has stated her point of view early on in the speech.

'I want you all' to take a good look around you' – student demonstrating she is conscious that this is a speech.

Appeals to her age group. Highlights the inevitable events that take place after school. This will appeal to her audience.

Good topic sentence.

Mixing short sentences in with long ones creates great impact.

She is controlling and distributing her ideas well. Each paragraph deals exclusively with one distinct topic at a time.

Acknowledges the audience again. Reminds the reader that she understands and is aware of genre.

Social networking offers endless hours of fun. Nothing helps me relax after an evening of study more than just going on Facebook or Twitter. I can indulge in a little mindless fun playing Candy Crush or Mafia Wars or Farmville. I can catch up with all my friends' gossip and check out what my favourite musician or sports star is doing. It's nice to see well-known personalities interacting directly with their fans. Every day on Twitter we see the likes of Paul Galvin offering to give something away for free to a fan or Tommy Bowe 'retweeting' your message and making you and your friends smile for days. These quirky little interactions between celebrities and fans remind us how much we appreciate them and how much they appreciate us.

Ladies and gentlemen, it is evident that social networking offers countless benefits and can be used to bring about positive change, but we persist in focussing only on the negatives. We sometimes like to shift the blame for social problems on to social networks without properly examining the real social cause. We should look instead at ourselves. Twitter and Facebook are merely tools. We have embraced them for a good reason and there's no reason why we should stop. Instead of trying to change these website's functions, we should really try to change how we ourselves behave. Thank you.

Acknowledges audience again, one last time.

Closes with a defence of social networking, thanks her listeners.

Comments:

» Clarity of purpose:

The student has been asked to write a speech arguing that social networks are either a positive or negative thing. She does this, taking a definite stance and arguing that Social Networking is a good thing.

She remains focussed on this argument throughout the speech and is careful to concentrate exclusively on the positive uses of social networking websites.

She demonstrates an awareness and understanding of the genre by addressing the audience at the beginning and end of the speech.

» Coherence of delivery:

The student makes her point of view clear from the opening of the speech ('I am here to talk to you about the positives of social networking') and reinforces this message throughout the speech using a variety of examples to prove his point.

She employs a friendly and light-hearted tone, which is likely to trigger a positive emotional reaction in the audience. Importantly, she maintains this tone throughout.

The student has gathered various ideas into coherent topics and has discussed these in a logical order – the body paragraphs highlight the many positive uses/functions of social networks and are knitted smoothly together.

» Efficiency of language:

She displays a solid vocabulary and varies the length of her sentences. This ensures the piece doesn't sound flat and repetitive. She controls the longer sentences through a well-structured approach, which prevents them becoming unwieldy.

» Mechanics:

Grammar, punctuation and syntax are all in good working order.

Past Exam Questions

1 (2008): '...the new global society.' (TEXT 1) Write a speech in which you argue for or against the necessity to protect national culture and identity.

2 (2008): '...fake, or worse...' (TEXT 2) Write the text of a talk you would deliver to your classmates on the topic: Appearances can be Deceptive.

3 (2009): '...science and research...' (TEXT 1) Write a persuasive speech in praise of science and technology.

4 (2010): 'But there is hopeful news as well ...' (TEXT 2) You have been elected by your classmates to deliver a speech at your school's graduation ceremony. Write the text of the speech you would give, encouraging your audience to be optimistic about the future.

5 (2011): 'There are people and possessions I could live without. But a cat is indispensable.' (TEXT 1) You have been asked to speak to your class about what you think is indispensable in your life. Write the text of the talk you would give.

6 (2012): '... shaped our national identity...' (TEXT 2) Write the text of an address you could deliver to an international gathering of young people outlining what you believe helps to define Ireland's distinctive national identity.

7 (2012): '... another book which I have read with enormous interest...' Write a persuasive speech about the importance of literature in people's lives.

8 (2013): In Text 2, William Trevor expresses his views on heroes. Write a speech in which you argue for or against the motion, We live in an un-heroic age.

Chapter 10: Short Stories

Introduction

IN THE LEAVING CERT YOU WILL BE ASKED TO WRITE A SHORT STORY ON A TOPIC YOU HAVE NEVER SEEN BEFORE IN APPROXIMATELY 70 MINUTES. IT IS VITAL, THEREFORE, THAT YOUR STORY IS CAREFULLY PLANNED BEFORE YOU COMMENCE.

If you are attempting the short story it is probably because something in the question has sparked your imagination or creativity. You have been asked to write a modern fairy tale or describe a mystery being solved and responded, 'Yes, I've got something here, I've got a story I can tell that fits this bill'. If you don't experience this Eureka moment, this sense of something clicking, you might be better advised to attempt a different question.

Beware of forcing square pegs into round holes: if a story 'comes to you' that only half fits the question, you'd also be better advised to try something else. Even if you feel genuinely inspired and think that you have something to write that addresses the question, don't rush in.

The short story is a genre in which the student often goes spectacularly off topic, spending paragraphs minutely describing a minor character or pages focusing on events that are little more than a prologue to the main action. Again and again, students find themselves running out of time before they've even gotten to the core of what their story is about. If you've been asked to write a short story about a reunion, the reunion should actually occur. You'll be punished severely if you spend paragraphs describing the weather but never get to the actual reunion itself.

CHARACTERS

The next important task is to determine how many characters will feature in the story. You have very limited space and time. It is advisable that your story, therefore, features three characters at most, though it is also fine for a story to have only two characters or to feature even a single protagonist.

Have a very clear idea about what role each of your characters is going to play. For instance, will my story feature a criminal who will threaten my main character or protagonist? Will it feature the victim of the crime he has witnessed? Will it feature his wife or other relative with whom he discusses his dilemma?

PLANNING THE PLOT

It is advisable to divide your story into eight or nine paragraphs. Before commencing the essay proper, write down what the focus of each paragraph will be. Many of the paragraphs will be used for advancing the plot. Some paragraphs will focus on describing characters or places. The important thing to do is establish what each paragraph will contain before you start writing your story.

PLANNING YOUR SHORT STORY

Imagine you've been asked to write an essay about a character facing a difficult decision. You're hit with the idea for a story about a character who witnesses a crime and must decide whether or not to report it to the police, knowing that doing so might endanger himself and his family. So far, so good. However, it is important not to just dive in now and commence writing. First you must plan.

SETTING

You have to have a very clear idea about where it is that your story takes place. Even if your story transpires in some random, anonymous room try to establish what the room looks and feels like: Does the room have a window? What furnishings does the room contain? Is the room pleasantly air-conditioned or is it hot and muggy?

The plan for my essay might, therefore, look something like this:

TITLE:

SETTING	Modern Dublin city centre
CHARACTERS	
Paragraph 1	Describe night-time Dublin scene: 'It was quiet that night as I made my way home from the gym, almost unnervingly quiet...
Paragraph 2	Describes suddenness of shooting. Car pulls up by passer-by/hooded gunman/incredible loudness of gunshots/ blood/ fear.
Paragraph 3	I was frozen stiff with fear. I knew I should help the guy, but he didn't have a cap lodged in his gut for nothing. Who knew what kind of dodgy stuff he was tangled up in? I had to make a decision.
Paragraph 4	The man was crumpled in a heap on the wet ground, bleeding slowly into a puddle of mud and rain...
Paragraph 5	I was staring, mesmerised, at the greasy film of blood on my hands..."
Paragraph 6	Being questioned by detective. I told him everything. Big mistake. Crooked cop! Tells me to keep quiet – or else.
Paragraph 7	Placing hand on the Bible as attorney swears in character: "I swear to tell the truth, the whole truth and nothing but the truth, so help me God."
Paragraph 8	"Mr Clyde, please tell the court what happened after the gunshots went off." For the second time, I had another big decision to make.

PLAYING WITH TIME

The above plan begins with the first event in the story and concludes with the final event. However, when writing stories you are always free to play games with how the passage of time is represented, and being able to do so will advertise your understanding of the language of narration. The following plan recounts exactly the same events as the one above, but does so beginning at the end, with the main character in the witness stand remembering the events that brought him to this point:

Paragraph 1	Placing hand on the Bible as attorney swears in characters: "I swear to tell the truth, the whole truth and nothing but the truth, so help me God."
Paragraph 2	"Mr. Clyde, please tell the court what happened after the gunshots went off." For the second time, I had another big decision to make.
Paragraph 3	Describe the night-time Dublin scene (a flashback, basically).
Paragraph 4	Describe suddenness of shooting, etc.
Paragraph 5	I was frozen stiff with fear. I knew I should help the guy, but he didn't have a cap lodged in his gut for nothing. Who knew what kind of dodgy stuff he was tangled up in? I had to make a decision.
Paragraph 6	The man was crumpled in a heap on the wet ground, bleeding slowly into a puddle of mud and rain...
Paragraph 7	I was staring, mesmerised, at the greasy film of blood on my hands..."
Paragraph 8	Being questioned by detective. I told him everything. Big mistake. Crooked cop! Tells me to keep quiet - or else.

It can also be very effective to begin the story in the middle, plunging the reader into action at the very beginning. The following plan begins with the victim of the shooting dying:

Paragraph 1	The man was crumpled in a heap on the wet ground, bleeding slowly into a puddle of mud and rain...
Paragraph 2	I started to panic. This guy didn't have a cap in his gut for nothing. What mess had he gotten into?
Paragraph 3	I was staring, mesmerised, at the greasy film of blood on my hands...
Paragraph 4	Being questioned by detective. Flashback to beginning. Describe the night-time Dublin scene – I was at the gym, it was around 10pm, dark, raining.
Paragraph 5	Describe the suddenness of the shooting.
Paragraph 6	I told him everything. Big mistake. He's a crooked cop! An inside man working for the gangs! Tells me to keep quiet – or else.
Paragraph 7	Later, placing hand on the Bible as attorney swears in character: "I swear to tell the truth, the whole truth and nothing but the truth, so help me God."
Paragraph 8	"Mr Clyde, please tell the court what happened after the gunshots went off." For the second time, I had another big decision to make.

CHARACTER DEVELOPMENT

In the Leaving Cert, constraints of time and space often make it difficult to fully flesh out the characters in the story. However, it is still possible for character development to take place.

Take a moment to visualise who the character is. Jot down a few details about him or her. You might ask yourself the following simple questions:

- Is the character male or female?
- Is the character old or young?
- Are they happy or sad, lonely or indifferent?
- What kind of clothes would you expect them to wear?
- What does the character look like?

One of the most effective ways in which you can conjure up a convincing picture of a character is to use language that precisely and evocatively describes their appearance and personality traits. It is important, however, that such descriptions be kept short and to the point. Remember, you've got a story to tell. The following are some examples of how this might be approached:

» EXAMPLE 1:

Donna was standing under the small bus shelter, waiting stoically for the 754 to arrive and rescue her, when the rain began to pour down. She brushed a stray wisp of dusty blonde hair back behind her ear and pulled the collar of her scuffed leather jacket up around her neck. She had nothing but the clothes in her duffel bag, a wad of birthday cash rolled into her boot and a cold determination to get out of Greenville.

» EXAMPLE 2:

Tommy Clark had the look of someone who'd spent his life working outdoors. The skin on his arms and the nape of his neck was bronzed from the long stare of the midday sun and the palms of his hands were calloused like sheets of sandpaper after countless hours gripping shovels, rakes and other tools of hard labour. The long, bright summer days had put crow's feet at the corner of Tommy's eyes and, though he was young, you could already see the older man he would someday become.

» EXAMPLE 3:

People used to say that Frank Howley Jr was just like his father – tall and pale, with a quiet way about him. He had a head for learning and everyone assumed he would go into teaching or accounting, just like Frank senior. People laughed when they found out he was enlisting in the army. Those scrawny arms could barely lift a pencil, they said, let alone a gun. The army would chew Frank up and spit him back out with nothing more than thick-framed glasses and a crew cut for his troubles. But it didn't. Not quite. In fact, the army chewed him and he just never came home. They sent his mother a folded flag and a cheap plastic box with a purple heart inside. The men in his platoon said he threw himself on a grenade. He was a good kid, Frank. Maybe too good.

SETTING AND ATMOSPHERE

In the Leaving Cert, creating a strong sense of setting and atmosphere will get you marks. Use descriptive language to create a picture of the setting in the reader's mind and to conjure up its atmosphere.

It is important to remember that it only takes a few words to make a setting seem vivid and atmospheric. For example, 'John walked through the dusty, sun-drenched schoolyard' is much more effective than 'John walked through the schoolyard'.

Here are some more examples of how brief passages of descriptive language can bring a setting to life:

» EXAMPLE 1:

The moon was rising slowly into the crisp night sky when the group finally came to a halt. They glanced furtively around the dark forest pines as they went about pitching their animal-skin tents. The snow crunched underfoot and a pack of wolves keened softly in the distant mountains. 'They won't bother us,' Cal told them gruffly. 'Wolves don't hunt at night.'

» EXAMPLE 2:

The autumn breeze swirled, sending coloured leaves skittering across the ground. Anticipation fluttered in Maria's chest as she stepped through the university gates and ventured with cautious curiosity around the quiet, manicured campus that would be her home for the next four years. The stately trees were hunched with age and the cobblestones were polished smooth from centuries of use. It was early still, but already there was a smattering of students about, marching across the quad to early classes with steaming cups of coffee in their clutches. She inhaled the dewy morning air and smiled softly to herself.

» EXAMPLE 3:

The empty house seemed to shift when she shut the front door behind her. She walked gingerly down the hall and when the floorboards creaked, she tensed and froze. She laughed nervously at herself and walked on towards the kitchen, swatting aside a thin veil of cobwebs as she moved. She emptied the cupboards and began to pack her grandmother's fine bone china wares in bubble wrap. She had turned back down the hall to retrieve some boxes from the car when she stopped dead. The door was open.

Remember that brevity is important here. Students often go wrong writing hundreds of words describing landscapes at the expense of character and plot.

A FURTHER NOTE ON BEGINNINGS AND ENDINGS

The vital thing about your opening is that it makes the reader want to read more. There are many, many ways of doing this.

- You could start with a dramatic or exciting event.
- You could begin by introducing a character that the reader will instantly find interesting and intriguing.
- You could beguile the reader by describing an atmospheric setting. (It is important that you don't spend too long describing the setting before you get down to the business of the plot.)

It is important that your story has a proper ending and doesn't look like you just stopped because you ran out of time. Some stories tie up all the loose ends and provide a very definite resolution. It is also possible to have an ending where the reader is left hanging, uncertain about how events will work out.

Example of a definite resolution:

The sun glinted on the silver trophy as Peter walked up the steps, mud on his boots and his sweat-soaked jersey. He looked down on the sea of smiling, cheering faces, one hand on the cup and one hand punching the air in ecstasy. He'd done it.

Example of an unresolved conclusion:

'I'm sorry,' she said, 'I never meant for this to happen,' and reached out to take his hand. In the distance, the traffic began its rush-hour drone and children laughed as they left the schoolyard. He turned away from her with tears in his eyes, and didn't know what to say.

Walk Thru 1

'It wasn't what I expected'. Write a short story in which your character is either surprised or disappointed by an unexpected event or occurrence.

PLANNING

There are three things that I need to take into consideration when planning a short story: plot; character(s) and setting. My short story must convince on all three fronts. I need to have a sense of a complete or self-contained story, a clear picture of the protagonist and any other characters in the story, and finally a good feel for the setting and atmosphere of the story.

As with other compositions, I will quickly jot down any ideas that come to me:

> Unmet expectation, disappointment. Teenage girl goes on road trip with friends to escape family problems – divorcing parents, awkwardness of new partners. Trip goes sour. Series of mishaps. Romantic betrayal by 'bff' and object of affection. Car breaks down. Hitch-hiking. Starts to rain. Splashed by truck. This is not what she expected.

I want my character to be realistic – I can select a style of thinking and conversing which is intuitive and casual. Her actions, and how I describe them, will help to paint a picture of how she feels, thinks and behaves. I want her to be flawed too (because nobody likes to read about a perfect goody-two-shoes!)

I want the reader to be able to digest a clear plot. This girl has just finished school, college is on the horizon and her family life is changing. Everything is in flux and she's struggling with it. She escapes a horrible domestic situation, only to be faced with another horrible situation on the road trip.

In terms of setting, I want her to be faced with a really awkward situation that she wants to escape and avoid at all costs – hanging out with her newly divorced father at his bachelor pad while he dates someone not much older than the protagonist. She gets out out on the road and sees a refreshing countryside, full of possibility.

1: Janet standing in the rain at the side of the road, hitch-hiking (end point).
2: Hanging out with friend Maria, road trip suggested. Discuss Janet's family situation.
3: Road trip begins.
4: Road trip detail. Beach, bonfire, marshmallows. Maria and Paul get together (shock!).
5: J leaves by herself. Describe emotional state.
6: Car breaks down, explaining why she's thumbing on the road.

WRITING

I would like to play with the passage of time in this story, so I will use a cyclical structure – i.e. I will start at the end to get the reader interested and then work backwards to explain how the character arrived at this point. I want to cut right into what my character is doing and give a strong impression of the environment she's in.

Janet Murray frowned into the rain as she stood on the hard shoulder of the road, holding her thumb out to passing cars. The cold damp was penetrating the layers of clothing and a shiver snaked through her petite limbs. Come on, guys, she thought as she paced backwards along the road. Cut me some slack. A truck appeared on the horizon and thundered in her direction. This guy would stop, surely. Truckers were known for it. She waved her thumb at it emphatically but was sprayed with mud as all 18 wheels passed through a puddle of filthy storm water. She lowered her arm, gave a growl of frustration and swore loudly to the empty road. She wiped the muck from her face and sighed. 'This,' she said. 'Is not what I expected.'

How did she get here...?

Now I want to describe the first awkward situation that Janet wants to get away from. Her mother and father have split up and her father is going out with someone new.

A road trip, her friend Maria suggested, as they lounged on the deck of Janet's father's two-bed house. Mr Murray had divorced Mrs Murray – Janet's mom – and his new 'friend', Suzie, was moving in with him at his new place. Suzie was an aerobics instructor, which was so clichéd that Janet thought she might puke. Her mom had sent her to spend the summer here with them, but she already knew she wouldn't last three weeks, let alone three months. Too many leotards. 'Think about it,' Maria said. 'No divorce, no spandex, no awkward dinners. Just you, me, Paul and the open road.' It did sound great. And she'd been hung up on the criminally attractive Paul for the past year. Maybe the road trip would give her the stones to ask him out.

Her mom didn't approve of the idea of her setting off for a few weeks without parental supervision, and her dad was wounded by her desire to skedaddle, but he was also so desperate to get into her good books after the divorce that he caved like a wet paper towel. They loaded up Janet's rickety old Corolla with their backpacks and a few cooler boxes of food and instant noodles, and then they set off into the sun. The first fortnight went great. They drove for miles, picnicked and hiked at the foothills of the mountains, took photographs, blared music and spoke sombrely to parents who checked in by phone. They made their way to the coast and checked into a hostel near a beach where they stayed for a weekend and attempted (badly) to surf.

Now for the second awkward situation that Janet gets landed with. Her best friend, Maria, becomes romantically involved with the guy that Janet has a huge crush on. This is a disappointing turn of events for Janet, who's already feeling let down by her father getting together with somebody else.

They were hanging out at the beach late one evening with a few other surfers, encamped around a fire to toast some marshmallows. Paul and Maria had gone to retrieve some snacks. Janet stood up and announced that she needed to use the ladies. She trudged barefoot over the silky, cool sand towards the hostel. She made her way upstairs to the communal restroom and stopped short when she saw Maria and Paul embraced in the kind of ardent gag-inducing kiss that made her think of her dad and Suzie the aerobics instructor. Her gut twisted hard with pain. They broke off, flustered and embarrassed. Maria stuttered an apology but Janet cut her off. 'You know what? I don't need this. I'm outta here.' She pushed past them into the dorm and grabbed her bag and her keys.

They tried to stop her, of course. But she was in the kind of bad mood that made PMS look like cute. She dumped her gear into the back of the car and set off. Her phone rung several times but she ignored it. Where the hell would she go now? Not back to dad and Suzie and her leotards and their inappropriate face-mauling. Her mom was too far away, at the other end of the country. Janet's eyes burned with tears that she refused to shed. With her parents splitting up and all the pressure of exams, things had been so crap. She thought she could get away from being disappointed by coming out here with her friends. And now this. Maria knew how she felt about him. Whatever about Paul, who wasn't always the sharpest tool in the shed, Maria knew. They would tell her it didn't mean anything, that it was an accident. Too many Bud Lights. Yeah, right. Like you just accidentally fall onto someone's face and then accidentally keep kissing them and accidentally enjoy it quite a bit and accidentally try to lie and excuse it to your best friend who'd actually liked him. Yeah, good call.

Okay, last paragraph. I've described the action of the story and Janet's emotional state fairly thoroughly. Now I need to detail the last action of the story that brings it all back to that opening scene.

She drove through the feelings of anger and betrayal that simmered in her chest. She cooled off a little eventually and realised that she didn't even know how long or how far she'd driven. The phone hadn't buzzed in a while. The road was dark, empty. Then the car began to putter and jump. Oh God... she thought. She pressed the accelerator pedal. 'Come on, Roxy...' she urged the car (Roxy was what she'd called the rust-bucket, in an effort to cool it up). The car jumped, slowed. She looked at the petrol gauge. Empty. Crap. She indicated and pulled over. The car slowed to a halt. She had no roadside assistance on her insurance. And if she called her mom she would probably never be allowed to leave the house again. She got out of the car and started to walk. She knew it was stupid and dangerous, but she was damned if she was gonna call her so-called friends and family to help her out. Thunder rumbled overhead and the rain came down. She stuck her thumb out to passing vehicles as she walked the lonely road. This just wasn't what she expected at all.

Walk Thru 2

Write a short story entitled "The Key"

PLANNING

Again, I want to think about the plot, the characters and the setting. This title is fairly open-ended, but is also specific enough in that I have to make a key – either literal or metaphorical – part of the central thrust of the story. I'll scribble down a few ideas.

> Old keys, skeleton keys, mystery. Not knowing what it unlocks. Having to figure it out. Two teenagers bored in one person's granny's house. Nothing to do. The key mystery gives them something to figure out. Granny is batty and loud. What has locks? Doors. Jewellery boxes. Cabinets. Cages. Prisons. Handcuffs. Clocks. What does it open? This is what they have to work out.

I want my characters to be two bored teenage friends who are having to stay with one person's old grandmother in her big country house. She's a bit deaf, shouts a lot without realising it, and makes them watch old movies. They're trying to be patient but find the experience both amusing and frustrating.

In a short story you don't always have to answer the questions that the action throws up. Sometimes, it's just as effective to leave it unresolved because this can create suspense and allows you to leave it on a cliff-hanger – perfect for a short story, especially if you're working to strict exam deadlines!

This story will be set in the grandmother's big, old house. It has to have a slightly funny smell, creaky floorboards, and nothing modern. The fanciest thing is, perhaps, an old cathode ray tube TV playing movies in black and white. I will reveal bits and pieces of this house and its décor as I go along – it's better to drip-feed these details to the reader in order to weave a picture than just describe things at length for a whole paragraph and then forget about them.

1: Jack and Sophie at Jack's grandmother's house. Grams is going deaf. Making them watch old films.

2: J&S leave the room. Brief description of the house. They're bored, have nothing to do.

3: J finds key on the ground. They theorise what it's for – chance to include some humour.

4: Briefly write that J spends the day thinking about the key – easy way to show that a certain amount of time has passed.

5: That week, J tries the key out on a bunch of different things around the house – none of them a match. Include quirky details and jokes – dead birds that Grams still feeds. Sophie suggests maybe it's for handcuffs.

6: Gets Grams's slippers, tries it on things in her room. No luck. Watching another movie. Bored and disappointed again.

7: Looks at a clock for the time. Sees that the face of clock has keyhole. Excitement. Key fits. What's inside?

WRITING

Short stories rely on the language of narration to be effective and interesting. I feel confident about my vocabulary, so this is a good opportunity to show it off – but it's important not overdo it, otherwise it'll seem pompous and ridiculous. If I shake up my verb selection and use a few different adverbs sparingly, it will help to paint a vivid picture.

> It was a cloying, warm day at the old Hennessey place. Jack Hennessey was slumped in the couch with his slightly deaf grandmother, now into her eighth decade, on one side and his best friend, Sophie, on the other. He stared dubiously at the grainy, monochrome image on the old cathode television. It was a real gung-ho war movie.
>
> 'TURN THAT UP, DEAR,' Grandma Hennessey instructed him. Her voice was so loud in his ear that he flinched. And there was his mom worrying about what rock concerts and earphones were doing to his hearing. Boy, was she wrong. He glanced sideways at Sophie, who pursed her lips together and bit back a laugh. He lifted the remote and raised the volume a notch.
>
> 'MORE, PLEASE.' She bellowed. He ground his teeth together and obeyed, wordlessly.

'Do you mind if me and Sophie head outside for a bit, Gran?' he asked her.

'WHAT, DEAR?'

He sighed internally and repeated his question with the appropriate volume in his voice.

'NO NEED TO SHOUT, DEAR... BUT OKAY. YOU GO AHEAD.'

Jack stood and they left the room, shuffling along the creaking floorboards of the hallway. The Hennessey house was cavernous and old. Everything about it was ancient. The floors, the furniture, the books – even the musty scent was from another era. That clunker of a television was the most sophisticated thing in there. He dug his hands into his jeans pockets and glanced apologetically at Sophie. 'Sorry, this sucks so much.'

Sophie shrugged. 'My thumbs will survive without the Xbox for a couple of days. It's no big deal.'

Okay, I've now set the scene a little. We've seen a little of what the grandmother is like, and what Jack is like. Now I can progress the plot a little bit more. I can feel free to use some humour and maybe some colloquial language from time to time to give the story some authenticity.

When Jack felt something hard under the soles of his worn, scuffed Converse, he stopped to look. A small key glinted in the beam of sunlight that flooded down the hall. Huh. He stooped to picked it up. The key was unlike any he'd ever seen. Small and ornate and silver. 'Wonder what this is for...'

Sophie looked at it and joked that, in this house, it probably unlocked a crypt where the crusty remains of Grandda Hennessey and his slobbery old pug, Arnold, were being stowed. Or, she said, some sort of treasure chest with blood diamonds – some of the Hennesseys were based in South Africa and there were plenty of mutterings about this more exotic connection. He laughed aloud but secretly was intrigued by this idea. She wasn't being serious, but Sophie was probably right.

He spent the day with the key in his pocket, where he thumbed it idly and dreamed up ever more wild ideas as to what the key unlocked. He could've just asked somebody, but something in him resisted this idea. What if it was for something mysterious? It's not like whoever knew would let him in on the secret. They would have to find out by themselves.

Dialogue is a great way to change the rhythm of the story and flesh out the characters' personalities. A little conversation can really do wonders for a story. You can be realistic in how you use dialogue – it doesn't have to be linguistically perfect.

As the week ticked slowly by, Jack admitted to Sophie that he now found himself looking at the house in ways he never had before. The key was too small for a door. The cabinets that housed collections of china wares and aged liquors wouldn't take it either. He tried it on the piano when nobody was looking. Too small for that too.

Grandma Hennessey used to keep a number of colourful birds in the conservatory. They were all dead now, including Señor Pablo, her beloved parakeet, but nobody had the heart to tell her about him, so they had him stuffed and Grandma H continued to feed him seed every day. He'd tried each elaborately constructed bird cage, but the key was not for these either.

'It's probably for a pair of handcuffs your granny used on your granda,' Sophie teased. Jack glared at her, horrified.

'Jesus, Sophie!' he hissed. 'Like... What...? Why, like? That's so disgusting.' He blinked hard. 'I actually can't believe you said that.'

She howled with laughter at his reaction, while he shuddered at the images that intruded in his brain and cursed to himself.

One day, Grandma H instructed Jack to fetch her slippers from her room. He trudged upstairs and while he was there he quickly tested out the key on whatever had a lock – jewellery boxes, wardrobes, a chest of drawers and a vanity case. None of them worked. He made his way back down to the sitting room, gave Grandma H her slippers and then sat down again, at her request, to sit through yet another black-and-white film. Sophie had her nose stuck in a book and earplugs in her ears while the on-screen characters gestured and spoke loudly on the box. Jack felt dejected. He loved his grandmother, but staying in that house and watching movies with her while his ears took a pounding was about as interesting as watching paint dry. That key had captured his imagination and he still couldn't figure out what it was for.

I'm now into the last paragraph. I need to create a sense of literary climax – by which I mean that the story must culminate in either a cliffhanger or in a satisfying resolution.

After a while Grandma H nodded off and slipped into a pattern of snoring so loud that it competed with volume of the television. Jack glanced at the old clock on the shelf behind the television. 7:20pm. They had a long night ahead of them. Then he stopped, craned his head.

'It's for the clock....' he murmured. With the earplugs wedged firmly into her ears, Sophie didn't hear him. He ran his thumb over the contours of the key again, unlatched his grandmother's arm from his elbow (which was creeping him out after Sophie's gross handcuff joke) and rose stealthily from the sofa. Sophie glanced up at him as he made his way over to the shelf. He opened the glass cover over the face of the clock and, with a quiver of excitement, smiled as the silver key slotted perfectly into the keyhole. He knew how this worked – it was just about winding the clock up to keep it ticking over. He couldn't stifle his surprise, however, when he twisted the key and heard a click. The clock face popped open. He stared inside. His eyes widened. There, inside the entrails of cogs, springs and wheels, was another, even smaller, key.

'Em. Sophie...?'

Walk Thru 3

'Reflection can lead to misery or mirth.' Write a short story about an older person reflecting on life.

PLANNING

This is another open title. I'll brainstorm quickly to get some ideas out and see what I can pursue.

> Reflection, mirrors, images. Thinking back on something. The past. Rueful. Wondering what could have been. Meeting an old flame, much later in your life. Café. Old age. Thinking about your youth. Ireland in the 50s. Dances. Flirting. Parents didn't approve. Emigration. Separation. Different lives, spouses. Chance reunion. Sense of possibility.

For my plot, I think I will go with the concept of two former lovers meeting by chance much later in life with both reflecting on how different things might have been.

Since they're older, I want to call on an authentic way of phrasing their thoughts and speech. Perhaps they're slightly annoyed by today's youth. But also, maybe there are some surprise attitudes in there that bust the stereotype.

The setting will be a café. It's got to be a comforting place for the characters – warm, social, offering them a treat.

Paragraph number and key concept

1: Old woman – Alice walks into a café, orders some grub.

2: Spots a familiar face walking past on the street outside.

3: Brief description of their time in the past, how they knew each other. Reunion conversation, how's the family etc.

4: Bit more detail – why she liked Jim, what happened that they lost touch.

5: What she ended up doing with her life.

6: What he ended up doing with his life.

7: How things could have been different if they'd ended up together. But also a sense of how that's all still a possibility.

WRITING

I want to start by showing Alice's age – this I'll do by showing her, perhaps, struggling with the heavy door into the café and being slightly dismissive of the teenagers there. I also want to show a side to her that reveals her still-youthful personality. Alice is a woman with a bit of fire in her. I'll use some euphemisms and phrases that will help to paint a picture of her personality and her age.

> Alice Stapleton pushed open the entrance of 'GoodBean' coffee shop. The heavy, glass door heaved slowly open and she teetered inside the warm café. She sidled past tables full of chattering youngsters – wouldja look at the state of their clothes! Mothera God. She made her way to the counter, ordering a cup of coffee and a slice of bakewell tart.
>
> 'How are ya, Mrs Stapleton? Have a sit down there and I'll bring it over to you.'
>
> Poor Barry, God bless him, thought that because she was a silver-haired fox that she must automatically be half deaf and incapable of lifting a tray. Leave him off, she thought to herself as she sat down on the chair near the window that overlooked the street. He dropped over the cake and coffee a minute later. She lifted a forkful of moist cake with a dollop of sweetened cream into her mouth and exhaled satisfactorily. She began to watch the people on the street go by. This was part of her Friday routine. Cake, coffee and comment.

Okay, great. My first paragraph is done. I've set the scene a little. Now I look at my plan and see that in the second paragraph I want to set in motion the main event – she sees an old friend passing by.

> One of the many faces breezing past the window caught her eye. An 'ould' fella, just like herself. There was something about the shape of his eyes and his square jaw. He seemed to feel her looking at him because he cast a glance in her direction and when his bifocals caught her bifocals, the spark of familiarity lit up her brain like a Christmas tree. He stopped flat in the street, sending other passersby bumping into him. His finely lined and slightly tanned face furrowed with fuzzy recognition. Then he raised his walking stick and decisively pointed it her way, as if to say, 'Eureka!'. Except that he said, in a somewhat muffled voice: 'Alice!'

I can see from my grid that, over the next few paragraphs, I should delve into these characters' pasts, explaining how they knew each other, what they liked about one another, and how they lost touch. I will be sure to use colloquial terms and natural conversation to infuse this story with some realism and energy.

James Ryan had danced many's the loose-hipped jig and polka with her at the céilís in the local town hall when they were kids. Her Da, God rest him, was scandalised when he found out. The daughter of a respectable doctor, in cahoots with a local mechanic. Imagine. Alice smiled and waved him inside. He sat down opposite her, slightly out of breath, and, eyeing her face said, 'Alice Molloy, my God. How long has it been?'

'Stapleton now, Jim. And I think the county final night in the Pav, wasn't it?'

He gave a hearty chuckle. 'That sounds about right. So. Mrs Stapleton, ha? Your father was thrilled, I suppose. Doctors and dentists, united in hygiene and matrimony.' He gave her a playful wink.

'Ah go on, ya codger!' she said. 'He wasn't so bad.'

'"Wasn't"?'

'Passed away 10 years ago, if you can believe it. Heart attack.'

'Jesus, I'm sorry to hear that, Alice. My own missus got cancer some years ago.'

Barry, the proprietor of GoodBean, stopped by the table and took his order.

'You've grandkids?' Alice queried. He nodded and rolled his eyes. 'Jesus, an army of them. All feasting on my wallet and my tin of sweets. Adorable little parasites.'

She chuckled and found herself reflecting bittersweetly on those dances in the 50s, wondering how different things could have been.

Jimmy was a vibrant man in his youth. He was a mechanic by trade and the goalkeeper for the local football team. Alice's uptight and overbearing parents were a pill, and Jim's easy-going *'qué será'* attitude appealed hugely to her. He was handsome too, of course. His blond hair was sun-burnished from days spent working and playing outdoors and he was fit as a fiddle. Her father nearly had a conniption fit when Esmé Murphy, who was at most of these dances, told her ma, told Alice's ma. Doctor Frank Molloy would not have his daughter hanging around with a 'common' fella like Jim Ryan. And that was the end of that.

He'd gone to 'Americae', as they used call it, like half the town back then. She would've loved America. But she went to London – her mother insisted. Her aunt was a nurse there and would give her a place to stay until she found a job. Alice spent 15 years in London working as a clerk and trying to hide her Irish accent, which was not popular at the time. Michael Stapleton moved there too, to practise as a dentist and later as an orthodontist. She married him, much to her father's delight, and they had a peaceful life, facilitated by Mike's secret love of brandy and cigars, which was ultimately what had caught him. Alice had hated London, with rain that reminded her of home and the anti-Irish sentiment that always let her know how far away she was. They had a family, of course. That was expected. But their slow and steady life never offered her the verve and exuberance she'd craved.

Jim, she'd heard – probably through Esmé Murphy, who told her ma, who told Alice's ma – rose up through the ranks in an engineering firm in New York and stayed there for many years. She asked him if he'd enjoyed the US, and Jim grinned, wistfully recalling the hot summers, icy winters and the colourful autumns. He told her how the raucous New Yoikers thronged the streets for work, play, peace protests, race riots and rock concerts alike. 'It was a brilliant place,' he said. 'But, no country for old men, as they say. I always woulda come home, ya see.'

Now that I've shown Alice reflecting on their past, I want them to reflect on an alternative hypothetical life they could've had together, and finish by suggesting that they could still have a future as a couple.

She reflected on how different things could have been for her over there in the sunny USA. They'd've lived in the leafy suburbs, she decided, after enjoying a few years in the city. A nice house and yard in Brooklyn, with a flag billowing on the porch. They'd've sipped lemonade on the hot summer days and driven to the Cape for a holiday with the kids. They'd've had Thanksgiving turkey and cranberry 'jelly', watched the fireworks in July and witnessed the whole world unravel and evolve in the great city on the horizon. They'd've sent their girls to good colleges, watch them fall in love with all-American boys – or girls, who knew? Sure, it all passed today. She looked at Jim, his pale blue eyes still a-twinkle with mischief. That's when she realised. For all that could've been, he still had come back and so had she. Probably they would've been talking in this café anyway, and there was nothing stopping them enjoying all that now.

'I know that smile, Ms Molloy. What are ye thinkin'?'

Alice quirked an eyebrow mischievously and said: 'Just that I'm glad I ran into ya, Jim.'

Walk Thru 4

'It was a gathering of minds as much as anything else.' Write a short story about a gathering.

PLANNING

The phrase 'The Gathering' now has a lot of well-known associations, which makes this – potentially – a really interesting and exciting title to work with. Sometimes, if a title or phrase conjures up certain obvious ideas, it can be a good idea to turn the idea on its head and go for something totally different and unexpected. Such a strategy, if planned well, can result in a really strong piece of writing. I'll do the same thing as before – brainstorm and write down some keywords.

> The Gathering. Positive take: a can-do, let's-fix-it event. Business people coming together to help. The reverse: negative, scary, corporate types assembling en masse to raid! Recession. People leaving. Empty streets. Abandoned homes. Few survivors. Apocalyptic.

I need to think about my plot a little bit. In this scenario, I want the gathering to be an eerie, nightmarish event – a meeting of suits and business people who march around like zombies, stealing and driving people away.

My characters: a plucky teenager who lives in a commune and monitors the suits who rove the city like a disease. She's accompanied by her kid brother who's learning the ropes.

This is a darker story. I want it to be set in a grim future, a bleak nether world that is populated by hordes of mindless suits. Most people have left, there are only a few survivors left. The streets are empty and dirty and dark.

1: Tessa and PJ watching the suits somewhere in the city centre. What are they doing?

2: T leaves, PJ hangs back. She gets mad, tells him it's dangerous. Tells him to throw away his money, because the suits will smell it and attack him.

3: Backtrack, explain the past, the transformation, what happened.

4: Describe and explain the present. Show T and PJ getting back to their 'settlement'.

5: T's job, what she does for the commune – monitoring the suits or 'Corps'. Reports to her chemistry teacher. The teacher is surrounded by books.

6: T tells teacher that the Corps are advancing. Teacher is fatalistic.

7: The end is nigh, so T decides ignorance is bliss for the survivors. Corps marching to the commune.

WRITING

I want to create an immediate sense that this world is dark, creepy and dangerous – almost inhospitable. I will introduce our characters, watching these zombie-like business people from the shadows. Tessa is older and more experienced, while her brother PJ is younger and must learn about the suits from her.

> 'What are they doing?' whispered PJ, his breath billowing out into the crisp night air. Tessa shook her head slowly, never taking her eyes away from the crowd of grunting, empty-eyed Corps who assembled in the square.
>
> 'They're gathering.'
>
> 'What are they saying?' he asked.
>
> 'They're not saying anything,' Tessa replied. 'It's just buzzwords and lingo. It doesn't mean anything. They can't think, they can't talk. It's just, like, a reflex for them.'
>
> She retreated slowly from their hiding space behind the collection of over-spilling wheelie bins and turned the corner up a small lane. The temperatures had dropped and there was a frosty bite in the clear night air. She glanced behind her to see her younger brother, PJ, still crouched by the bins with the rubbish and rats, peering, entranced, at the suits in the square below. Rolling her eyes, she strode back, grabbed him by the collar of his tattered coat and dragged him quickly away.

Great, my first paragraph is done. I feel I've made a good start. I've introduced the characters in the action, in the moment, I've described the scene – it's cold, night time, it's dirty. I've also used character dialogue to explain a lot having to write lots of exposition.

'What did I tell ya?' she hissed. PJ shrugged.

'It's fine. We were miles away.'

'It's not fine!' she muttered, and began to stride up the lane whilst throwing furtive glances about the empty buildings around them.

'They can smell you, you know. Do you have any money?'

PJ hesitated for a second too long. If he'd just flat out lied and said 'no', Tessa would've let it go. But he hesitated, and before he could say anything at all, she held out a gloved hand, open-palmed, and said stoically: 'Give it to me.'

PJ sulkily dug his hands into his pockets and slapped the loose change and crumpled fivers into Tessa's paw.

'Is that all of it?' she asked. 'Yes,' he muttered. With that, she flung the money far away. The coppers chimed delicately as they hit the cracked road surface in the distance behind. She could hear the distress in his breath. She relented, and with more patience, explained to him how they scented money like sharks scented blood. They would stop at nothing, she told him. You're nothing to them. They don't care about you. They would tear him limb from limb to get at it. They retrieved their bikes, which were chained to the wrought-iron fence of the empty, ruinous cathedral.

Less than 10 years before, the entire country had buzzed with life. No, Tessa told herself firmly. It just seemed like that. The plague was already there. Even then. It was just dormant. Near the end of that decade, things started to change. The first of the plague-ridden Corps arrived in the capital and infected the leaders, turning them into nothing more than mindless, aggressive underlings who were compelled to do the Corps' bidding. They began to loot their own country and people, funnelling everything back to the chief Corps. As the years wore on, the nation began to fall apart and the people began to fade away. The plague, it seemed, was incurable and the Corps unstoppable. Turn by turn, the lights went off in the streets and the houses emptied out. The ports filled and emptied, filled and emptied, as people escaped this dark and choking future. They stopped using money – they just couldn't risk the Corps sniffing them out. The roads became quiet. The televisions went blank and the radios broadcast nothing but eerie white noise.

I take a quick look back at my plan. I see that to move the story on, I should paint a picture that succinctly explains the past, and the changes that occurred in the place these characters live.

Now I see from my plan that I want to clarify what the world is like now, and I also want to return a little to the action of the story itself and reveal a little more of the environment the characters live in as well as some of the people they live with.

There weren't many people left now. Most of them had fled the plague that had swept the country. There were pockets of survivors in the major urban centres. In this city, they kept to the north. The Corps never travelled north because their sorcery didn't work there. But now Tessa was seeing signs that this was changing. The square was as far north as she'd ever seen them venture. And they looked hungry. She and PJ went back to the commune, where a few hundred of the last hard-nosed survivors were residing on school grounds and sports facilities. There were a couple of young guys standing guard at the gate, kitted out with unwieldy hurleys and helmets that didn't fit them. They hopped down from the top of the fence when they saw Tessa and PJ zipping towards them on their bikes. The gates were unchained and they slipped inside the grounds, where small children played in a schoolyard of faded hopscotch and basketball court markings.

Tessa was respected here. She was one of the top scouts, cycling down into the belly of the city every day to watch the ever-growing hordes of Corps. She reported back to the last leaders – those few haggard doctors, nurses and teachers who chose to stay, to try to give the new generation a fighting chance, even though it seemed pretty much like a losing battle now. She made her way inside the maze of dilapidated prefabs and made her way to McCarthy's office. Beaker, they called her, because she was Tessa's former chemistry teacher. Beaker managed this particular commune. Tessa rapped on the door of her office and heard a muffled voice say, 'Come in.'

She squeezed inside the small room, where precious dog-eared books were stacked ceiling-high all around her. Beaker believed the cure of the Plague and the destruction of the Corps was in these pages somewhere and she spent her free time poring over them, looking for the answer. Much and all as Tessa admired Beaker, she wondered more and more now if the woman wasn't just slowly losing her mind.

'Tessa,' she smiled pleasantly. 'What did your research yield today?'

Tessa was quiet for a second. She thought about how she could sugar-coat it. How she might see the positives, where there was some thin crack of light. But she couldn't.

'They're migrating,' she said eventually, and felt even herself deflate with disappointment once she openly voiced these words. 'They was a gathering at the square today. I've never seen them come that far before. But there's a pattern. And they're moving north.'

Beaker looked back at her book and was quiet for a moment. She sighed eventually and said, 'We held out as long as we could.'

Tessa's heart sank when she heard this. This was Beaker, man. Beaker was tough as nails. She'd taught the most stubborn and troublesome of classes. She'd lived through a terrifying run-in with the Corps, surviving their vicious, clawing snatches as they drained the pennies from her person. She'd held this entire commune together with her own sheer will and invention. It killed Tessa to hear her say this. She left the office and walked out of the prefab maze. She told no-one what Beaker had said. She didn't have the heart, because she knew deep-down Beaker was right, and with this heavy knowledge resting on her shoulders, Tessa decided that, for the rest of the survivors, ignorance was bliss.

I want to change the tone and atmosphere of the story now. I want to create a sense of foreboding. Tessa's hero, Beaker, has admitted that they can do no more. This nightmarish world is getting the better of them. I'll try to end it on a gloomy and unnerving note.

She stopped scouting after that. PJ never asked why. He seemed to know. By the end of the following week, the Corps were shuffling en-masse slowly up the hilly northside terrain towards the commune. The guards at the gate called Tessa and pointed them out to her. She stared grimly at the horizon of the dark-suited Corporates, who lumbered towards them, their bony hands outstretched, grunting and wailing their incoherent babble.

'What's happening?' one of the guards asked anxiously, as though it wasn't already obvious. A strange calm washed over Tessa as she observed the Corps march slowly towards them.

'Throw away your money,' she told them. 'They're coming.'

Walk Thru 5

'The only thing we have to fear is
fear itself.' Write a short story in
which our character must face
his/her darkest fears.

PLANNING

Fear must be the theme of this short story, so it's
an obvious strategy to write about phobias. These
are often irrational fears – seemingly small or
insignificant things that shouldn't inspire so much
terror in a person. As with other short stories, I'll
write down some keywords and see what ideas I can
come up with.

Fears, phobias, often silly things eliciting terror. Spiders.
Very common fear. Sporting teen, fears nothing but
spiders. A popular kid, liked because of his on-pitch
heroics. Keeps his phobia secret. Hurling match. Spiders
in dressing room. Freaked out. Plays the match. One
hidden in his jersey or helmet. Flips out. Adrenaline helps
him to score match-winning goal.

1: Sporting young guy, Neil Sullivan. Paint picture
of strong youngster, inspiring to his friends and
teammates. Allude to a crippling fear.

2: Neil can take a lot, but can't handle spiders.

3: Fear came to haunt him for important
hurling match.

4: Lots of spiders in the 'away' changing room.
Neil flips out, starts striking out with hurley.

5: Everyone else copies him, not realising it's
because of a spider. Match begins.

6: Overview of match progress. All square at half
time, down a point in last few mins of second
half. Suddenly spider crawls in front of his face.

7: Ball sent into him. His fear drives him to feats
of athleticism. He scores winning goal. Nobody
realises it's because he was terrified by a spider.

8: Finish with newspaper report of, 'Sullivan
played like a man possessed'.

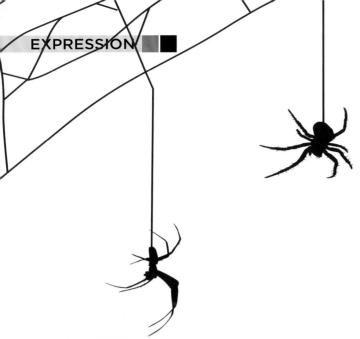

WRITING

I want to give a strong impression of Neil as a confident young guy, whose peerless athleticism has made him an icon in his school. I will paint this picture as vividly and humorously as possible in the first two paragraphs.

Neil Sullivan's reputation had been enhanced by many years of sporting bravery. He was only 17 years old, but still had an impressive résumé of nasty, faint-worthy injuries that had garnered the respect of friends and teachers alike – broken wrist, torn cruciate, dislocated shoulder (twice), not to mention endless black eyes and stitched cuts. All in the name of whatever jersey he donned, whatever flag was flying. This was a guy who put his body on the line for his team. His bloody-minded disregard for his own body meant that he was feared and respected in equal measure. But the bigger they come, the harder they fall, and Neil knew this just as well as anybody. Everyone had weaknesses – fears and phobias that, if preyed on, rendered them helpless. Neil's fear was a closely guarded secret, but his solitary awareness of it meant that he'd had more cold, sweaty nightmares about it entering the public domain than he cared to think about.

He was capable of dealing with a lot, Neil was, but spiders were beyond him. When Seanie Maguire came off his bike and broke the bone of his thumb so badly that it popped out through his skin, Mikey Fitz threw up, his girlfriend Suzie O'Leary literally ran away crying, and his mother started saying the Rosary. But Neil, with an appreciative grimace, took a photo of it on his iPhone and Instagram'd it before driving all and sundry to the hospital in his Civic with Kanye thumping loudly in the background while Seanie's mother, unable to look at her son's bloody hand, lectured him vociferously. But those disgusting critters made his blood run cold and his bowels jiggle. His mind just couldn't get around the way the legs protruded from the bodies, let alone the fact that there were eight of them. They were deceptively fast too. He'd marked and tackled some fast fellas in his time, but those things were in a league of their own.

I look back at my plan and see that the next step is to show Neil's phobia interfering at the worst possible time – during a crucial hurling match. I must build the sense of match anticipation and spider-related fear over the next three paragraphs. I want to call on some colloquial phrases and vocabulary to infuse this story with a sense of the protagonist's personality and give it a humorous kick.

His arachnophobia was, at times, terribly unhelpful and inconvenient. He had to keep it under wraps. It was difficult to be the captain of the school hurling team when you possessed an unmanly fear of bugs that, more often than not, were smaller than your big toe. He'd kept it successfully hidden for a long time, but one day it all started to come undone. It was the day of a crucial Croke Cup match. They were playing an away fixture against some rural shower. Big lads, the lot of them. Fellas who, when they weren't hurling, were shifting hay-bales or man-handling cows. Neil's team were underdogs. This was the school's first time even making it out of the provincial competition. They had a good team but no pedigree, and after winning the Harty for the first time since Jesus was a boy, the coaches, teachers and parents seemed happy enough. Anything else was a bonus and expectation wasn't high. It suited some fellas. He was feeling the pressure a little, Neil.

They got off the bus and slopped out through the muck to a squalid prefab of a dressing room that was being slowly eaten alive by an overspill of ivy and other green growth. Neil's heart pumped hard as they all filed into the tiny room. He set his kit down and then stopped in horror when he saw the thick, grey cobweb in the corner of the small window of the changing room, just above his head. It was peppered with dead blue bottles and what seemed like a fist-sized spider, sitting smugly in one corner. He backpedalled for a second, his eyes wide, his heart half way up his throat, along with his breakfast. Ciarán 'Flah' Flaherty was effing and blinding in one corner, riling the lads up, and the coach was roaring at them to remember the basics. Neil barely heard them. He stared at the spider, gripped his hurley tightly, shivered

a little, and then, without thinking, released a roar and swung at the spider once, twice, three times, like a mad-man.

Everyone stopped and stared for a second and then started to mimic him, bellowing and and shouting at one another, lashing one another with hurleys to prepare for the battle that awaited them on the pitch. They slapped Neil hard on the shoulder. Jesus, he thought frantically, Did I get...? Did I get it?! The coach gathered them around for one final, curse-ridden pep talk. Neil grabbed his helmet, fear still coursing through him. They jogged out, did a quick warm up and, a short while later, the ref threw the ball in.

Now I can start to move the action forward, by offering a short overview of the game. Neil's team are fronting up and hanging tough in the match. It's coming to the last few minutes. It's a crucial time. Neil is suddenly forced to confront his fears at this critical moment.

The game went by in a blur. Miraculously, they were level pegging at half time. The coach threw on a few subs and they battled through the second half. The opposition pulled ahead by a point with a few minutes to go. Coach was losing the rag altogether, screaming at the players to pull forward for the last puck out. There was a break in play as one of the players cried off injured. Then he saw something in the corner of his eye. That fat-arsed spider from the dressing room crawled precariously down the side of his face guard. The sight of it hit his brain like fire hits your skin. The goalie pucked the ball out. Neil's pulse went through the roof and he slapped at his face frantically.

The fear is intense, but bizarrely, Neil manages to put it to good use. His fight-or-flight instinct inspires amazing feats of athleticism that help him to win the game for his teammates.

'Neiiilllll!' the coach screamed hoarsely. Suddenly he spotted the sliotar dropping down out of the grey sky. It dropped behind him and the centre-back. He broke into a sprint, legs pumping like pistons knowing that the spider was trailing from a web at the back of his helmet. Get it away from me! he thought as he legged towards the goal. He'd outpaced his man, and there was the ball. He scooped it up and raced forward with it glued to his hurl. Sweat tickled his back and he flipped out at the thought that it was the spider. He writhed and jinked, until all of a sudden he was only 20 yards from the goal. He brought the sliotar to his hand, released it and fired it like a bullet into the top corner. There was a roar from his teammates and the ref blew the whistle. His friends flocked toward him with whoops and cheers. Neil kept running, ripping off his helmet, raking his fingers through his hair, then pulling off his jersey. He stopped to check himself and then got floored by 14 other young fellas. Well. Whatever was crawling on him was dead now anyway. He nearly passed out with relief.

I'll finish now, as planned, with a short excerpt from a newspaper report.

In the local paper the next day, there was a report on the match.

'Inspired by their captain Neil Sullivan, St Martin's beat the favourites and progressed to the Croke Cup semis for the first time in their history. Sullivan played like a man possessed in the final moment of the game, scoring a freak goal to put his side ahead by two points in the last few seconds of play.'

Exercises

1. Take a moment to consider the room you are sitting in. Now try to describe it in a paragraph. Pay attention to the light, the temperature, the overall feel and atmosphere, the furnishings.

2. Describe the view from your bedroom window in the afternoon. Is it quiet or busy? Are you looking onto lush greenery or a built-up urban setting? What's the weather like?

3. Now describe the view from your bedroom window after dark has fallen. Examine the scene closely. Is the sky clouded over? Are the stars visible? What sounds do you hear? Are these sounds human or animal? What lights can be seen? What can you smell?

4. Think of a place that you visited in the past couple of years that stuck in your mind. This might be a beach, a village in Ireland, a holiday resort in a foreign country. Write a paragraph describing this place.

5. Think of a venue that you attended recently. It might be the local cinema or dancehall, a concert venue or football stadium. Describe this venue in a paragraph.

6. Think of two people that you don't know very well but that you see reasonably often. It might be the local bus driver or shopkeeper. Write a paragraph describing their appearance and personality. It can be useful here to highlight two or three details that reveal the person's character.

7. Imagine one of the people you described in question 6 in one of the locations you described in question 4 and 5. Imagine it is a specific time of day. What are they doing there? Brainstorm and write down four or five possibilities.

8. Imagine your character unexpectedly meeting someone that they have not met for a long time in the location you described. Think about this second character and take the time to describe them. Is this person young or old? Rich or poor? Happy or sad?

9. Jot down why you think these two characters have not met for a long time. Are they former lovers? Friends who drifted apart? Ex-soldiers who served in the same platoon? Write a paragraph describing why they drifted apart.

10. How do they react now that they have met again? Is their meeting tense and awkward or joyful and celebratory?

11. Drawing on everything you have written so far, write a short story entitled 'The Reunion'.

12. The following is a plan for a story entitled 'The Bridge'. The plan moves forward in a very simple fashion dealing with events as they occur in time. The first paragraph deals with the earliest events in the story and the final paragraph deals with the latest events. Rework the plan so that it begins at the end. The first paragraph should deal with the final events of the story. The other paragraph should look back at how the protagonist reached this point.

ORIGINAL VERSION

Paragraph 1	The character is walking home from work across a bridge. It is a normal day and he is expecting nothing out of the ordinary to happen.
Paragraph 2	He sees a person whose car has broken down and stops to offer to help. He wishes after that he had asked for her number.
Paragraph 3	They meet again at a friend's party some weeks later. Describe party atmosphere – people everywhere, their eyes meeting.
Paragraph 4	Describe their surprise at seeing each other again, their conversation,
Paragraph 5	The 'blur' of walks and happy meetings of the next few months as they get to know each other. 'Often we would find ourselves walking across the bridge where we first met.'
Paragraph 6	The wedding. The happiest day of his life.
Paragraph 7	Finds out that she is cheating on him. How does he discover this?
Paragraph 8	He's back on the bridge, filled with sorrow. What's going through his head?

REWORKED VERSION

Paragraph 1	
Paragraph 2	
Paragraph 3	
Paragraph 4	
Paragraph 5	
Paragraph 6	
Paragraph 7	
Paragraph 8	

Now pick one of the above plans and use it to write a short story.

13. **The following is a plan for a story about a rebellious teenager. The plan moves forward in a very simple fashion dealing with events as they occur in time. The first paragraph deals with the earliest events in the story and the final paragraph deals with the latest events. Rework the plan so that it begins in the middle. The first paragraph deals with the dramatic events at the centre of the story. Some of the other paragraphs will have the character thinking back, whilst others will describe events that follow the dramatic events.**

ORIGINAL VERSION

Paragraph 1	The character is staring despondently at a maths equation, glances at the clock, and then closes the book and starts drawing instead.
Paragraph 2	The character is sitting mutely in the classroom while a teacher roars at her, gesturing furiously at a blank copybook.
Paragraph 3	Later on, the character is doodling in her maths copy while waiting out a spell in detention. One of the other 'detainees' befriends her.
Paragraph 4	From here, the character loses interest in academics and starts drawing more and more, receiving artistic encouragement from her detention buddy.
Paragraph 5	The character starts to skip school to work on a comic book. She falls for detention buddy. The character's parents have a stern conversation with her about her behaviour.
Paragraph 6	Eventually she drops out of school. Her relationship with her parents worsens. She moves out, but life is not as rosy in her dingy shared flat.
Paragraph 7	She finds an unfulfilling job in a shop, continues drawing at breakfast, on lunch breaks and after work, all the while going out with her partner in crime, detention buddy. Sometimes, when things get tough, she wonders if she's done the right thing or not.
Paragraph 8	One day she gets home from work and picks up the post. Bills, bills, bills. But there's one from DC comics. She opens it to find that her graphic novel has been accepted for publication.

REWORKED VERSION

Paragraph 1	
Paragraph 2	
Paragraph 3	
Paragraph 4	
Paragraph 5	
Paragraph 6	
Paragraph 7	
Paragraph 8	

Now pick one of the above plans and use it to write a short story.

14. **'A Night to Remember'. Come up with three plans for this title: one where the opening paragraph is set on events during the night in question, one where the opening paragraph is set on the lead-up to the night, and one where the opening paragraph is set on the morning after.**
Now take one of these plans and use it to write a short story.

15. **Write a short story entitled 'My Lucky Day'.**

16. **Write a short story entitled 'There's nothing stranger than the everyday'.**

17. **Write a short story in which a character is forced to leave home against his or her will.**

18. **Write a short story entitled 'It wasn't what I expected'.**

19. **Write a short story in which a character makes a decision they will regret forever.**

Past Exam Questions

1 (2008): '...17-year-old male protagonist with a darting gaze...' (TEXT 1) Write a short story in which the central character is a rebellious teenager (male or female).

2 (2008): Write a short story in which setting/location is a significant feature. (Your story may be prompted by one or more of the locations depicted in Text 3.)

3 (2009): '...the decisive moment...' (TEXT 3) Write a short story in which the central character is faced with making an important decision.

4 (2009): Write a short story in which a photograph, or a set of photographs, plays a part in the plot. Your story may be prompted by one or more of the photographs in TEXT 3.

5 (2010): 'Isn't that funny, and sad, too?' (TEXT 3) Write a short story suggested by the above quotation.

6 (2010): 'What a strange meeting!' (TEXT 3) Write a short story in which two unusual or eccentric characters meet for the first time.

7 (2011): '...the waiting had been magical...' (TEXT 2) Write a story to be included in a collection of modern fairytales.

8 (2011): 'The man above remained rigid, and yet his mystery was mobile.' (TEXT 2) Write a short story in which a mystery is solved.

9 (2012): 'When I was eighteen, I couldn't wait to get out of that town ...' (TEXT 1) Write a short story in which a young character is eager to leave home.

10 (2012) '... an inferior rock band howling for fame.' (TEXT 3) Write a short story inspired by the phrase, '... an inferior rock band howling for fame'.

11 (2013) '...they make manipulation a virtue.' (TEXT 1) Write a short story in which a central character is either manipulated or is manipulative.

12 (2013) In TEXT 3, the writer refers to two short stories on the theme of reunion. Write a short story about a reunion.

Chapter 11:
Comprehension

Introduction

WHEN IT COMES TO THE READING
COMPREHENSION THERE ARE THREE
STAGES TO PRODUCING A GOOD
ANSWER.

READING

Once you have decided which text you are going to
answer on, read it from start to finish.

Read the questions carefully and underline key
phrases in them to ensure that you understand
what specifically is being asked of you. It's tempting
to rush this part but skimming could easily cause
you to misinterpret the question.

Then read the text again with the questions in
mind, underlining relevant passages.

Quickly read through the text for a third time.

PLANNING

Briefly plan your first answer, jotting down the main
points you want to make. You should also jot down
the order in which these points should be dealt with.
This will guide you as you write, and prevent you
wandering off the point.

WRITING

As you write your first answer, remember to quote
from and refer to the text at all times. This is essential
in order to support the points you wish to make.

As you write keep one eye on your plan in order to
ensure your answer remains relevant and focused.

Avoid going on and on. Wrap up your answer once
you've addressed each point you wish to make.

Briefly read through your answer, checking for
spelling and other errors, before moving on to the
next question.

Walk Thru 1

Extract from *Gilead* by Marilynne Robinson

This novel is the fictional autobiography of the Reverend John Ames, an elderly pastor in the small, secluded town of Gilead, Iowa. In this passage the Reverend recalls a trip he made with his father to find the grave of his grandfather.

When I was twelve years old, my father took me to the grave of my grandfather. At the time my family had been living in Gilead for about ten years, my father serving the church here. His father, who was born in Maine and had come out to Kansas in the 1830s, lived with us for a number of years after his retirement. Then the old man ran off to become a sort of itinerant preacher, or so we believed. He died in Kansas and was buried there, near a town that had pretty well lost its people. A drought had driven most of them away, those who had not already left for towns closer to the railroad.

It took my father months to find where the old man had ended up, lots of letters of inquiry to churches and newspapers and so on. He put a great deal of effort into it. Finally someone wrote back and sent a little package with his watch and a beat up old bible and some letters, which I learned later were just a few of my father's letters of inquiry, no doubt given to the old man by people who thought they had induced him to come home.

It grieved my father bitterly that the last words he said to his father were very angry words and there could never be any reconciliation between them in this life. He did truly honour his father, generally speaking, and it was hard for him to accept that things should have ended the way they did.

That was in 1892, so travel was still pretty hard. We went as far as we could by train, and then my father hired a wagon and team. That was more than we needed, but it was all we could find. We took some bad directions and got lost, and we had so much trouble keeping the horses watered that we boarded them at a farmstead and went the rest of the way on foot. The roads were terrible, anyway, swamped in dust where they travelled and baked into ruts where they were not. My father was carrying some tools in his gunnysack so he could try and put the grave to rights a little, and I was carrying what we had for food, hardtack and jerky and the few little yellow apples we picked up along the road here and there, and our changes of shirts and socks, all by then filthy.

He didn't really have enough money to make the trip at that time, but it was so much in his thoughts that he couldn't wait until he had saved up for it. I told him I had to go, too, and he respected that, though it did make many things harder. My mother had been reading about how bad the drought was west of us, and she was not at all happy when he said he planned to take me along. He told her it would be educational, and it surely was. My father was set on finding that grave despite any hardship. Never before in my life had I wondered where I would come by my next drink of water, and I number it among my blessings that I have not had occasion to wonder since. There were times when I truly believed we might just wander off and die. Once, when my father was gathering sticks for firewood into my arms, he said we were like Abraham and Isaac on the way to Mount Moriah. I'd thought as much myself.

It was so bad out there we couldn't buy food. We stopped at a farmstead and asked the lady, and she took a little bundle down from a cupboard and showed us some coins and bills and said, 'It might as well be Confederate for all the good it does me'. The general store had closed, and she couldn't get salt or sugar or flour. We traded her some of our miserable jerky – I've never been able to stand the sight of it since then – for two boiled eggs and two boiled potatoes, which tasted wonderful even without salt.

Then my father asked after his father and she said, why, yes, he'd been in the neighbourhood. She didn't know he had died, but she knew where he was likely to have been buried, and she showed us to what remained of a road that would take us right to the place, not three miles from where we stood. The road was overgrown, but as you walked along you could see the ruts. The brush grew lower in them, because the earth was still packed so hard. We walked past that graveyard twice. The two or three headstones in it had fallen over and it was all grown up with weeds and grass. The third time, my father noticed a fence post, so we walked over to it, and we could see a handful of graves, a row of maybe seven or eight, and below it a half row, swamped with that dead brown grass. I remember that the incompleteness of it seemed sad to me. In the second row we found a marker someone had made by stripping a patch of bark off a log and then driving nails partway in and bending them down flat so they made the letters REV AMES. The R looked like the A and the S was a backward Z, but there was no mistaking it.

It was evening by then, so we walked back to the lady's farm and washed at her cistern and drank from her well and slept in her hayloft. She brought us a supper of cornmeal mush. I loved that woman like a second mother. I loved her to the point of tears. We were up before daylight to milk and cut kindling and draw her a bucket of water, and she met us at the door with a breakfast of fried mush with blackberry preserves melted over it and a spoonful of top milk on it, and we ate standing there at the stoop in the chill and the dark, and it was perfectly wonderful.

Question A

(i) The extract describes a very difficult journey. Referring to paragraphs 4 to 6, describe three hardships that the father and son endured.

(ii) Based on your reading of the above passage, what impression do you have of the father? Support your view with reference to the text.

(iii) Marilynne Robinson has been described as 'one of the world's most compelling English-speaking novelists'. Based on your reading of this passage, identify three aspects of the author's style that you found most effective.

I have already read the text and questions several times and have highlighted relevant passages.

I am going to tackle the **first question**. Because the question asks me to base my answer on particular sections of the text, I will count and number the paragraphs just to be sure that I'm referring to the right parts in my answer. I must now find three hardships described in these paragraphs.

I will identify the three difficulties I am going to discuss and then I will write my answer.

- Travel was tough: Trains only went so far, hired wagon, got lost, horses lacked water and left behind, travel on foot.
- No money: 'He didn't really have enough money…'
- No water or food: 'My mother had been reading of the drought…', 'store had closed'. Etc.

The author writes that three things made their journey difficult. The first challenge they had to overcome was the fact that travelling to their destination was tricky. They spanned the distance by train, wagon and on foot. They got lost once and had to leave the horses behind: 'we boarded them at a farmstead'. The second issue was lack of money. His father didn't have the patience to save: 'He didn't really have enough money … but it was so much in his thoughts that he couldn't wait until he had saved up for it.' The final hardship they encountered was the lack of food and water. The narrator recalls that his mother was aware that 'the drought was west of us'. He notes that he never before questioned where the next drink of water might come from. This, in turn, affected the food. They found a local who had money but no food to buy: 'It was so bad out there we couldn't buy food … She showed us some coins and bills and said, 'It might as well be Confederate for all the good it does me'. The general store had closed and she couldn't get salt or sugar or flour.

Now I will turn to the **second question**:

'Based on your reading of the above passage, *what impression* do you have *of the father*? Support your view with reference to the text.'

I've already underlined key passages in the text relevant to the question. I'll just a have quick look through to ensure I have not missed anything obvious. I will now list what seem to me to be the father's main traits and then I'll write my answer.

- Religious, pious.
- Dedicated, persistent.
- He regrets not making amends, has a conscience, cared about his own father.
- Conscientious man. Considerate of others.
- Perhaps foolhardy. Stubborn to the point of stupidity – leaving the family and heading to a tough drought-stricken place simply to find a grave.

The narrator's father seems to be very morally-minded and conscientious, but also very stubborn. The first clues we get as to his piety is in the first paragraph where it says that he 'served the church' in Gilead. Later on, the father also compares himself and his son (the speaker) to 'Abraham and Isaac on the way to Mount Moriah.' He clearly has a strong sense of faith and as a result is very conscientious. On their way to Kansas, he makes a point to tidy up graves – and this is something he planned for: 'My father was carrying some tools in his gunnysack so he could try and put the grave to rights a little.'

There is much that suggests that the father was persistent and hard-working. It took him 'months to find where the old man had ended up, lots of letters of inquiry to churches and newspapers and so on. He put a great deal of effort into it.' However, this perseverance and single-mindedness leads him to sometimes make foolhardy choices. He leaves his family and marches into a drought-stricken state simply to find a grave, and he does so even though he has no money. This decision, which does not seem very wise, angered his wife: 'My mother had been reading about how bad the drought was west of us, and she was not at all happy when he said he planned to take me along.'

Great. **Last question**.

'Marilynne Robinson has been described as 'one of the world's most compelling English-speaking novelists'. Based on your reading of this passage, *identify three aspects of the author's style that you found most effective*'
This question is asking me to pick out three aspects of her writing that I think work best. I'm going to quickly jot down aspects of the writing that I like.

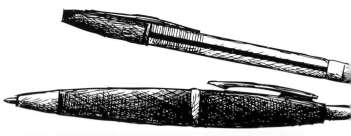

The first thing that strikes me about the extract from Marilynne Robinson's novel is her attention to detail. She creates a vivid picture of the American countryside with her aesthetic use of language. For example, she describes the roads in Kansas as being 'swamped in dust ... and baked into ruts'. This depiction makes it easy to imagine a place that has become barren and hostile. Later, when they are approaching the grandfather's grave, she writes that 'the road was overgrown' and 'the earth was still packed so hard ... The two or three headstones in it had fallen over and it was all overgrown with weeds and grass.' Her choice of words offers the reader a strong sense of the loneliness and desolation of the drought-stricken terrain.

Her decision to use informal or colloquial terminology imbues the piece with an authenticity that makes it more interesting to read. She tells us that her father carried a 'gunnysack' and that they ate simple foods such 'hardtack, 'jerky' and 'cornmeal mush'. Again this gives a clear indication of the stark circumstances they faced in Kansas and makes you admire the characters for enduring such a tough journey just to find Reverend Ames's final resting place.

The author's narrative skill is excellent. In just a few short paragraphs, she offers us a short history of the final years of Reverend Ames's life as well as details of the protagonists' long, arduous trek to Kansas. She does this efficiently, without burdening the reader with too much descriptive detail and yet, at the same time, with some considered writing, she has managed to give us many insights into the character of the father while also sketching a sharp picture of their bleak environment. She seems to contrast that austere world with the humanity of the people. The father, for example, goes to great lengths to locate Reverend Ames, to reach out to him and find his grave, which is a strong sign of his love. Elsewhere, the woman on the farm offers these strangers a place to stay as well as food and water – despite the fact that the drought meant there was almost none available. This is an act of extraordinary generosity, just as the father's efforts were an act of extraordinary love. I really enjoyed this element of the story.

I will quickly read through my answers to check for errors and move on.

Walk Thru 2

Are text messages destroying our language? Eric Uthus takes a look at the evidence.

I have speculated on this for many years, but it seems to have finally come true: mobile phones are evil. That is, grammatically speaking.

In a report released from the State Examination Commission in Ireland, our ability to write in English is slowly deteriorating. And the main culprit behind this deterioration, believe it or not, is text messaging. According to this report, all those messages you send your friends and family at work, on the bus or during class are leading to a weaker understanding of correct grammar and spelling. We are forming shorter sentences, using simpler tenses of verbs and, worst of all, little or no punctuation.

I knew this was coming. From the first time one of my friends sent me the message "I've got 2 go, talk to U later," I knew the end was approaching like black clouds foreshadow the storm. The English language as we once knew it is out the window, and replacing it is this hip and cool slang-induced language given to taking the vowels out of words and spelling phonetically.

I'm glad they finally found something to blame 4 this mess. For a long time, I thought ppl had just become lazy and didn't want to take the time or effort to write complete and coherent sentences. But, apparently, it's the technology itself causing the downfall of writing.

Forget the fact that most mobile phones these days have the option to use T9 or similar technologies that will spell words 4 U, making txt msging even faster. Some people don't have a 2nd to spare; they have jobs, classes and people to luv, so contemplating the time it takes to write correctly seems ridiculous when the information they wish to pass on can be done so quicker.

I guess I feel kinda like a hypocrite, because I remember reading old English novels and thinking, "Man, I can't believe people actually wrote like this! This is soooooo boring and goes on forever." But now here I am, complaining that people are writing in a way that I can't appreciate.

Maybe it's coz I'm afraid of the fast-paced society we live in, which is partly 2 blame 4 the breakthrough of txt msgs. We are always on the run, never stopping to say "Hi!" or have an actual conversation. Instead, we send a couple of words to tell people that we still luv them. But really, who looks at "I <3 you" and feels loved? Or worse yet, has NE 1 actually laughed out loud when they claimed that they were LOL?

Yet what's really sad about the deterioration is that it doesn't appear to bother us. Which brings up the question: where is the line going 2 be drawn? At what point do we begin to realise that our language, something that can be beautiful, eloquent and can paint pictures to rival da Vinci's, is almost in the can? Has txt msging begun a downward spiral that will bring about the end of good writing? Can you imagine reading a good novel with its narrative in text speak? Can you imagine reading Hemingway or Tolstoy as a txt msg?

I hope that this report from Ireland gets more attention and leads to some serious discussion among the populace. As small as this issue may seem, it has a bigger impact on the way we communicate than most people care to admit. I can't, of course, speak for you, but I can't bear to see just how far the destruction can go. I hope U feel da same way.

Question A

(i) What negative consequence of text messaging does the writer highlight at the beginning of the piece?

(ii) 'I hope you feel da same way'. Do you agree with the writer's point of view? Support your answer with reference to the text.

(iii) Uthus is often considered to be a very persuasive writer. What features of good persuasive writing are evident in this piece?

I've read the piece carefully several times. I have also studied the questions and I have highlighted passages in the text that most relate to each one.

I am now going to plan my **first answer**. I am going to read the question carefully again to make sure I understand what is being asked. I have been asked to outline the negative consequences outlined by Uthus in the first three paragraphs. Before writing I'll plan my answer by quickly listing the relevant points:

- Language 'slowly deteriorating'
- Weaker understanding
- Shorter sentences
- Using simpler tenses
- Little or no punctuation
- Out the window → phonetically

As I write my answer I'll keep this little plan in front of me. It will ensure I address every relevant point without wandering off track.

The writer makes the case that text messaging is causing a decline in English around the world. He claims that our writing ability is 'slowly deteriorating' because text messaging causes a 'weaker understanding of correct grammar and spelling'. He mentions how people today are using 'shorter sentences', 'simpler tenses' and 'little or no punctuation' in their writing. In his opinion text messaging has thrown correct English 'out the window' and has replaced it with a slang phonetically spelled language.

I have addressed each of the points in my plan so there is no need to say any more. I have also backed up each of my points with quotations and references to the text. I'll quickly read through what I have written looking for any obvious errors before moving on to the next question.

I will now plan my **second answer**. I am being asked if I agree with the author's point of view and have been told to refer to the text when answering.

The first thing I need to be clear about is what the author's point of view is. Uthus is of the view that text messaging is damaging our ability to write and communicate well. I now need to decide whether or not I agree with his point of view.

I think that the author is right and I think that he has made a number of good points to back up his claim.

Before writing I'll plan my answer by quickly listing the relevant points.

Glancing at the text, I see that I have already highlighted certain lines that are relevant to this question.

- The technology itself causing the downfall of writing: 2 blame 4 the breakthrough of txt msgs
- People are writing in a way that I can't appreciate
- It doesn't appear to bother us
- We are always on the run, never stopping to say "Hi!" or have an actual conversation

I now have the main points that I will refer to in my answer. As I write my answer I'll keep this little plan in front of me. It will ensure I address every relevant point without wandering off track.

I strongly agree with the author that text messaging is 'causing the downfall of writing'. Mobile phones have been in existence for a relatively short period of time and already the way people write has utterly changed. Uthus demonstrates this in a very effective way by using text-speak throughout the essay. For example, he writes '2 blame 4 the breakthrough of txt msgs' instead of 'to blame for the breakthrough in text messaging'. Perhaps it is the 'fast-paced society we live in' that is to blame for this new style, but such writing strikes me as both ugly and lazy, especially considering that, as the author points out, most phones have the technological ability to spell the words for you.

Like the author I find it sad that 'it doesn't appear to bother us' that our use of the English language is deteriorating. We seem to be eager to replace long sentences, proper words and correct grammar with shorter sentences, simpler tenses of verbs and, 'worst of all, little or no punctuation'. Yet we do not seem to be conscious of what is being lost every time we write in this manner. I too fear what lies ahead if we continue down this road. It is quite possible that text messaging has begun a 'downward spiral that will bring about the end of good writing'.

I also agree with the author's concern that we do not communicate properly with one another anymore. It might be the case that we live in a faster-paced world, but I sometimes think that we use this as an excuse to avoid deep conversations. As the author says, we are always on the run, never stopping to say "Hi!" or have an actual conversation'. This is certainly a sad thing.

Again, I have addressed each of the points in my plan so there is no need to say any more. I have also backed up each of my points with quotations and references to the text. I'll quickly read through what I have written looking for any obvious errors before moving on to the next question.

I am now ready to address the **final question** about the author's writing style. This is a question about the author's style of writing. Uthus is considered to be a very persuasive writer. I must find examples of good persuasive writing within the text to support this claim.

Before writing I will once again plan my answer by quickly listing the relevant points:

- Establishes his POV early and stays focused throughout.
- Backs his points up with evidence: personal experience/report released from the State Examination Commission in Ireland/uses the very language he despises.
- Has an engaging style that enables reader to easily support his POV. Uses sarcasm well.

As I write my answer I'll refer to this plan to ensure I make relevant points and stay focused track.

Having read the article, I can see why Mr Uthus is considered a very persuasive writer. He establishes his point of view early on in the article, but he couches it in humorously dramatic terms. For example, 'mobile phones are evil. That is, grammatically speaking.' Using humour makes his opinions seem convincing but not aggressive. Uthus calls on research to support his theory ('a report from the State Examinations Commission in Ireland') and this strengthens his claim that text messaging negatively impacts on our use of English.

To persuade the reader to agree with his way of thinking, he slowly starts to integrate 'text speak' into the article. For example, 'something to blame 4 this mess', 'ppl', 'has txt msging caused a downward spiral', etc. This echoes the claims made in the research he mentioned in the first paragraph, but it also deliberately annoys the reader. Seeing this slang being used where we don't expect it will bother the reader and makes us much more likely to agree with him.

The final feature of his writing that makes it persuasive is his style. He adopts a sarcastic tone throughout the piece: 'Forget the fact that most mobile phones these days have the option to use T9 or similar technologies that will spell words 4 U, making txt msging even faster. Some people don't have a 2nd to spare; they have jobs, classes and people to luv, so contemplating the time it takes to write correctly seems ridiculous.' This makes it very entertaining as well as rendering his criticism sharper and more effective.

Comprehension 1:

"The Bankrupt Man" by John Updike

In his essays, the author John Updike observed the ordinary life around him and prodded us to take a fresh look at stereotypes and shed preconceived notions. In 'The Bankrupt Man' Updike turns upside-down how people normally think of an insolvent man by portraying a lifestyle that isn't down in the dumps.

The bankrupt man dances. Perhaps, on other occasions, he sings. Certainly he spends money in restaurants and tips generously. In what sense, then, is he bankrupt?

He has been declared so. He has declared himself so. He returns from the city agitated and pale, complaining of hours spent with the lawyers. Then he pours himself a drink. How does he pay for the liquor inside the drink, if he is bankrupt?

One is too shy to ask. Bankruptcy is a sacred state, a condition beyond conditions, as theologians might say, and attempts to investigate it are necessarily obscene, like spiritualism. One knows only that he has passed into it and lives beyond us, in a condition not ours.

He is dancing at the Chilblains Relief Association Fund Ball. His heels kick high. The mauve spotlight caresses his shoulders, then the gold. His wife's hair glistens like a beehive of tinsel above her bare shoulders and dulcet neck. Where does she get the money, to pay the hairdresser to tease and singe and set her so dazzlingly? We are afraid to ask but cannot tear our eyes from the dancing couple.

The bankrupt man buys himself a motorcycle. He is going to hotdog it all the way to Santa Barbara and back. He has a bankrupt sister in Santa Barbara. Also, there are business details to be cleared up along the way, in Pittsburgh, South Bend, Dodge City, Santa Fe, and Palm Springs. Being bankrupt is an expansionist process; it generates ever new horizons...

We wish to destroy him, this clown of legerity, who bounces higher and higher off the net of laws that would enmesh us, who weightlessly spiders up the rigging to the dizzying spotlit tip of the tent-space and stands there in a glittering trapeze suit, all white, like the chalk-daubed clown who among the Australian aborigines moves in and out of the sacred ceremonial, mocking it. We spread ugly rumours; we mutter that he is not bankrupt at all, that he is as sound as the pound, as the dollar, that his bankruptcy is a sham. He hears of the rumour and in a note on one-hundred-percent-rag stationery, with embossed letterhead, he challenges us to meet him on West Main Street, by the corner of the Corn Exchange, under the iron statue of Cyrus Shenanigan, the great Civil War profiteer. We accept the challenge. We experience butterflies in the stomach. We go look at our face in the mirror. It is craven and shrivelled, embittered by ungenerous thoughts.

Comes the dawn. Without parked cars, West Main Street seems immensely wide. The bankrupt man's shoulders eclipse the sun. He takes his paces, turns, swiftly reaches down and pulls out the lining of both pants pockets. Verily, they are empty. We fumble at our own, and the rattle of silver is drowned in the triumphant roar of the witnessing mob. We would have been torn limb from limb had not the bankrupt man with characteristic magnanimity extended to us a protective embrace, redolent of cologne and smoking turf and wood violets.

In the locker room, we hear the bankrupt man singing. His baritone strips the tiles from the walls like cascading dominoes. He has just shot a minus sixty-seven, turning the old course record inside out.

He ascends because he transcends. He deals from the bottom of the deck. He builds castles in the air. He makes America grow. His interests ramify. He is in close touch with Arabian oil. With Jamaican bauxite. With Antarctic refrigeration. He creates employment for squads of lawyers. He gets on his motorcycle. He tugs a thousand creditors in his wake, taking them over horizons they had never dreamt of hitherto.

He proves there is an afterlife.

Question A

(i) Based on your reading of the above text, what sort of life does the bankrupt man lead?

(ii) What, in your opinion, is the author's attitude towards the bankrupt man?

(iii) John Updike is known for his keen observations of human life which are often considered to be both witty and insightful. Discuss this view with reference to the extract opposite.

Comprehension 2:

Reading the world in 196 books. Writer Ann Morgan set herself a challenge – to read a book from every country in the world in one year. She describes the experience and what she learned.

I used to think of myself as a fairly cosmopolitan sort of person, but my bookshelves told a different story. Apart from a few Indian novels and the odd Australian and South African book, my literature collection consisted of British and American titles. Worse still, I hardly ever tackled anything in translation. My reading was confined to stories by English-speaking authors.

So, at the start of 2012, I set myself the challenge of trying to read a book from every country (well, all 195 UN-recognised states plus former UN member Taiwan) in a year to find out what I was missing.

With no idea how to go about this beyond a sneaking suspicion that I was unlikely to find publications from nearly 200 nations on the shelves of my local bookshop, I decided to ask the planet's readers for help. I created a blog called A Year of Reading the World and put out an appeal for suggestions of titles that I could read in English.

The response was amazing. Before I knew it, people all over the planet were getting in touch with ideas and offers of help. Some posted me books from their home countries. Others did hours of research on my behalf. In addition, several writers, like Turkmenistan's Ak Welsapar and Panama's Juan David Morgan, sent me unpublished translations of their novels, giving me a rare opportunity to read works otherwise unavailable to the 62% of Brits who only speak English. Even with such an extraordinary team of bibliophiles behind me, however, sourcing books was no easy task. For a start, with translations making up only around 4.5 per cent of literary works published in the UK and Ireland, getting English versions of stories was tricky.

This was particularly true for francophone and lusophone (Portuguese-speaking) African countries. There's precious little on offer for states such as the Comoros, Madagascar, Guinea-Bissau and Mozambique – I had to rely on unpublished manuscripts for several of these. And when it came to the tiny island nation of Sao Tome & Principe, I would have been stuck without a team of volunteers in Europe and the US who translated a book of short stories by Santomean writer Olinda Beja just so that I could have something to read.

Then there were places where stories are rarely written down. If you're after a good yarn in the Marshall Islands, for example, you're more likely to go and ask the local iroij's (chief's) permission to hear one of the local storytellers than you are to pick up a book. Similarly, in Niger, legends have traditionally been the preserve of griots (expert narrators-cum-musicians trained in the nation's lore from around the age of seven). Written versions of their fascinating performances are few and far between – and can only ever capture a small part of the experience of listening for yourself.

If that wasn't enough, politics threw me the odd curveball too. The foundation of South Sudan on 9 July 2011 – although a joyful event for its citizens, who had lived through decades of civil war to get there – posed something of a challenge. Lacking roads, hospitals, schools or basic infrastructure, the six-month-old country seemed unlikely to have published any books since its creation. If it hadn't been for a local contact putting me in touch with writer Julia Duany, who penned me a bespoke short story, I might have had to catch a plane to Juba and try to get someone to tell me a tale face to face.

All in all, tracking down stories like these took as much time as the reading and blogging. It was a tall order to fit it all in around work and many were the nights when I sat bleary-eyed into the small hours to make sure I stuck to my target of reading one book every 1.87 days.

But the effort was worth it. As I made my way through the planet's literary landscapes, extraordinary things started to happen. Far from simply armchair travelling, I found I was inhabiting the mental space of the storytellers. In the company of Bhutanese writer Kunzang Choden, I wasn't simply visiting exotic temples, but seeing them as a local Buddhist would. Transported by the imagination of Galsan Tschinag, I wandered through the preoccupations of a shepherd boy in Mongolia's Altai Mountains. With Nu Nu Yi as my guide, I experienced a religious festival in Myanmar from a transgender medium's perspective.

In the hands of gifted writers, I discovered, bookpacking offered something a physical traveller could hope to experience only rarely: it took me inside the thoughts of individuals living far away and showed me the world through their eyes. More powerful than a thousand news reports, these stories not only opened my mind to the nuts and bolts of life in other places, but opened my heart to the way people there might feel.

And that in turn changed my thinking. Through reading the stories shared with me by bookish strangers around the globe, I realised I was not an isolated person, but part of a network that stretched all over the planet.

One by one, the country names on the list that had begun as an intellectual exercise at the start of the year transformed into vital, vibrant places filled with laughter, love, anger, hope and fear. Lands that had once seemed exotic and remote became close and familiar to me – places I could identify with. At its best, I learned, fiction makes the world real.

Question A

(i) What problems did the author encounter in her efforts to read a book from every country in the world?

(ii) 'But the effort was worth it.' In your opinion was the effort expended by Ann Morgan on this project worthwhile? Support your answer with reverence to the text.

(iii) Comment on three stylistic features which contribute to making this an interesting and informative text.

Comprehension 3:

Extract from *Super-Cannes* by J.G. Ballard

In his novel *Super-Cannes*, J. G. Ballard describes a community of European elite living in the hills above Cannes in the business park Eden-Olympia. The park is a closed society that offers its privileged residents luxury homes, private doctors and other conveniences required by the modern businessman. The book's protagonist, Paul, quits his job as an editor and moves to Eden-Olympia with his wife Jane. At first glance, Eden-Olympia seems the ideal workers' paradise, but beneath its glittering surface, all is not well.

In the meantime I explored Eden-Olympia on foot, logging miles along the simulated nature trails that ended abruptly when they were no longer visible from the road. Ornamental pathways led to the electricity substations feeding power into the business park's grid. Surrounded by chain-link fences, they stood in the forest clearings like mysterious and impassive presences. I circled the artificial lakes, with their eerily calm surfaces, or roamed around the vast car parks. The lines of silent vehicles might have belonged to a race who had migrated to the stars.

By the early afternoon Charles's e-mails brought me final proof pages, cheery gossip about the latest office romances, and queries over the editorial copy of our aviation journals. I missed Jane, who never returned home before seven o'clock, but I was happy to doze on the sun-lounger and listen to the droning engines of light aircraft trailing their pennants across the cloudless sky, new from the sun of furniture sales, swimming pool discounts and the opening of a new aqua-park.

A lawnmower sounded from a nearby garden as the roving groundstaff trimmed the grass. Sprinklers hissed a gentle drizzle across the flowerbeds of the next-door villa, occupied by Professor Ito Yasunda, chairman of a Japanese finance house, his serious-faced wife and even more serious three-year-old son. On Sundays they played tennis together, a process as stylized as a Kabuki drama, which involved endless ball retrieval and virtually no court action.

My other neighbours were a Belgian couple, the Delages, among the earliest colonists of the business park. Alain Delage was the chief financial officer of the Eden-Olympia holding company, a tall, preoccupied accountant lost somewhere behind the lenses of his rimless glasses. But he was kind enough to give Jane a lift to the clinic each morning. I had met the couple, Delage and his pale watchful wife Simone, but our brief conversation across the roof of their Mercedes would have been more expressive if carried out by semaphore between distant peaks in the Alpes-Maritimes.

Intimacy and neighbourliness were not features of everyday life at Eden-Olympia. An invisible infrastructure took the place of traditional civic virtues. At Eden-Olympia there were no parking problems, no fears of burglars or purse snatchers, no rapes or muggings. The top-drawer professionals no longer needed to devote a moment's thought to each other, and had dispensed with the checks and balances of community life. There were no town councils or magistrates' courts, no citizens' advice bureaus. Civility and polity were designed into Eden-Olympia, in the same way that mathematics, aesthetics and an entire geopolitical world-view were designed into the Parthenon and the Boeing 747. Representative democracy had been replaced by the surveillance camera and the private police force.

By the afternoon, all this tolerance and good behaviour left me feeling deeply bored. After a light lunch I would set off on foot around the business park. A few days earlier, while circling one of the largest lakes, I came across a curious human settlement in the woods. This was the lavish sports centre advertised in the brochure, a complex that contained two swimming pools, saunas, squash courts and a running track. It was fully staffed by helpful young instructors, but otherwise deserted. I assumed that the senior administrators at Eden-Olympia were too tired after a day's work to do more than eat supper from a tray and doze in front of the adult movie channel.

Question A

(i) What does this extract tell us about Eden-Olympia? Identify three different aspects of life there.

(ii) Would you consider Eden-Olympia a pleasant place in which to live? Support your answer with reference to the text.

(iii) J.G. Ballard uses a number of vivid images to conjure the world of Eden-Olympia. Identify three of these and say why you find them effective.

Comprehension 4:

Extract from *On the Road by* Jack Kerouac

I first met Dean not long after my wife and I split up. I had just gotten over a serious illness that I won't bother to talk about, except that it had something to do with the miserably weary split-up and my feeling that everything was dead. With the coming of Dean Moriarty began the part of my life you could call my life on the road. Before that I'd often dreamed of going West to see the country, always vaguely planning and never taking off. Dean is the perfect guy for the road because he actually was born on the road, when his parents were passing through Salt Lake City in 1926, in a jalopy, on their way to Los Angeles. First reports of him came to me through Chad King, who'd shown me a few letters from him written in a New Mexico reform school. I was tremendously interested in the letters because they so naively and sweetly asked Chad to teach him all about Nietzsche and all the wonderful intellectual things that Chad knew. At one point Carlo and I talked about the letters and wondered if we would ever meet the strange Dean Moriarty. This is all far back, when Dean was not the way he is today, when he was a young jailkid shrouded in mystery. Then news came that Dean was out of reform school and was coming to New York for the first time; also there was talk that he had just married a girl called Marylou.

One day I was hanging around the campus and Chad and Tim Gray told me Dean was staying in a cold-water ~~rad~~ in East Harlem, the Spanish Harlem. Dean had arrived the night before, the first time in New York, with ~~~s~~ beautiful little sharp chick Marylou; they got off the Greyhound bus at 50th Street and cut around the ~~~ner~~ looking for a place to eat and went right in Hector's, and since then Hector's cafeteria has always been ~~~g~~ symbol of New York for Dean. They spent money on beautiful big glazed cakes and creampuffs.

All this time Dean was telling Marylou things like this: "Now, darling, here we are in New York and although I haven't quite told you everything that I was thinking about when we crossed Missouri and especially at the point when we passed the Booneville reformatory which reminded me of my jail problem, it is absolutely necessary now to postpone all those leftover things concerning our personal lovethings and at once begin thinking of specific worklife plans..." and so on in the way that he had in those early days.

I went to the cold-water flat with the boys, and Dean came to the door in his shorts. Marylou was jumping off the couch; Dean had dispatched the occupant of the apartment to the kitchen, probably to make coffee, while he proceeded with his loveproblems, for to him sex was the one and only holy and important thing in life, although he had to sweat and curse to make a living and so on. You saw that in the way he stood bobbing his head, always looking down, nodding, like a young boxer to instructions, to make you think he was listening to every word, throwing in a thousand "Yeses" and "That's rights." My first impression of Dean was of a young Gene Autry – trim, thin-hipped, blue-eyed, with a real Oklahoma accent – a sideburned hero of the snowy West. In fact he'd just been working on a ranch, Ed Wall's in Colorado, before marrying Marylou and coming East. Marylou was a pretty blonde with immense ringlets of hair like a sea of golden tresses; she sat there on the edge of the couch with her hands hanging in her lap and her smoky blue country eyes fixed in a wide stare because she was in an evil gray New York pad that she'd heard about back West, and waiting like a longbodied emaciated Modigliani surrealist woman in a serious room. But, outside of being a sweet little girl, she was awfully dumb and capable of doing horrible things. That night we all drank beer and pulled wrists and talked till dawn, and in the morning, while we sat around dumbly smoking butts from ashtrays in the gray light of a gloomy day, Dean got up nervously, paced around, thinking, and decided the thing to do was to have Marylou make breakfast and sweep the floor. "In other words we've got to get on the ball, darling, what I'm saying, otherwise it'll be fluctuating and lack of true knowledge or crystallization of our plans." Then I went away.

During the following week he confided in Chad King that he absolutely had to learn how to write from him; Chad said I was a writer and he should come to me for advice. Meanwhile Dean had gotten a job in a parking lot, had a fight with Marylou in their Hoboken apartment – God knows why they went there – and she was so mad and so down deep vindictive that she reported to the police some false trumped-up hysterical crazy charge, and Dean had to lam from Hoboken. So he had no place to live. He came right out to Paterson, New Jersey, where I was living with my aunt, and one night while I was studying there was a knock on the door, and there was Dean, bowing, shuffling obsequiously in the dark of the hall, and saying, "Hello, you remember me – Dean Moriarty? I've come to ask you to show me how to write."

Question A

(i) What is the narrator's impression of Dean Moriarty prior to their first meeting? How does his view of Dean change afterwards?

(ii) 'Dean is the perfect guy for the road.' Based on your reading of this text would you consider undertaking a long journey with Dean Moriarty as your travelling companion? Give reasons for your answer.

(iii) What features of the writer's style help to make this an interesting piece to read?

Comprehension 5:

Extract from *Goodbye to all that* by Joan Didion.

It is easy to see the beginnings of things, and harder to see the ends. I can remember now, with a clarity that makes the nerves in the back of my neck constrict, when New York began for me, but I cannot lay my finger upon the moment it ended, can never cut through the ambiguities and second starts and broken resolves to the exact place on the page where the heroine is no longer as optimistic as she once was. When I first saw New York I was twenty, and it was summertime, and I got off a DC-7 at the old Idlewild temporary terminal in a new dress which had seemed very smart in Sacramento but seemed less smart already, even in the old Idlewild temporary terminal, and the warm air smelled of mildew and some instinct, programmed by all the movies I had ever seen and all the songs I had ever read about New York, informed me that it would never be quite the same again. In fact it never was. Some time later there was a song in the jukeboxes on the Upper East Side that went 'but where is the schoolgirl who used to be me,' and if it was late enough at night I used to wonder that. I know now that almost everyone wonders something like that, sooner or later and no matter what he or she is doing, but one of the mixed blessings of being twenty and twenty-one and even twenty-three is the conviction that nothing like this, all evidence to the contrary notwithstanding, has ever happened to anyone before.

Of course it might have been some other city, had circumstances been different and the time been different and had I been different, might have been Paris or Chicago or even San Francisco, but because I am talking about myself I am talking here about New York. That first night I opened my window on the bus into town and watched for the skyline, but all I could see were the wastes of Queens and big signs that said MIDTOWN TUNNEL THIS LANE and then a flood of summer rain (even that seemed remarkable and exotic, for I had come out of the West where there was no summer rain), and for the next three days I sat wrapped in blankets in a hotel room air conditioned to 35 degrees and tried to get over a cold and a high fever. It did not occur to me to call a doctor, because I knew none, and although it did occur to me to call the desk and ask that the air conditioner be turned off, I never called, because I did not know how much to tip whoever might come – was anyone ever so young? I am here to tell you that someone was. All I could do during those years was talk ng-distance to the boy I already knew I would never marry in the spring. I would stay in New York, I told n, just six months, and I could see the Brooklyn Bridge from my window. As it turned out the bridge was Triborough, and I stayed eight years.

In retrospect it seems to me that those days before I knew the names of all the bridges were happier than the ones that came later, but perhaps you will see that as we go along. Part of what I want to tell you is what it is like to be young in New York, how six months can become eight years with the deceptive ease of a film dissolve, for that is how those years appear to me now, in a long sequence of sentimental dissolves and old-fashioned trick shots – the Seagram Building fountains dissolve into snowflakes, I enter a revolving door at twenty and come out a good deal older, and on a different street. But most particularly I want to explain to you, and in the process perhaps to myself, why I no longer live in New York. It is often said that New York is a city for only the very rich and the very poor. It is less often said that New York is also, at least for those of us who came there from somewhere else, a city only for the very young.

Question A

(i) Describe the narrator's first impressions of New York City and how she felt when she first arrived there.

(ii) What does this text say about what it's like to be young and about youth's passing?

(iii) Did the author's description of New York bring the city to life for you as a reader? Support your answer with reference to the text.

Comprehension 6:

It is a simply-styled, silent camera that has produced some of photography's most memorable images. Jonathan Glancey writes in praise of the Leica.

Richard Nixon doubted its authenticity, but then as the US president who stepped up the bombing of North Vietnam by the USAF that Christmas to levels unknown since the late stages of WWII, he would, wouldn't he? Armed with nothing more than a Leica M2 35mm rangefinder camera, Nick Ut, a 21-year-old Vietnamese photographer with AP (Associated Press), had caught what is perhaps the most poignant and disturbing image of the terrible nineteen-year war that tore South East Asia apart.

The photograph was published around the world on 12 June 1972. It showed a naked, nine-year-old girl, Kim Phuc – her skin scorched by Napalm – running for her life with fellow villagers. 'Napalm Girl' is said to have helped put an end to the Vietnam War soon afterwards. It was not a fake. Nick Ut even helped Kim to safety – an author, she is alive, well, married and a mother of two in Canada today – before rushing to an AP darkroom and printing negative number seven from the roll of 35mm film wound tightly inside his bombproof Leica.

Many of the world's great photojournalists have used Leica's evergreen range of 35mm rangefinder cameras for their most memorable work, among them Robert Doisneau – who can forget his 1950 shot of two young Parisian lovers kissing in front of the Hotel de Ville? – Diane Arbus, Henri Cartier-Bresson, Rene Burri, Robert Capa, Elliott Erwitt and Sebastiao Salgado. And, of course, there was that image of Che Guevara – the Heroic Guerilla – which Alberto Korda said he took with a Leica M2, and which has been reproduced on millions of t-shirts, posters and coffee mugs ever since.

Some of photography's most important images – such as Robert Capa's picture of a soldier killed in the Spanish Civil War – were taken on Leicas. **(Photo: Robert Capa/Magnum)**

Leicas travelled the world, allowing photographers such as Eve Arnold to take classic portraits unobtrusively; the Leica's shutter was almost silent. **(Photo: Eve Arnold/Magnum)**

BRASS TACKS

Compact, crafted, solid – all brass and manganese alloy – silent and reliable, the Leica rangefinder camera that made its debut in 1932 remains one of the best-loved of all cameras by photographers in tumultuous times and challenging locations. Here is a camera that, because of its size, discreet looks and superb lens can be relied on to capture publishable images at the most demanding moments, especially when the click of a shutter release, let alone a blaze of flash light or even the glow from a digital phone camera, could spell the arrest, deportation or even death of the photographer. The fact that Leica's M-range (M is for Messsucher or rangefinder) has a spare, old-fashioned look means that it is often considered quaint and quirky – hardly the type of camera a war reporter or a celebrity-hunting paparazzo would choose.

But they do, and have done so ever since the quietly revolutionary camera designed by Oskar Barnack for the Leitz Optische Werke of Wetzlar, Germany, went on general sale in 1925. Barnack had produced the first of his new generation cameras in 1914; World War I and its disastrous effect on the German economy held production back. The lightweight, hand-held camera used 35mm cinema film; a custom-made lens ensured that prints from those small negatives could be blown up to a large scale. Barnack thought of his Leica as a camera that would be used for landscape and mountain photography. It was, but, with its compact dimensions and unrivalled performance, it quickly became a favourite of journalists.

Cuban photographer Alberto Korda took the famous portrait of Argentine revolutionary Che Guevara on a Leica. The image became a counterculture icon.
(Photo: AP)

PRODUCTION LINE

Not surprisingly, copies of the Leica were soon in production in other parts of the world, notably the Soviet Union, where the FED camera produced in the Ukraine was to follow the fortunes of its German source. In 1941, the Germans destroyed the FED factory; towards the end of World War II, the Red Army plundered the Leica factory allowing FED to re-tool and to begin manufacturing a new generation of Leica lookalikes from 1946; production ended in 1990. Today, these cameras – Pablo Picasso preferred a FED to a Leica – can be bought in good condition for less than $150, a fraction of the cost of a German-made Leica.

Barnack's camera has mutated slowly over the decades into Leica's current M-range, including the M7 that uses traditional 35mm film and the M9, a digital version; the lenses of analogue and digital cameras are interchangeable and, from a distance, they look much of a muchness. Their simple styling means they will never appeal to those in need of ostentation, status symbols or bling: an M-series Leica is a refined tool, not a design statement. As Leica itself says: 'Classics are works that are immune to the passing whims of the present. They are never rewritten, but re-interpreted on the basis of a changed world.' And, yet, as the world changes – and sometimes dramatically so, in front of photographers' eyes – the M-series Leica carries on superficially heedless of new fads, fashions, faces and wars.

Street photographers loved the Leica. Leitz's lenses were famed for their sharpness, allowing an enormous amount of detail to be captured on film. **(Photo: Rene Burri/Magnum)**

Question A

(i) Identify four of the features and advantages that helped the Leica become some such a successful brand.

(ii) Select three features of the author's style in the written element of the text and comment on their effectiveness.

(iii) Write a personal response to the visual image in the above piece that makes the greatest impact on you. You might consider the subject matter, setting, mood, caption, photographic qualities and so on.

Comprehension 7:

Are Grimm's Fairy Tales too twisted for children? Stephen Evans explores the twisted world of Grimm's Fairy Tales – bedtime stories complete with mutilation, cannibalism, infanticide and incest.

On the covers are the most innocent of titles: Grimm's Fairy Tales in their English version or Children's and Household Tales in the original German editions published two hundred years ago. Nice tales for nice children.

But behind the safe titles lie dark stories of sex and violence – tales of murder, mutilation, cannibalism, infanticide and incest, as one academic puts it. They are far from anything we might imagine as acceptable today. If they were a video game, there would be calls to ban them.

Jacob and Wilhelm Grimm were writing in a different world. They lived in the town of Kassel in Germany and studied law and language as well as writing more than 150 stories which they published in two volumes between 1812 and 1814.

Some stories have fallen out of favour but some – Red Riding Hood, Cinderella, Hansel and Gretel, Snow White – seem eternal. They have morphed into countless adaptations; Disney disneyfied them and new filmmakers and novelists continue to rework them. Comics from Japanese Manga to the erotic and 'adult' depict the characters of the Grimm brothers' tales.

But even in their original, they are far from saccharine, according to Maria Tatar, professor of Germanic folklore and mythology at Harvard University: 'These tales are not politically correct. They are full of sex and violence. In Snow White, the stepmother asks for the lungs and liver of the little girl. She's just seven years old and she's been taken into the woods by the huntsman. That's pretty scary.

'And then the evil stepmother is made to dance to death in red-hot iron shoes. In Cinderella, you've got the stepsisters whose heels and toes are cut off.'

ADULT THEMES

These tales of gore and sexuality – John Updike called them the pornography of an earlier age – are still going strong. 'I can't even keep track of the number of new versions of Snow White,' says Professor Tatar. 'And these aren't just Disney productions – you have film-makers making very adult versions of the fairy tales, drawing out the perverse sexuality of some of these tales.'

They are tales of right and wrong. There are clear morals to be drawn – deception and dishonesty are punished; honest hard work is rewarded; promises must be honoured; beware of strangers – and especially the forest.

But that can't be the enduring appeal. Moralistic lectures never entertained anyone – but gory tales of suspense are a different thing. They do have an eternal following. As Professor Tatar puts it: 'They give us these 'what if' scenarios – what if the most terrible thing that I can imagine happened? – but they give us these scenarios in the safe space of 'once upon a time'. I'm going to tell you the story and I'm going to show you how this hero or this heroine manages to come out of it alive.' And not just alive, but also 'happily ever after'.

It's clear that many children love the gory bits. And it's clear that many parents don't. A survey last year found that many reported that their children had been left in tears by the gruesome fate of Little Red Riding Hood. Some parents wouldn't read Rumpelstiltskin to their children because it was about kidnapping and execution. And many parents felt that Cinderella was a bad role model for daughters because she did housework all day.

Some pop culture versions of the tales have sugar-coated their more unpalatable aspects. It's true that the Cinderella made by Disney in 1950 is a work of schlock – the titles of the songs (A Dream is a Wish Your Heart Makes', Bibbidi-Bobbidi-Boo and Sing Sweet Nightingale) give the flavour. But Disney's older animated versions of Grimm's Fairy Tales are much darker.

'In *Snow White* which was made in 1937,' says Professor Tatar, 'the Wicked Queen goes down into the basement where she's got a chemistry set which she's going to use to turn the apple into a poisoned apple.'
There are ravens down there and skulls and mysterious dusty tomes.

'And then she transforms herself into an old hag. She goes from the fairest of all to the ugliest of all.

'I think that's really an adult moment which enacts our anxieties about aging. First, her voice changes and then her hands begin to change and there she is a decrepit old woman.

'I think Disney picked up on the scariness of fairy tales as something which appeals to both children and adults.'

EVIL THOUGHTS

You get a flavour of these debates and nuances in the town of Kassel in Germany at the moment. It's where the two brothers grew up and lived (in the same house, Wilhelm married to Henriette; Jacob single until his death).

There have been productions of some of the tales in the Botanical Gardens and a thought-provoking exhibition in the city's documenta-Halle. It displays the original publications of the tales and the dictionaries and other works produced by the brothers.

But the most interesting exhibits are the ones designed to make people think. There are videos of glossy perfume adverts featuring a radiant Little Red Riding Hood taming the wolf with her fragrance. There is a section marked 'No Access for Minors' where, behind a thick curtain, you can read the most violent extracts from the tales through slits in the wall.

One of the curators, Louisa Dench, said these extracts show that good triumphs over evil and that the bad get punished. There are clear choices. 'There is good and there is bad and you know what's good and what's bad and there's no question about it. And that's very understandable for children. It's very clear, and good always wins. That's important.'

She thinks the secret of the enduring appeal is that much is left to the imagination. 'You have only limited characterisation so there's a lot you can imagine yourself,' she says. 'If someone reads them to you, your mind can build up its own picture. That's part of the magic.'

It is a magic based on fantasy and that may be what protects the tales from the unmitigated wrath of parents. Children – some children – do seem to like the darkness of horror but, perhaps, not if it becomes too realistic. Some parents feel uneasy about tales for children where a child's hands are cut off ('The Girl without Hands') or where a man is pushed down stairs ('The Story of the Youth Who Went Forth to Learn What Fear Was') – but children know it is fantasy.

Their fantastical darkness may have protected today's video games from the wrath of tougher laws. Two years ago, the Supreme Court of the United States struck down a lower court's ruling that video games should be banned. Justice Scalia ruled that depictions of violence had never been regulated. 'Grimm's Fairy Tales, for example, are grim indeed,' he wrote, referring to the gory plots of Snow White, Cinderella and Hansel and Gretel.

Grim, indeed. And exciting, too, to generations of children and adults for two hundred years – and perhaps for another two hundred.

Question A

(i) What, according to the author and other experts, gives the fairy tales their lasting appeal? Support your answer with quotes from the text.

(ii) 'These tales are not politically correct.' What is your opinion on this debate about whether fairy tales are appropriate for children? In your answer refer to the text above.

(iii) Do you find the style of writing in this article appealing? Support your answer with detailed reference to the text.

Comprehension 8:

Extract from *Notes From A Small Island* by Bill Bryson

I awoke early and hit the drizzly streets determined to form some fixed impression of the city. My problem with Manchester, you see, is that I have no image of it, none at all. Every other great British city has something about it, some central motif that fixes it in my mind: Newcastle has its bridge, Liverpool has the Liver Buildings and docks, Edinburgh its castle, Glasgow the great sprawl of Kelvingrove Park and the buildings of Charles Rennie Mackintosh, even Birmingham has the Bull Ring (and very welcome it is to it, too). But Manchester to me is a perennial blank – an airport with a city attached. Mention Manchester to me and all that swims into my mind is a vague and unfocused impression of Ena Sharples, L.S. Lowry, Manchester United football club, some plan to introduce trams because they have them in Zurich or some place and they seem to work pretty well there, the Halle Orchestra, the old *Manchester Guardian* and these rather touching attempts every four years or so to win the bid for the next summer Olympics, usually illustrated with ambitious plans to build a £400-million velodrome or a £250-million table tennis complex or some other edifice vital to the future of a declining industrial city.

Apart from Ena Sharples and L.S. Lowry, I couldn't name a single great Mancunian. It's clear from the abundance of statues outside the town hall that Manchester has produced its share of worthies in its time, though it is equally clear from all the frock coats and mutton chops that it has either stopped producing worthies or stopped producing statues. I had a look around them now and didn't recognize a single name.

If I haven't got a very clear image of the city, it's not entirely my fault. Manchester doesn't appear to have a very fixed image of itself. 'Shaping Tomorrow's City Today' is the official local motto, but in fact Manchester seems decidedly of two minds about its place in the world. At Castlefield, they were busy creating yesterday's city today, cleaning up the old brick viaducts and warehouses, recobbling the quaysides, putting fresh coats of glossy paint on the old arched footbridges and scattering about a generous assortment of old-fashioned benches, bollards and lampposts. By the time they have finished, you will be able to see exactly what life was like in nineteenth-century Manchester – or at least what it would have been like if they had had wine-bars and cast-iron litter bins and directional signs for heritage trails and the G-Mex Centre. At Salford Quays, on the other hand, they have taken the opposite tack and done everything they can to obliterate the past, creating a kind of mini-Dallas on the site of the once-booming docks of the Manchester Ship Canal. It's the most extraordinary place – a huddle of glassy modern office buildings and executive flats in the middle of a vast urban nowhere, all of them seemingly quite empty.

The one thing you have a job to find in Manchester is the one thing you might reasonably expect to see – row after row of huddled Coronation Streets. These used to exist in abundance, I'm told, but now you could walk miles without seeing a single brick terrace anywhere. But that doesn't matter because you can always go and see the real Coronation Street on the Granada Studios Tour, which is what I did now – along with, it seemed, nearly everyone else in the North of England. For some distance along the road to the studios there are massive waste-ground car and coach parks, and even at 9.45 in the morning they were filling up. Coaches from far and wide – from Workington, Darlington, Middlesbrough, Doncaster, Wakefield, almost every northern town you could think of – were decanting streams of sprightly white-haired people, while from the car parks issued throngs of families, everyone looking happy and good natured.

I joined a queue that was a good 150 yards long and three or four people wide and wondered if this wasn't a mistake, but when the turnstiles opened the line advanced pretty smartishly and within minutes I was inside. To my deep and lasting surprise, it was actually quite wonderful. I had expected it to consist of a stroll up the *Coronation Street* set and a perfunctory guided tour of the studios, but they have made it into a kind of amusement park and done it exceedingly well. It had one of those Motionmaster Cinemas, where the seats tilt and jerk, so that you actually feel as if you are being hurled through space or thrown off the edge of a mountain, and another cinema where you put on plastic glasses and watched a cherishably naff 3D comedy. There was an entertaining demonstration of sound effects, an adorably gruesome show about special effects make-up and a lively, hugely amusing debate in an ersatz House of Commons, presided over by a troupe of youthful actors. And the thing was, all of these were done not just with considerable polish but with great and genuine wit.

Even after twenty years here, I remain constantly amazed and impressed by the quality of humour you find in the most unlikely places – places where it would simply not exist in other countries. You find it in the patter of stallholders in places like Petticoat Lane and in the routines of street performers – the sort of people who juggle flaming clubs or do tricks on unicycles and keep up a steady stream of jokes about themselves and selected members of the audience – and in Christmas pantomimes and pub conversations and encounters with strangers in lonely places.

Question A

(i) Based on your reading of the above text what impression do you form of the writer Bill Bryson? Support your view with reference to the text.

(ii) The author writes that he cannot get a picture of Manchester because it does not have a picture of itself. What does he mean by this? Refer especially to the text's third and fourth paragraphs in your answer.

(iii) Bill Bryson is a successful travel writer. Based on the above passage what do you think makes his writing attractive to so many readers? In your answer you should refer to both the content and style of the text.

Comprehension 9:

The life and works of photojournalist Robert Capa

One of the great war photographers, the photojournalist Robert Capa (1913-1954), born in Hungary, but a naturalized US citizen, photographed the tumultuous 1930s and the wars that followed. After World War II he helped found Magnum Photos, an international photographic agency.

In a sense Robert Capa invented himself. The son of middle class Jewish parents, he was born Endre Friedmann in Budapest in what was then Austro-Hungary. He grew up under the dictatorship of Regent Nicholas Horthy but accepted the ideas of the artist Lajos Kassák, who spear-headed the avant garde movement in Hungary. Kassák's anti-authoritarian, anti-fascist, pro-labor, egalitarian, and pacifist beliefs influenced Robert Capa for the rest of his life. At age 18 Capa was arrested by the secret police for his political activities. He was released through the intervention of his father but was banished from Hungary.

Moving to Berlin in 1931, he worked as a darkroom assistant at Dephot (Deutscher Photodienst), the leading photo-journalist enterprise in Germany. This agency was distinguished by its use of the new small cameras and fast film that allowed photographers to capture fleeting gestures and to take pictures even in poor light. With these advances the photographer could focus on human events and move away from the carefully posed rows of diplomats that had characterised news photography until then. Capa soon mastered the new cameras and was occasionally sent out on small photographic assignments. In his first major break, he was sent to Copenhagen to photograph Leon Trotsky. His photos of an impassioned Trotsky addressing the crowd captured Trotsky's charismatic oratorical style.

With Hitler's rise to power, Capa eventually moved to Paris. There he met Gerda Pohorylles, who called herself Gerda Taro, and fell in love with her. She wrote the text for his stories and acted as his agent. Taro found she could charge much more for a photo taken by a "rich American" photographer named Robert Capa than she could for the photographs of a poor Hungarian named Endre Friedmann. Thus the internationally known Robert Capa was born.

Capa and Taro were sent to Spain to cover the Spanish Civil War, where Capa took the picture that made him famous – a dying Loyalist soldier falling from the impact of a bullet. In July 1937 Taro was killed by a tank which sideswiped the car she had clambered onto in the retreat from Brunete. She was 26. Capa later dedicated his book *Death in the Making*, "to Gerda Taro, who spent one year at the Spanish front and who stayed on. R. C."

From 1941 to 1945 Capa photographed World War II in Europe as correspondent for Collier's and then *Life* magazine. On D-Day, 1944, he landed in the second wave on Omaha Beach. The soldiers, pinned down by unexpectedly heavy fire, sought shelter wherever they could. Capa, crouching with them, snapped pictures of the incoming troops. In London the lab assistant who was processing the films as quickly as possible turned up the heat in the print dryer and melted the emulsion on the negatives. The 11 that survived are slightly out of focus due to the melted emulsion, but the blurring adds to their effectiveness by conveying the confusion and danger.

After the war the photographer became what he always claimed he wanted to be – an unemployed war correspondent. He worked on a variety of projects, including a book about Russia with text by John Steinbeck. He returned to war photography briefly to cover the Israeli war of independence, 1948-1949.

In 1948 he had put into effect his long held dream of a cooperative photographic agency that would free photographers to concentrate on stories that interested them rather than spending their time scrounging for assignments. The other founders of the Magnum Photo Agency were Henri Cartier-Bresson, David Seymour ("Chim"), William Vandivert, and George Rodger. Capa's legacy, beyond his wonderful photographs, included his commitment to nurturing young photographers, for his help extended beyond mere mentoring to ensuring that they had enough to eat and the freedom to work as they pleased. Though he was often short of cash himself, he was extremely generous in his support of others.

1 Bidding farewell to the International Brigades, Spain, October 25th, 1938 **2** Republican militia members, Barcelona, 1936 **3** Landing of the American troops on Omaha Beach, Normandy, June 6th 1944 **4** Crowds running for shelter, Bilbao, 1937.

While on an assignment in Japan Capa was asked to fill in for a photographer covering the French Indochina War. He was killed when he stepped on a land mine on May 25, 1954, at Thai-Binh.

For Capa, war always had a human face. His photographs, a deeply moving account of the boredom, terror, and insanity of war, are characterized by a direct appeal to the emotions, the response of average people to events beyond their control. Close-up photos of a few people express the emotional impact of the whole. And his pictures were inevitably of people; beautiful compositions of inanimate objects did not interest him unless they somehow expressed the human element, as for instance his photo of an airplane propeller used as a German pilot's tombstone. He was impassioned, and therefore his photos always had a certain bias, but it was a humane bias. He hated war, never glorified it, and never saw himself as heroic. Despite his saying, "If your photos aren't good enough, you aren't close enough," he never took chances unless the photo demanded it.

Question A

(i) Capa took photographs of war. But what specifically did he like to focus on in these photographs, and why? Back up your answer with quotes from the text.

(ii) Select three features of the author's style in the written element of the text and comment on their effectiveness.

(iii) Write a personal response to the visual image in the above piece that makes the greatest impact on you. You might consider the subject matter, setting, mood, caption, photographic qualities and so on.

Comprehension 10:

Should restaurants do away with tipping?
We explore both sides of this heated debate.

NO, according to Ty Batirbek-Wenzel, author of *Behind Bars: The Straight-Up Tales of a Big City Bartender,* **who believes that tips supplement paltry paycheques.**

'Tip or Die.'

That was written in black permanent marker on a can that lived next to the cash register at the bar where I mixed drinks for over a decade.

The cash I earned tending bar, which involved 10-hour shifts on my feet and drunks vomiting on me, bought groceries, health care and peace of mind.

I've had to defend tipping more than a handful of times. I actually had to deal with an anti-tipping heckler while on book tour for my bartending memoir. I've had born-again Christians leave me pamphlets on finding God – in lieu of a tip – after drinking themselves into heaven.

Sure, I made decent money from tips; there was rarely a night that I didn't clear two or three hundred dollars. 'You're making money hand-over-fist!' some would declare, as if I didn't deserve it. Care to look at my $30 weekly paycheck? Care to subsidize my health insurance? I didn't get any. Care to work over 10 hours a night on your feet and shuffle home at 5 in the morning? McDonald's workers had bigger paychecks, and I doubt they had to deal with people vomiting on them on a fairly regular basis.

Getting rid of tipping would be bad business. Prices at restaurants would rise if the burden of paying servers were turned over to the house. And then there is the question of motivation. Think it's hard to find your waitress now? Think your waiter was a little surly? Wait until their income is no longer linked to their performance at your table.

Of course, if all restaurants offered a living wage – say, at least $25 per hour with health care and other benefits – then this could be a game-changer. Until then, though, those five- and 10-dollar bills left on tables and bars across the country are paying for rent, doctor visits and child care. Without tipping in this current environment, I fear that we would be just a stone's throw away from inflicting the same kind of poverty on servers that is endured by the employees at Wal-Mart, to give just one example.

Tipping counters the actions of powerful restaurant lobbies that spare no expense in driving down wages to near poverty levels.

So until salaries are generous, tip or die.

YES, according to food critic Steven A. Shaw, who believes that managers should decide who gets paid more, not customers.

Sushi Yasuda, following the lead of most of the world's best restaurants, was right to do away with tipping.

I find that those who support capitalism – and many who usually don't – reflexively believe that tipping creates an incentive, controlled by the customer, for servers to provide better service. Were that true, there might be a market-based argument against doing away with it. But all the accumulated evidence and experience indicates that tipping disrupts rather than encourages healthy workplace incentives.

Managers should decide who gets paid more, not customers. This way servers won't have to resort to up-selling or obsequious behaviour.

The No. 1 activity the tipping system encourages is "up-selling". Because most customers tip a standard percentage of the bill regardless of what happens during the dining experience, the most significant driver of a tip is the total cost of the meal. The more bottled water, coffee, alcohol, dessert and side dishes servers

can sell, the more money they make. Neither servers nor customers actually enjoy this state of affairs, but the mythology of tipping as incentive is so firmly entrenched in American restaurant culture that most of us, regardless of our actual opinions, find it impossible to imagine a world without it.

Other bad behaviours encouraged by tipping include obsequiousness, which is one of the only activities other than up-selling that studies show increases tips, along with servers who use their looks to win over customers. Many establishments encourage this practice, some more subtly than others. The restaurant chain Hooters is the most obvious about it, but every restaurant manager knows that when there are two equally skilled servers "on the floor", the more physically attractive and flirtatious one will generate more in tips.

Sushi Yasuda now explains on its receipts: 'Following the custom in Japan, Sushi Yasuda's service staff are fully compensated by their salary. Therefore gratuities are not accepted.' But this is not only the custom in Japan. It is the custom in other countries where I have experienced superior restaurant service, namely France and Singapore.

The best way to encourage quality service and a humane workplace is to follow the compensation structure of most successful, ethical corporations under the free-enterprise system: employees receive a living wage, as well as increased pay and career advancement when their superiors feel that they've earned it.
Tipping is not capitalism. It's a failed exception. And it's high time we end it.

Question A

(i) Based on your reading of the above text, outline the views of both authors on tipping.

(ii) Having considered the views expressed in the text, do you think that restaurants should do away with tipping? Give reasons for your answer.

(iii) Select four features of argumentative and/or persuasive writing in the texts and comment on their effectiveness.

Comprehension 11:

Extract from 'Falk' by Joseph Conrad

'Falk' tells the tale of a young seaman who travels to Bangkok to take charge of a ship.
Here he becomes acquainted with Falk, a Scandinavian tugboat captain who harbours a dark secret.

Falk was the other assiduous visitor on board, but from his behaviour he might have been coming to see the quarter-deck capstan. He certainly used to stare at it a good deal when keeping us company outside the cabin door, with one muscular arm thrown over the back of the chair, and his big shapely legs, in very tight white trousers, extended far out and ending in a pair of black shoes as roomy as punts. On arrival he would shake Hermann's hand with a mutter, bow to the women, and take up his careless and misanthropic attitude by our side. He departed abruptly, with a jump, going through the performance of grunts, handshakes, bow, as if in a panic. Sometimes, with a sort of discreet and convulsive effort, he approached the women and exchanged a few low words with them, half a dozen at most. On these occasions Hermann's usual stare became positively glassy and Mrs. Hermann's kind countenance would colour up. The girl herself never turned a hair.

Falk was a Dane or perhaps a Norwegian, I can't tell now. At all events he was a Scandinavian of some sort, and a bloated monopolist to boot. It is possible he was unacquainted with the word, but he had a clear perception of the thing itself. His tariff of charges for towing ships in and out was the most brutally inconsiderate document of the sort I had ever seen. He was the commander and owner of the only tug-boat on the river, a very trim white craft of 150 tons or more, as elegantly neat as a yacht, with a round wheel-house rising like a glazed turret high above her sharp bows, and with one slender varnished pole mast forward. I daresay there are yet a few shipmasters afloat who remember Falk and his tug very well. He extracted his pound and a half of flesh from each of us merchant-skippers with an inflexible sort of indifference which made him detested and even feared. Schomberg used to remark: "I won't talk about the fellow. I don't think he has six drinks from year's end to year's end in my place. But my advice is, gentlemen, don't you have anything to do with him, if you can help it."

This advice, apart from unavoidable business relations, was easy to follow because Falk intruded upon no one. It seems absurd to compare a tugboat skipper to a centaur: but he reminded me somehow of an engraving in a little book I had as a boy, which represented centaurs at a stream, and there was one, especially in the foreground, prancing bow and arrows in hand, with regular severe features and an immense curled wavy beard, flowing down his breast. Falk's face reminded me of that centaur. Besides, he was a composite creature. Not a man-horse, it is true, but a man-boat. He lived on board his tug, which was always dashing up and down the river from early morn till dewy eve.

In the last rays of the setting sun, you could pick out far away down the reach his beard borne high up on the white structure, foaming up stream to anchor for the night. There was the white-clad man's body, and the rich brown patch of the hair, and nothing below the waist but the 'thwart-ship white lines of the bridge-screens, that lead the eye to the sharp white lines of the bows cleaving the muddy water of the river.

Separated from his boat to me at least he seemed incomplete. The tug herself without his head and torso on the bridge looked mutilated as it were. But he left her very seldom. All the time I remained in harbour I saw him only twice on shore. On the first occasion it was at my charterers, where he came in misanthropically to get paid for towing out a French barque the day before. The second time I could hardly believe my eyes, for I beheld him reclining under his beard in a cane-bottomed chair in the billiard-room of Schomberg's hotel.

It was very funny to see Schomberg ignoring him pointedly. The artificiality of it contrasted strongly with Falk's natural unconcern. The big Alsatian talked loudly with his other customers, going from one little table to the other, and passing Falk's place of repose with his eyes fixed straight ahead. Falk sat there with an untouched glass at his elbow. He must have known by sight and name every white man in the room, but he never addressed a word to anybody. He acknowledged my presence by a drop of his eyelids, and that was all. Sprawling there in the chair, he would, now and again, draw the palms of both his hands down his face, giving at the same time a slight, almost imperceptible, shudder.

Question A

(i) Read the second paragraph carefully. Why was Falk 'detested and even feared' by other sailors?

(ii) Pick three adjectives that in your opinion best describe Falk. In each case support your choice with reference to the text.

(iii) Would you consider this piece of writing a vivid and effective character sketch?
Support your answer with reference to the text.

Appendix 1: Punctuation

The Comma (,)

» TO SEPARATE ITEMS IN A LIST OR SERIES

We use commas to clearly separate items in a list or series. The following examples show how commas are used in such instances:

EXAMPLE 1	They ate turkey, ham, potatoes and sprouts.
EXAMPLE 2	Mike went to the zoo with Luke, Sarah, Jill and Paul.
EXAMPLE 3	The invention of the printing press by Johannes Gutenberg brought about huge social change by spreading literacy, knowledge and scientific revolution.

» TO SEPARATE ADJECTIVES

Sometimes we use more than one adjective to describe a noun. In these instances a comma is used to separate the different adjectives:

EXAMPLE 1	The girl had short, black hair.
EXAMPLE 2	A strong, cold wind met them when they stepped outside.
EXAMPLE 3	The author wrote in powerful, stirring sentences.

›› TO INTRODUCE AND SET OFF COMMENTS AND NEW PHRASES WITHIN A SENTENCE

If you introduce a phrase or any information that is relevant but separate to the central thrust of a sentence, it must be defined using commas.

EXAMPLE 1	Late that night, as Lucy stirred feverishly in her sleep, Emma rode out to track down Doctor Morten.
EXAMPLE 2	Firemen and policemen, in the course of their work, put their own lives at risk on a daily basis.
EXAMPLE 3	Apples, for instance, are an excellent source of fibre and essential vitamins.

›› AFTER AN INTRODUCTORY PHRASE

Sometimes a sentence has an opening phrase that is set off from the rest of the sentence using a comma.

EXAMPLE 1	By the time it got dark, there was nobody left in the village.
EXAMPLE 2	After three years, they were happier than ever.
EXAMPLE 3	Building this unusual house was stressful, but worth it in the end.

Exercises:

Complete the following exercises by inserting commas where necessary in the following sentences.

TIP: IF YOU ARE UNSURE, READ THE SENTENCE OUT LOUD. THIS WILL GIVE YOU A SURPRISINGLY GOOD SENSE OF WHETHER OR NOT THE SENTENCE IS WORKING OR IF IT IS LACKING ANYTHING.

1. For breakfast I had porridge eggs and bacon.
2. I learned mathematics English French and Latin.
3. On my first day of school I brought my sack my copies and an ocean of tears.
4. It was a bright warm day.
5. The hills were barren black and lonely.
6. The battle had left him tired bruised and disheartened.
7. The time was nearly up and much as it pained her to admit it they could not win this match.
8. That night as the dew settled on the blades of grass something extraordinary happened.
9. She was at school late one afternoon grumbling her way through solitary detention when she heard a clatter in the lab. Strange she thought to herself everyone should be gone by now.
10. Naturally enough he felt dejected by the whole experience.
11. Without really understanding why she opened the attic door.
12. Desperate to catch the scout's attention he gritted his teeth and ran through the pain in his knee.
13. He learned music not by reading notes on a sheet but by listening to the melody over and over again.
14. He had served his country well and deserved recognition, not ridicule, for his efforts.
15. The clerk was arrogant not stupid.
16. They had won votes by campaigning aggressively among the public, not by brushing shoulders with the wealthy elite.

Insert and/or delete commas in the following:
17. The winter nights were dark, cold, and long.
18. While she believed she had the ability to get to the very top she knew Daniels would try to undermine her at every turn.
19. This he, realised, was the ultimate honour.
20. For once, it was not he who had screwed up but, the Captain.

The Colon (:)

» TO INTRODUCE A LIST

The following examples indicate how we use colons to introduce a list:

EXAMPLE 1	The steps are as follows: 1. Chop the chicken into bite-size pieces. 2. Fry for three minutes on each side. 3. Serve with your salad.
EXAMPLE 2	Munster comprises six counties: Clare, Cork, Kerry, Limerick, Tipperary and Waterford.
EXAMPLE 3	'Holiday essentials' checklist: passport, phone, charger, wallet, cash, boarding pass.

» TO INTRODUCE A QUOTE

The following examples indicate how we use colons to introduce a quotation:

EXAMPLE 1	When the judge asked the defendant how he would plead to the charges laid out against him, the defendant replied: 'Not guilty, your honour'.
EXAMPLE 2	In this famous soliloquy, Hamlet ponders life and death: 'To be or not to be, that is the question.'
EXAMPLE 3	With this in mind, I would like to leave you with the famous words of Oscar Wilde: 'We are all in the gutter, but some of us are looking at the stars.'

» TO CLARIFY OR EXPLAIN

We also use a colon when the information following the colon proves or clarifies what has gone before.

EXAMPLE 1	Here's what I think about the lottery: you have as much chance of winning as anyone, but if you're not in, you can't win.
EXAMPLE 2	There is only one thing we can do: someone must take the ring to Mordor.
EXAMPLE 3	There could only be one logical reason for Smith not to show: someone had killed him.

Exercises:

Insert the missing colons in the sentences below.

1. For dinner we will need to buy fish, vegetables and potatoes.
2. To set up a bank account you will need proof of identity (a valid passport or Garda ID) and proof of address. Proof of address can include any of the following a current utility bill, insurance policy, tax documents or other government correspondence.
3. The New Testament is composed of four Gospels Matthew Mark Luke and John.
4. I have three siblings Mike, Colin and Jessica.
5. I questioned him about what had happened and he said 'We were in a car accident.'
6. He asked if there was a bed free in the hospital. She shook her head and replied 'No. You will be waiting for around seven hours.'
7. She recited the poem verbatim 'There is another sky,/Ever serene and fair...'
8. He opened the envelope and, in his best dramatic falsetto, said to the crowd 'And the 1977 UK Battle of the Bands winner is… Marseille!'
9. We tested how effective this procedure is and what we found was nothing short of extraordinary In a sample of 1,021 patients, surgery significantly reduced the severity of symptoms in 87 per cent.
10. The website wasn't responding and he knew why it had been hacked.
11. She worked hard, staying late every night, and she did it with one purpose in mind to prove to the people that mattered that she was good enough for the senior job.
12. When Tom finished reading her notes and journals, he finally understood why she'd skipped town it wasn't safe for her to stay.

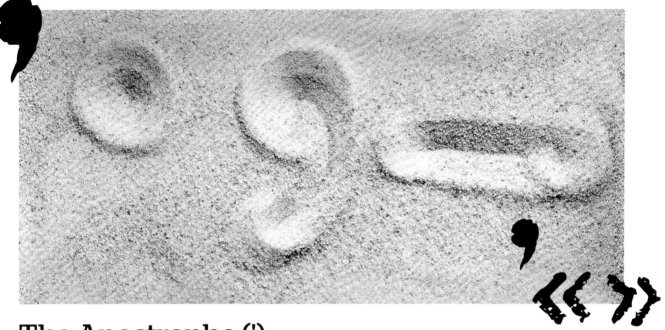

The Apostrophe (')

» POSSESSION

With singular nouns we use an apostrophe followed by the letter 's' to indicate possession:

EXAMPLE 1	The hawk's talons (meaning the talons of a single hawk).
EXAMPLE 2	The player's jersey (meaning the jersey that belongs to one player).
EXAMPLE 3	The dog's bone (meaning the bone that belongs to the dog).

Note how this changes with plural nouns: we use the letter 's' followed by an apostrophe to indicate possession.

EXAMPLE 1	The hawks' talons were sharp (meaning the talons of multiple hawks).
EXAMPLE 2	The players' jerseys were new (meaning all of the players had new jerseys).
EXAMPLE 3	The students' union (meaning the union that represents many students).
EXAMPLE 4	The sisters' get-together (meaning the get-together of multiple sisters).

Note how 'men', 'women' and 'children' are irregular.

EXAMPLE 1	The men's changing room
EXAMPLE 2	The women's group
EXAMPLE 3	The children's playground

What happens when a word already ends in 'S' or 'Z'?
- Should you say 'Jesus' life and death' or 'Jesus's life and death'?
- 'Martin Amis' book', or 'Martin Amis's book'?
- 'Kurtz' army', or 'Kurtz's army'?

Both forms are correct, but consistency is very important. Make a decision about which one you prefer and stick to it.

» CONTRACTIONS

Many common phrases are shortened by omitting letters, making one's use of language more natural and fluid. In the following examples note how the apostrophe is inserted in place of the omitted letter or letters:

EXAMPLE 1	Shouldn't, wouldn't, couldn't (instead of 'should not', 'would not', 'could not')
EXAMPLE 2	Didn't (instead of 'did not')
EXAMPLE 3	Won't, don't, shan't (instead of 'will not', 'do not', 'shall not')
EXAMPLE 4	He'll, she'll, they'll, you'll (instead of 'he will', 'she will', 'they will', 'you will')
EXAMPLE 5	It'd (instead of 'it would' or 'it had')
EXAMPLE 6	It's (instead of 'it is' or 'it has', depending on the context. And be careful not to mix it up with the possessive pronoun 'its' which has no apostrophe!)
EXAMPLE 7	They're, you're, we're (instead of 'they are', 'you are', 'we are')

» IT'S AND ITS

Its is a possessive pronoun meaning **of it** or **belonging to it**:

EXAMPLE 1	The cat licked **its** paws.
EXAMPLE 2	She enjoyed the glass of wine to **its** last drop.
EXAMPLE 3	His car looked good with **its** new coat of paint.
EXAMPLE 4	The match wore on to **its** predictable conclusion.
EXAMPLE 5	The dawn broke with **its** vivid display of light and colour.

It's is a contraction of 'it is' or 'it has':

EXAMPLE 1	**It's** raining. (This is a contraction of '**It is** raining.')
EXAMPLE 2	**It's** time to go. (**It is** time to go.)
EXAMPLE 3	I'm so happy that **it's** the weekend. (This is a contraction of '**it is** the weekend.')
EXAMPLE 4	I don't know if **it's** working or if **it's** broken. (I don't know if **it is** working or if **it is** broken.)
EXAMPLE 5	**It's** been a bad year for the country. (**It has** been a bad year for the country.)
EXAMPLE 6	It's been great meeting you. (It **has been** great meeting you.)

Exercises:

Correct, where necessary, the following sentences:

1. John doesnt like movies.
2. Mary wasnt allowed to go to the club.
3. Its a sad state of affairs.
4. The rocket makes its way slowly skyward.
5. The tiger gave a swipe of it's huge paw.
6. If I dont study hard, Ill fail my exams.
7. She stopped and admired an old Ford Thunderbird whose wheels gleamed brilliantly in the sunshine.
8. Pat, whose bike was now mangled under the tyre of a huge truck, sat up and stared in disbelief.
9. John couldnt find his wallet anywhere. He later discovered that one of the security staff had stolen it. The companys reputation was damaged badly by it.
10. Shirleys purse was stolen by a thief who's sole purpose was to spend her hard-earned money on drink.
11. Lieutenant Murrays ensign, George Smith, who's job it was to carry the flag into battle, lay injured in a medical tent.
12. He was slave to the supervisors mood swings and as long as he was stuck in the warehouse, he couldnt do anything to assuage his friends plight.
13. Bruno, the captains portly bulldog, sat nearby, licking it's chops and panting in the humid summer air.
14. 'I shouldnt be here!' Murphy yelled. 'I've done nothing wrong! You cant keep me here. Its not right! It's not right!'
15. Theyre out there in the cold, begging for money, for food, for medicines and for shelter. But they shouldnt have to. Were not doing enough to help these refugees.
16. They opened the box but the idol wasnt there. 'Its gone…' Lilly murmured.
17. The childrens' efforts paid off.
18. Theyll die if they dont get help and well be the ones to blame for it. We cant just sit here and think the situation will magically improve by itself

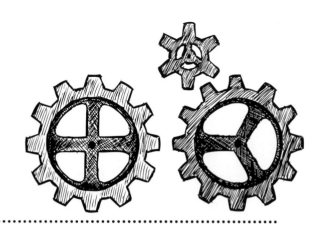

The Hyphen (-)

We use a hyphen to join two words together, creating a new compound word.
Many prefixes require hyphenation:

EXAMPLE 1	Semi: semi-industrial, semi-skimmed, semi-detached, semi-darkness
EXAMPLE 2	Anti: anti-apartheid, anti-ageing, anti-inflationary, anti-inflammatory
EXAMPLE 3	Pre: pre-book, pre-pay, pre-war, pre-Christian, pre-empt, pre-existing

We use a hyphen with phrases like these involving better, best, well, lower, little or ill:

EXAMPLE 1	His best-known work. Her better-known art. The better-prepared player.
EXAMPLE 2	A well-known actress. A well-adjusted child. It was a well-attended event.
EXAMPLE 3	The lower-priced tickets. The lower-grade medicine.
EXAMPLE 4	The little-understood theory of relativity. The little-travelled road.
EXAMPLE 5	The ill-advised expedition. The ill-informed politician.

We use a hyphen when combining a noun and a verb ending in ing or ed:

EXAMPLE 1	The alcohol-fuelled car
EXAMPLE 2	Her hate-motivated resilience
EXAMPLE 3	The conflict-resolving initiative
EXAMPLE 4	The terror-inducing examination

We also use a hyphen when combining a number and a noun:

EXAMPLE 1	thirteenth-floor apartment
EXAMPLE 2	nineteenth-century history

Finally, we hyphenate coequal nouns.

EXAMPLE 1	The critically acclaimed actor-director
EXAMPLE 2	The popular singer-songwriter
EXAMPLE 3	The talented writer-illustrator

Appendix 2:
PCLM

Purpose 30%

In the Leaving Cert 30 per cent of the marks are awarded for Clarity of Purpose. What you write **must be a clear response to what you've been asked to write. Your composition must serve the purpose intended for it by the examiners. There are several ways to ensure you get the marks on offer here.**

ANSWER THE QUESTION YOU'VE BEEN ASKED

Your composition must address the question or essay title that actually appears on the Exam Paper. There's no point answering the question you think you see on the paper or the question you'd like to see. Therefore, you must take the time to read, re-read and understand the question you've chosen to answer. This really can't be stressed enough.

WARNING: IF YOUR COMPOSITION STRAYS TOO FAR FROM THE QUESTION YOU HAVE BEEN ASKED YOU WILL BE PENALISED SEVERELY AND MAY, IN FACT, LOSE FAR MORE THAN THE 30% OF THE MARKS USUALLY AWARDED FOR PURPOSE.

WHERE NECESSARY ADOPT A POINT OF VIEW

Some questions specifically require you make the case for a particular point of view. Some don't. However, it is often best to adopt a definite point of view anyway. Doing so will lend your writing a sense of purpose and focus: you can state your point of view in the first or second paragraph, and use the rest of the essay to support it.

REMAIN FOCUSED FROM BEGINNING TO END

Your composition must be focused. It is no good to start writing in response to the question or essay title if, by the halfway stage, you have drifted off the topic completely. Every single paragraph must be relevant to your chosen title and serve your overall purpose.

BE CONSCIOUS OF GENRE

You will often be asked to write in a specific genre: a speech, a letter, a magazine article and so on. It is vital that you remain conscious of this as you proceed and tailor your writing accordingly.

Coherence 30%

It is vital that your composition holds together as a coherent and well-organised piece of writing. The Leaving Cert examiners refer to this as 'Coherency of Delivery'. Thirty per cent of all marks are awarded for this.

CONTROL YOUR TONE

It's important to be conscious of the tone in which you are writing. Are you going to be formal, semi-formal or light-hearted? Every year the examiners' report stresses how marks are lost in this area through lack of consistency. It is nearly always best, therefore, to maintain the same tone throughout. If you slip from a formal to an informal tone halfway through your composition, you will lose marks unless it is for a very, very good reason.

MANAGE YOUR IDEAS, REFERENCES AND EXAMPLES

In your composition, you will probably deal with a number of topics, introducing various ideas, references and examples. Always ensure that they are a hundred per cent relevant to your aim. Furthermore, don't let them sidetrack you. If you mention Live Aid in a composition on charity, don't start writing about Bob Geldof's love life. Just make the relevant point about Live Aid and then move on to your next topic.

SEQUENCE YOUR TOPICS CAREFULLY

Your composition will make several different points and introduce different topics. It is important that these are arranged in a coherent order: a sequence that makes the composition easy to read and allows it to achieve its aim. Two things are important here: planning and practise. Before you start writing your essay, think this through carefully. Sketch out several different sequences and decide on which one works best. This is time well spent. The more you practise, the easier this will become.

Efficiency of Language Use 30%

This aspect of the marking scheme deals with how well you use and manipulate language. Thirty per cent of all marks are awarded for this.

VARY YOUR VOCABULARY

Displaying a large and varied vocabulary in the Leaving Cert testifies to your ability to manipulate language, and it is advisable to vary your vocabulary in order to avoid repetition. However, always use vocabulary that serves the aim of your composition. For example, if you are writing a short talk aimed at foreign students, you will want to avoid long, complicated and unusual words. Never use a word unless you know what it means and how to use it properly.

VARY YOUR SENTENCE PATTERNS

It is vital that your sentences are not all in the same type. All too often students write sentence after sentence that follows the exact same pattern: I went...I saw... I bought... I caught. Such repetitious sentence patterns will turn the reader off or bore her to tears. It will also cost you marks.

USE LIVELY AND INTERESTING PHRASING

You will be rewarded for using language in a lively and interesting way, so if you have a flair for language, let the examiner see it. However, always be conscious of the genre in which you are writing. Flowery and poetic language, for instance, might be fine in a personal essay, but might be out of place in a newspaper article.

IN GENERAL KEEP YOUR SENTENCES SHORT

Again and again, students use long, over-complicated sentences that confuse the reader. Long sentences also lead to 'errors of syntax': the words in the sentence are arranged in the wrong order. In general, it is best to keep your sentences short. The longer your sentences are, the more likely you are to confuse both yourself and the reader. This is not to say you should never use long sentences – sometimes they can't be avoided – but try to use them sparingly. As the old mantra goes: the more full stops you have, the less mistakes you make.

Mechanics 10%

Ten per cent of the marks are awarded for spelling and grammar, which is known as 'Accuracy of Mechanics'. There is nothing for you to do except learn how to spell and apply the rules of grammar consistently. This means learning how to spell new words as you encounter them, and familiarising yourself with the rules of grammar.

Get Up To Speed
With The Regs

STOP

To comply with the new Building Regulations (Part L)
Aerobord Limited is introducing **Aerobord Platinum**
a new range of **high performance** expanded
polystyrene insulation products.

CHECK

Check that the insulation you buy

- Complies with 2002 Building Regulations
  and EN standards
- Is competitively priced.
- Is tongued & grooved for cavity wall applications.
- Has a high thermal performance.
- Maintains its declared lambda value throughout the
  life time of the building.
- Is recyclable.
- Is totally CFC and HCFC free with zero O.D.P

GO

Go to your local merchant and insist on the new
Aerobord Platinum range of high performance
products. Aerobord has been serving the construction
industry since the 1950's, with high quality products
and excellent customer service, we look forward to
continuing to do so.
Aerobord Platinum
Products of the future built on the Past.

Outstanding Performance
in a New Environment

Aerobord Ltd. Askeaton, Co. Limerick, Tel: 061 604600. Aircell Ltd. Loch Gowna, Co. Cavan, Tel: 043 83550.

Gypsum Industries
High Performance Boards
provide a variety of solutions

Tom O'Callaghan

*Sales and Marketing Director,
Gypsum Industries*

Market demand for high performance products has risen significantly over recent years. Architects and specifiers are constantly seeking ways of more effectively achieving improved build quality in terms of impact resistance, moisture resistance, thermal and acoustic insulation and fire protection.

Gypsum Industries works closely with the trade to develop product solutions which meet these specific performance demands. As a result it has developed the most comprehensive range of high performance products and systems available to the market. Our innovative products and systems speed up the construction process and save valuable time and labour costs on site.

WHERE IMPACT RESISTANCE IS NEEDED

Gyproc Duraline was developed in response to market demand for applications which need a resilient and durable drylining finish for high traffic areas. It is an extremely impact resistant product with twice the compressive and breaking strength of standard plasterboard. Gyproc Wall Lining and partition systems lined with Gyproc Duraline carry a Heavy Duty rating.

Gyproc Gyptone

A dense glass fibre reinforced core and extra strong paper liners help give the product its inherent strength. It is particularly suitable for use in public and commercial buildings like schools, hospitals, hotels and offices, as well as in high traffic areas in industrial buildings.

ABSORBING SOUND

Gyproc Gyptone is a perforated plasterboard designed to offer a combination of an exceptionally decorative and aesthetically appealing building board with a high sound absorption performance.

It has been designed specifically for use in high quality environments, offices, retail outlets and leisure buildings, where a designer or architect does not want to compromise the visual concept to satisfy acoustic requirements. Gyproc Gyptone's sound absorption performance is achieved through a combination of the perforated surface and an acoustic-felt, factory bonded to the back of the board.

It is primarily used in concealed grid ceiling systems such as the Gyproc M/F System but can also be used as a drylining with the Gyproc Gyplyner system to create flat or curved surfaces.

EXCELLENT SOUND INSULATION

Noise pollution is perhaps one of the most significant of today's construction issues, Gyproc SoundBloc provide the market with a wallboard which, whilst maintaining the qualities of regular plasterboards, can provide acoustic insulation to the most demanding levels.

The high acoustic performance of Gyproc SoundBloc is obtained by careful product design resulting in a modified higher mass gypsum core encased in strong paper liners. Its sound insulation performance is coupled with the excellent fixing and finishing qualities of standard plasterboard.

Gyproc SoundBloc was developed for use in partitions for commercial and public buildings where, for example, improved sound insulation is required between areas of occupancy.

MOISTURE RESISTANT

Gyproc Moisture Resistant Board was developed as a high performance board to offer the benefits of drylining in areas of high moisture content, such as bathrooms and shower areas. It was introduced in reply to Irish market demand for a drylining that was more tolerant to moisture for particular applications and provides a tough solution to the damage problems caused by water in intermittently wet and damp locations.

It is ideal for use on general construction processes where exposure to external conditions can be expected, or when the board is to be used internally as a substrate for ceramic tiling in wet areas.

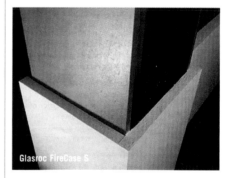

Glasroc FireCase S

FIRE PROTECTION

The Glasroc brand range of non-combustible, glass reinforced gypsum boards are developed to meet high performance requirements in terms of passive fire protection.

The Glasroc range consists of two main products, Glasroc Multi-board and Glasroc FireCase S Board.

Glasroc Multi-board combines excellent protection properties with a high degree of impact resistance with exceptionally smooth surfaces suitable for direct decorating with Gyproc plaster application. Glasroc Multi-Board's inherent flexibility also makes it ideal for curved surfaces. Glasroc FireCase S Board is principally used in the fire protection of structural steel columns and beams by means of a frameless encasement system.

Blueprint Homes

Design No. 80 Vanguard

Design No.103 Rushbrook

Design No.125 Pembrok

Underfloor Heating Systems - The Future of Home Heating

you are buying or uilding the house of your eams, don't you owe it to urself to install the best eating system available?

Comfort - Gentle and even heat - creates a feeling of well being.

Flexibility - Make use of that extra wall space.

Economic - Don't waste money heating the airspace above your head. Distribute the heat exactly where you need it.

Control - Easy control at your fingertips.

REHAU - Distinguish the best from the rest:-

- Over 40 years experience
- Full technical and sales service available
- System fully tested to BS7291
- System designed to BS1264
- Worldwide installations from small domestic to large industrial projects
- BBA approved
- WRAS approved

Available at:

Branches Almost Nationwide
Tel: 090 - 642 4083   www.heatmerchants.ie   E-mail: ufhinfo@heatmerchants.ie

REHAU Ltd, 9 St John's Court, Business Park, Swords Road, Santry, Dublin 9
Tel: 01 816 5020 Fax: 01 816 5021

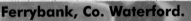

BLUEPRINT HOME PLANS
SINCE 1981

PROFESSIONALLY DESIGNED HOME PLANS BY MAIL ORDER

CONTENTS

PLANS.

9TH EDITION 2003

Architect & Designer:

Michael J. Allen FASI. MRICS. FGIS. FCIOB.
Architect & Chartered Building Surveyor
Beechlawn, Kells,
County Meath.

Telephone: 046-9240349
Fax: 046-9241638
Email: bphp@eircom.net
Web: www.allenarchitect.com

House Design Artwork:

Sharon Gaynor BA

© **Published by:**

Oisin Publications
4 Iona Drive, Dublin 9.
Tel. (01) 8305236 Fax. (01) 8307860
email: oisinpr@iol.ie

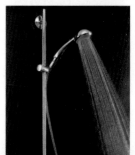

Welcome to BLUEPRINT HOME PLANS

THIS IS OUR NINTH EDITION of Blueprint Home Plans, presenting two hundred and fifty home designs. Since our first publication in 1981, the range of designs has grown from fifty four in number and the majority of the most popular designs remain included in the current edition. Over the years, major improvements have taken place in the quality and variety of our designs and the current range meets all the requirements of the Building Regulations. As in previous editions of our book, the drawings remain clear and without elaborate artistic treatment. Each illustration includes the frontage measurement and the gross floor area of the house, expressed in metric format. The old days of imperial measurement are now gone, and with respect to those who still think in "feet and inches", we have included a conversion sheet.

The construction cost guideline for our designs is just that! The costing cannot be taken as a quotation for the construction of the design indicated, and the information is based on labour and material rates current at the time of publication. We design and prepare the detailed drawings for your new home, but we do not offer to construct the house. You should seek a detailed estimate from your local Building Contractor. Local knowledge will inform you who the competent builders are and if necessary, you could contact Home Bond for a list of contractors registered. Our cost guideline includes for a completed house ready for painting, including kitchen fittings, plumbing and heating fixtures, wardrobes where indicated; but excluding all external services, ground development and entrance. The Architect is engaged in the practice of architecture in Ireland since 1972 and is a specialist in home design. It is important that your design brief is prepared by an architect who is appropriately qualified, who holds professional indemnity insurance and who is in practice on his/her own account.

BLUEPRINT HOME PLANS designs have been constructed throughout Ireland for many years and the vast number of satisfied clients is testimony to the service offered. If you do not find a suitable design in our book, please consult us in respect of alterations or a personalised design. Our book is a consistent seller throughout Ireland and always in demand.

All **BLUEPRINT HOME PLANS** are designed to satisfy current regulations and provide up to date design features including full insulation and ventilation proposals. The designs provide for central heating systems and open fireplaces. Some designs feature a solid fuel or oil-fired cooker in the kitchen. In all houses a regulation fire detection and alarm system is specified. All design drawings comply with part M of the Building Regulations 2000 in relation to visitable access, where a level platform must be provided at the main entrance, ramped from path level. The layout of the bathroom, corridor width, door width and the location of electrical fittings comply with such regulations also.

The technical editorial has been kept to a minimum in our latest edition, but we believe, at the same time, that you will find it important. We have given particular importance to the new planning regulations where they affect the preparation of a planning application. Clear instructions are given on how to order your plans and specifications and an official order form is provided. A photocopy of the order form may be used. We will accept an order by email if required.

At **BLUEPRINT HOME PLANS**, we pay tribute to the countless clients who have consulted us over the years. In each new edition, we improve our design criteria, as a direct result of our client's instructions, and of constantly improving design awareness. We look forward to being of continued professional assistance to those intending to construct a new home.

SELECTING YOUR DESIGN

WITH CARE, consider the environment in which you intend to place your new home, prior to making your design choice. Do not site your new home on the top of a hill, or in a location that will break the horizon. Avoid complicated roof lines and elevational treatments; always aim for simplicity of external finish. Some Local Authority guidelines favour a plain plaster finish or a dry dash finish rather than features of stone and brick. With a little thought and consideration for the existing environment, your new home will blend happily with the surrounding landscape. To assist you, the local library will have books and leaflets on how to site a new house sensitively in the local landscape. In particular look for guidelines by An Taisce, Wexford County Council and a publication produced by Tony Lowes on building sensitively in the West Cork landscape.

You should consider the extension of the existing environment by way of tree planting, the proposed floor levels for your new home and a variety of shrub groupings. Seek out information on local species and try to avoid exotic species, not native to the area. New road side fences should be of natural materials, except where the Local Authority specifies walls. Urban or near urban sites will need particular consideration of course and again the Local Authority may have recommendations on how the site boundary will be finished. All these considerations will affect your design choice and consultation with your local Planning Department will assist you.

Observations of existing developments in the area of your site will assist you in making a design choice. For example, an area where either single storey, two storey or dormer designs are predominant will determine that you must choose a design that does not conflict with the existing allowed development in the area. Planners and Architects must accept constructive criticism in relation to some housing developments that were permitted in the past, but the overall situation has changed for the better and we must all continue with our efforts to promote good design concepts and encourage ourselves to design and site our new homes sensitively within the existing landscape. Our book of plans contains a wide cross section of design ideas, but we do not pretend that all or any of the designs shown would suit a particular site. Through our Clients' continued appreciation of design, our design criteria improves on a day to day basis, and, by keeping in touch with our client base, our designs reflect current design preferences.

You will listen to remarks about poor design concepts, particularly relating to building shapes, window designs, roof designs and exterior finishes. Seldom you will hear remarks about interior design and layout, as those who comment on house design mainly concern themselves with the exterior views in relation to the local environment. It is easy to lay blame on books of house plans for unsuitable housing development in the countryside, but of course this would be far from the truth. Your design concepts are influenced by many factors, including the media, photographs, holiday memories, film, our own particular design preferences and of course your budget. As we travel and research more, we are bound to be influenced by European and American design ideas and already we see the better design ideas from other countries manifest themselves in the Irish landscape. We now live in a multi-cultural society and we are bound to see the influence in our home designs of the future.

A fair balance will need to be achieved and when we view the older urban and rural buildings, the design influence of many countries can easily be observed. The architect does not pretend that any of the designs in this publication will suit any particular site and the involvement of your local architect, designer, engineer and or Local Authority is always highlighted as advisable. Discuss your proposal at the earliest opportunity with the Officers in the Local Authority Planning Department. In some counties, the Planners hold pre-planning clinics or advice meetings in surrounding towns from the main planning office. In some counties we are seeing the establishment of "one stop shops" and this may include area planning offices as branch offices, where you can discuss matters of planning applications and lodge applications. At the planning clinics, you will be able to discuss your proposal in general terms and satisfy the planners in relation to your local need to construct a new family home.

The selection of your design will be based on many considerations, not least your budget. We give you a cost indicator for each of our designs and your local building contractor will also give you an indication of construction cost. If you are totally unfamiliar with construction costs, you may well choose to take your plans to a qualified Quantity Surveyor who will cost the entire project with detailed precision. As part of you costs exercise, take into account a reasonable amount to cover ground preparation work, landscaping, decoration and provision of services such as electricity, water, grounds development and professional fees. When you finally arrive at an approximate floor area, use the following check list to assist you further:

1. How many living rooms do we require?

Sitting room, living room, study, kitchen dining room or working kitchen only with separate dining room. Do we require a sun room or conservatory?

2. Circulation between rooms.

Is direct connection required between the kitchen and the living room or the dining room? Should we directly connect the dining room with the sitting room? Should we have an open plan hall, or should the hall be large enough as a living space?

3. Fireplaces and heating.

Will we provide an open fire in the sitting room and living room? Do we require an oil-fired, gas fired or solid fuel cooker in the kitchen? What type of central heating should we have, oil-fired, solar, gas fired, under floor heating, radiator heating, warm air, economy electric storage? Where will we locate the boiler?

4. Utility Areas.

Utility areas are quite important and you could choose to have just a rear entrance hall and locate all appliances in the kitchen. You might choose to enlarge the rear hall to accommodate the laundry equipment. The utility room could be self-contained and the general utility areas could incorporate a separate entrance hall and a toilet facility. Consider the equipment that must be accommodated in the utility room- washer, dryer, sink, warm coats press, freezer, work units and presses.

5. Sunlight.

The living rooms and kitchen areas should be located to take full advantage of the sunlight. As a guideline, locate the window of the master bedroom facing east to capture the morning sun, locate the kitchen and living room windows facing south to capture the day-time sun and locate the sitting room and sun room towards south and west to capture the afternoon and evening sun. This may not always be possible due to the orientation of your site and may prove difficult if your site is urban located. However, with some thought, it will be possible to take as much advantage as possible of natural sunlight.

6. Bedrooms.

You will need to decide on the number of bedrooms and whether they are to be designated double bedrooms, single or to accommodate twin beds. Decide if you wish to have free standing or built in wardrobes, this will affect the room dimensions. If any bedroom will also be used for study purposes, allow extra floor space. You might consider allowing for the provision of a wash hand basin in some bedrooms.

7. Bathrooms.

How many bathrooms do we require? Decide if you are having one main bathroom or, as additional, some bathrooms en-suite. List the fittings you require within the bathroom as this will determine the size of the room. Bath, toilet, bidet, shower unit or shower over bath, one wash basin or two, standard bath, bath in centre of floor, jacuzzi bath, corner bath and/or sauna. A bathroom facility will have to be included to cater for visitable disabled within your house and accessible from the main living areas to comply with regulations. Needless to say such regulations also allow for specific corridor and door widths, location of electrical fittings and detailed specifications for the entrance and the approach to your new home. The hot press should be located within a reasonable distance from the bathrooms. The hot press should be as large as possible and accommodate a reasonable amount of spar shelving and plain shelving for winter storage. A small warm press is a consideration in bathrooms and bedrooms.

8. Finishes.

List your preferences for external finishes, window design, attic spaces, internal door types, patio or french doors, roof finishes, ceiling heights, kitchen presses, ceiling finishes, cornices, fireplaces, porches, stairs, floor finishes, driveways, garages, and landscaping. All of these matters will affect your budget.

9. Disabled access.

Part M of the Building Regulations 2000 provides detailed requirements for all dwellings in relation to visitable access for disabled persons and the specifications are mandatory. In the case of a dwelling to suit special needs, your architect will be fully familiar with all requirements and all special requirements must be included at initial design stage.

From the Architect's many years of experience in designing new homes in Ireland, you can be assured that a simple check list such as the foregoing will greatly simplify your design choice. Now it's over to you!

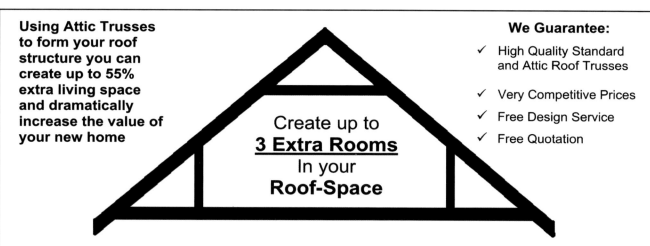

THE BUILDING SITE

If you are lucky enough to have the choice of a building site for your new home, then there are many considerations. Firstly, make sure that the orientation is reasonably favourable to your proposed design, and that the new house will sit well into the existing environment. The local environment should be capable of easy development. Look at the dimensioins, and make sure that the site is adequate in dimension to contain the proposed house, and the services.

If there is no public sewer available, the site will need to accommodate a septic tank and percolation area, constructed to the SR6 recommendations. If the ground is not suitable for the disposal of septic tank effluent by means of a percolation area, a specialist disposal system may have to be employed.

The Standard Recommendation 6 is published by Eolas, and is available from the NSAI, Glasnevin, Dublin 9. The general recommendation is that the septic tank must be located a minimum of seven metres from the house, and the percolation area must commence twenty metres from the house. The length of the percolation area is determined by percolation tests. A water table test may also be required. Both tests require that test holes be prepared on site, and the land owner should be made aware of these procedures in advance. Some Local Authorities now insist on such tests being carried out, and the results submitted with the planning application. Your local engineer or architect will arrange to have the tests carried out on your behalf.

Surface water from your site, and rainwater from the building, will need to be disposed of to soakways located on the site, or directly to local drains or a public storm water drain. Your site design will need to incorporate a disposal system for rainwater at the entrance to the site, to prevent water running onto the surface of the public road. The proposed site may have trees and shrubs already existing, and, in this case, a preservation order may be in place to retain such plantations. You are advised to check with the Local Authority in this matter, as such an order may affect the position of the proposed house on the site.

A visit to the local Planning Office will determine if there are any road improvement schemes that might affect your proposal, or whether there are any other current or recent planning applications which might influence your decision to acquire the proposed site. You should determine if there is a planning history on the site, and whether any previous applications were approved or refused. If you feel put off by the prospect of such investigations, ask your local architect or engineer to undertake the work for you. The fee will be reasonable, and you will have a written report. When purchasing your site, complete the sale only subject to full planning permission being granted. In all matters of site purchase, confirmation of Land Registry boundaries, and reasonable conditions of sale, you should consult your solicitor, who will play a vital role in such proceedings.

Make a detailed survey or your site proper. See if there are overhead cables, and make enquiries from the ESB and Eircom in relation to connections. Take note of the ground conditions, and avoid a low lying or filled site. A hilltop site may not be suitable. Read the Ordnance Survey map of the area, and make note of local place names and townland names, as this information may give you an indication of local ground conditions. 'Railwayland' may suggest filled ground. 'Stonefield' may suggest rock or gravel, and 'Marshtown' may suggest low lying, or waterlogged, ground. These townland examples are fictional, of course! Talk to local site owners who will have experience with the ground conditions and may assist you with information. In the case of suspect ground, consult your local engineer and request ground tests. Suspect ground conditions may require special foundation design, and this could seriously affect your proposed budget.

If the site boundaries have already been established, check the measurements from the site map provided, and confirm accuracy. If there is any doubt, arrange with the vendor to have the matter corrected. If the boundaries have not yet been established, request the vendor to place permanent markers on the lands and on a scaled map. Always remember that timber posts can be lost or altered, and you should place permanent markers, set in each corner point. When purchasing an urban site, check that the boundaries are correct, and confirm that all services have been taken onto the site proper. Early and accurate site investigations may save you money later.

PLANNING PERMISSION

YOU MUST OBTAIN PLANNING PERMISSION to construct your home. If you are purchasing a site with full planning permission and intend to use a **BLUEPRINT HOME PLAN**, then your application will be for a change of house type. A site with the benefit of outline planning permission will require an application for permission consequent on the grant of outline permission. If you are in doubt whether permission will be granted at all, then you should first make an application for outline permission. Planning applications are now made under the terms of the Planning & Development Act 2000 and the Planning and Development Regulations 2001. Such regulations are effective from March 11th 2002 and affect the manner and documents required in making a planning application. The documents required and the format of such documents are outlined in the following text.

If you are purchasing a site with the benefit of planning permission, you are advised to research the history of the property prior to making a decision to purchase. You should have a search carried out at the offices of the Local Authority. Such a search involves examination of the appropriate planning file, the register maps, and the plans and maps submitted.

Your application for planning permission will also encompass an application under the terms of the Building Regulations. When the planning permission is granted you will be furnished with a Commencement Notice under the terms of the Building Control Act. You are required to complete and furnish this notice to the Local Authority, giving notice to the Building Control Authority not less than fourteen days and not more than twenty eight days before the commencement date.

HOUSE PLANS

You must submit six copies of your house plans and building specifications. The plans must be drawn to a scale of 1:50 or 1:100 and detail all features of the building; plans, elevations, technical sections, overall height of the building and all specifications required to show compliance with the regulations. Important matters to bear in mind in the design of your house include compliance with part M of the Building Regulations 2000 which sets out requirements for visitable disabled access, layout of bathrooms, corridor widths and door widths, and location of electrical fittings. **BLUEPRINT HOME PLANS** are detailed to satisfy the requirements referred to in the Republic of Ireland. All drawings must now be completed in metric format, so the days of "feet and inches" are finally gone!

SPECIFICATIONS

Six copies of the written specification for the works are required for your planning application. This document sets out the quality and standards of the material to be used in the construction of the building and the **BLUEPRINT HOME PLANS** specification sets out the required standards. This document enables the Local Authority determine and approve the standards of construction to be employed.

It is not a list of materials required for the construction of the house.

SITE MAPS AND SITE LAYOUT PLANS

Six copies of a site location map will be required with your application. This map must be based on an Ordnance Survey map. Such maps, known as a Rural Place Map are available from your local Ordnance Survey agent, from the Ordnance Survey Office in Phoenix Park Dublin or from the National Map Centre in Dublin. The site must be clearly outlined in red and all adjoining properties must be shown. The maps must show the north point and the ordnance sheet number. **BLUEPRINT HOME PLANS** will detail your site map if one copy of the appropriate Rural Place Map is supplied.

The site layout plan should be to a scale of 1:500. The layout plan must describe to location of the proposed house, and distances from the site boundaries. Full details of the boundary treatment, the entrance and the effluent disposal system must be shown. The site boundary is to be edged in red, and the land holding adjoining the proposed site is to be edged in blue. Any wayleaves must be shown in yellow. If there is any significant change in levels, the Applicant is required to submit a drawing showing contours and levels of the proposed structure. **BLUEPRINT HOME PLANS** will prepare your site layout plans from information supplied. If the contour map is supplied, we will incorporate the details in the layout plan.

APPLICATION FORMS AND FEES

The planning application forms are available from your Local Authority Planning Department and now require extensive information under the terms of the Planning & Development Regulations 2001. In some areas, you may be required to complete a Local Needs form in addition to the planning application form. Where a local needs form is not required, you are well advised to submit supplementary information with the planning application. Such supplementary information should outline your family status, your reasons for selecting the particular site and your relationship to the land owner, if any. Ideally, you should be a native of the area in which the site is located or a long term resident of the area; and working in the vicinity of the proposed site. There is no need to disclose details of a personal nature unless your application is being made on compassionate grounds. A letter of consent to make the application will be required from the land owner, if you are not the owner of the site. The planning application fee for a single dwelling is €65-00. The content of the newspaper notice and the site notice is expanded and word specific. The site notice must be on a white background. Where a second application for permission is being made on the same site within six months of making a previous application, the site notice of the subsequent application must be inscribed on a yellow background. A submission or observation may be made by a third party in writing to the Planning Authority on payment of a fee of €20-00 within a period of five weeks beginning on the date of receipt of the application.

INVALID APPLICATIONS.

Planning applications must now be validated by the Planning Authority before it processes the application. A valid application must comply with the requirements set out for the newspaper notice, site notice, content of planning application, and the plans, maps and drawings to accompany an application. Where an application does not comply with any of these requirements, the application will be declared invalid and must be returned to the applicant with the fee paid. The Planning Authority must explain to the applicant why the application is not valid, when it returns the application.

FURTHER INFORMATION.

The Planning Authority may seek further information in respect of the application. They have four weeks from the receipt of further information from the applicant to make a decision in an ordinary application. Where further information is sought and the request is not complied with within six months, the application will be deemed withdrawn.

TIME LIMITS FOR DEALING WITH PLANNING APPLICATIONS.

The minimum period for determination of an application is five weeks from receipt of the planning application. Under the Planning Act, a planning authority must make a decision on an ordinary planning application within eight weeks of receipt of the application. After the appropriate period, the planning authority will issue a decision in the application, which will be either a decision to grant planning permission or a decision to refuse planning permission. Assuming that the decision is to grant planning permission, conditions will be embodied within the decision. If you are unhappy with the conditions, you may appeal the decision to An Bord Pleanala. After a period of one month, if no appeal is lodged, either by the applicant or by a third party, a full grant of permission will be issued.

The requirements stated are only a brief interpretation and relevant to the making of a planning application for a single house. From March 11th 2002 there are only two pieces of relevant legislation, the Planning & Development Act 2000 and the Planning & Development Regulations 2001, S.I. No. 600 of 2001. A Planning Authority can only ask for the information that is specified in the legislation. It would be very much simpler if a standard application form were introduced as part of the legislation and which would be mandatory in the case of all planning applications to any Planning Authority. In all cases therefore, our advice is simple; study the application form with care prior to completion, make sure that all your plans and maps satisfy the requirements and conduct a check list prior to submitting your application. Pay particular attention to the content of the newspaper notice and site notice, the wording for the proposal must match in both cases and with the description given in the application form. If you overlook any matter in preparing the application, the Planning Authority will have no choice but to return the application as invalid and you must start all over again!

THE ELECTRICITY CONNECTION
AND INSTALLATION

YOU HAVE MADE THE DECISION to build your own home. The site has been selected and the plans drawn up, but before you can go any further, there is one important thing you have to arrange - your electricity connection.

As a starting point you will need to find out whether or not an electricity connection is reasonably available to your new site. Before you sign a contract to buy the site call to your local ESB Networks office with your site map. ESB will advise you whether an electricity connection is available and at what cost. This is particularly important if the site is in an isolated rural location. To ensure that a connection will be available in time make your application as early as possible. Your local ESB staff will be happy to assist you.

The ESB connection is usually taken underground from the connection point or pole to an outdoor cabinet (meter box) positioned at the side or front of the house. The ESB meter and isolating switch will be located in the cabinet. The customers' distribution unit (fuse box) is usually located inside the house for convenience.

ELECTRICAL INSTALLATION

The electrical installation in your new home must be carried out to the standards set by the ETCI (Electro Technical Council of Ireland). Before the electricity connection can be made live by ESB you must supply an ETCI-recognised completion certificate from your Electrical Contractor. This Certificate is also your guarantee from the contractor that the installation has been carried out to the specified standards. It is important to remember that the safety of the installation on the customer's side of the ESB meter is the responsibility of the customer alone.

POWER AND LIGHTING POINTS

The first 'fixing', as architects call it, will determine where permanent lights, switches, power points, heating and ventilation points will eventually be located. First fixing involves the positioning of cables, chasing walls for cabling, and fixing back boxes. As the work progresses, changing these positions will be difficult, so you will need to decide in advance of first fixing where the points will be eventually required.

When locating the power points, it is important to note that sockets should be of twin design and switched. It is recommended that general wall sockets in living rooms, circulation areas and bedrooms are located a minimum of eighteen inches above floor level. Special consideration should be given to disabled persons, and sockets should be fit-

ted at a height above floor level that is suitable. Sockets should all be of a safety type, and are usually fitted with an in-built indicator lamp.

Each room should be wired for general lighting, usually with a ceiling rose fitting in the centre of the room. This is the minimum requirement, but there are lots of imaginative ways of lighting your rooms, and many new fittings available. In the kitchen area, for example, you could consider recessed ceiling fittings, and strip-lighting under high-level presses. The bedrooms could have wall lights fitted. Wall fittings and picture lamps are popular for sitting rooms or dining rooms, with table lamps for added atmosphere. Make sure you have adequate power points in every room for extra lamps, etc. For areas where lighting is left on for longer periods, CFLs (Compact Fluorescent Lamps) are convenient and economical. They last 10 times as long as an ordinary bulb, and use only one-fifth the electricity for equivalent light. They are particularly useful for those awkward-to-reach places, because they do not need to be replaced very often.

THE KITCHEN AND BATHROOM

Water and electricity do not mix, so there are rooms in the house which need special attention when it comes to the safe use of electricity – the bathroom(s) and the kitchen. Remember, the only power outlet allowed in the bathroom is an approved light and shaver point. Switches for lighting and for any other approved fixed appliance in the bathroom, such as a wall-mounted fan heater or an electric shower, must be located external to the bathroom. When you are deciding on your fitted kitchen, make sure that the sockets are not placed anywhere close to the sink, or where they might be subjected to water splashes.

Remember, all new domestic installations must be provided with an RCD protecting the socket and water heater circuit. An electric shower circuit must also be fitted with one.

The current building regulations insist on an approved smoke alarm. The unit, which should be wired through the mains supply, can be located in the bedroom corridor in a single storey dwelling, and on the top landing over the stairwell in a dormer or two-storey house. Although not a requirement, we suggest that you have a recessed emergency light fitting in the corridor, landing or hallway, and also in the kitchen ceiling. Having this fitting means an end to the search for candles and torches in the event of fire or power failure, and the immediate danger of stumbling in the darkness. It also removes the danger associated with lighted candles, especially those balanced on old saucers!

Much of electrical safety has to do with commonsense and having respect for a powerful source of energy. To help you make the best and safest use of electricity, ESB has produced a booklet, Electrical Safety in the Home, which is available, free of charge, from your local ESB office.

ELECTRIC HEATING OPTIONS

When designing the services, you should consider incorporating electric heating and water heating specifications, which will maximise the benefits of Nightsaver electricity. The recommended water heating system, for example, is a factory-insulated hot water cylinder fitted with two separate side-entry immersion heaters (one fitted at the base of the cylinder to heat a full cylinder of water; the other fitted closer to the top to heat a smaller amount). This arrangement will facilitate making use of less than half price Nightsaver electricity for water heating. Install wiring for storage heating. The current design of slim-line storage heaters blends with most interior design schemes, and the units are modern and fully controlled.

There are also exciting new developments in electric heating, such as under-floor or over-ceiling heating. This form of heating leaves your living space free of visible heat source. It is a fully controllable and efficient way to heat your home. While storage heating or under-floor and ceiling heating are efficient, most people still like to have a focal point in their living room. The open fireplace still has an attraction, though nowadays people might prefer not to use solid fuel. By fitting a modern, flame-effect electric fire into the fireplace, it is still possible to retain the focal point of the chimney-breast, and the visual effect of the open fire. Gone are the days of the two-bar electric fire, as current models offer a very realistic effect.

It is important to apply for your electricity connection and also decide on the installation and heating requirements as early as possible. You will find useful information on ESB's Website relating to the application for connection and on-building energy efficiency into your new home right from the beginning.

ESB CONTACT NUMBERS

New Connections
1850 372 757
General Enquiries
1850 372 372
Emergencies
1850 372 999

 # Beware of overhead lines

- Before work begins on your site **Look Up and Look Out** for overhead power lines.

- Make sure your staff and subcontractors always observe safe working practices where overhead lines cross or pass close to your site.

- Remember, contact or even near contact, with power lines can be fatal.

Take particular care with:

✓ Tipper Trucks
✓ Concrete Trucks (with conveyor belts or pumps)
✓ Conveyors and Hoists
✓ Mobile Cranes
✓ Scaffolding and Ladders

Supporting safety in the Construction Industry.

ELECTRICITY IS A GREAT FORCE OF NATURE. RESPECT ITS POWER. Networks

Flogas Cosy Home Heating

Flogas, the Drogheda-based LPG company, has developed the Flogas Cosy Home Heating concept which tailors their unique home-heating system to the individual needs of your home. Flogas Cosy Home Heating gives you instant, versatile and clean central heating, instant hot water, economical gas cooking, a choice of coal-effect fires and now even a gas-powered tumble dryer. The Flogas Cosy Home Heating system can be installed quickly and easily into your home as one integrated system, a system which has long proved itself in numerous homes throughout Ireland for efficiency, economy, flexibility and reliability.

What's more, with Flogas' latest offer of a full 25% off every gas bill you receive in your first two years on the Flogas Cosy Home Heating system, there's no need to worry about increased fuel bills over the winter months. Flogas Cosy Home Heating system ensures that all your home's energy needs are catered for, with Flogas' combination of modern, stylish appliances, and their technical expertise and back-up.

Central Heating
Our installers' expertise and experience mean that conversion to Flogas is a speedy and straightforward operation. We simply replace your old boiler with a Flogas boiler to allow you to benefit instantly from the cleanliness, controllability and economy of Flogas. As far as possible, we will retain your existing pipework and radiators, and you begin to enjoy the benefits of your conversion immediately.

Modern digital time-clocks enable you to programme your Flogas Cosy Home Heating system to provide you with a warm reception at home – at whatever time suits you.

Super Sers
There are times when instant heat, in one or two rooms, is what you want, rather than activating your entire central heating system – this is where Flogas' Super Ser excels. Early in the morning, for example, heat is instantly available at the press of a button. Super Sers provide quality, mobile and economic heating in your home.

Hot Water
Unlimited supplies of hot water at the turn of a tap – a further element of the Flogas Cosy Home Heating system. Your supply of hot water can be controlled by a time clock, giving you as much hot water as you want – when you want it. Alternatively, individually installed instant and cost-effective water heaters, which are completely independent of the central heating system, will provide you with instant hot water as you need it.

Cooking
Flogas Cosy Home Heating system offers you the latest cooker technology in choosing appliances, from free-standing cookers to separate up-to-the-minute built-in ovens and hobs.

Ever wondered why top chefs rely on gas in their kitchens? Convert to Flogas and you'll see. Gas is instant, controllable, and, with up to 30% savings to be made on conversion from electricity, it's very economical.

Coal Effect Gas Fires
Toastie toes in a living room filled with life with the dancing flames and cosy comfort of a Flogas coal effect fire. Traditional fire comforts are avilable to you within seconds, without the usual back-breaking chores, or family rows, of setting a fire and cleaning the grate. Flogas Cosy Home Heating system offers you a range of efficient economical and attractive gas fires from which to choose.

What's more, you can install a back boiler system when combined with certain gas fires – in your existing fireplace if you like. Not only can you use your fire to provide heat for your hot water and central heating requirements, but you can operate both systems independently – using the coal effect fire on its own, independent of the back boiler, or the boiler itself can be operated separately if you only require hot water or radiators.

Gas Tumble Dryers
Flogas have recently added a stylish, high-tech gas tumble dryer to their Cosy Home Heating system. Simple to install and use, the dryer will save you up to 50% in running costs. The dryer is designed to be highly energy efficient, and drying times are less than with an electric model. The machine will automatically shut off the heat should your clothes dry before the drying cycle has finished – this saves you money and is kinder on the environment. The machine is extremely quiet in operation. It also reduces static, minimises creasing and ensures that clothes are never over-dried.

The Perfect Home Heat System
So it's clear that the Flogas Cosy Home Heating system is the perfect choice for an integrated solution to all your home heating needs – be they central heating, hot water, cooking, coal effect gas fires or gas tumble dryers.

25% OFF YOUR GAS BILLS FOR 2 YEARS...

Wouldn't that make you feel warm inside.

Flogas Cosy Home Heating is the most versatile and environmentally friendly energy system available. Designed specifically for your needs, nothing compares with it for convenience, economy and efficiency.

Flogas Cosy Home Heating will provide trouble free efficient central heating, instant hot water, economical cooking, attractive coal effect fires and energy efficient gas tumble dryers.

If you install a Flogas Cosy Home Heating system now, we'll give you

*25% off your gas bills for the next 2 years!

*This offer will apply only to bulk tank installations.

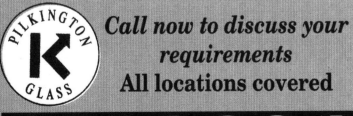

PROJECTED CONSTRUCTION COSTS FOR BLUEPRINT HOME PLANS. COSTS EXCLUDE SITE AND SITE DEVELOPMENTS COSTS, LOCAL AUTHORITY CHARGES, GOOD STANDARD INTERNAL FINISHES AND ALL DECORATION.

Design No. 1 — **Kilmore**
Floor area: 68.39 sq.m.
Frontage dimension: 10.30m

Cost indicator:
€43,428 - €52,318

Design No. 2 — **Connaught**
Floor area: 61.15sq.m.
Frontage dimension: 10.17m

Cost indicator:
€38,830 - €46,780

Design No. 3 — **Beaufort**
Floor area: 82.41sq. m.
Frontage dimension: 11.27m

Cost indicator:
€52,330 - €63,044

Design No. 4 — **Hawthorn**
Floor area: 82.26sq.m.
Frontage dimension: 10.98m

Cost indicator:
€56,680 - €68,284

Design No. 5 — **Melville**
Floor area: 102.30sq.m.
Frontage dimension: 14.12m

Cost indicator:
€64,961 - €78,260

Design No. 6 — **Kylemore**
Floor area: 103.38sq.m.
Frontage dimension: 14.12m

Cost indicator:
€65,646 - €79,086

Design No. 7 — **Mayberry**
Floor area: 85.55sq.m.
Frontage dimension: 11.40m

Cost indicator:
€54,324 - €65,446

Design No. 8 — **Nevada**
Floor area: 149.50sq.m.
Frontage dimension: 17.57m

Cost indicator:
€94,933 - €114,368

Design No. 9 — **Princeton**
Floor area: 124.43sq.m.
Frontage dimension: 15.55m

Cost indicator:
€79,013 - €95,189

Design No. 10 — **Balrath**
Floor area: 57.66sq.m
Frontage dimension: 9.60m

Cost indicator:
€36,614 - €44,110

Design No. 11 — **Stanwell**
Floor area: 137sq.m.
Frontage dimension: 12.77m

Cost indicator:
€86,995 - €104,805

Design No. 12 — **Bredon**
Floor area: 87sq.m.
Frontage dimension: 12.98m

Cost indicator:
€55,245 - €66,555

Design No. 13 — **Rothley**
Floor area: 105.46sq.m.
Frontage dimension: 13.91m

Cost indicator:
€66,967 - €80,677

Design No. 14 — **Dalton**
Floor area: 63.48sq.m
Frontage dimension: 10.09m

Cost indicator:
€40,310 - €48,562

Design No. 15 — **Whitby**
Floor area: 69.19sq.m.
Frontage dimension: 10.31m

Cost indicator:
€43,936 - €52,930

Design No. 16 — **Galena**
Floor area: 86.11sq.m.
Frontage dimension: 12.62m

Cost indicator:
€54,680 - €65,874

Design No. 17 — **Millhouse**
Floor area: 65.75sq.m.
Frontage dimension: 10.13m

Cost indicator:
€41,751 - €50,299

Design No. 18 — **Lakefield**
Floor area: 80.66sq.m.
Frontage dimension: 11.81m

Cost indicator:
€51,219 - €61,705

Design No. 19 — **Miami**
Floor area: 94.54sq.m.
Frontage dimension: 13.53m

Cost indicator:
€60,033 - €72,323

Design No. 20 — **Kilglin**
Floor area: 73.42sq.m.
Frontage dimension: 11.22m

Cost indicator:
€46,622 - €56,166

Design No. 21 — **Cherokee**
Floor area: 90.21sq.m.
Frontage dimension: 13.41m

Cost indicator:
€57,283 - €69,011

Design No.22 — **Lemington**
Floor area: 91sq.m.
Frontage dimension: 12.60m

Cost indicator:
€57,785 - €69,615

Design No. 23 — **Marsdon**
Floor area: 100.71sq.m.
Frontage dimension: 13.55m

Cost indicator:
€63,951 - €77,043

Design No. 24 — **Brooklyn**
Floor area: 87.02sq.m.
Frontage dimension: 7.78m

Cost indicator:
€55,258 - €66,570

Design No. 25 — **Leicester**
Floor area: 98.34sq.m.
Frontage dimension: 13.52m

Cost indicator:
€62,446 - €75,230

Design No. 26 — **Kenmare**
Floor area: 102.10sq.m.
Frontage dimension: 13.94m

Cost indicator:
€64,834 - €78,107

Design No. 27 — **Chelsem**
Floor area: 90.02sq.m.
Frontage dimension: 12.80m

Cost indicator:
€57,163 - €68,865

Design No. 28 — **Hanwell**
Floor area: 96.51sq.m.
Frontage dimension: 13.72m

Cost indicator:
€61,284 - €73,830

Design No. 29 — **Trent**
Floor area: 101sq.m.
Frontage dimension: 9.34m

Cost indicator:
€64,135 - €77,265

Design No. 30 — **Wellington**
Floor area: 105sq.m.
Frontage dimension: 13.87m

Cost indicator:
€66,675 - €80,325

Design No. 31	Ferndale	Design No. 42	Sorrento	Design No. 53	Castlecoole
Floor area:	106.86sq.m.	Floor area:	116.32sq.m.	Floor area:	124.18sq.m.
Frontage dimension:	14.30m	Frontage dimension:	15.60m	Frontage dimension:	16.53m

Cost indicator:
€67,856 - €81,748 | **Cost indicator:** €74,863 - €88,985 | **Cost indicator:** €78,854 - €94,998

Design No. 32	Glenfarne	Design No. 43	Montrose	Design No. 54	Newhaven
Floor area:	103.14sq.m.	Floor area:	119.04sq.m.	Floor area:	124.62sq.m.
Frontage dimension:	13.72m	Frontage dimension:	16.45m	Frontage dimension:	18.87m

Cost indicator:
€65,494 - €78,902 | **Cost indicator:** €75,590 - €91,066 | **Cost indicator:** €79,134 - €95,334

Design No. 33	Weyburn	Design No. 44	Fiona	Design No. 55	Olympus
Floor area:	109.46sq.m.	Floor area:	97.29sq.m.	Floor area:	121.55sq.m.
Frontage dimension:	14.58m	Frontage dimension:	16.65m	Frontage dimension:	17.76m

Cost indicator:
€69,507 - €83,737 | **Cost indicator:** €61,779 - €74,427 | **Cost indicator:** €77,184 - €92,986

Design No. 34	Richmond	Design No. 45	Verona II	Design No. 56	Algarve
Floor area:	106.17sq.m.	Floor area:	172.50sq.m.	Floor area:	143.03sq.m.
Frontage dimension:	14.29m	Frontage dimension:	18.28m	Frontage dimension:	13m

Cost indicator:
€67,418 - €81,220 | **Cost indicator:** €109,538 - €131,963 | **Cost indicator:** €90,824 - €109,418

Design No. 35	Lincoln	Design No. 46	Charmont	Design No. 57	Portland
Floor area:	106.65sq.m.	Floor area:	124.71sq.m.	Floor area:	124.53sq.m.
Frontage dimension:	15.91m	Frontage dimension:	14.63m	Frontage dimension:	17.40m

Cost indicator:
€67,723 - €81,587 | **Cost indicator:** €79,191 - €95,403 | **Cost indicator:** €79,077 - €95,266

Design No. 36	Gwent	Design No. 47	Hampton	Design No. 58	Winnipeg
Floor area:	105.09sq.m.	Floor area:	124.62sq.m.	Floor area:	116.43sq.m.
Frontage dimension:	14.02m	Frontage dimension:	14.83m	Frontage dimension:	16.45m

Cost indicator:
€66,732 - €80,394 | **Cost indicator:** €79,134 - €95,334 | **Cost indicator:** €73,933 - €89,069

Design No. 37	Montana	Design No. 48	Newcastle	Design No. 59	Dominique
Floor area:	109.65sq.m.	Floor area:	124.25sq.m.	Floor area:	120sq.m.
Frontage dimension:	14.88m	Frontage dimension:	15.91m	Frontage dimension:	18.95m

Cost indicator:
€69,628 - €83,882 | **Cost indicator:** €78,899 - €95,051 | **Cost indicator:** €76,200 - €91,800

Design No. 38	Vienna	Design No. 49	Kiltormer	Design No. 60	Verona
Floor area:	97.89sq.m.	Floor area:	124.15sq.m.	Floor area:	136.15sq.m.
Frontage dimension:	13.38m	Frontage dimension:	17.06m	Frontage dimension:	18.31m

Cost indicator:
€62,160 - €74,886 | **Cost indicator:** €78,835 - €94,975 | **Cost indicator:** €86,455 - €104,155

Design No. 39	Greenville	Design No. 50	Leinster	Design No. 61	Trinity
Floor area:	121.45sq.m.	Floor area:	137.92sq.m.	Floor area:	124.43sq.m.
Frontage dimension:	16.33m	Frontage dimension:	13.11m	Frontage dimension:	18.14m

Cost indicator:
€77,121 - €92,909 | **Cost indicator:** €87,579 - €105,509 | **Cost indicator:** €79,013 - €95,189

Design No. 40	Cherryvale	Design No. 51	Rathbrack	Design No. 62	Ashwood
Floor area:	120.20sq.m.	Floor area:	123.23sq.m.	Floor area:	124.09sq.m.
Frontage dimension:	15.77m	Frontage dimension:	16.76m	Frontage dimension:	16.48m

Cost indicator:
€76,327 - €91,953 | **Cost indicator:** €78,251 - €94,271 | **Cost indicator:** €74,797 - €94,929

Design No. 41	Primrose	Design No. 52	Dunbarton	Design No. 63	Miltown
Floor area:	114.76sq.m.	Floor area:	123.88sq.m.	Floor area:	90.28sq.m.
Frontage dimension:	15.55m	Frontage dimension:	16.05m	Frontage dimension:	14.18m

Cost indicator:
€72,873 - €87,791 | **Cost indicator:** €78,664 - €94,768 | **Cost indicator:** €57,328 - €69,064

Design No. 64	Ballina	Design No. 75	Topaz	Design No. 86	Ballyhale
Floor area:	169sq.m.	Floor area:	125.28sq.m.	Floor area:	123.69sq.m
Frontage dimension:	15m	Frontage dimension:	17.07m	Frontage dimension:	15.16m

Cost indicator: €107,315 - €129,285   **Cost indicator:** €79,553 - €95,839   **Cost indicator:** €78,543 - €94,623

Design No. 65	Loughan	Design No. 76	Cheldon	Design No. 87	Crawford
Floor area:	124.08sq.m.	Floor area:	138.85sq.m.	Floor area:	124.99sq.m.
Frontage dimension:	17.46m	Frontage dimension:	19.07m	Frontage dimension:	17.07m

Cost indicator: €78,791 - €94,921   **Cost indicator:** €88,170 - €106,220   **Cost indicator:** €79,369 - €95,617

Design No. 66	Canada	Design No. 77	Clonard	Design No. 88	Clonmore
Floor area:	87.78sq.m.	Floor area:	123.67sq.m.	Floor area:	132sq.m.
Frontage dimension:	12m	Frontage dimension:	16.86m	Frontage dimension:	17.60m

Cost indicator: €55,740 - €67,152   **Cost indicator:** €78,530 - €94,608   **Cost indicator:** €83,820 - €100,980

Design No. 67	Woodgreen	Design No. 78	Hanover	Design No. 89	Sussex
Floor area:	162.27sq.m.	Floor area:	124.71sq.m.	Floor area:	118.66sq.m.
Frontage dimension:	18.19m	Frontage dimension:	17.02m	Frontage dimension:	13.93m

Cost indicator: €103,041 - €124,137   **Cost indicator:** €79,191 - €95,403   **Cost indicator:** €75,349 - €90,775

Design No. 68	Gatwick	Design No. 79	Merland	Design No. 90	Bracknell
Floor area:	109.40sq.m.	Floor area:	124.12sq.m.	Floor area:	124.10sq.m.
Frontage dimension:	14.89m	Frontage dimension:	16.75m	Frontage dimension:	17.60m

Cost indicator: €69,469 - €83,691   **Cost indicator:** €78,816- €94,952   **Cost indicator:** €78,804 - €94,937

Design No. 69	Meadows	Design No. 80	Vanguard	Design No. 91	Connemara
Floor area:	84.69sq.m.	Floor area:	124.61sq.m	Floor area:	112.81sq.m.
Frontage dimension:	9.60m	Frontage dimension:	17.12m	Frontage dimension:	15.27m

Cost indicator: €53,778 - €64,788   **Cost indicator:** €79,127 - €95,327   **Cost indicator:** €71,634 - €86,300

Design No. 70	Sanford	Design No. 81	Ascot	Design No. 92	Bellcroft
Floor area:	124.62sq.m.	Floor area:	124.89sq.m.	Floor area:	124.96sq.m.
Frontage dimension:	14.42m	Frontage dimension:	16.80m	Frontage dimension:	18.20m

Cost indicator: €79,134 - €95,334   **Cost indicator:** €79,305 - €95,541   **Cost indicator:** €79,350 - €95,594

Design No. 71	Linwood	Design No. 82	Galway	Design No. 93	Riversdale
Floor area:	124.62sq.m.	Floor area:	106.86sq.m.	Floor area:	120.34sq.m.
Frontage dimension:	15.69m	Frontage dimension:	15.24m	Frontage dimension:	9.63m

Cost indicator: €79,134 - €95,334   **Cost indicator:** €67,856 - €81,748   **Cost indicator:** €76,416 - €92,060

Design No. 72	Martok	Design No. 83	Ashgrove	Design No. 94	Elmwood
Floor area:	111.60sq.m.	Floor area:	124.89sq.m.	Floor area:	123.97sq.m.
Frontage dimension:	15.23m	Frontage dimension:	16.98m	Frontage dimension:	16.97m

Cost indicator: €70,866 - €85,374   **Cost indicator:** €79,305 - €95,541   **Cost indicator:** €78,721 - €94,837

Design No. 73	Weston	Design No. 84	Dunmore	Design No. 95	Pemberton
Floor area:	122sq.m.	Floor area:	123.69sq.m.	Floor area:	124.67sq.m.
Frontage dimension:	17.11m	Frontage dimension:	16.05m	Frontage dimension:	17.11m

Cost indicator: €77,470 - €93,330   **Cost indicator:** €78,543 - €94,623   **Cost indicator:** €79,165 - €95,373

Design No. 74	Sable	Design No. 85	Albany	Design No. 96	Willow
Floor area:	123.78sq.m.	Floor area:	122sq.m.	Floor area:	96.12sq.m
Frontage dimension:	16.15m	Frontage dimension:	8.28m	Frontage dimension:	10.58m

Cost indicator: €78,600 - €94,692   **Cost indicator:** €77,470 - €93,330   **Cost indicator:** €61,036 - €73,532

Design No. 97 **Woodside**
Floor area: 124sq.m.
Frontage dimension: 15.98m

Cost indicator:
€78,740-€94,860

Design No. 98 **Roscommon**
Floor area: 119.60sq.m.
Frontage dimension: 9.30m

Cost indicator:
€75,946 - €91,494

Design No. 99 **Glasdrum**
Floor area: 124sq.m.
Frontage dimension: 15.39m

Cost indicator:
€78,740 - €94,860

Design No. 100 **Kinsale**
Floor area: 124.73sq.m.
Frontage dimension: 17m

Cost indicator:
€79,204 - €95,418

Design No. 101 **Newbridge**
Floor area: 132.80sq.m.
Frontage dimension: 17.17m

Cost indicator:
€84,328 - €101,592

Design No. 102 **Guildford**
Floor area: 124.62sq.m.
Frontage dimension: 15.39m

Cost indicator:
€79,134 - €95,334

Design No. 103 **Rushbrook**
Floor area: 121.27sq.m.
Frontage dimension: 14.07m

Cost indicator:
€77,007 - €92,772

Design No. 104 **Pampas**
Floor area: 122.29sq.m.
Frontage dimension: 16.86m

Cost indicator:
€77,654 - €93,552

Design No. 105 **Tyrone**
Floor area: 123.23sq.m.
Frontage dimension: 14.94m

Cost indicator:
€78,251 - €94,271

Design No. 106 **Castlekelly**
Floor area: 112.53sq.m.
Frontage dimension: 15.09m

Cost indicator:
€71,457 - €86,085

Design No. 107 **Brampton**
Floor area: 114.48sq.m.
Frontage dimension: 7.92m

Cost indicator:
€72,695 - €87,577

Design No. 108 **Drumcar**
Floor area: 107.07sq.m.
Frontage dimension: 14.56m

Cost indicator:
€67,989 - €81,909

Design No. 109 **Wagner**
Floor area: 128.81sq.m
Frontage dimension: 16.92m

Cost indicator:
€81,794 - €98,540

Design No. 110 **Hazelmere**
Floor area: 123.11sq.m.
Frontage dimension: 17.23m

Cost indicator:
€78,175 - €94,179

Design No. 111 **Brackenfield**
Floor area: 124.08sq.m
Frontage dimension: 20.75m

Cost indicator:
€78,791 - €94,921

Design No. 112 **Mansfield**
Floor area: 127.15sq.m.
Frontage dimension: 16.47m

Cost indicator:
€80,740 - €97,270

Design No. 113 **Norfolk**
Floor area: 124.24sq.m.
Frontage dimension: 15.80m

Cost indicator:
€78,892 - €95,044

Design No. 114 **Seville**
Floor area: 124.90sq.m.
Frontage dimension: 17.16m

Cost indicator:
€79,312 - €95,549

Design No. 115 **Kent**
Floor area: 118.83sq.m.
Frontage dimension: 9.42m

Cost indicator:
€75,457 - €90,905

Design No. 116 **Rosevale**
Floor area: 112.48sq.m.
Frontage dimension: 17.37m

Cost indicator:
€71,425 - €86,047

Design No. 117 **Rochdale**
Floor area: 133.27sq.m.
Frontage dimension: 17.15m

Cost indicator:
€84,627 - €101,952

Design No. 118 **Ashford**
Floor area: 152.61sq.m.
Frontage dimension: 19.66m

Cost indicator:
€96,907 - €116,747

Design No. 119 **Nashville**
Floor area: 123.04sq.m.
Frontage dimension: 16.91m

Cost indicator:
€78,130 - €94,126

Design No. 120 **Kileen**
Floor area: 142.66sq.m.
Frontage dimension: 16.91m

Cost indicator:
€90,589 - €109,135

Design No. 121 **Arran**
Floor area: 150sq.m.
Frontage dimension: 18.43m

Cost indicator:
€95,250 - €114,750

Design No. 122 **Somerset**
Floor area: 144.71sq.m.
Frontage dimension: 17.37m

Cost indicator:
€91,891 - €110,703

Design No. 123 **Canberra**
Floor area: 138.57sq.m.
Frontage dimension: 17.83m

Cost indicator:
€87,992 - €106,006

Design No. 124 **Setanta**
Floor area: 138.05sq.m.
Frontage dimension: 19.93m

Cost indicator:
€87,662 - €105,608

Design No. 125 **Pembroke**
Floor area: 152.71sq.m.
Frontage dimension: 18.49m

Cost indicator:
€96,971 - €116,823

Design No. 126 **Ontario**
Floor area: 151.29sq.m.
Frontage dimension: 18.27m

Cost indicator:
€96,069 - €115,737

Design No. 127 **Tunbridge**
Floor area: 170.28sq.m.
Frontage dimension: 15.85m

Cost indicator:
€108,128 - €130,264

Design No. 128 **Wicklow**
Floor area: 124.62sq.m.
Frontage dimension: 16.31m

Cost indicator:
€79,134 - €95,334

Design No. 129 **Classic**
Floor area: 158.10 sq.m.
Frontage dimension: 19.15m

Cost indicator:
€100,394 - €120,947

18

Design No. 130   **Webster**
Floor area: 149.82sq.m.
Frontage dimension: 18.30m

Cost indicator:
€95,136 - €114,612

Design No. 131   **Washington**
Floor area: 149.73sq.m.
Frontage dimension: 16.15m

Cost indicator:
€95,079 - €114,544

Design No. 132   **Ashford**
Floor area: 134.66sq.m.
Frontage dimension: 18.29m

Cost indicator:
€85,509 - €103,--015

Design No. 133   **Meridian**
Floor area: 160.29sq.m.
Frontage dimension: 10.50m

Cost indicator:
€101,784 - €122,622

Design No. 134   **Canticle**
Floor area: 159.77sq.m.
Frontage dimension: 19.38m

Cost indicator:
€101,454 - €122,224

Design No. 135   **Rodez**
Floor area: 171.86sq.m.
Frontage dimension: 19.61m

Cost indicator:
€109,131 - €131,473

Design No. 136   **Concordia**
Floor area: 169.53sq.m.
Frontage dimension: 22m

Cost indicator:
€107,652 - €129,690

Design No. 137   **Fenwick**
Floor area: 149.85sq.m.
Frontage dimension: 23.25m

Cost indicator:
€95,155 - €114,635

Design No. 138   **Bedford**
Floor area: 190.79sq.m.
Frontage dimension: 23.31m

Cost indicator:
€121,152 - €145,954

Design No. 139   **Moylough**
Floor area: 176.42sq.m.
Frontage dimension: 20.07m

Cost indicator:
€112,027 - €134,961

Design No. 140   **Brooklodge**
Floor area: 165.45sq.m.
Frontage dimension: 19.65m

Cost indicator:
€105,696 - €127,334

Design No. 141   **Lisdornan**
Floor area: 179.50sq.m.
Frontage dimension: 20.11m

Cost indicator:
€113,983 - €137,318

Design No. 142   **Lissarda**
Floor area: 195.35sq.m.
Frontage dimension: 19.91m

Cost indicator:
€124,047 - €149,443

Design No. 143   **Killarney**
Floor area: 215.30sq.m.
Frontage dimension: 24.69m

Cost indicator:
€136,716 - €164,705

Design No. 144   **Gallow**
Floor area: 179.42sq.m.
Frontage dimension: 21.79m

Cost indicator:
€113,932 - €137,256

Design No. 145   **Danestown**
Floor area: 145.64sq.m.
Frontage dimension: 18.29m

Cost indicator:
€92,481 - €111,415

Design No. 146   **Kilnew**
Floor area: 151.59sq.m.
Frontage dimension: 17.91m

Cost indicator:
€96,260 - €115,966

Design No. 147   **Douglas**
Floor area: 183.21sq.m.
Frontage dimension: 20.27m

Cost indicator:
€116,338 - €140,156

Design No. 148   **Humber**
Floor area: 138sq.m.
Frontage dimension: 19.45m

Cost indicator:
€87,630 - €105,570

Design No. 149   **Holbrook**
Floor area: 152.61sq.m.
Frontage dimension: 17.88m

Cost indicator:
€96,907 - €116,747

Design No. 150   **Hadley**
Floor area: 125sq.m.
Frontage dimension: 16.60m

Cost indicator:
€79,375 - €95,625

Design No. 151   **Dauphin**
Floor area: 124.60sq.m.
Frontage dimension: 17m

Cost indicator:
€79,121 - €95,319

Design No. 152   **Dalgan**
Floor area: 199.09sq.m.
Frontage dimension: 21.20m

Cost indicator:
€126,422 - €152,304

Design No. 153   **Abbeyland**
Floor area: 227.31sq.m.
Frontage dimension: 20.50m

Cost indicator:
€144,342 - €173,892

Design No. 154   **Stanbury**
Floor area: 207.39sq.m.
Frontage dimension: 25.98m

Cost indicator:
€131,693 - €158,653

Design No. 155   **Tredfort**
Floor area: 147.59sq.m.
Frontage dimension: 17.77m

Cost indicator:
€93,720 - €112,906

Design No. 156   **Loxton**
Floor area: 175.11sq.m.
Frontage dimension: 18.28m

Cost indicator:
€111,195 - €133,959

Design No. 157   **Tarnwood**
Floor area: 140.43sq.m.
Frontage dimension: 19.46m

Cost indicator:
€89,173 - €107,429

Design No. 158   **Glendara**
Floor area: 175.77sq.m.
Frontage dimension: 17.12m

Cost indicator:
€111,614 - €134,464

Design No. 159   **Meadowvale**
Floor area: 124.43sq.m.
Frontage dimension: 9.70m

Cost indicator:
€79,013 - €95,189

Design No. 160   **Colebrook**
Floor area: 133sq.m.
Frontage dimension: 10m

Cost indicator:
€84,455 - €101,745

Design No. 161   **Mountemple**
Floor area: 124.99sq.m.
Frontage dimension: 10.36m

Cost indicator:
€79,369 - €95,617

Design No. 162   **Canterbury**
Floor area: 124sq.m.
Frontage dimension: 9.93m

Cost indicator:
€78,740 - €94,860

Design No. 163   **Kilbeggan**
Floor area: 124.31sq.m.
Frontage dimension: 9.73m

Cost indicator:
€78,937 - €95,097

Design No. 164   **Bailey**
Floor area: 124.99sq.m.
Frontage dimension: 9.14m

Cost indicator:
€79,369 - €95,617

Design No. 165   **Moorefield**
Floor area: 124.90sq.m
Frontage dimension: 10.06m

Cost indicator:
€79,312 - €95,549

Design No. 166   **Rockwell**
Floor area: 143sq.m.
Frontage dimension: 10.46m

Cost indicator:
€90,805 - €109,395

Design No. 167   **Newport**
Floor area: 139.22sq.m.
Frontage dimension: 10.36m

Cost indicator:
€88,405 - €106,503

Design No. 168   **Virginia**
Floor area: 185sq.m.
Frontage dimension: 9.87m

Cost indicator:
€117,475 - €141,525

Design No. 169   **Kingfisher**
Floor area: 124.71sq.m.
Frontage dimension: 9.75m

Cost indicator:
€79,191 - €95,403

Design No. 170   **Daytona**
Floor area: 176sq.m.
Frontage dimension: 10.71m

Cost indicator:
€111,760 - €134,640

Design No. 171   **Kilkee**
Floor area: 154.66sq.m.
Frontage dimension: 10.52m

Cost indicator:
€98,209 - €118,315

Design No. 172   **Hawkfield**
Floor area: 124.06sq.m.
Frontage dimension: 16.66m

Cost indicator:
€78,778 - €94,906

Design No. 173   **Oldbridge**
Floor area: 124.62sq.m.
Frontage dimension: 9.45m

Cost indicator:
€79,134 - €95,334

Design No. 174   **Emyvale**
Floor area: 183.95sq.m.
Frontage dimension: 16.31m

Cost indicator:
€116,808 - €140,722

Design No. 175   **Brunswick**
Floor area: 174.06sq.m.
Frontage dimension: 14.48m

Cost indicator:
€110,528 - €133,156

Design No. 176   **Belmont**
Floor area: 159.03sq.m.
Frontage dimension: 11.18m

Cost indicator:
€100,984 - €121,658

Design No. 177   **Garrybawn**
Floor area: 124.25sq.m.
Frontage dimension: 13.89m

Cost indicator:
€78,899 - €95,051

Design No. 178   **Moyvore**
Floor area: 171.93sq.m.
Frontage dimension: 10.03m

Cost indicator:
€109,176 - €131,526

Design No. 179   **Aisling**
Floor area: 175.70sq.m.
Frontage dimension: 18.60m

Cost indicator:
€111,570 - €134,411

Design No. 180   **Kilcormack**
Floor area: 179.49sq.m.
Frontage dimension: 17.52m

Cost indicator:
€113,976 - €137,310

Design No. 181   **Mondego**
Floor area: 144.24sq.m.
Frontage dimension: 10.38m

Cost indicator:
€91,592 - €110,344

Design No. 182   **Pinewood**
Floor area: 180.98sq.m.
Frontage dimension: 17.88m

Cost indicator:
€114,922 - €138,450

Design No. 183   **Aylesbury**
Floor area: 172.40sq.m.
Frontage dimension: 11.26m

Cost indicator:
€109,474 - €131,886

Design No. 184   **Avignon**
Floor area: 181.07sq.m.
Frontage dimension: 16.15m

Cost indicator:
€114,980 - €138,519

Design No. 185   **Frumpton**
Floor area: 114.76sq.m.
Frontage dimension: 9.50m

Cost indicator:
€72,873 - €87,791

Design No. 186   **Limerick**
Floor area: 151.96sq.m.
Frontage dimension: 19.05m

Cost indicator:
€96,495 - €116,249

Design No. 187   **Hamwood**
Floor area: 122.40sq.m.
Frontage dimension: 10.03m

Cost indicator:
€77,724 - €93,636

Design No. 188   **Ashpark**
Floor area: 269sq.m.
Frontage dimension: 12.60m

Cost indicator:
€170,815 - €205,785

Design No. 189   **Newbury**
Floor area: 194.18sq.m.
Frontage dimension: 15.85m

Cost indicator:
€123,304 - €148,548

Design No. 190   **Carlton**
Floor area: 214.37sq.m.
Frontage dimension: 14.94m

Cost indicator:
€136,125 - €163,993

Design No. 191   **Vermont**
Floor area: 205sq.m.
Frontage dimension: 15.39m

Cost indicator:
€130,175 - €156,825

Design No. 192   **Thornwood**
Floor area: 198sq.m.
Frontage dimension: 16.37m

Cost indicator:
€125,730 - €151,470

Design No. 193   **Arizona**
Floor area: 194.37sq.m.
Frontage dimension: 15.85m

Cost indicator:
€123,425 - €148,693

Design No. 194   **Kilsharvin**
Floor area: 168.25sq.m.
Frontage dimension: 11.38m

Cost indicator:
€106,839 - €128,711

Design No. 195   **Garfield**
Floor area: 232.71sq.m.
Frontage dimension: 17.90m

Cost indicator:
€147,771 - €178,023

Design No. 196   **Waldorf**
Floor area: 221.81sq.m.
Frontage dimension: 17.11m

Cost indicator:
€140,849 - €169,685

Design No. 197   **Southford**
Floor area: 225sq.m.
Frontage dimension: 12.90m

Cost indicator:
€142,875 - €172,125

Design No. 198   **Valiant**
Floor area: 279sq.m.
Frontage dimension: 14.99m

Cost indicator:
€177,165 - €213,435

Design No. 199   **Knockbride**
Floor area: 141.36sq.m.
Frontage dimension: 10.36m

Cost indicator:
€89,764 - €108,140

Design No. 200   **Morrell**
Floor area: 198.30sq.m.
Frontage dimension: 13.65m

Cost indicator:
€125,920 - €151,670

Design No. 201   **Moyfin**
Floor area: 113.27sq.m.
Frontage dimension: 9.04m

Cost indicator:
€71,927 - €86,652

Design No. 202   **Fassaroe**
Floor area: 180.98sq.m.
Frontage dimension: 17.83m

Cost indicator:
€114,922 - €138,450

Design No. 203   **Caranbrook**
Floor area: 145.82sq.m.
Frontage dimension: 10.47m

Cost indicator:
€92,596 - €111,552

Design No. 204   **Vernon**
Floor area: 114.76sq.m.
Frontage dimension: 9.50m

Cost indicator:
€72,873 - €87,791

Design No. 205   **Hermitage**
Floor area: 168.65sq.m.
Frontage dimension: 10.18m

Cost indicator:
€107,093 - €129,017

Design No. 206   **Taltean**
Floor area: 153.89sq.m.
Frontage dimension: 10.64m

Cost indicator:
€97,720 - €117,726

Design No. 207   **Trimton**
Floor area: 198.78sq.m.
Frontage dimension: 15.05m

Cost indicator:
€126,225 - €152,067

Design No. 208   **Kilkerly**
Floor area: 170.36sq.m.
Frontage dimension: 10.50m

Cost indicator:
€108,179 - €130,325

Design No. 209   **Winsford**
Floor area: 153.54sq.m.
Frontage dimension: 10.60m

Cost indicator:
€97,498 - €117,458

Design No. 210   **Cashel**
Floor area: 133.38sq.m.
Frontage dimension: 8.52m

Cost indicator:
€84,696 - €102,036

Design No. 211   **Ballincar**
Floor area: 114.86sq.m.
Frontage dimension: 9.75m

Cost indicator:
€72,936 - €87,868

Design No. 212   **Monroe**
Floor area: 122.85sq.m.
Frontage dimension: 14.42m

Cost indicator:
€78,010 - €93,980

Design No. 213   **Ballykilty**
Floor area: 146.66sq.m.
Frontage dimension: 17.53m

Cost indicator:
€93,129 - €112,194

Design No. 214   **Dungloe**
Floor area: 186.47sq.m.
Frontage dimension: 13.36m

Cost indicator:
€118,409 - €142,650

Design No. 215   **Balrenny**
Floor area: 116sq.m.
Frontage dimension: 9.40m

Cost indicator:
€73,660 - €88,740

Design No. 216   **Sobrando**
Floor area: 119sq.m.
Frontage dimension: 11.90m

Cost indicator:
€75,565 - €91,035

Design No. 217   **Carlingford**
Floor area: 116.35sq.m.
Frontage dimension: 10.29m

Cost indicator:
€73,882 - €89,008

Design No. 218   **Cheshire**
Floor area: 105.81sq.m.
Frontage dimension: 10.30m

Cost indicator:
€67,189 - €80,945

Design No. 219   **Chester**
Floor area: 159.80sq.m.
Frontage dimension: 12.90m

Cost indicator:
€101,473 - €122,247

Design No. 220   **Ballybrew**
Floor area: 173.35sq.m.
Frontage dimension: 13.41m

Cost indicator:
€110,077 - €132,613

Design No. 221   **Saxony**
Floor area: 119.69sq.m.
Frontage dimension: 11.43m

Cost indicator:
€76,003 - €91,563

Design No. 222   **Ashbrook**
Floor area: 138.20sq.m.
Frontage dimension: 10.31m

Cost indicator:
€87,757 - €105,723

Design No. 223   **Preston**
Floor area: 153sq.m.
Frontage dimension: 13.61m

Cost indicator:
€97,155 - €117,045

Design No. 224   **Afton**
Floor area: 166.01sq.m.
Frontage dimension: 14.33m

Cost indicator:
€105,416 - €126,998

Design No. 225   **Broadfort**
Floor area: 207.73sq.m.
Frontage dimension: 15.70m

Cost indicator:
€131,909 - €158,914

Design No. 226   **Kilmoon**
Floor area: 158.17sq.m.
Frontage dimension: 13.10m

Cost indicator:
€100,438 - €121,000

Design No. 227   **Domingo**
Floor area: 141.27sq.m.
Frontage dimension: 11.58m

Cost indicator:
€89,707 - €108,072

Design No. 228   **Northville**
Floor area: 161.72sq.m.
Frontage dimension: 11.07m

Cost indicator:
€102,692 - €123,716

Design No. 229	Provincial	Design No. 237	Dorset	Design No. 245	Newtown
Floor area:	188.31sq.m.	Floor area:	136.54sq.m.	Floor area:	214.11sq.m.
Frontage dimension:	15.77m	Frontage dimension:	11.73m	Frontage dimension:	18.90m

Cost indicator:	Cost indicator:	Cost indicator:
€119,577 - €144,057	€86,703 - €104.453	€135,960 - €163,794

Design No. 230	Provincial	Design No. 238	Kimberlin	Design No. 246	Wexford
Floor area:	171.40sq.m.	Floor area:	209.34sq.m.	Floor area:	129.91sq.m.
Frontage dimension:	16m	Frontage dimension:	17.47m	Frontage dimension:	11.30m

Cost indicator:	Cost indicator:	Cost indicator:
€108,839 - €131,121	€132,931 - €160,145	€82,493 - €99,381

Design No. 231	Provincial	Design No. 239	Yeovil	Design No. 247	Lisclougher
Floor area:	179.58sq.m.	Floor area:	194.83sq.m.	Floor area:	367.67sq.m.
Frontage dimension:	15.85m	Frontage dimension:	14.93m	Frontage dimension:	20m

Cost indicator:	Cost indicator:	Cost indicator:
€114,033 - €137,379	€123,717 - €149,045	€233,471 - €281,268

Design No. 232	Provincial	Design No. 240	Clayton	Design No. 248	Lislea
Floor area:	123.78sq.m.	Floor area:	175.86sq.m.	Floor area:	187.11sq.m.
Frontage dimension:	15.81m	Frontage dimension:	15.23m	Frontage dimension:	16.64m

Cost indicator:	Cost indicator:	Cost indicator:
€78,575 - €94,661	€111,671 - €134,533	€118,815 - €143,139

Design No. 233	Provincial	Design No. 241	Kelton	Design No. 249	Kilfannan
Floor area:	214.11sq.m.	Floor area:	123.46sq.m.	Floor area:	270.15sq.m.
Frontage dimension:	18.88m	Frontage dimension:	12m	Frontage dimension:	18.88m

Cost indicator:	Cost indicator:	Cost indicator:
€135,960 - €163,794	€78,397 - €94,447	€171,545 - €206,665

Design No. 234	Provincial	Design No. 242	Crusade	Design No. 250	Whitewood
Floor area:	172.33sq.m.	Floor area:	125.09sq.m.	Floor area:	150.18sq.m.
Frontage dimension:	15.24m	Frontage dimension:	9.96m	Frontage dimension:	12m

Cost indicator:	Cost indicator:	Cost indicator:
€109,430 - €131,833	€79,432 - €95,694	€95,364 - €114,888

Design No. 235	Provincial	Design No. 243	Rathcoon
Floor area:	190.17sq.m.	Floor area:	190sq.m.
Frontage dimension:	16.72m	Frontage dimension:	12.82m

Cost indicator:	Cost indicator:
€120,758 - €145,480	€120,650 - €145,350

Design No. 236	Provincial	Design No. 244	Stonefield
Floor area:	179sq.m.	Floor area:	143.46sq.m
Frontage dimension:	15.90m	Frontage dimension:	16.25m

Cost indicator:	Cost indicator:
€113,665 - €136,935	€91,097 - €109,747

2 Bedroom Homes

FRONT ELEVATION

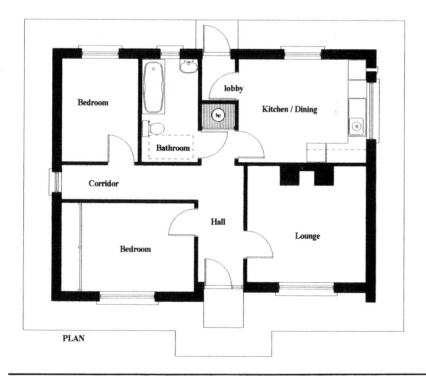

PLAN

No. 1
Kilmore

An ideal first home, holiday home or retirement dwelling, the Kilmore provides two good sized bedrooms, one with built-in wardrobe, a fully fitted bathroom and large living rooms. Provision has been made in the kitchen for a solid fuel or oil boiler. This house can easily be extended later to become a full sized four bedroomed bungalow. The front elevation features a natural stone feature panel, the roof is of concete tiles and the fabric of the house is insulated.

ROOM DIMENSIONS
Kitchen/Dining Room:4190mm x 3200mm
Lounge: 3510mm x 3430mm
Bedroom: 3200mm x 2440mm
Bedroom: 3510mm x 2740mm
Bathroom: 3200mm x 1520mm

Floor area: 68.39 sq. metres
Frontage dimension: 10.30 metres

No. 2
Connaught

This cottage style bungalow is of modest proportions and features a large living area and two fine bedrooms, one with a built in wardrobe. Front and rere access is by means of double glazed sliding doors. The bedroom is fitted with a shower, toilet and washbasin. The design features full insulation, a plaster finish externally and a concrete tiled roof. Access from hall to sitting room is via glazed doors. Note the cottage style entry to the bedrooms.

elevation

ROOM DIMENSIONS

Sitting Room:	3860mm x 3660mm
Kitchen/Dining Room:	4120mm x 2440mm
Bathroom:	2440mm x 1680mm
Hall:	3860mm x 1520mm
Bedroom:	3250mm x 3150mm
Bedroom:	3300mm x 3150mm

Floor Area:	61.15 sq. metres
Frontage dimension:	10.17 metres

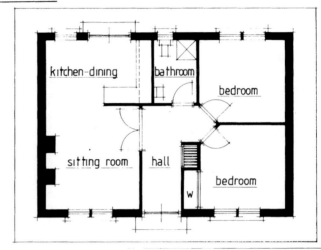

plan

FRONT ELEVATION

PLAN

No. 3
Beaufort

This two bedroomed bungalow has a dormer roof capable of providing two further bedrooms and a bathroom in the roof space. Windows are described on the elevation to light the roof area and the stairs is indicated in dotted line. Initial accommodation provides a large kitchen/dining room with provision for a solid fuel cooker. The sitting room has an open fireplace. The ground floor bathroom is adjacent to the two generously dimensioned bedrooms.

ROOM DIMENSIONS

Sitting Room:	4170mm x 3860mm
Kitchen/Dining Room:	4720mm x 3350mm
Utility Room:	2130mm x 1070mm
Bathroom:	2130mm x 1830mm
Bedroom:	4010mm x 2740mm
Bedroom:	3860mm x 3510mm
Hall:	2080mm wide
Future Attic Rooms:	2590mm x 2540mm
	3860mm x 3000mm
	2900mm x 1680mm

Floor Area:	82.41 sq. metres
Frontage Dimension:	11.27 metres

No. 4
Hawthorn

Two bedroom bungalow with full size living and sleeping accommodation, ideal as a starter or holiday home. This residence can be easily extended to become a four bedroom home at a future date. The front elevation treatment gives the impression of a much larger house and is attractive with quoins and Jacobean glass. Provision has been made for a solid fuel cooker firing a radiator central heating system. The proximity of the hot water cylinder to the heating source makes the design heat efficient.

elevation

plan

ROOM DIMENSIONS

Sitting Room:	4270mm x 4270mm
Kitchen/Dining Room:	4270mm x 3660mm
Hall:	1630mm wide
Utility Room:	1980mm x 1630mm
Bathroom:	2440mm x 1680mm
Bedroom:	3610mm x 3100mm
Bedroom:	3610mm x 3050mm
Floor Area:	89.26 sq. metres
Frontage Dimension:	10.98 metres

No. 5
Melville

This two bedroomed home is designed to facilitate future extensions suited to the provision of two further bedrooms. Note the attractive recess detail and brick features to the front. The design has a large utility room, two open fireplaces and built-in wardrobes. As with all **BLUEPRINT HOME PLANS** we have specified full insulation.

ELEVATION

PLAN

ROOM DIMENSIONS

Living Room:	3960mm x 4140mm
Kitchen:	4880mm x 3050mm
Lounge:	3960mm x 3560mm
Utility Room & HP:	3050mm x 2130mm
Bathroom:	2290mm x 3050mm
Bedroom:	3960mm x 3560mm
Bedroom:	3050mm x 2970mm
Floor Area:	102.30 sq. metres
Frontage Dimension:	14.12 metres

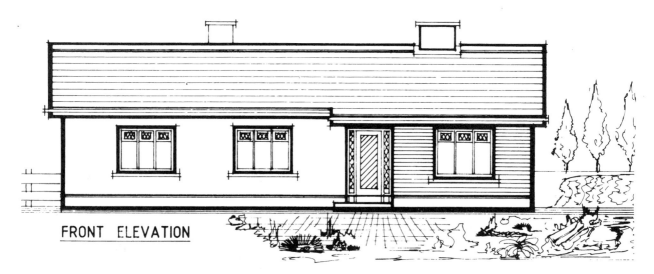

FRONT ELEVATION

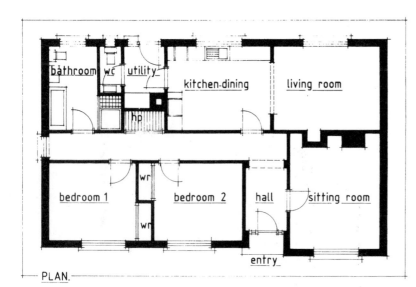

bathroom | wc | utility

kitchen-dining

living room

bedroom 1

wr

bedroom 2

wr

hp

hall

sitting room

entry

PLAN.

No. 6
Kylemore

Two bedroomed bungalow having family sized living accommodation. Fireplaces in living room and sitting room. Provision for solid fuel cooker in Kitchen. Fully fitted bathroom including shower area. Natural daylight in corridor. Built-in wardrobes in two bedrooms.

ROOM DIMENSIONS

Sitting Room:	4520mm x 3660mm
Living Room:	4320mm x 3300mm
Kitchen/Dining Room:	4270mm x 3300mm
Utility Room:	2440mm x 1680mm
Toilet:	1830mm x 970mm
Bathroom:	3300mm x 1980mm
Bedroom:	3660mm x 3050mm
Bedroom:	3560mm x 3050mm

Floor Area:	103.38sq. metres
Frontage Dimension:	14.12 metres

Send your order to:

Michael J. Allen. FASI. MRICS. FGIS. FCIOB.
Architect & Chartered Building Surveyor

BLUEPRINT HOME PLANS
Beechlawn, Kells, Co. Meath.
Telephone: (046) 9240349 Fax: (046) 9241638

No. 7
Mayberry

Similar in elevation to our Hawthorn No. 4 but don't let this deceive you. This house has provision for two further bedrooms in the roof space, without the need for dormer windows. The upper floor also accommodates a half-bathroom. We have included an integral garage with easy access to the dwelling. Provision has been made for a Solid fuel cooker in the Kitchen and an open fireplace in the Sitting Room. Both bedrooms have built-in wardrobes. A practical house design suitable for Town and Country.

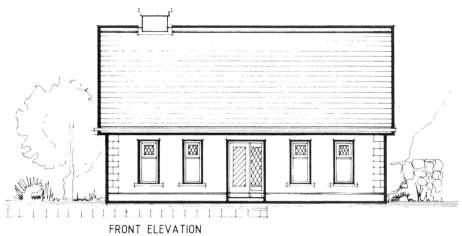

FRONT ELEVATION

ROOM DIMENSIONS

Sitting Room:	4270mm x 3910mm
Kitchen/Dining Room:	4270mm x 3910mm
Utility Room:	2080mm x 2030mm
Bathroom:	2440mm x 1630mm
Garage:	4720mm x 2900mm
Bedroom:	3660mm x 3050mm
Bedroom:	3660mm x 3050mm
Hall:	2080mm wide

Floor Area excluding
Garage: 85.55 sq. metres
Frontage Dimension: 11.40 metres

PLAN

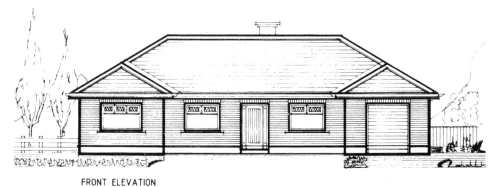

FRONT ELEVATION

No. 8
Nevada

Hipped roof bungalow with integral garage. The sitting room in this design is to the back of the house; has an open fireplace and patio doors opening to the rear garden area. The large kitchen dining room has provision for a solid fuel cooker. Note the covered porch affording access from house to garage. Two bathrooms are provided and built-in wardrobes are indicated in the two generously dimensioned bedrooms.

ROOM DIMENSIONS

Sitting Room:	5840mm x 3960mm
Kitchen/Dining Room:	8280mm x 3510mm
Hall:	1830mm wide
Bedroom:	3050mm x 3050mm
Bedroom:	4270mm x 3660mm
En-suite:	2290mm x 1830mm
Bathroom:	3200mm x 2290mm
Utility Room:	3200mm x 1830mm
Garage:	6100mm x 3660mm

Floor Area including
Garage & Porch: 149.50 sq. metres
Frontage Dimension: 17.57 metres

PLAN

No. 9
Princeton

This attractive two bedroom dormer home has an integral garage. A ground floor shower room is provided. Open fireplaces are shown in the family room and sitting room. The upper floor has two generously dimensioned bedrooms, a bathroom and a walk-in hot press. A further room may be provided over the garage if required.

ROOM DIMENSIONS

Garage: 7320mm x 3660mm
Sitting Room: 4570mm x 4320mm
Family Room: 4320mm x 3760mm
Kitchen/Dining Room: 5990mm x 3560mm
Utility Room: 3350mm x 2640mm
Shower Room: 2640mm x 1420mm
Main Hall: 2130mm wide
Bedroom: 4320mm x 3660mm
Bedroom: 4320mm x 3660mm
Bathroom: 2130mm x 1730mm

Floor Area excluding Garage: 124.43 sq.m
Front Dimension: 15.55 metres

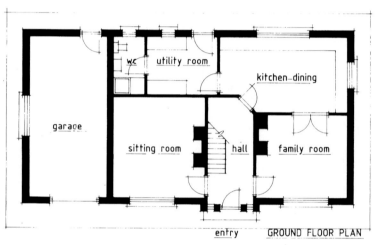

FRONT ELEVATION

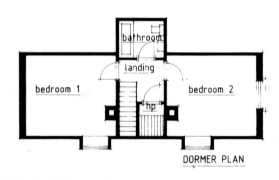

DORMER PLAN

GROUND FLOOR PLAN

entry

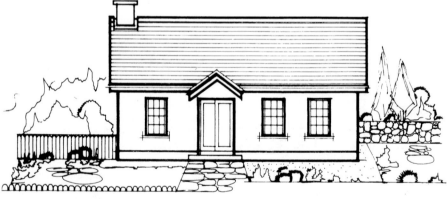

elevation

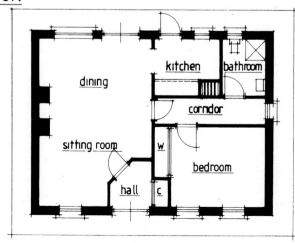

plan

No. 10
Balrath

Here we introduce our one bedroomed holiday cottage. A substantial house with a huge living-dining area featuring an open fireplace and patio doors at the rere. The kitchen is self contained. The unusual shaped entrance hall has a built-in coats press and the bathroom is fully fitted with shower, toilet and wash basin. Dimensions of the master bedroom with built-in wardrobe are generous. This house is fully insulated and features concrete floors, plaster finish externally, concrete roof tiles and double leaf insulated walls. The floor plan can easily be extended to provide two further bedrooms.

ROOM DIMENSIONS

Sitting/Dining Room: 6400mm x 4420mm
(including hall)
Kitchen: 2590mm x 2130mm
Bathroom: 2130mm x 1780mm
Bedroom: 3810mm x 3050mm
Hall: 1680mm x 1680mm

Floor Area: 57.66 sq. metres
Frontage Dimension: 9.60 metres

No. 11
Stanwell

An unusual two bedroomed home offering practical accommodation and traditional design sense. The study on the ground floor can be utilised as a third bedroom. The sitting room has an open fireplace. Two bedrooms with generous dimensions are located on the upper floor, together with a fully fitted bathroom. The elevation features raised and capped gables, and two dormer windows.

FRONT ELEVATION

ROOM DIMENSIONS

Kitchen:	4320mm x 3860mm
Toilet:	1600mm x 1600mm
Dining Room:	3970mm x 3000mm
Study:	3550mm x 3550mm
Sitting Room:	4570mm x 3300mm
Hall:	2430mm wide
Utility Room:	3550mm x 1550mm
Bedroom:	4000mm x 2829mm
Bedroom:	4000mm x 3000mm
Bathroom:	2186mm x 2300mm

Floor Area: 137 sq. metres
Frontage Dimension: 12.77 metres

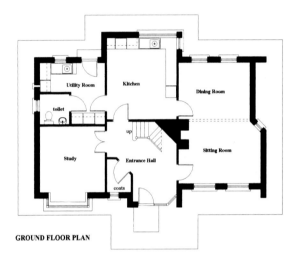

GROUND FLOOR PLAN

DORMER PLAN

29

No. 12
Bredon

This well designed two bedroomed home has a fully insulated fabric. Double glazed windows in pvc with Georgian design are fitted and the front elevation has brick features. The accommodation is nicely laid out and both bedrooms have built-in wardrobes. The sitting room has an open fireplace and provision is made for a boiler or cooker in the kitchen

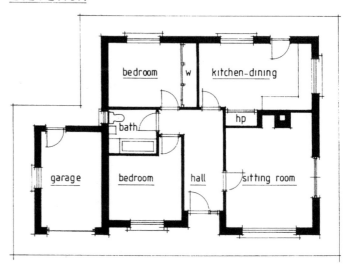

elevation

plan

ROOM DIMENSIONS

Sitting Room:	5180mm x 3960mm
Kitchen/Dining Room:	5130mm x 2950mm
Bedroom:	3350mm x 2950mm
Bedroom:	4120mm x 2850mm
Bathroom:	2180mm x 1930mm
Garage:	4270mm x 2740mm
Hall:	1830mm wide
Floor Area:	87.00 sq. metres
Frontage Dimension:	12.98 metres

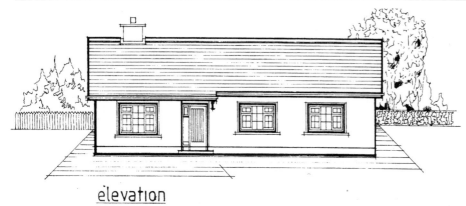

elevation

plan

No.13
Rothley

A traditional elevation with dry dash finish to this attractive two bedroomed bungalow will allow the building to settle well into an existing environment. The accommodation is well laid out and the corridor arrangement will allow for future bedroom extension. The building is fully insulated.

ROOM DIMENSIONS

Sitting Room:	4520mm x 3910mm
Living Room:	4370mm x 3200mm
Kitchen/Dining Room:	4120mm x 3200mm
Utility Room:	2490mm x 1680mm
Bathroom:	3200mm x 1830mm
Hall:	1680mm wide
Bedroom:	3510mm x 3510mm
Bedroom:	3510mm x 3510mm
Floor Area:	105.46 sq. metres
Frontage Dimension:	13.91 metres

No.14
Dalton

This two bedroomed bungalow is ideal as a starter home or a holiday bungalow. The bedrooms are double sized and the kitchen living room is well fitted and provided with an open fireplace. The fabric of the building is fully insulated and the windows are double glazed. Sliding patio doors are provided at the side of the living room. There are built-in wardrobes in both bedrooms.

front elevation

ROOM DIMENSIONS
Kitchen/Living Room: 6710mm x 3760mm
Bedroom: 4120mm x 3150mm
Bedroom: 4120mm x 2740mm
Bathroom: 2130mm x 1730mm
Hall: 1320mm wide

Floor Area: 63.48 sq. metres
Frontage Dimension: 10.09 metres

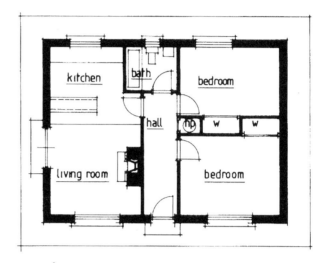

plan

front elevation

No. 15
Whitby

A compact two bedroomed dwelling-house with easy to extend construction. This bungalow has an attractive but simple elevation, finished with dry dash and a tiled roof. All rooms are well appointed and provision is made for a cooker or heating boiler in the kitchen.

ROOM DIMENSIONS
Sitting Room: 3860mm x 3660mm
Kitchen/Dining Room: 4220mm x 3150mm
Bathroom: 3150mm x 1630mm
Bedroom: 4270mm x 2490mm
Bedroom: 3560mm x 2740mm
Hall: 1630mm wide

Floor Area: 69.19 sq. metres
Frontage Dimension: 10.31 metres

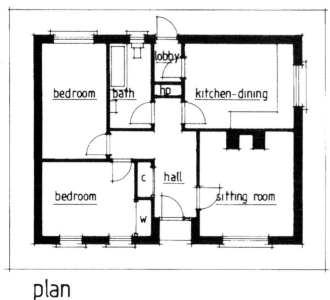

plan

No. 16
Galena

This practical two bedroomed home is easily exended to provide two additional bedrooms later. The accommodation is well laid out and features a large utility room and integral garage. The front elevation features a recessed area with stone panel. The roof is finished with concrete tiles and the building fabric is fully insulated.

front elevation

ROOM DIMENSIONS

Sitting Room	3510mm x 3350mm
Kitchen/Dining Room:	4390mm x 3200mm
Bedroom:	3050mm x 2720mm
Bedroom:	3200mm x 2440mm
Bathroom:	2240mm x 1750mm
Garage:	4750mm x 2460mm
Utility Room:	2460mm x 2130mm
Hall:	1520mm wide

Floor Area: 86.11 sq metres
Frontage Dimension: 12.62metres

plan

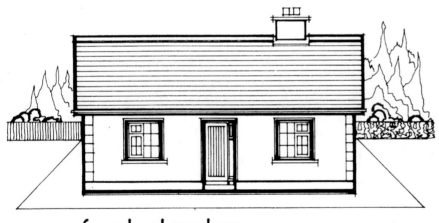

front elevation

No. 17
Millhouse

Start with two bedrooms and extend later with two further bedrooms. This two bedroomed starter home offers well laid out accommodation within a reasonable floor area. The sitting room is provided with an open fireplace and provision is made for a cooker or boiler in the kitchen. All floors are in concrete. The roof is finished with concrete tiles and the exterior is finished with dry dash.

ROOM DIMENSIONS

Kitchen/Dining Room:	4780mm x 2900mm
Sitting Room:	3910mm x 3660mm
Bathroom:	2900mm x 1630mm
Bedroom:	3660mm x 2740mm
Bedroom:	2900mm x 2440mm
Hall:	1520mm wide

Floor Area: 65.75 sq. metres
Frontage Dimension: 10.13 metres

plan

3 Bedroom Bungalows

FRONT ELEVATION

No. 18
Lakefield

This three bedroomed bungalow of modest floor area embraces all the accommodation required for family living. We have located the hot press to open into the kitchen and provision can be made for a solid fuel cooker if required. The master bedroom incorporates a built-in wardrobe. The sitting room has an open fireplace with a boiler grate providing central heating.

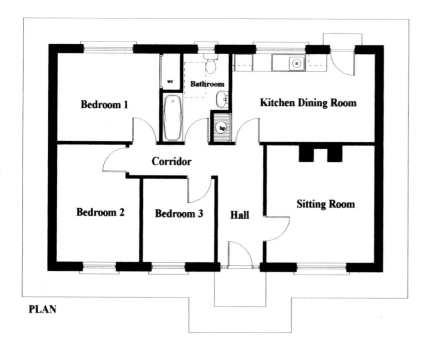

PLAN

ROOM DIMENSIONS

Sitting Room:	4056mm x 3810mm
Kitchen/Dining Room:	5040mm x 3040mm
Bathroom:	1630mm x 3040mm
Bedroom:	3616mm x 3040mm
Bedroom:	4056mm x 2940mm
Bedroom:	2890mm x 2540mm
Entrance Hall:	1620mm wide

Floor Area:	80.66 sq. metres
Frontage:	11.81 metres

No. 19
Miami

An ideal starter home, this three bedroomed bungalow offers ease of construction with good sensible accommodation. Within a very modest floor area we have provided generously sized rooms and an en-suite shower to service the Master bedroom. The roof is comprised of timber trusses and concrete tiles. We have trimmed the front elevation with stone. The kitchen has a solid fuel cooker with hot press nearby and the lounge has an open fireplace.

FRONT ELEVATION

ROOM DIMENSIONS

Sitting Room and Hall:	5340mm x 4570mm
Kitchen/Dining Room:	4830mm x 3350mm
Master Bedroom:	3330mm x 3350mm
En Suite:	2520mm x 910mm
Bathroom:	3350mm x 1780mm
Bedroom 2:	3580mm x 2740mm
Bedroom 3:	3400mm x 2740mm
Utility Room:	2130mm x 1520mm

Floor Area: 94.54 sq. metres
Frontage Dimension: 13.53 metres

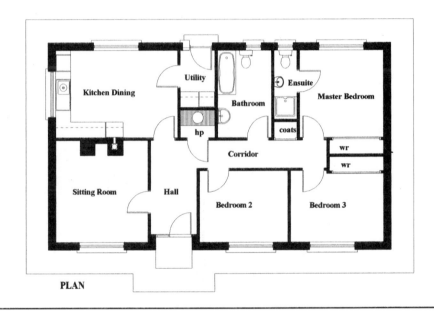

PLAN

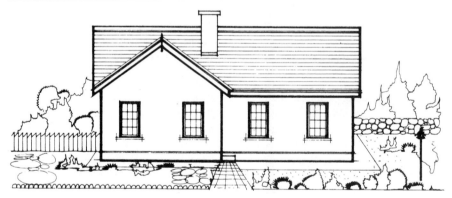

elevation

plan

No. 20
Kilglin

This 'School-house' type design has proved very popular with its attractive layout plan and distinctive front elevation. A modest floor area and well laid out accommodation offers a reasonably costed new home. Roof covering is of concrete tiles, all walls and floors are insulated and the external finish comprises napped plaster.

ROOM DIMENSIONS

Sitting Room and Hall:	5330mm x 4570mm
Kitchen/Dining Room:	4570mm x 2740mm
Bathroom:	2740mm x 1980mm
Bedroom:	2740mm x 2440mm
Bedroom:	3560mm x 2440mm
Bedroom:	2390mm x 2390mm

Floor Area: 73.42 sq. metres
Frontage Dimension: 11.22 metres

No. 21
Cherokee

This bungalow has remained in our design book since 1975. An old reliable, one might say, that has stood the test of time. We have re-designed the elevation to give an up to date appearance with smart white dash and attractive windows. The emphasis here is on a large living/dining area and a compact kitchen. Central heating is provided via the inset fire in the sitting room. Two of the bedrooms have built-in wardrobes.

front elevation

ROOM DIMENSIONS

Sitting/Dining Room: 7010mm x 3960mm
Kitchen: 3510mm x 2590mm
Bathroom: 2590mm x 1730mm
Bedroom: 3610mm x 3350mm
Bedroom: 3000mm x 2620mm
Bedroom: 4060mm x 2640mm
Entrance Hall: 1550mm wide

Floor Area: 90.21 sq. metres
Frontage Dimension: 13.41 metres

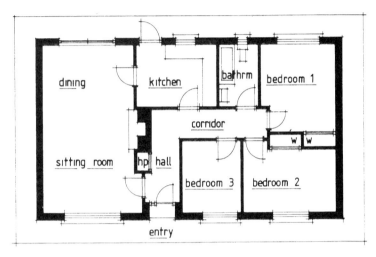

plan

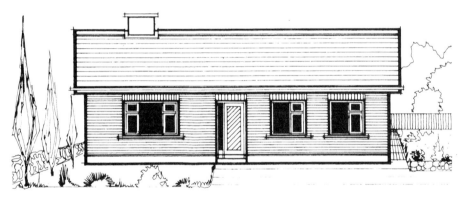

front elevation

No. 22
Lemington

This attractive brick fronted bungalow incorporates three good sized bedrooms and two living rooms within a floor area of a mere 91 sq. metres. The Utility Room is large enough to accommodate a washing machine and deep freeze. We have described a solid fuel cooker in the kitchen and an open fireplace in the sitting room. The roof is finished with concrete tiles. This design is available also in timber frame construction.

ROOM DIMENSIONS

Sitting Room: 4900mm x 3600mm
Kitchen Dining Room: 3900mm x 3900mm
Utility Room: 2000mm x 2000mm
Bathroom: 2700mm x 1700mm
Bedroom: 4100mm x 2700mm
Bedroom: 4800mm x 2900mm
Bedroom: 3600mm x 2400mm
Entrance Hall: 1500mm

Floor Area: 91.00 sq. metres
Frontage: 12.60 metres

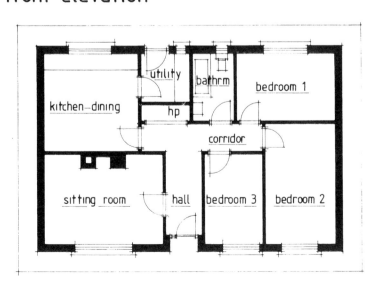

plan

No. 23
Marsdon

A traditionally styled three bedroomed bungalow with capped gables and slated roof. The kitchen dining room has provision for a solid fuel or oil fired cooker and the sitting room has an open fireplace. Two of the three fine bedrooms have built-in wardrobes. A large Utility room is a feature of the design. A recessed entrance with projecting roof and traditional style windows enhance the front elevation.

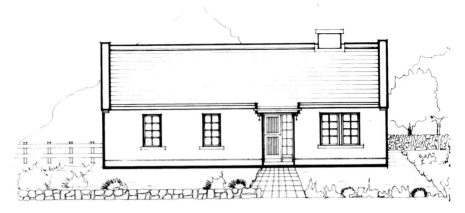

elevation

ROOM DIMENSIONS

Sitting Room:	4420mm x 3810mm
Kitchen/Dining Room:	5490mm x 3350mm
Utility Room:	2490mm x 2440mm
Bathroom:	3350mm x 2440mm
Hall:	1830mm wide
Bedroom:	3660mm x 3050mm
Bedroom:	3200mm x 3050mm
Bedroom:	3350mm x 3200mm

Floor Area: 100.71 sq. metres
Frontage Dimension: 13.55 metres

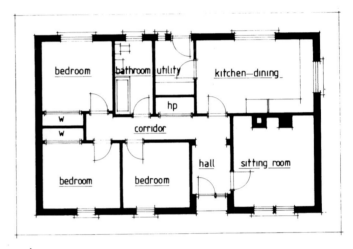

plan

No. 24
Brooklyn

A compact gabled facing bungalow with an amazing 7.80M frontage measurement. The Architect's brief here was to reduce corridor space and we feel he has achieved this requirement. The bedroom block is self contained and provides access with privacy to the bathroom. The large kitchen dining room has provision for a solid fuel cooker. The traditional elevation allows for a balanced brick trim and roofed entrance porch.

ROOM DIMENSIONS

Sitting Room:	4190mm x 3580mm
Kitchen/Dining Room:	7190mm x 3050mm
Bathroom:	2820mm x 1730mm
Bedroom:	4040mm x 3050mm
Bedroom:	3050mm x 3050mm
Bedroom:	2820mm x 2820mm

Floor Area: 87.02 sq. metres
Frontage: 7.78 metres

Plan

Front Elevation

No. 25
Leicester

This attractive brick fronted bungalow provides three good sized bedrooms and an ensuite bathroom with bedroom No. 1. A separate Dining Room is located off the front hall. This room may be used as an extra bedroom if required. Open fireplaces as described in the kitchen and sitting room. We have recessed the front entrance

front elevation

ROOM DIMENSIONS

Kitchen:	4010mm x 3150mm
Utility:	2180mm x 1070mm
Sitting Room:	3760mm x 3505mm
Hall:	1580mm wide
Dining Room:	3660mm x 3505mm
Bedroom 1:	3660mm x 3505mm
En Suite:	2290mm x 2540mm
Bedroom 2:	3710mm x 2900mm
Bathroom:	2900mm x 2030mm
Bedroom 3:	2900mm x 2600mm

Floor Area: 98.34sq. metres
Frontage Dimension: 13.52 metres

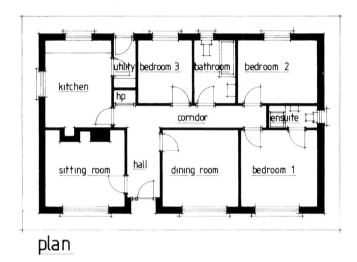

plan

FRONT ELEVATION

No. 26
Kenmare

This three bedroomed bungalow has a hipped roof and attractive styling on the front elevation. The Sitting Room is provided with a bay window. Central heating may be serviced from boiler grates located in the open fireplaces. The master bedroom has an en-suite bathroom. This house will blend with any landscape.

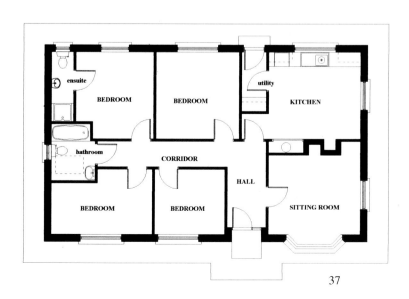

ROOM DIMENSIONS

Sitting Room:	3960mm x 3906mm
Kitchen/Dining Room:	3960mm x 3650mm
Utility Room:	2484mm x 1066mm
Dining Room:	3600mm x 3650mm
Bedroom:	3350mm x 3650mm
En Suite:	2928mm x 960mm
Bathroom:	2382mm x 1900mm
Bedroom:	4366mm x 2740mm
Bedroom:	3040mm x 2740mm
Hall:	1670mm wide

Floor Area: 102.10 sq. metres
Frontage Dimension: 13.94 metres

No. 27
Chelsem

A cottage style bungalow of modest floor area and yet offering full accommodation. The large kitchen-dining room and the well proportioned sitting room each have open fireplaces. Provision has been made for wardrobes in each bedroom. The front entrance is recessed and we have provided a coats press in the hall.

front elevation

ROOM DIMENSIONS

Master Bedroom:	3760mm x 3350mm
Bathroom:	3350mm x 1830mm
Dining/Kitchen Room:	6400mm x 3660mm
Sitting Room:	4270mm x 3610mm
Hall:	1780mm wide
Bedroom:	2740mm x 2590mm
Bedroom:	3250mm x 2740mm

Floor Area: 90.02 sq. metres
Frontage Dimension: 12.80 metres

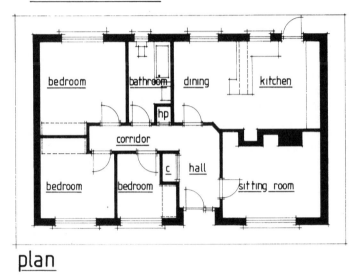

plan

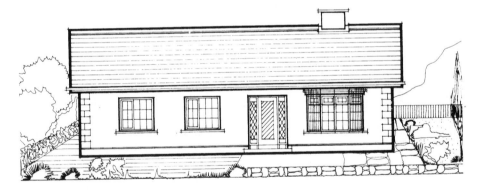

front elevation

No. 28
Hanwell

A fine three bedroomed bungalow with a medium pitch tiled roof and feature bow window to the sitting room. Fireplaces are provided in the kitchen and sitting room. All bedrooms have built-in wardrobes and we have provided an en-suite shower with bedroom No. 1.

ROOM DIMENSIONS

Bedroom 1:	3350mm x 3200mm
Shower Room:	1980mm x 1070mm
Bedroom 2:	3350mm x 2900mm
Bedroom 3:	2900mm x 2900mm
Bathroom:	3200mm x 1370mm
Utility:	2440mm x 1420mm
Kitchen/Dining Room:	6050mm x 3200mm
Lounge:	4220mm x 4060mm
Hall:	2900mm x 1730mm

Floor Area: 96.51sq. metres
Frontage Dimension: 13.72 metres

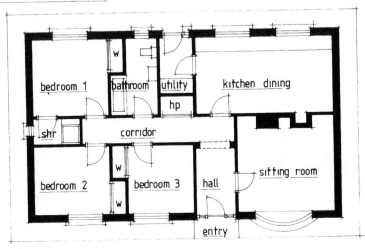

plan

No. 29
Trent

An ideal starter home, this bungalow offers full accommodation and simplicity of construction. All rooms open off a central corridor and the dwelling can be extended with ease. Provision has been made for a dining room. We have included built-in wardrobes in two bedrooms and the bathroom has been provided with a separate shower unit. This residence will suit a town or country site and has an attractive stone feature on the front elevation.

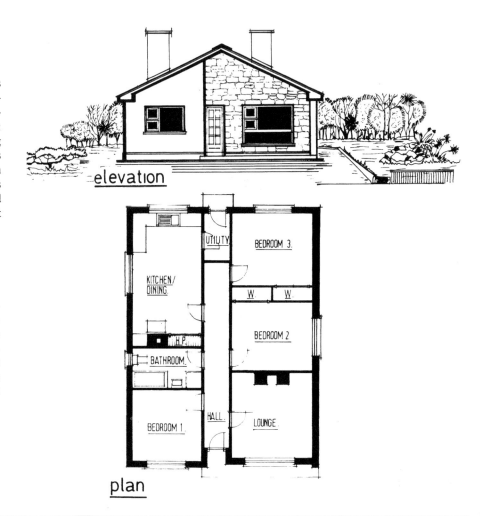

elevation

plan

ROOM DIMENSIONS

Kitchen/Dining Room:	6250mm x 3350mm
Lounge:	3960mm x 3960mm
Bathroom:	3350mm x 1830mm
Utility Room:	2240mm x 1270mm
Bedroom:	3960mm x 3400mm
Bedroom:	3960mm x 3200mm
Bedroom:	3350mm x 3350mm

Floor Area:	101 sq. metres
Frontage Dimension:	9.34 metres

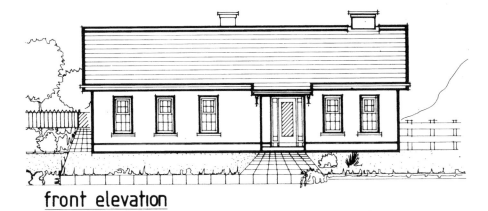

front elevation

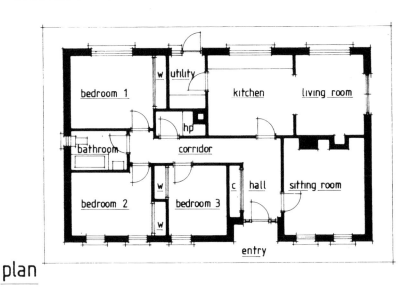

plan

No. 30
Wellington

A well laid out three bedroomed bungalow with a tradional style elevation. We have provided three good sized rooms and three well proportioned bedrooms, each having built-in wardrobes. Open fireplaces are shown in both the living room and sitting room. Central heating may be provided from a solid fuel cooker or from a boiler located in the utility room. We have provided a walk in hot press and a fully fitted bathroom.

ROOM DIMENSIONS

Sitting Room:	4270mm x 3660mm
Living Room:	3560mm x 3050mm
Kitchen:	3960mm x 3560mm
Utility Room:	2340mm x 1630mm
Entrance Hall:	1730mm wide with
	coat press
Bathroom:	2590mm x 1780mm
Bedroom:	3760mm x 3200mm
Bedroom:	3760mm x 2740mm
Bedroom:	3100mm x 2640mm

Floor Area:	105 sq. metres
Frontage Dimension:	13.87 metres

No. 31
Ferndale

We have grouped the living areas together in this reasonably costed bungalow. The bedrooms have fitted wardrobes. Provision has been made for a solid fuel cooker in the kitchen and open fireplaces in the sitting room and dining area. Note the proximity of the walk-in hot press to the solid fuel cooker, ensuring virtually no heat loss between cooker and cylinder. A second toilet is located off the utility room. The elevation is well styled with its open portico and a bow window lighting the sitting room.

FRONT ELEVATION

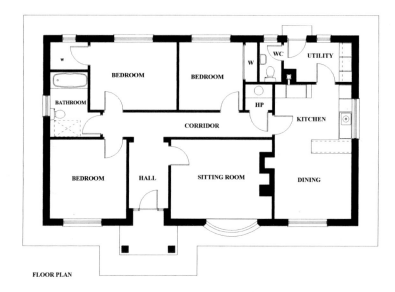

FLOOR PLAN

ROOM DIMENSIONS

Kitchen Dining Room: 5950mm x 3500mm
Utility Room: 3100mm x 1750mm
Toilet: 1750mm x 1000mm
Bedroom: 2900mm x 3000mm
Bedroom: 3900mm x 3000mm
Bedroom: 3500mm x 3500mm
Bathroom: 2885mm x 1750mm
Sitting Room: 4600mm x 3500mm
Hall: 1800mm wide

Floor Area: 106.86 sq. metres
Frontage Dimension: 14.30 metres

elevation

No. 32
Glenfarne

An attractive three bedroomed bungalow with large living rooms. The sitting room has an open fire and provision has been made in the kitchen for a solid fuel cooker. Two of the fine bedrooms have built-in wardrobes and the master bedroom has a shower en-suite. The front elevation is finished with napped plaster and features hardwood decorative shutters.

ROOM DIMENSIONS

Sitting Room: 5080mm x 4170mm
Kitchen/Dining Room: 4880mm x 4170mm
Hall: 1980mm wide
Utility Room: 1980mm x 1680mm
Bathroom: 3050mm x 2290mm
Bedroom: 3960mm x 3050mm
Bedroom: 3050mm x 3000mm
Bedroom: 3200mm x 2740mm

Floor Area: 103.14 sq. metres
Frontage Dimension: 13.72 metres

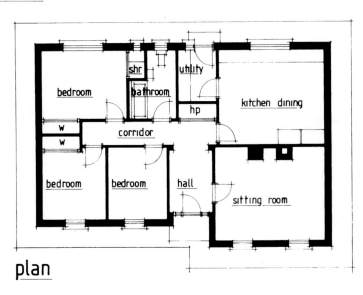

plan

No. 33
Weyburn

The Weyburn three bedroomed bungalow has appeared in all our previous publications. Certainly a measure of popularity! We have however re-vamped the features. The walk-in hot press is located directly behind the solid fuel cooker making the design heat efficient. All three bedrooms now have fitted wardrobes and open fireplaces are described in the family room and sitting room. Features on the front elevation such as granite panels, recessed entrance and Jacobean glazing make our re-vamped Weyburn a very attractive bungalow.

front elevation

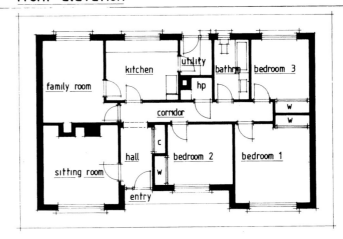

plan

ROOM DIMENSIONS

Sitting Room:	3960mm x 3960mm
Dining Room:	4140mm x 3200mm
Kitchen:	3860mm x 3300mm
Utility Room:	1830mm x 1630mm
Bathroom:	3050mm x 1830mm
Entrance Hall:	1680mm wide with
Bedroom:	coat press
Bedroom:	3960mm x 3730mm
Bedroom:	3050mm x 3050mm
	3400mm x 3050mm

Floor Area:
109.46 sq. metres
Frontage dimension: 14.58 metres

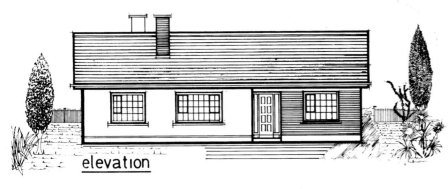

elevation

plan

No. 34
Richmond

This three bedroomed bungalow allows a view to the front of the house from the large kitchen/dining room. We have made provision for a solid fuel or oil fired cooker in the Kitchen with an adjacent hot press. A second toilet facility is provided opening off the utility room. The bedrooms are of adequate dimension and two of them have been provided with built in wardrobes. The front elevation has Georgian styled windows and an attractive brick feature. The front entrance is recessed.

ROOM DIMENSIONS

Kitchen/Dining Room:	5900mm x 3510mm
Lounge:	4570mm x 3450mm
Utility Room:	2850mm x 1730mm
Bathroom:	2440mm x 1830mm
Entrance Hall:	1830mm wide
Bedroom:	3960mm x 3050mm
Bedroom:	3510mm x 3450mm
Bedroom:	3050mm x 2900mm

Floor Area:	106.17 sq. metres
Frontage Dimension: 14.29 meters	

No. 35
Lincoln

Compact simplicity is an apt description for this three bedroomed bungalow with integral garage. The large kitchen/dining room is provided with a solid fuel or oil fired cooker. A service door connects the single car garage with the utility room. The hot press is located in the bathroom. Two of the bedrooms are provided with built-in wardrobes. Externally the dwelling is finished with napped plaster and a tiled roof.

ROOM DIMENSIONS

Kitchen Dining Room:	5440mm x 3050mm
Sitting Room:	3960mm x 3560mm
Bathroom:	3050mm x 1980mm
Utility Room:	3050mm x 1600mm
Garage:	4880mm x 3050mm
Bedroom:	4270mm x 3050mm
Bedroom:	3560mm x 3000mm
Bedroom:	2950mm x 2440mm

Floor Area:	106.65 sq. metres
Frontage Dimension:	15.91 metres

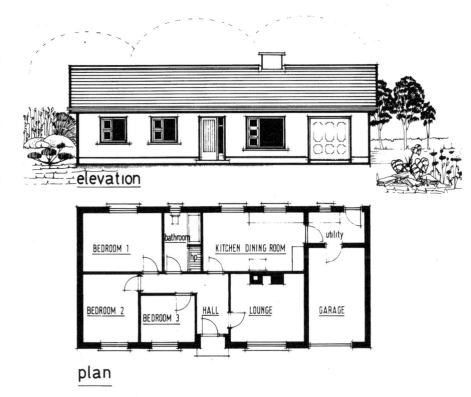

elevation

plan

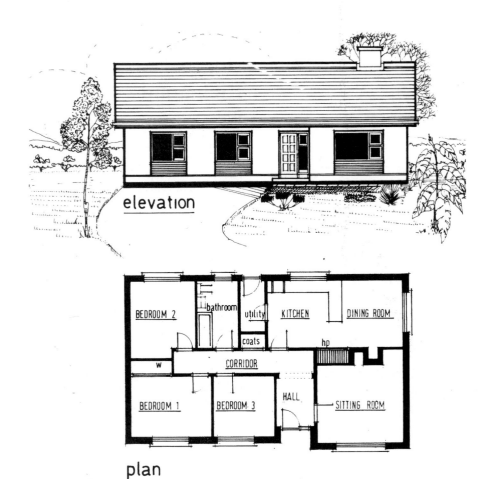

elevation

plan

No. 36
Gwent

A compact three bedroomed bungalow without frills and simple front elevation styling. Open fireplaces in the Dining room and sitting room provide source for the radiator central heating system and the hot press is located adjacent to the firebreast. The bathroom is fully fitted and the master bedroom has a fitted wardrobe. Floors throughout are of concrete insulated and the roof is covered with concrete tiles. Bedrooms are of generous dimensions and you will note that we have provided a fitted coats press in the corridor.

ROOM DIMENSIONS

Sitting Room:	4370mm x 3660mm
Kitchen/Dining Room:	6710mm x 3200mm
Lobby:	2490mm x 1220mm
Bathroom:	3200mm x 1980mm
Bedroom:	3960mm x 2900mm
Bedroom:	3050mm x 2900mm
Bedroom:	3660mm x 3300mm
Entrance Hall:	1930mm wide

Floor Area:	105.09 sq. metres
Frontage Dimension:	14.02 metres

No. 37
Montana

One of the most popular in our range. This three bedroomed bungalow offers good room sizes throughout. Features L shape and stone trim. Two open fireplaces. Two bedrooms having built in wardrobes.

FRONT

ROOM DIMENSIONS

Sitting Room:	4720mm x 4120mm
Dining Room:	4040mm x 3510mm
Kitchen:	4010mm x 2950mm
Rear Lobby, Hot Press, Fitted Bathroom	
Bedroom:	3050mm x 2950mm
Bedroom:	3050mm x 2970mm
Bedroom:	4270mm x 3200mm

Floor Area: 109.65 sq. metres
Frontage Dimension: 14.88 metres

PLAN

FRONT ELEVATION

No. 38
Vienna

No fuss or frills are attached to this compact three bedroomed home. Provision has been made for a solid fuel cooker in the kitchen and an open fireplace in the sitting room. The large utility room, good sized bedrooms and a recessed front door make this a popular design.

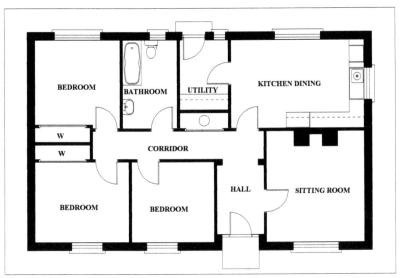

ROOM DIMENSIONS

Sitting Room:	4210mm x 3810mm
Kitchen/Dining Room:	5180mm x 3350mm
Utility Room:	1870mm x 2650mm
Bathroom:	3350mm x 2130mm
Bedroom:	3300mm x 3216mm
Bedroom:	3650mm x 3044mm
Bedroom:	3200mm x 3044mm
Hall:	1820mm wide

Floor Area: 97.89 sq. metres
Frontage: 13.38 metres

No. 39
Greenville

A tradional style three bedroomed bungalow. We have provided an L shape with brick trim and medium pitch concrete tiled roof. The accommodation is fully detailed, each bedroom having fitted wardrobes and vanity units. The master bedroom is serviced with an en-suite bathroom. Note our rear lobby detail with fitted coats press. The kitchen has a solid fuel cooker and the lounge has an open fireplace. Natural daylight is provided in the access corridor by means of a feature window in the gable end wall of the dwelling.

ROOM DIMENSIONS

Lounge:	4060mm x 3960mm
Living/Dining Room:	4120mm x 3960mm
Kitchen:	3660mm x 2970mm
Lobby:	2970mm x 1220mm
Bathroom:	2970mm x 1630mm
En Suite:	2130mm x 1120mm
Bedroom 1:	3560mm x 2850mm
Bedroom 2:	2900mm x 2850mm
Bedroom 3:	3400mm x 2970mm

Floor Area:	121.45 sq. metres
Frontage Dimension:	16.33 metres

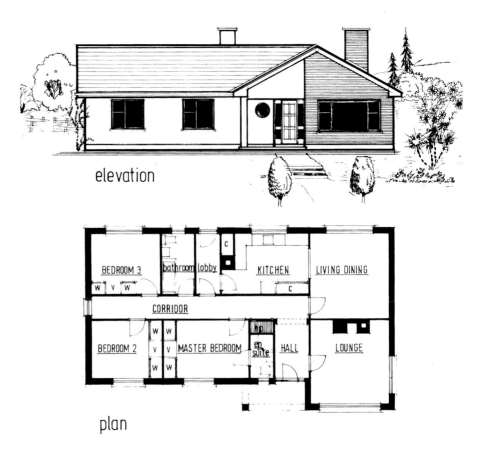

elevation

plan

front elevation

plan

No. 40
Cherryvale

This three bedroomed bungalow is a revamped design from our previous editions and remains one of our most popular designs. We have incorporated three good sized bedrooms with built-in wardrobes. The bathroom is fully fitted and has a shower cabinet. Central heating can be provided from a solid fuel cooker in the kitchen. Note the proximity of the walk-in hot press to the heat source. The bungalow is finished externally in white dash and has a tiled roof.

ROOM DIMENSIONS

Sitting Room:	4780mm x 4170mm
Kitchen/Dining Room:	6250mm x 3350mm
Utility Room:	2130mm x 1520mm
Bathroom:	3350mm x 1830mm
Entrance Hall:	1830mm wide
Bedroom:	3660mm x 3450mm
Bedroom:	3350mm x 3150mm
Bedroom:	3960mm x 3350mm

Floor Area:	120.20 sq. metres
Frontage Dimension:	15.77 metres

No. 41
Primrose

A three bedroomed bungalow of modest proportions and well laid out. The elevation is
along simple lines with stone trim. We have
given a view to the front of the residence
from the kitchen area. All bedrooms have fitted wardrobes. The bathroom is fully fitted
and we have provided a second toilet facility
opening off the utility room. The lounge is
serviced by an open fireplace and provision
has been made for a solid fuel cooker to the
kitchen. Roof covering comprises concrete
tiles.

elevation.

ROOM DIMENSIONS

Kitchen/Dining Room:	6100mm x 3660mm
Lounge:	4570mm x 4270mm
Utility Room:	2440mm x 1980mm
Toilet:	1780mm x 1220mm
Bathroom:	2440mm x 1830mm
Bedroom:	3050mm x 3050mm
Bedroom:	3610mm x 2740mm
Bedroom:	3050mm x 2440mm

Floor Area: 114.76 sq. metres
Frontage Dimension: 15.55 metres

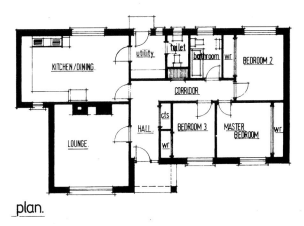

plan.

front elevation

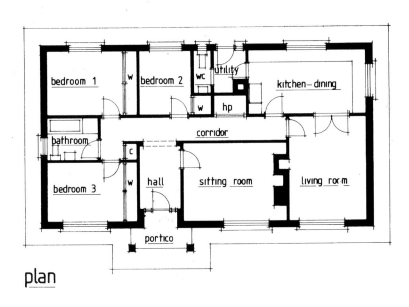

plan

No. 42
Sorrento

Another of our classic style bungalows with
three good bedrooms and an interesting
overall floor plan. The kitchen has a solid
fuel cooker. A second toilet facility is provided opening off the utility room. A pair of
glazed doors lead you from the kitchen to the
large living room. We have located the bathroom at the end of the bungalow giving privacy of access from the three fine bedrooms.
All bedrooms have fitted wardrobes. The sitting room and living room both have open
fireplaces.

ROOM DIMENSIONS

Kitchen:	5540mm x 2950mm
Living Room:	4720mm x 3660mm
Sitting Room:	4830mm x 3560mm
Entrance Hall:	1930mm wide
Utility Room:	1930mm x 1520mm
Toilet:	1930mm x 810mm
Bathroom:	2440mm x 1880mm
Bedroom:	3660mm x 2740mm
Bedroom:	3660mm x 2950mm
Bedroom:	2950mm x 2440mm

Floor Area: 116.32 sq. metres
Frontage Dimension: 15.60 metres

No. 43
Montrose

Full sized three bedroomed bungalow with integral garage. The garage may be converted later to become a fourth bedroom. The gross size of this dwelling with garage included amounts to C. 119.04 sq.m.

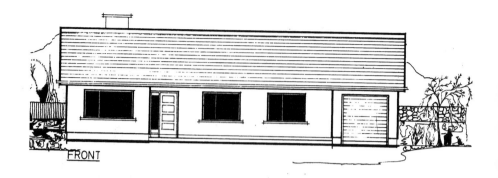
FRONT

ROOM DIMENSIONS

Lounge:	4270mm x 3660mm
Dining Room:	3660mm x 3050mm
Kitchen:	3660mm x 3050mm
Bedroom:	4010mm x 3050mm
Bedroom:	3050mm x 2740mm
Bedroom:	3050mm x 2740mm

Floor Area including garage: 119.04 sq.m
Frontage: 16.45 metres

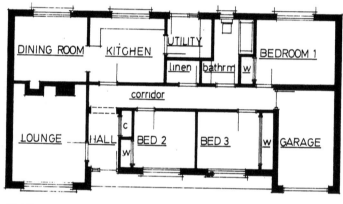
PLAN

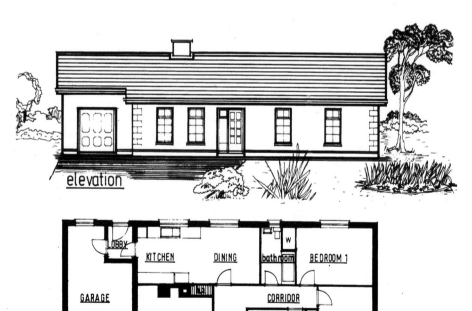
elevation

plan

No. 44
Fiona

A delightful three bedroomed bungalow with integral garage and traditional front elevation. The exterior is finished with napped plaster and raised corner quoins. We have a cut-back feature on the garage roof. The roof pitch is medium with concrete tile finish. Ease of construction makes this a reasonably costed home. The lounge has an open fireplace and provision has been made for a solid fuel cooker in the kitchen. The bathroom is fully fitted with recessed bath, toilet and washbasin and all bedrooms have fitted wardrobes. We have recessed the front entrance door.

ROOM DIMENSIONS

Lounge:	4200mm x 4050mm
Kitchen/Dining Room:	6850mm x 3050mm
Garage:	6000mm x 3600mm
Lobby:	1750mm x 1400mm
Bathroom:	1900mm x 3050mm
Bedroom:	4200mm x 3050mm
Bedroom:	4050mm x 3000mm
Bedroom:	3200mm x 2850mm

Floor Area: 97.29 sq. metres
Frontage: 16.65 metres

No. 45
Verona II

The overall profile of this house is similar to No. 60 Verona but in extended format. We have provided five bedrooms with the master bedroom having a bathroom en-suite. All bedrooms have built in wardrobes. The dining area extends into a semi-circular window space. This house is featured in photographs in our book with a brick finish to the front.

FRONT ELEVATION

ROOM DIMENSIONS

Kitchen Dining:	4260mm x 6850mm
Sitting Room:	4920mm x 4360mm
Hall:	1820mm wide
Utility:	2000mm x 2390mm
Bathroom:	2125mm x 3250mm
En-suite:	1575mm x 3250mm
Master Bedroom:	3975mm x 3250mm
Bedroom:	3183mm x 3225mm
Bedroom:	2983mm x 3350mm
Bedroom:	2750mm x 3268mm
Bedroom:	2750mm x 3268mm

Gross Floor Area: 172.50 sq. metres
Frontage Dimension: 18.28 metres

FLOOR PLAN

front elevation

No. 46
Charmont

Behind this simple elevation we have provided an easy way to heat this compact three bedroom bungalow. Open fireplaces are provided in the family room and sitting room and a solid fuel cooker in the kitchen. Note the proximity of the hot press to the solid fuel cooker and cylinder. The three bedrooms are well proportioned and incorporate built-in wardrobes. An en-suite shower is located off the master bedroom.

ROOM DIMENSIONS

Family Room:	3960mm x 3510mm
Kitchen/Dining Room:	5490mm x 3960mm
Sitting Room:	4170mm x 3810mm
Utility Room:	2180mm x 1780mm
Toilet:	1780mm x 1070mm
Bathroom/Hot Press:	3200mm x 2740mm
Bedroom:	3810mm x 3200mm
Bedroom:	3200mm x 3200mm
Bedroom:	3200mm x 3150mm
Entrance Hall:	1730mm wide

Floor Area: 124.71 sq. metres
Frontage Dimension: 14.63 metres

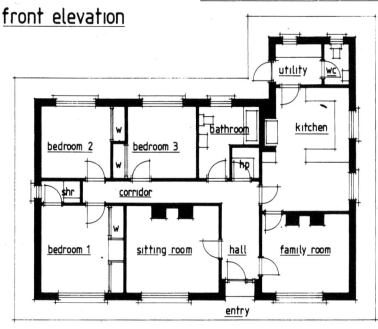

plan

No. 47
Hampton

This three bedroomed bungalow is ideal for future expansion. We have continued the corridor to meet the gable end wall and provided natural light to this area. Central heating is provided from a solid fuel cooker in the kitchen and a boiler grate in the family room. A toilet is provided opening off the utility area. The living rooms are well laid out and dimensioned and the three family sized bedrooms have built-in wardrobes.

ROOM DIMENSIONS

Sitting Room:	5030mm x 4450mm
Kitchen:	4120mm x 3710mm
Family Room:	4720mm x 3660mm
Utility Room:	2240mm x 1680mm
Toilet:	1680mm x 1370mm
Bathroom:	3350mm x 2240mm
Bedroom:	3660mm x 3350mm
Bedroom:	3200mm x 2850mm
Bedroom:	3200mm x 2850mm
Entrance Hall:	1830mm wide

Floor Area: 124.62 sq. metres
Frontage Dimension: 14.83 metres

front elevation

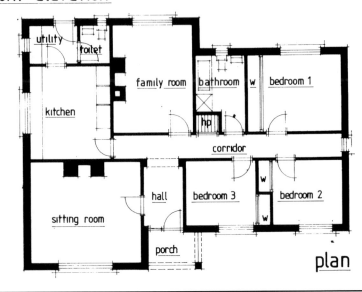

plan

front elevation

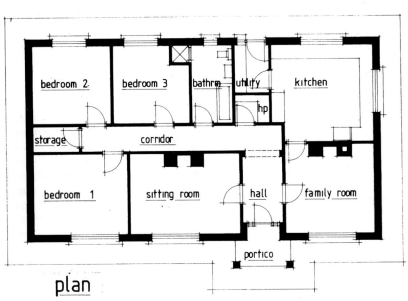

plan

No. 48
Newcastle

This fine bungalow is similar in elevation to our Classic range of houses. The layout describes a sensible three bedroomed bungalow with three good sized living rooms. Open fireplaces are shown in the sitting room and family room. Provision is made for a solid fuel cooker in the kitchen. The fully fitted bathroom includes a shower cabinet. We have indicated a storage area at the end of the corridor and this space could be utilised later to provide an en-suite bathroom. The design incorporates a hipped end slated roof and Georgian windows.

ROOM DIMENSIONS

Family Room:	3960mm x 3860mm
Kitchen:	4570mm x 4170mm
Sitting Room:	5030mm x 3510mm
Utility Room:	1980mm x 1520mm
Bathroom:	3350mm x 1830mm
Bedroom:	4270mm x 3510mm
Bedroom:	3510mm x 3350mm
Bedroom:	3510mm x 3350mm
Entrance Hall:	1780mm wide

Floor Area: 124.25 sq. metres
Frontage Dimension: 15.91 metres

No. 49
Kiltormer

This bungalow is in our now familiar Classic style incorporating three spacious bedrooms each with built-in wardrobes. The master bedroom is provided with an en-suite bathroom. The large kitchen/dining room has provision for a solid fuel cooker. Open fireplaces arc described in the family room and sitting room. A bow window sets off the front elevation. The roof is finished with slates. The detail plans for this design describe a matching detached garage.

ROOM DIMENSIONS

Sitting Room:	5180mm x 3810mm
Family Room:	3710mm x 3660mm
Kitchen/Dining Room:	4670mm x 3400mm
Utility Room:	2030mm x 1730mm
Bathroom:	3400mm x 2240mm
Entrance Hall:	2130mm wide
Bedroom:	4570mm x 3050mm
Bedroom:	3910mm x 2870mm
Bedroom:	3610mm x 2870mm

Floor Area:	124.15 sq. metres
Frontage Dimension:	17.06 metres

front elevation

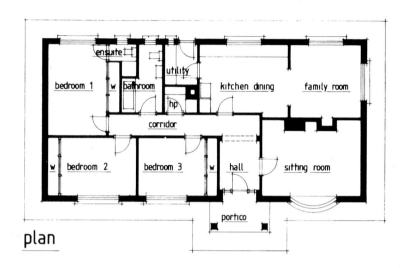

plan

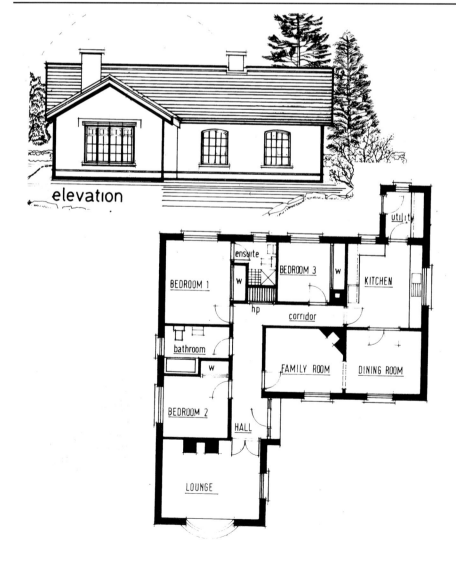

elevation

No. 50
Leinster

This three bedroomed bungalow will sit happily on any town or country site and has a remarkably short frontage dimension. The layout is both interesting and practical. The pleasant L shape allows for a front facing lounge, family room and dining room. Built in wardrobes are provided in each bedroom. The bathroom is fully fitted and an en-suite bathroom services the master bedroom. An open archway connects the family room with the dining room and the family room has a corner fireplace, now presently in vogue. The kitchen is fitted with a solid fuel or oil fired cooker and the utility room is provided with plumbing to cater for your laundry machines.

ROOM DIMENSIONS

Lounge:	4780mm x 3810mm
Dining Room:	3660mm x 3050mm
Family Room:	3860mm x 3050mm
Kitchen:	3910mm x 3660mm
Utility Room:	2130mm x 1830mm
Bathroom:	3150mm x 2240mm
Bedroom:	3910mm x 3150mm
Bedroom:	2790mm x 2690mm
Bedroom:	3150mm x 2850mm

Floor Area:	137.92 sq. metres
Frontage Dimension:	13.11 metres

No. 51
Rathbrack

This fine bungalow in our Classic style offers generous accommodation within an affordable floor area. Two open fireplaces are provided together with provision for a solid fuel or oil fired cooker. The master bedroom features a full wall wardrobe and a shower ensuite. The remaining two bedrooms each have built-in wardrobes. The bathroom is fully fitted and incorporates a separate shower cabinet. This design also features a large utility room with toilet facility opening off and a walk-in hotpress

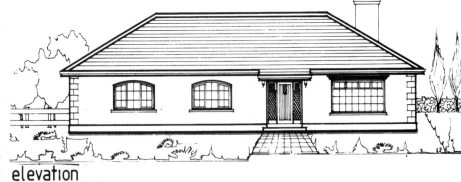

elevation

ROOM DIMENSIONS

Sitting Room:	4980mm x 3960mm
Dining Room:	3300mm x 3200mm
Kitchen:	4720mm x 3300mm
Utility Room:	2130mm x 1680mm
Toilet:	2130mm x 910mm
Bathroom:	3300mm x 2290mm
Hall:	2080mm wide
Bedroom:	4170mm x 3250mm
Bedroom:	3300mm x 2640mm
Bedroom:	3560mm x 3250mm

Floor Area: 123.23 sq. metres
Frontage Dimension: 16.76 metres

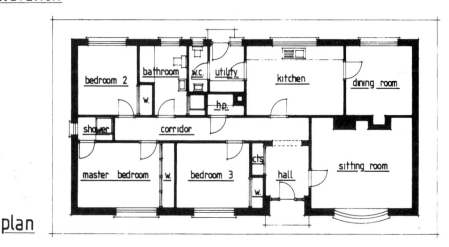

plan

front elevation

No. 52
Dunbarton

This elegant three bedroomed bungalow is suited to a rural location. Note the utility and shower room arrangement and the family room opening adjacent to the kitchen. We have included a solid fuel cooker and two open fireplaces. All bedrooms have built-in wardrobes and a fully fitted bathroom is located at the end of the access corridor. Despite its compact area, this bungalow has a dormer trussed roof that will accommodate two further bedrooms and a half bathroom at a future date.

ROOM DIMENSIONS

Kitchen:	4570mm x 3250mm
Family Room:	4420mm x 3510mm
Sitting Room:	4270mm x 3510mm
Utility Room:	2540mm x 1630mm
Toilet & Shower:	2540mm x 1470mm
Bathroom:	2690mm x 1830mm
Bedroom:	3810mm x 3250mm
Bedroom:	3960mm x 2740mm
Bedroom:	3250mm x 2900mm

Floor Area: 123.88 sq. metres
Frontage Dimension: 16.05 metres

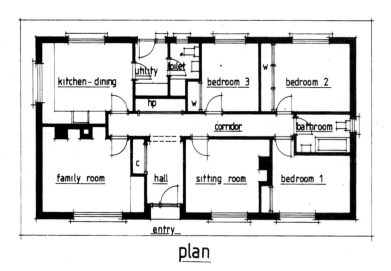

plan

No. 53
Castlecoole

A full sized three bedroomed family home with a distinctive elevation and roof lines. The picture windows and plaster quions compliment the elevation. Accommodation is well laid out and all bedrooms have built-in wardrobes. The master bedroom has a bathroom en-suite. Provision has been made for a solid fuel cooker in the kitchen/dining room. The family room and sitting room have open fireplaces. You will see that we have isolated the sleeping areas from the living areas.

front elevation

ROOM DIMENSIONS

Sitting Room:	5330mm x 4170mm
Family Room:	4270mm x 3960mm
Kitchen/Dining Room:	4780mm x 3100mm
Utility Room:	2080mm x 1730mm
Bathroom:	3100mm x 2080mm
Bedroom:	3910mm x 3250mm
Bedroom:	3100mm x 3100mm
Bedroom:	3050mm x 2950mm
Entrance Hall:	2130mm wide

Floor Area: 124.18 sq. metres
Frontage Dimension: 16.53 metres

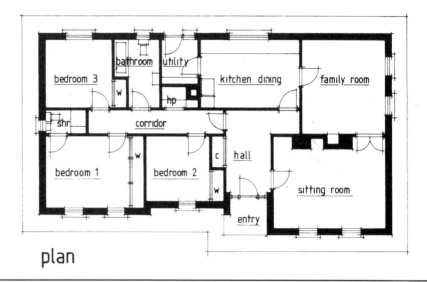

plan

elevation

No. 54
Newhaven

This is one of our more popular designs, being the reverse of our design No. 47, with an integral garage added. Again we have grouped the living areas together for heat efficiency and ease of circulation. Front elevation remains simple with attractive curved lintels and Georgian windows. The roof is of medium pitch and is finished with slates.

plan

ROOM DIMENSIONS

Lounge:	5030mm x 4450mm
Kitchen:	4120mm x 3710mm
Family Room:	4720mm x 3660mm
Utility Room:	2240mm x 1680mm
Toilet:	1680mm x 1370mm
Bathroom:	3350mm x 2240mm
Bedroom 1:	3660mm x 3350mm
Bedroom 2:	3200mm x 2850mm
Bedroom 3:	3200mm x 2850mm
Garage:	7470mm x 3810mm

Floor Area: 124.62 sq. metres
Frontage Dimension: 18.87 metres

No. 55
Olympus

Interesting roof lines and a sensible layout make this bungalow one of the most popular with our clients. The integral garage is ideal for future conversion. The three living rooms, two with open fireplaces and a solid fuel cooker in the kitchen are of generous dimensions. A second toilet facility is provided opening off the utility room. Two bedrooms have fitted wardrobes and the fully fitted bathroom has a separate shower cabinet.

elevation

ROOM DIMENSIONS

Sitting Room:	4880mm x 3960mm
Dining Room:	4370mm x 3660mm
Kitchen:	4720mm x 3200mm
Utility Room:	2290mm x 1220mm
Bathroom:	3200mm x 2290mm
Hall:	1680mm wide
Bedroom:	4270mm x 3200mm
Bedroom:	3530mm x 2900mm
Bedroom:	2900mm x 2900mm
Garage:	4880mm x 3960mm

Floor Area:	121.55 sq. metres
Frontage Dimension:	17.76 metres

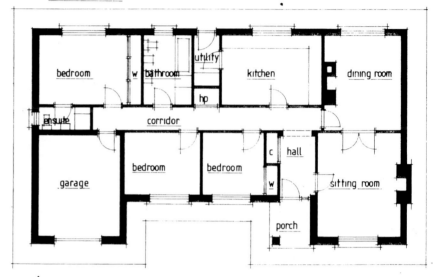

plan

elevation

plan

No. 56
Algarve

This bungalow has a touch of class. Observe the brick trim to the front. This finish returns along the wall of the cloistered walkway to the front entrance. Internally an exposed brick wall divides the hall and the bedroom behind it. The cloistered theme is carried through across to the garage and conceals a private patio behind. A pair of matching bow windows are fitted on the dining room and living room, both rooms having open fireplaces. The large family kitchen has a solid fuel cooker. Each of the three double sized bedrooms have fitted wardrobes. Bedroom No. 3 has its own private shower cabinet.

ROOM DIMENSIONS

Living Room:	4880mm x 3960mm
Dining Room:	3960mm x 3660mm
Kitchen:	4720mm x 3960mm
Utility Room:	3250mm x 1880mm
Toilet:	1980mm x 1020mm
Bathroom:	2740mm x 2130mm
Bedroom 1:	3960mm x 3960mm
Bedroom 2:	3990mm x 3660mm
Bedroom 3:	4270mm x 3070mm
Garage:	5490mm x 3050mm

Floor Area:	143.03 sq. metres
Frontage Dimension:	13.00 metres

No. 57
Portland

The Portland Bungalow gives you circa 124.53 sq.m. of living area initially and circa 21.39 sq.m. convertible garage area. The bungalow contains one fireplace and a boiler house under the main roof, Georgian style windows and a 25 degree pitched and tiled roof. Separate shower and toilet facilities adjoin the main bathroom.

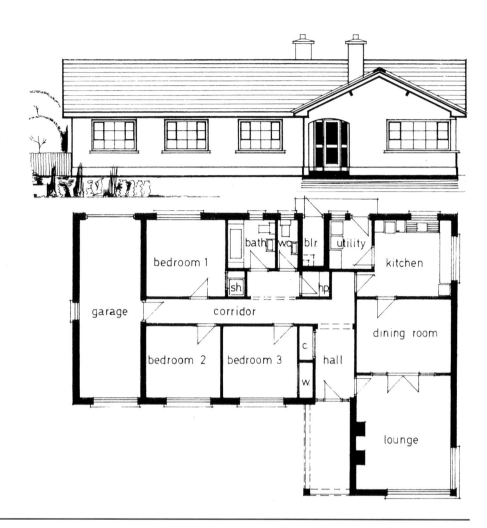

ROOM DIMENSIONS

Lounge:	4880mm x 4320mm
Dining Room:	4320mm x 3200mm
Kitchen:	3660mm x 3350mm
Entrance Hall:	1830mm wide
Bathroom:	2130mm x 2130mm
Bedroom:	3580mm x 3350mm
Bedroom:	3350mm x 3100mm
Bedroom:	3350mm x 3100mm

Future Bedrooms:

Bedroom:	3350mm x 3100mm
Bedroom:	3350mm x 3100mm

Floor Area excluding
convertible garage area: 124.53 sq. metres
Frontage: 17.40 metres

FRONT ELEVATION

plan

No. 58
Winnipeg

A delightful three bedroomed home with integral garage. The garage can be converted later to a bedroom. Stone features to the front elevation. This design dispenses with the need for gable end windows and therefore makes the plan suitable for a town site.

ROOM DIMENSIONS

Sitting Room:	4880mm x 3960mm
Dining Room:	4370mm x 3510mm
Kitchen:	3660mm x 3200mm
Garage:	4880mm x 2670mm
Bedroom:	4270mm x 3200mm
Bedroom:	3510mm x 2900mm
Bedroom:	2850mm x 2900mm

Floor Area: 116.43 sq. metres
Frontage: 16.45 metres

No. 59
Dominique

This fine three bedroomed bungalow with it's integral garage and traditional front elevation provides for full family living. We have provided a study opening off the front hall that may in fact be used as an extra bedroom, if required. A second toilet facility is located opening off the utility room. The kitchen has provision for a solid fuel cooker and the sitting room has an open fireplace. Note the proximity of the hot press to the solid fuel cooker. All bedrooms have fitted wardrobes.

front elevation

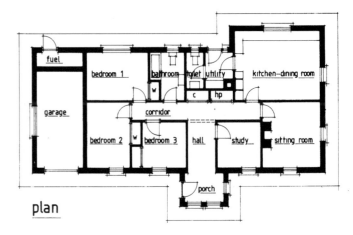

plan

ROOM DIMENSIONS

Sitting Room:	4100mm x 3800mm
Study:	2900mm x 2800mm
Kitchen Dining Room:	5500mm x 4300mm
Utility Room:	2300mm x 1900mm
Toilet:	2300mm x 1100mm
Bathroom:	3000mm x 2200mm
Garage:	6000mm x 3000mm
Bedroom:	4000mm x 3000mm
Bedroom:	4100mm x 2800mm
Bedroom:	2900mm x 2800mm
Entrance Porch:	2500mm x 1800mm

Floor Area: 120.00 sq. metres
Frontage: 18.95 metres

front elevation

plan

No. 60
Verona

This magnificent three bedroomed bungalow with integral Garage offers full design features from the elegant elevation to the semicircular window detail at the dining area. All bedrooms have fitted wardrobes and the master bedroom is provided with an en-suite bathroom. The garage is ideal for later conversion for use as a fourth bedroom. A boiler room in the garage area takes care of the central heating boiler.

ROOM DIMENSIONS

Sitting Room:	4930mm x 4370mm
Kitchen:	4270mm x 3810mm
Dining Room:	5790mm x 3050mm
Utility Room:	1980mm x 2440mm
Bathroom:	3250mm x 2030mm
En Suite:	2440mm x 1220mm
Entrance Hall:	1830m wide
Bedroom:	3810mm x 3250mm
Bedroom:	3200mm x 2740mm
Bedroom:	3200mm x 2740mm
Garage:	5490mm x 3350mm
Boiler Room:	1850mm x 1370mm

Floor Area excluding
Garage: 136.15 sq.metres
Frontage Dimension: 18.31 metres

No. 61
Trinity

This is one of our Classic style bungalows with an integral garage. Built in wardrobes are provided in each bedroom and the garage is suited to later conversion as a fourth bedroom. Two open fireplaces are provided and we have made provision for a solid fuel cooker in the kitchen. The bathroom is fully fitted and incorporates a separate shower cabinet. A second toilet facility is described opening off the utility room. The building features a slated roof and an attractive entrance portico.

front elevation

ROOM DIMENSIONS

Kitchen:	4320mm x 3660mm
Utility:	2130mm x 1730mm
Toilet:	2130mm x 1020mm
Bathroom:	3150mm x 2340mm
Bedroom 2:	3350mm x 3150mm
Bedroom 1:	4270mm x 3150mm
Garage:	4550mm x 2900mm
Bedroom 3:	3960mm x 3510mm
Hall:	1830mm wide
Sitting Room:	3990mm x 3510mm
Family Room:	3660mm x 3510mm

Floor Area: 124.43 sq. metres
Frontage Dimension: 18.14 metres

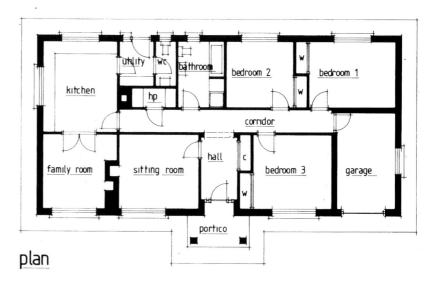

plan

elevation

plan

No. 62
Ashwood

This fine three bedroomed bungalow has a traditionally styled hipped end roof, finished with slates. Three bedrooms are provided, each with built in wardrobes. The master bedroom has a bathroom en-suite. Provision is made for two open fireplaces and a Myson boiler in the utility room. The living rooms are generously proportioned. Full insulation is provided throughout.

ROOM DIMENSIONS

Living Room:	4600mm x 3600mm
Bathroom:	3400mm x 2300mm
Kitchen/Dining Room:	4900mm x 3400mm
En Suite:	2100mm x 1200mm
Sitting Room:	4600mm x 3300mm
Bedroom:	4600mm x 3300mm
Hall:	2000mm wide
Bedroom:	3400mm x 3200mm
Utility Room:	2400mm x 1600mm
Bedroom:	3800mm x 2800mm
Garage & Store:	8100mm x 3000mm

Floor Area: 124.09 sq. metres
Frontage: 16.48 metres

No. 63
Miltown

A traditional appearance externally and an exciting and different layout internally, this three bedroomed home offers adequate living and sleeping areas within a modest floor area.

ROOM DIMENSIONS

Kitchen/Dining Room:	4270mm x 3660mm
Study:	2590mm x 2440mm
Utility:	2440mm x 1520mm
Living Room:	3960mm x 3660mm
Bathroom:	2440mm x 2440mm
Bedroom:	2740mm x 2440mm
Bedroom:	2740mm x 2590mm
Bedroom:	3350mm x 2740mm

Floor Area: 90.28 sq. metres
Frontage Dimension: 14.18 metres

elevation

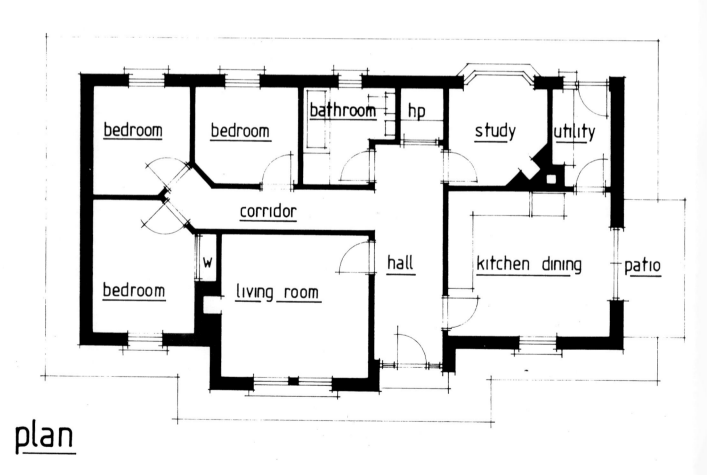

plan

No. 64
Ballina

A simple elevation that uncovers an impressive layout incorporating three Bedrooms, sitting room, dining room, kitchen, utility room, workroom and garage. This design would be particularly suited to a south facing elevation.

ROOM DIMENSIONS

Bedroom:	3600mm x 3900mm
Bedroom:	2800mm x 3900mm
Bathroom:	2300mm x 3900mm
Bedroom:	4700mm x 3900mm
Dining Room:	3800mm x 4000mm
Kitchen:	3600mm x 4000mm
Hall:	1900mm wide
Sitting Room:	5400mm x 4000mm

Floor Area:	169 sq. metres
Frontage:	15.00 metres

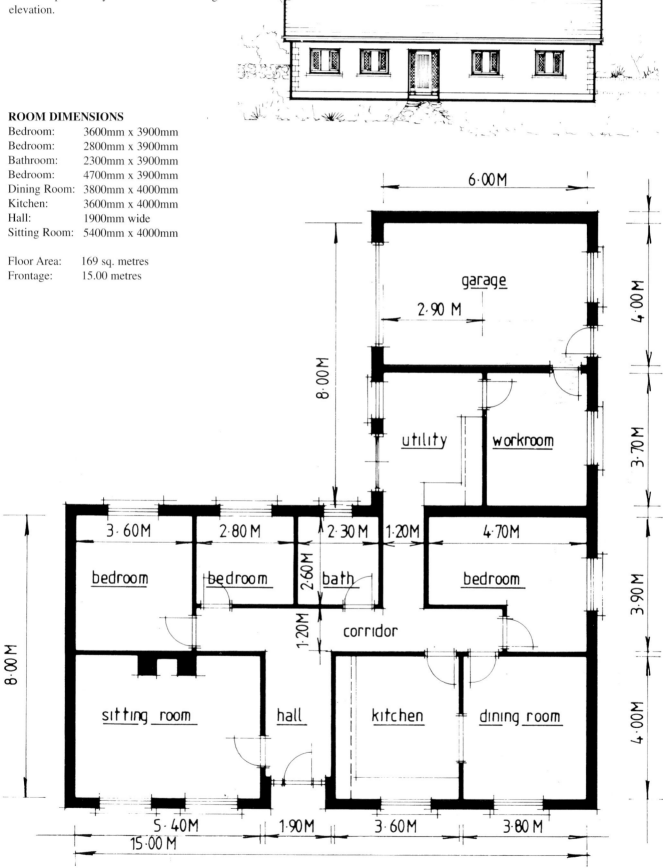

No. 65
Loughan

A well trusted design concept featured in our original publication in 1981, this Classic style bungalow has well laid out accommodation with the living rooms and bedrooms in separate wings. All bedrooms have built in wardrobes.

elevation

ROOM DIMENSIONS

Sitting Room:	4120mm x 3660mm
Family Room:	3910mm x 3400mm
Kitchen/Dining Room:	7370mm x 3350mm
Utility Room:	2240mm x 2180mm
Entrance Hall:	1980mm wide
Bedroom:	3300mm x 2790mm
Bedroom:	3910mm x 3350mm
Bedroom:	3660mm x 3350mm
Bathroom:	3350mm x 2590mm

Floor Area:	124.08 sq. metres
Frontage:	17.46 metres

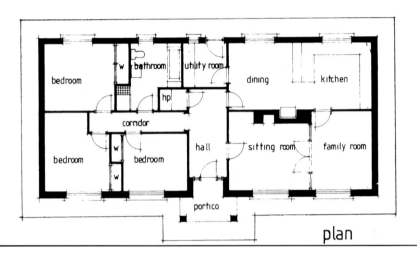

plan

ELEVATION

No. 66
Canada

A compact three bedroomed bungalow that has been popular with our design office for over ten years now. This home gives practical accommodation within a modest floor area. The external finish is white dash and the roof has concrete tiles.

PLAN

ROOM DIMENSIONS

Kitchen / Dining:	5800mm x 3500mm
Sitting Room:	4000mm x 3500mm
Bathroom:	2000mm x 2000mm
Bedroom:	3380mm x 3500mm
Bedroom:	2400mm x 3000mm
Bedroom:	2400mm x 2700mm

Floor Area:	87.78 sq metres
Frontage:	12.00 metres

No. 67
Woodgreen

This three bedroomed bungalow has brick features at the front elevation and bay windows featured at the sitting room and master bedroom. A large kitchen/dining room and living area with open plan design, leads into an attractive sun room. The utility room is fully fitted and the master bedroom has a bathroom en-suite. This dwelling can be extended into the roof space later and the stairs location is shown in the hall. The upper floor would have two bedrooms and a bathroom.

ROOM DIMENSIONS

Living Area:	4500mm x 3810mm
Kitchen/Dining Room:	4970mm x 3810mm
Utility:	1800mm x 2685mm
Bathroom:	2300mm x 3610mm
Bedroom 1:	4500mm x 4650mm
En-suite:	2554mm x 1400mm
Bedroom 2:	4250mm x 3350mm
Bedroom 3:	3720mm x 3610mm
Hall:	2740 wide
Sitting Room:	4500mm x 5950mm
Sun Room:	3200mm x 3650mm

Floor Area: 162.27 sq.m. (excl. sun room)
Frontage: 18.19 metres

FRONT ELEVATION

FLOOR PLAN

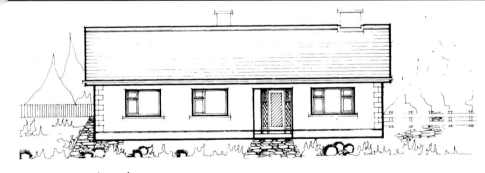

elevation

No. 68
Gatwick

This three bedroomed bungalow of modest floor area offers well laid out accommodation. Three good bedrooms have built-in wardrobes. Open fireplaces are provided in the living room and sitting room. Provision is made for a solid fuel or oil fired cooker in the kitchen. External finish is in white dash.

ROOM DIMENSIONS

Sitting Room:	4220mm x 4060mm
Living Room:	3350mm x 3100mm
Kitchen/Dining Room:	4320mm x 3350mm
Utility Room:	2130mm x 1680mm
Entrance Hall:	1830mm wide
Bedroom:	3050mm x 3050mm
Bedroom:	3760mm x 3050mm
Bedroom:	4520mm x 2900mm
Bathroom:	3350mm x 1930mm

Floor Area: 109.40 sq. metres
Frontage: 14.89 metres

plan

No. 69
Meadows

This compact three bedroomed bungalow features a large sitting room and kitchen/dining room. The three bedrooms are good sized and two have built-in wardrobes. A walk-in hot press is included. The roof is finished in concrete tiles and the front elevation has a brick panel and an attractive roof detail over the front entrance.

front elevation

ROOM DIMENSIONS

Sitting Room:	5180mm x 3660mm
Kitchen/Dining Room:	4420mm x 3660mm
Bathroom:	3050mm x 1580mm
Bedroom:	3610mm x 3050mm
Bedroom:	2440mm x 2440mm
Bedroom:	3610mm x 3050mm
Hall:	1580mm wide

Floor Area: 84.69 sq. metres
Frontage Dimension: 9.60 metres

plan

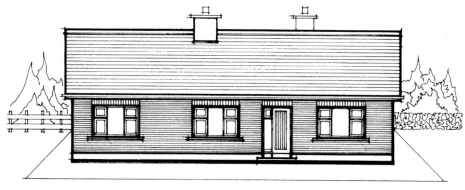

front elevation

No. 70
Sanford

This full-sized family home has a brick outer leaf wall all around. Three good sized bedrooms have provision for built-in wardrobes and one bedroom has a shower ensuite. The large family kitchen is well fitted and has provision for boiler or solid fuel cooker. Floors are in concrete and the roof may be finished with tiles or slates.

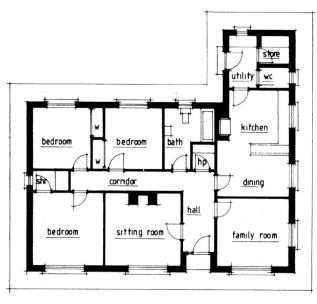

plan

ROOM DIMENSIONS

Family Room:	3910mm x 3510mm
Sitting Room:	4120mm x 3760mm
Kitchen/Dining Room:	5490mm x 3910mm
Utility Room:	2690mm x 1520mm
Bathroom / Hot Press:	3150mm x 2740mm
Bedroom:	3760mm x 3760mm
Bedroom:	3150mm x 3100mm
Bedroom:	3150mm x 3100mm

Floor Area: 124.62 sq. metres
Frontage Dimension: 14.42 metres

No. 71
Linwood

This attractive three bedroomed dwelling has brick features on the front elevation. The layout is well designed and has three full-sized bedrooms, all with built-in wardrobes. Provision is made in the utility room for a heating boiler and open fireplaces are provided in the living room and sitting room. The roof is finshed with slates or tiles and all floors are concrete. The fabric of the building is fully insulated.

front elevation

ROOM DIMENSIONS

Living Room:	5390mm x 3660mm
Sitting Room:	4880mm x 3610mm
Kitchen/Dining Room:	4880mm x 3050mm
Bedroom:	3200mm x 3050mm
Bedroom:	3660mm x 3050mm
Bedroom:	3660mm x 2850mm
Bathroom:	2440mm x 1830mm
Utility Room:	2340mm x 1520mm
Hall:	1980mm wide

Floor Area: 124.62 sq. metres
Frontage Dimension: 15.69 metres

plan

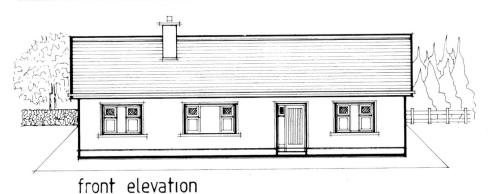

front elevation

No. 72
Martok

This dwelling house has a large kitchen/living room that extends from the front of the house through to the rear wall with provision for a solid fuel or oil-fired cooker. A second toilet is located opening off the Utility Room. The bedrooms are well appointed and two bedrooms have built-in wardrobes. Two fireplaces are provided. The elevation is simple and finished with dry dash, allowing this dwelling to complement a rural or urban environment.

ROOM DIMENSIONS

Kitchen/Living Room:	7620mm x 3660mm
Sitting Room:	4880mm x 3660mm
Utility Room:	1830mm x 2690mm
Bathroom:	2690mm x 1830mm
Bedroom:	3960mm x 3000mm
Bedroom:	3860mm x 2850mm
Bedroom:	2950mm x 2690mm
Hall:	1830mm wide

Floor Area: 111.60 sq. metres
Frontage Dimension: 15.23 metres

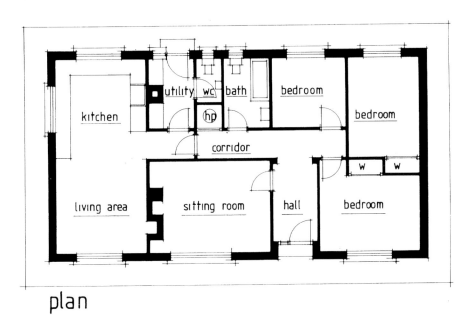

plan

No. 73
Weston

The front elevation on this fine bungalow features a bow window and dry dash finish. The roof is finished with concrete tiles. An integral garage forms part of the design, connecting with a large utility room. The accommodation is well laid out and all bedrooms feature built-in wardrobes. The design incorporates a large kitchen/dining room. Two open fireplaces are provided. All floors are in concrete and insulated.

front elevation

ROOM DIMENSIONS

Sitting Room:	4220mm x 4060mm
Kitchen/Dining Room:	7570mm x 3200mm
Bathroom:	3200mm x 2030mm
Bedroom:	2900mm x 2900mm
Bedroom:	3350mm x 2900mm
Bedroom:	3350mm x 3200mm
Hall:	1730mm wide
Utility Room:	3050mm x 1830mm
Garage:	5310mm x 3050mm

Floor Area: 122 sq. metres
Frontage Dimension: 17.11 metres

plan

front elevation

No. 74
Sable

Generous living accommodation is provided in this bungalow. The Kitchen/Dining Room extends from front to rear and provision is made for two fireplaces and an oil-fired cooker. The proximity of the cooker to the hot press and bathroom ensures efficient water heating. The bathroom is fully fitted and includes a shower cabinet and bath. The sitting room has an open fire. The bedroom accommodation is adequately dimensioned and located away from the living room.

ROOM DIMENSIONS

Kitchen/Living Room:	7820mm x 4060mm
Sitting Room:	4880mm x 3660mm
Utility Room:	2180mm x 2030mm
Bathroom:	3050mm x 1830mm
Bedroom:	4880mm x 3660mm
Bedroom:	4470mm x 3660mm
Bedroom:	4170mm x 3250mm
Hall:	1830mm wide

Floor Area: 123.78 sq. metres
Frontage Dimension: 16.15 metres

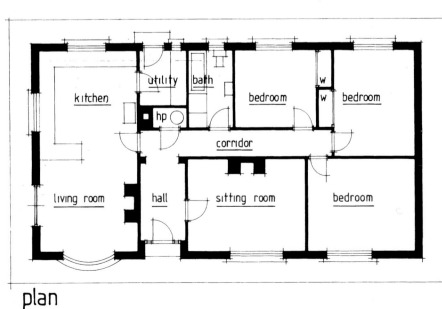

plan

No. 75
Topaz

A full sized family home with a brick exterior and a slated roof, this three bedroomed bungalow is well laid out and has a study which could be used as a fourth bedroom. The design features a large kitchen/dining room and a large sitting room. A large utility room houses the laundry equipment and the heating boiler. All bedrooms have built-in wardrobes and the main bedroom has a bathroom ensuite. All floors arc concrete insulated.

front elevation

ROOM DIMENSIONS

Sitting Room:	5180mm x 3810mm
Kitchen/Dining Room:	5180mm x 3660mm
Utility Room:	2540mm x 1830mm
Study:	3400mm x 2340mm
Bathroom:	2160mm x 1470mm
Bedroom:	4570mm x 3050mm
Bedroom:	4220mm x 2900mm
Bedroom:	3610mm x 2900mm
Hall:	1830mm wide

Floor Area: 125.28 sq. metres
Frontage Dimension: 17.07 metres

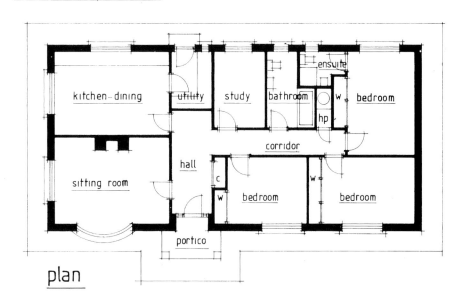

plan

elevation

No. 76
Cheldon

This three bedroomed bungalow has a large integral garage, suitable for later conversion to two bedrooms. The large kitchen/dining room has provision for an oil fired cooker or central heating boiler. Two bedrooms have built-in wardrobes. The front elevation has a limestone feature and the roof may be finished with tiles or slates. All floors are concrete and the entire fabric of the building is fully insulated

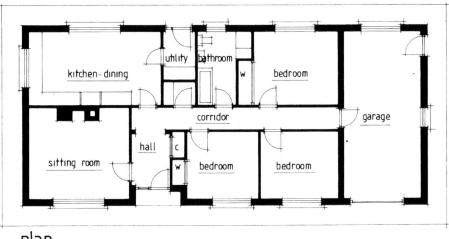

plan

ROOM DIMENSIONS

Sitting Room:	4780mm x 4170mm
Kitchen/Dining Room:	6250mm x 3350mm
Utility Room:	2180mm x 1520mm
Bathroom:	3350mm x 2540mm
Hall:	1830mm wide
Bedroom:	3350mm x 3050mm
Bedroom:	3660mm x 3050mm
Bedroom:	4010mm x 3350mm
Garage:	7620mm x 3660mm

Floor Area: 138.85 sq. metres
Frontage Dimension: 19.07 metres

4 Bedroom Bungalows

FRONT ELEVATION

FLOOR PLAN

No. 77
Clonard

A straightforward four bedroomed bungalow with well proportioned rooms. The elevation features a slated roof. Living rooms are well laid out and provision has been made for two open fireplaces and a solid fuel cooker. An en-suite bathroom is located off the master bedroom. Three bedrooms have built-in wardrobes. The design features a walk-in hot press.

ROOM DIMENSIONS

Sitting Room:	4206mm x 4100mm
Family Room:	3700mm x 3300mm
Kitchen/Dining Room:	4000mm x 3300mm
Utility Room:	2300mm x 1800mm
Toilet:	2300mm x 1000mm
Bathroom:	2330mm x 3300mm
Hall:	1980mm wide
Bathroom En Suite:	1764mm x 1316mm
Bedroom:	3500mm x 2890mm
Bedroom:	2740mm x 3040mm
Bedroom:	2740mm x 3040mm
Bedroom:	2890mm x 3040mm

Gross Floor Area: 123.67 sq. metres
Frontage Dimension: 16.86 metres

No. 78
Hanover

A traditional style bungalow with four good sized bedrooms and three living rooms. Provision has been made for a solid fuel cooker in the kitchen. An en-suite bathroom is described on the plan and all bedrooms have built in wardrobes. The exterior has a plaster finish and the roof is covered with concrete tiles.

elevation

plan

ROOM DIMENSIONS

Living Room:	4220mm x 3050mm
Kitchen/Dining Room:	4170mm x 3050mm
Utility:	2290mm x 1520mm
Bathroom:	3050mm x 1830mm
En Suite:	3300mm x 1170mm
Master Bedroom:	3610mm x 3050mm
Bedroom 2:	3910mm x 2900mm
Bedroom 3:	2740mm x 2590mm
Bedroom 4:	2740mm x 2590mm
Hall:	2740mm x 1830mm
Sitting Room:	4780mm x 3960mm
Corridor:	1070mm wide

Floor Area: 124.71 sq. metres
Frontage Dimension: 17.02 metres

elevation.

plan.

No. 79
Merland

Four bedroomed bungalow with hipped roof and granite feature to front elevation. This popular style bungalow has two open fireplaces and provision for a solid fuel or oil fired cooker. Minimal heat loss between cooker and hot water cylinder due to proximity of both fittings. Built in wardrobes to all bedrooms. Utility room off kitchen with separate toilet and basin adjacent. Open porch protecting front entrance door

ROOM DIMENSIONS

Toilet:	2440mm x 970mm
Utility Room:	2030mm x 1680mm
Hall:	1830mm wide
Lounge:	4420mm x 4120mm
Living Room:	4370mm x 3050mm
Kitchen:	4120mm x 3250mm
Bathroom:	3200mm x 1730mm
Bedroom:	4060mm x 3050mm
Bedroom:	3510mm x 3200mm
Bedroom:	2900mm x 2590mm
Bedroom:	2900mm x 2590mm

Floor Area: 124.12 sq. metres
Frontage: 16.75 metres

No. 80
Vanguard

A compact bungalow with an unusual portico giving the front elevation a well balanced appearance. An en-suite bathroom is provided along with a fully fitted bathroom. We have located the boiler room as part of the floor plan. Access is provided directly connecting the kitchen with the sitting room. Open fireplaces as described in the sitting room and dining room. Three bedrooms have built in wardrobes.

ROOM DIMENSIONS

Kitchen/Dining Room:	4980mm x 3200mm
Utility:	2130mm x 1220mm
Bathroom:	3200mm x 1830mm
Bedroom 4:	3200mm x 2440mm
Bedroom 1:	4170mm x 3200mm
En Suite:	1830mm x 1420mm
Boiler Room:	2620mm x 1520mm
Bedroom 2:	3450mm x 3330mm
Bedroom 3:	3330mm x 3050mm
Hall:	3330mm x 1830mm
Dining Room:	3350mm x 3330mm
Sitting Room:	4470mm x 3810mm
Corridor:	1040mm wide

Floor Area:	124.61 sq. metres
Frontage:	17.12 metres

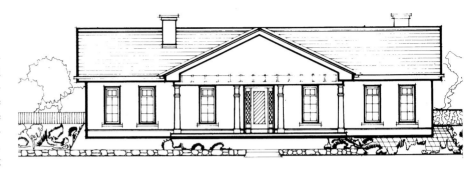

front elevation

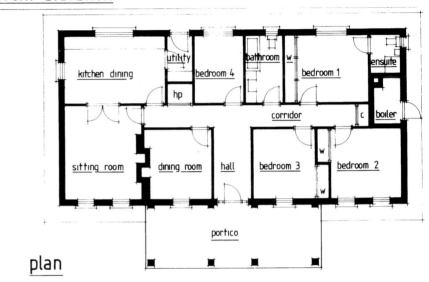

plan

No. 81
Ascot

The front elevation features on this bungalow include a bow window on the lounge and an attractive portico supported by styled glass fibre columns. The roof is of medium pitch and finished with concrete tiles. Natural daylight enters the corridor from a feature window on the gable end of the bungalow. The kitchen is fitted with a solid fuel cooker and the hot press is adjacent ensuring minimal heat loss between heat source and hot water cylinder. Open fireplaces service the dining room and lounge. The hall is divided from the corridor by means of a segmental arch. A second toilet facility is provided opening off the utility room. The four bedrooms are of adequate dimension and three have fitted wardrobes.

ROOM DIMENSIONS

Lounge:	4220mm x 4190mm
Dining Room:	3530mm x 3300mm
Kitchen:	4320mm x 3300mm
Utility Room:	2080mm x 1830mm
Toilet:	2080mm x 1020mm
Bathroom:	3300mm x 2340mm
Bedroom 1:	3510mm x 3050mm
Bedroom 2:	3050mm x 2950mm
Bedroom 3:	3050mm x 2740mm
Bedroom 4:	3300mm x 2850mm

Floor Area:	124.89 sq. metres
Frontage:	16.80 metres

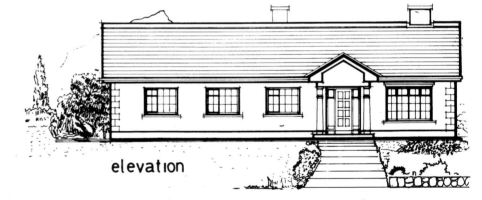

elevation

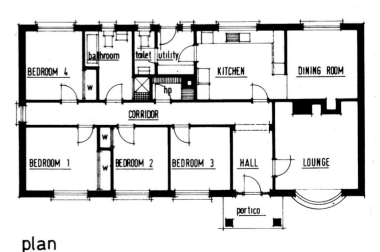

plan

No. 82
Galway

This four bedroomed bungalow has a brick front and a tiled roof. Three bedrooms have built-in wardrobes. The master bedroom en-suite. Provision is made for a cooker in the kitchen and an open fireplace in the sitting room. All floors are concrete, insulated and the fabric of the building is fully insulated. An open plan layout is featured at the kitchen and sitting room area.

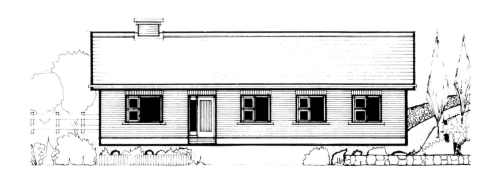

ROOM DIMENSIONS

Kitchen/Dining Room: 5180mm x 3200mm
Utility: 3200mm x 1680mm
Bathroom: 3200mm x 1730mm
En Suite: 3200mm x 1320mm
Bedroom 1: 3660mm x 3200mm
Bedroom 2: 4320mm x 2740mm
Bedroom 3: 3100mm x 2690mm
Bedroom 4: 3100mm x 2740mm
Sitting Room: 4010mm x 3710mm
Hall: 4320mm x 1420mm

Floor Area: 106.86 sq. metres
Frontage: 15.24 metres

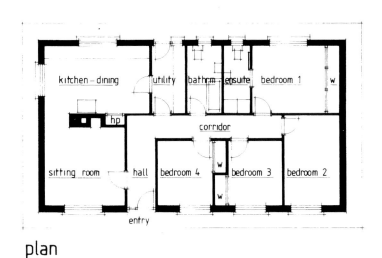

plan

elevation.

plan.

No. 83
Ashgrove

A Classic with four respectable sized bedrooms, three with built-in wardrobes. Natural light in the corridor is provided by a feature window in the gable wall. Bathroom and bath and shower compartment and provision for secondary toilet facilities off the utility room. Provision has been made for a solid fuel cooker with adjacent hot press. Feature bow window to lounge. Generously dimensioned kitchen and dining room.

ROOM DIMENSIONS

Lounge: 4190mm x 4220mm
Dining Room: 3150mm x 3300mm
Kitchen: 4700mm x 3300mm
Bathroom: 3300mm x 2340mm
Bedroom: 3510mm x 3050mm
Bedroom: 3050mm x 2740mm
Bedroom: 3050mm x 2740mm
Bedroom: 3300mm x 2850mm
Hall: 1980mm x 3050mm

Floor Area: 124.89 sq. metres
Frontage: 16.98 metres

No. 84
Dunmore

The roof space of this well proportioned bungalow may be developed at a later date and we have made provision in the hall width to take a stairs. All bedrooms have built-in wardrobes. We have indicated an open fireplace in the sitting room and a solid fuel cooker in the kitchen/dining room. The elevations are dashed and the roof is covered with slates.

front elevation

ROOM DIMENSIONS

Kitchen/Dining Room: 4570mm x 3250mm
Utility: 2540mm x 1630mm
Toilet: 1830mm x 1470mm
Bedroom 2:   3250mm x 2900mm
Bedroom 1:   3810mm x 3250mm
Bathroom: 2690mm x 1830mm
Bedroom 4:   3960mm x 3510mm
Bedroom 3:   3660mm x 3510mm
Hall: 1830mm
Sitting Room: 4420mm x 3510mm

Floor Area: 123.69 sq. metres
Frontage: 16.05 metres

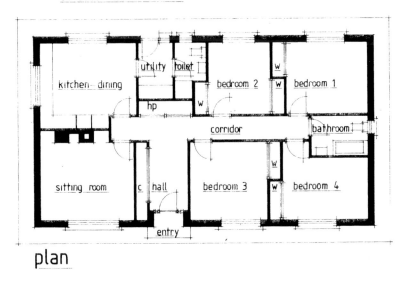

plan

---

plan

No. 85   Albany

If your site frontage dimension is restricted, then this fine bungalow will suit you. Although narrow, the front elevation presents a respectable appearance with its arched entry, covered porch and granite trim surrounding the lounge window. The main hall leads to an access corridor off which all main rooms open. The living section contains a large kitchen, utility room, dining room and lounge. Both lounge and dining room are serviced with an open fireplace. The hot press is a walk-in type. We have provided four good sized wardrobes and a fully fitted bathroom. The roof is covered in concrete tiles to a medium pitch.

elevation

ROOM DIMENSIONS

Lounge: 4880mm x 3860mm
Dining Room: 3350mm x 3200mm
Kitchen: 3960mm x 3350mm
Utility Room: 2130mm x 1520mm
Bathroom: 3050mm x 1830mm
Bedroom: 3810mm x 3350mm
Bedroom: 3510mm x 2900mm
Bedroom: 3050mm x 2740mm
Bedroom: 3050mm x 2590mm
Main Hall: 2740mm x 2440mm

Floor Area: 122 sq. metres
Frontage: 8.28 metres

No. 86
Ballyhale

A simple elevation conceals a full sized family home with a large kitchen/dining room and sitting room. Note the proximity of the hot press to the solid fuel cooker in the kitchen. Three bedrooms have built in wardrobes and a coats press is located in the entrance hall.

front elevation

ROOM DIMENSIONS

Bedroom 4:	3580mm x 2900mm
Bedroom 3:	3810mm x 3300mm
Utility:	2490mm x 1520mm
Kitchen/Dining Room:	5180mm x 4220mm
Sitting Room:	5180mm x 4270mm
Hall:	1520mm
Bedroom 2:	3510mm x 3300mm
Bedroom 1:	3580mm x 3510mm
Bathroom:	2290mm x 1980mm
Corridor:	1070mm wide

Floor Area:	123.69 sq. metres
Frontage:	15.16 metres

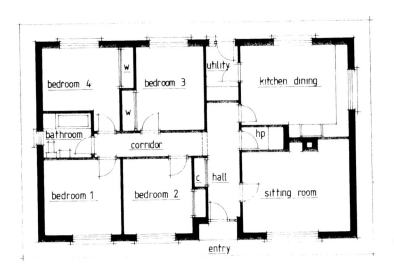

plan

elevation

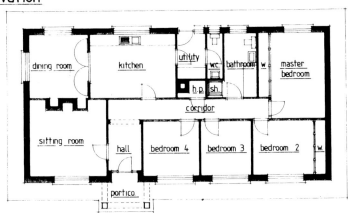

plan

No. 87
Crawford

A well balanced four bedroomed bungalow in our Classic style. Two of the bedrooms have built-in wardrobes. The living rooms are well proportioned and we have provided open fireplaces in both rooms. The familiar lines of the hipped roof and complementary portico set off the front elevation. Provision has been made for a solid fuel cooker in the kitchen.

ROOM DIMENSIONS

Dining Room:	3560mm x 3050mm
Sitting Room:	4220mm x 4170mm
Kitchen:	4670mm x 3300mm
Utility:	2290mm x 1520mm
Toilet:	2130mm x 810mm
Bathroom:	3300mm x 1730mm
Bedroom:	4470mm x 3000mm
Bedroom:	3350mm x 3000mm
Bedroom:	3000mm x 2950mm
Bedroom:	3050mm x 3000mm
Hall:	1830mm wide

Floor Area:	124.99 sq. metres
Frontage:	17.07 metres

No. 88
Clonmore

Four bedroomed bungalow with hipped roof and feature entrance. The living room has a bay window and patio doors. A toilet and basin is provided opening off the utility room. Wardrobes are built-in to bedrooms 1&2 and the master bedroom has a bathroom en-suite.

FRONT ELEVATION

ROOM DIMENSIONS

Family Room:	4660mm x 3400mm
Kitchen/Dining Room:	5224mm x 3000mm
Sitting Room:	4600mm x 3500mm
Utility Room:	2300mm x 1810mm
Toilet:	2300mm x 1066mm
Bedroom:	3500mm x 3500mm
Bedroom 2:	3500mm x 2650mm
Bedroom 3:	3500mm x 2716mm
Bedroom 4:	3000mm x 3000mm
Bathroom:	3000mm x 1900mm
Hall:	1800mm wide
En-suite Bathroom:	2334mm x 1350mm

Floor Area:	132 sq. metres
Frontage Dimension:	17.60 metres

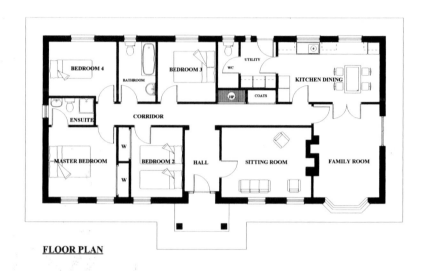

FLOOR PLAN

elevation

plan

No. 89
Sussex

This elegant four bedroomed bungalow is well laid out and is contained within a modest frontage dimension. The twin roof adds character to the design and is finished with concrete tiles. Space has been allowed in the building for later fitted wardrobes in three bedrooms. The hot press is located close to the solid fuel cooker in the kitchen/dining room. The bathroom is fully fitted and we have provided an en-suite shower and wash basin to service the Master Bedroom. Georgian windows are fitted on the front elevation and the lounge and hall face wall is trimmed in brick.

ROOM DIMENSIONS

Lounge:	4620mm x 3860mm
Kitchen/Dining Room:	6250mm x 3860mm
Utility Room:	2740mm x 1830mm
Bathroom:	3050mm x 1630mm
En Suite:	1980mm x 1070mm
Bedroom 1:	4010mm x 3200mm
Bedroom 2:	3200mm x 3200mm
Bedroom 3:	3050mm x 3050mm
Bedroom 4:	3050mm x 2440mm

Floor Area:	118.66 sq. metres
Frontage Dimension:	13.93 metres

No. 90
Bracknell

The well balanced elevation on this bungalow features neo-georgian windows, an open portico and a slated roof. Both living rooms are generously dimensioned and all bedrooms have fitted wardrobes. The main bedroom has a Bathroom En-Suite. An open archway divides the sitting room and formal dining area. This design is also available with a hipped roof.

elevation

ROOM DIMENSIONS

Sitting Room/Dining:	7440mm x 3910mm
Kitchen/Dining Room:	5740mm x 3350mm
Utility:	2180mm x 1600mm
Toilet:	1600mm x 1070mm
Bathroom:	2670mm x 2180mm
Hall:	1980mm wide
Bedroom / En Suite:	3530mm x 3530mm
Bedroom:	3530mm x 2790mm
Bedroom:	3330mm x 2790mm
Bedroom:	3530mm x 2390mm

Floor Area:	124.10 sq. metres
Frontage:	17.60 metres

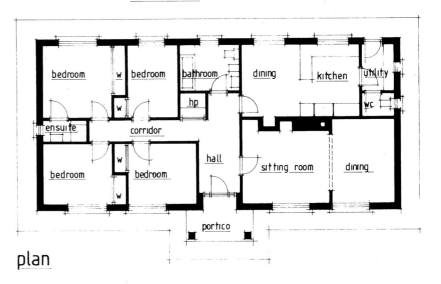

plan

front elevation

No. 91
Connemara

This well laid out bungalow has a large kitchen/dining room with an open fireplace. A separate utility room may be provided later as a conservatory infill to open directly off the kitchen. A toilet facility is located off the main entrance hall. The bedroom block is self contained. Externally the elevation is well balanced with tiled roof and brick trim.

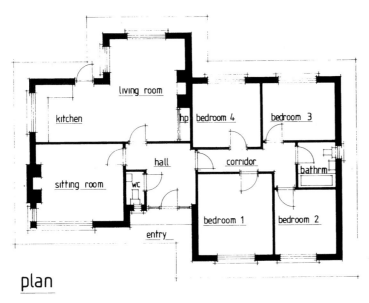

plan

ROOM DIMENSIONS

Kitchen/Living Room:	7320mm x 4880mm
Bedroom 4:	3660mm x 3050mm
Bedroom 3:	3510mm x 2740mm
Bathroom:	2180mm x 1830mm
Bedroom 2:	3050mm x 3050mm
Bedroom 1:	3810mm x 3660mm
Toilet:	1580mm x 914mm
Sitting Room:	4270mm x 3660mm

Floor Area:	112.81 sq. metres
Frontage:	15.27 metres

No. 92
Bellcroft

This is one of our more popular bungalows. A central portico leads you through to the main hall. From this point you will notice that the design separates the living and sleeping blocks of the residence. Four bedrooms, three with built-in wardrobes and the master bedroom having an en-suite bathroom. The lounge, dining room and kitchen have interconnecting doors and the kitchen has provision for a solid fuel or oil fired cooker. The dining room and lounge each have an open fireplace. The hot press has dual access from the utility room and main corridor and the utility room itself is physically separated from the rear hall.

ROOM DIMENSIONS

Kitchen:	4120mm x 3050mm
Dining Room:	3610mm x 3380mm
Lounge:	4450mm x 3610mm
Bathroom:	2440mm x 2130mm
Utility Room:	1680mm x 1600mm
Bedroom:	3580mm x 2870mm
Bedroom:	3580mm x 2870mm
Bedroom:	3430mm x 2870mm
Bedroom:	3430mm x 3050mm

Floor Area:	124.96 sq. metres
Frontage:	18.20 metres

elevation

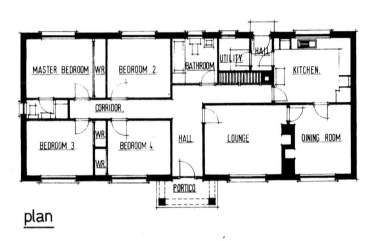

plan

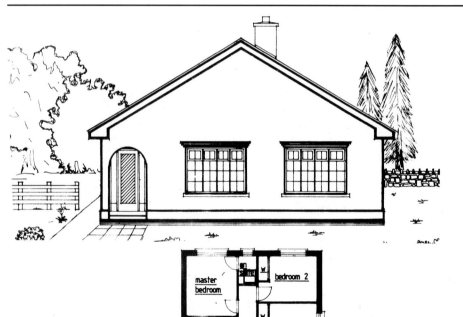

No. 93
Riversdale

A gable facing bungalow with a frontage dimension of a mere 9.63 metres. This fine dwelling offers three fine living rooms and four well proportioned bedrooms. Three bedrooms have fitted wardrobes. Two open fireplaces are provided. A shower is located ensuite to the master bedroom. The front elevation is along simple clean lines and the roof is finished with concrete tiles.

ROOM DIMENSIONS

Sitting Room:	4780mm x 3910mm
Living Room:	3860mm x 3450mm
Kitchen:	4220mm x 3450mm
Utility Room:	2820mm x 1220mm
Bathroom:	3050mm x 1520mm
Bedroom/En Suite:	4060mm x 3050mm
Bedroom:	3450mm x 2590mm
Bedroom:	3450mm x 2590mm
Bedroom:	3050mm x 2740mm

Floor Area:	120.34 sq. metres
Frontage:	9.63 metres

No. 94
Elmwood

The elevation of the **Elmwood** home has stone features and an arched recess. The accommodation is well laid out and provides for four bedrooms and a study. The kitchen has provision for a solid fuel cooker and the lounge has an open fireplace. We have included for a coats press in the kitchen, backing on to the hot press. The hot press itself is a walk-in type. Two bedrooms feature built in wardrobes.

front elevation

ROOM DIMENSIONS

Lounge:	4950mm x 3560mm
Dining Room:	3120mm x 3050mm
Kitchen:	3510mm x 3120mm
Bedroom:	3510mm x 2740mm
Bedroom:	3860mm x 3560mm
Bedroom:	4220mm x 2790mm
Bedroom:	3120mm x 2740mm
Study:	2850mm x 2740mm

Floor Area:	123.97 sq. metres
Frontage:	16.97 metres

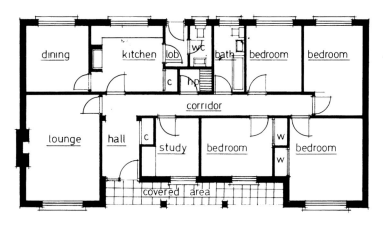

plan

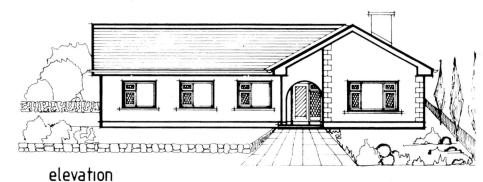

elevation

No. 95
Pemberton

This traditional style bungalow has simple lines. The front elevation is finished with white dash and the roof is covered with concrete tiles. The well proportioned kitchen/dining room is large and has provision for a solid fuel cooker. The sitting room has an open fireplace. All bedrooms have fitted wardrobes and the master bedroom has a shower en-suite.

ROOM DIMENSIONS

Sitting Room:	4880mm x 3960mm
Kitchen/Dining Room:	6550mm x 4220mm
Utility Room:	2340mm x 1470mm
Toilet:	2340mm x 1400mm
Bathroom:	3050mm x 1830mm
Bedroom/En Suite:	4010mm x 3050mm
Bedroom:	3910mm x 2900mm
Bedroom:	2740mm x 2590mm
Bedroom:	2740mm x 2590mm
Hall:	1830mm wide

Floor Area:	124.67 sq. metres
Frontage:	17.11 metres

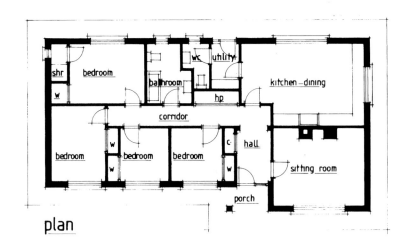

plan

No. 96
Willow

A two bedroom bungalow with a frontage to suit a narrow site. The dwelling has self contained sleeping accommodation, a full bathroom and one bathroom en-suite. The kitchen/dining room and sitting room areas are of open plan design. A sun room is designed to open off the dining area via french doors. Bedrooms have built-in wardrobes. The front elevation has a brick feature.

FRONT ELEVATION

ROOM DIMENSIONS

Bedroom:	3040mm x 5358mm
Bedroom:	2810mm x 2810mm
En-suite:	1720mm x 1740mm
Bathroom:	1720mm x 2810mm
Kitchen/Dining Room:	7178mm x 3040mm
Sitting Room:	4190mm x 3580mm
Sun Room:	2500mm x 3640mm

Floor Area:	96.12 square metres
Frontage:	10.58 metres

FLOOR PLAN

front elevation

No. 97
Woodside

We feature a large kitchen/dining room with solid fuel cooker in this design with a view towards the front and side of the dwelling. The Master Bedroom has a shower en-suite and three of the four bedrooms have built-in wardrobes. The elevation is in our Classic style and features a bow window lighting the sitting room.

ROOM DIMENSIONS

Bedroom 2:	3200mm x 2950mm
Bedroom 3:	3200mm x 2640mm
Bedroom 4:	3200mm x 2640mm
Bathroom:	3200mm x 2440mm
Utility:	3710mm x 1420mm
Kitchen/Dining Room:	6550mm x 3710mm
Hall:	1930mm wide
Sitting Room:	5280mm x 3660mm
Bedroom 1:	3660mm x 3510mm
Shower Room:	1780mm x 1020mm

Floor Area:	124.00 sq. metres
Frontage:	15.98 metres

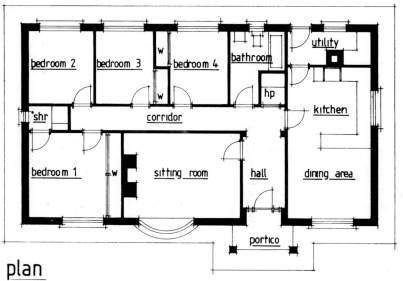

plan

No. 98
Roscommon

This bungalow is suited to a site with restricted frontage and features brick trim to the front elevation. A particular feature of this home is the large kitchen and sitting room. Three bedrooms have built in wardrobes.

ROOM DIMENSIONS

Bedroom 4:	3350mm x 3050mm
Lounge:	5490mm x 3710mm
Kitchen:	5840mm x 3710mm
Utility:	1830mm x 1730mm
Toilet:	1730mm x 810mm
Bathroom:	2740mm x 2390mm
Bedroom 1:	3710mm x 3510mm
Bedroom 2:	3050mm x 2590mm
Bedroom 3:	3050mm x 3050mm
Hall:	2130mm wide
Floor Area:	119.60 sq. metres
Frontage:	9.30 metres

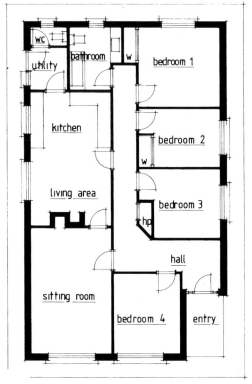

plan

front elevation

elevation

plan

No. 99
Glasdrum

Traditional styling with excellent accommodation make this design very popular with our customers. Without doubt the layout is heat efficient, the hot water cylinder being located a mere eight inches from the solid fuel or oil fired cooker. Glazed doors connect the lounge with the dining room. The utility room is of sufficient dimension to contain your washing machine and deep freeze. Bedrooms are well proportioned with particular emphasis on the master bedroom which has an en-suite bathroom. The main bathroom is provided with recessed bath, vanity basin, W.C. and bidet.

ROOM DIMENSIONS

Lounge:	4830mm x 4220mm
Dining Room:	3610mm x 3200mm
Kitchen:	4620mm x 3200mm
Utility Room:	1830mm x 1930mm
Bathroom:	3200mm x 2240mm
Bedroom:	4220mm x 3710mm
Bedroom:	3200mm x 3050mm
Bedroom:	2850mm x 2740mm
Bedroom:	2850mm x 2740mm
Floor Area:	124 sq. metres
Frontage:	15.39 metres

No. 100
Kinsale

An attractive bungalow in our Classic style featuring a large kitchen/dining room with solid fuel cooker. A walk-in hot press is provided with access from the kitchen. Three bedrooms have built-in wardrobes. The master bedroom has a bathroom en-suite. Side windows are indicated to the kitchen/dining room and sitting room. Georgian styled windows and open portico set off the front elevation.

front elevation

ROOM DIMENSIONS

Kitchen/Dining Room:	6100mm x 3300mm
Utility:	2080mm x 1830mm
Toilet:	2080mm x 1020mm
Bathroom:	3300mm x 2340mm
Master Bedroom:	4700mm x 3300mm
En Suite:	1070mm wide
Bedroom 2:	3510mm x 3050mm
Bedroom 3:	3050mm x 2740mm
Bedroom 4:	3050mm x 2950mm
Hall:	3050mm x 1980mm
Sitting Room:	4220mm x 4190mm

Floor Area:	124.73 sq. metres
Frontage:	17.00 metres

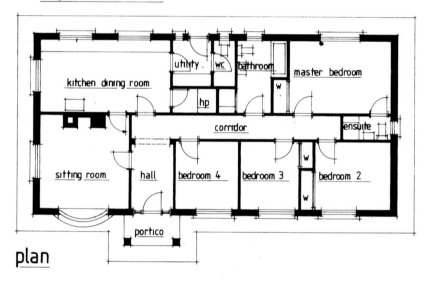

plan

front elevation

No. 101
Newbridge

This four bedroomed bungalow offers a practical layout with four bedrooms, three good sized living rooms and two bathrooms. The boiler room under the main roof ensures an efficient heating layout with minimum heat loss. All floors are concrete and the roof is finished with slates. The front elevation has cut stone features.

ROOM DIMENSIONS

Sitting Room:	4470mm x 3810mm
Kitchen/Dining Room:	4980mm x 3200mm
Family Room:	4570mm x 3350mm
Hall:	1830mm wide
Bathroom:	3200mm x 1830mm
En Suite:	1830mm x 1420mm
Utility Room:	2210mm x 1220mm
Bedroom:	3560mm x 3200mm
Bedroom:	3450mm x 3330mm
Bedroom:	3330mm x 3050mm
Bedroom:	3200mm x 2440mm

Floor Area:	132.80 sq. metres
Frontage:	17.17 metres

plan

No. 102
Guildford

A no-nonsense brick fronted design with a large kitchen/dining room. Three bedrooms have built-in wardrobes. The entrance door is recessed. One open fireplace is described and we have provided a solid fuel cooker in the kitchen. The fabric of the house is fully insulated and the roof is finished with concrete tiles.

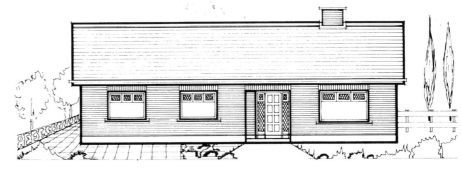

front elevation

ROOM DIMENSIONS

Bedroom 1:	3350mm x 3100mm
Bedroom 2:	4170mm x 2740mm
Bedroom 3:	4620mm x 3120mm
Bedroom 4:	3450mm x 2740mm
Bathroom:	3450mm x 2210mm
Kitchen/Dining Room:	6400mm x 3450mm
Utility:	2440mm x 1830mm
Sitting Room:	4570mm x 4520mm
Hall:	2740mm x 1980mm

Floor Area:	124.62 sq. metres
Frontage:	15.39 metres

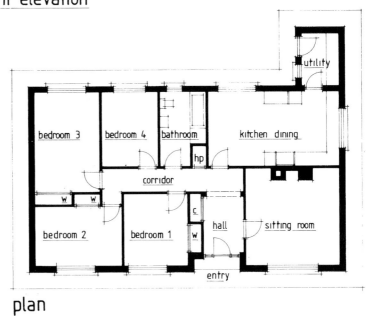

plan

No. 103
Rushbrook

This bungalow with hipped roof is suited to a narrow fronted site. The in-line living areas are well proportioned. Natural light is provided to the corridor and all four bedrooms have built-in wardrobes. An attractive covered porch leads you to the main entrance door. The roofed area to the rere of this bungalow can easily be utilised later to provide a conservatory.

ROOM DIMENSIONS

Bedroom 1:	3660mm x 3710mm
Bedroom 2:	3660mm x 2740mm
Bedroom 3:	3150mm x 3050mm
Bedroom 4:	3660mm x 3050mm
Bathroom:	3660mm x 2590mm
Roofed Area:	3960mm x 3960mm
Kitchen/Dining Room:	6760mm x 3960mm
Sitting Room:	4570mm x 3960mm
Hall:	4220mm x 1730mm

Floor Area:	121. 27 sq. metres
Frontage:	14.07 metres

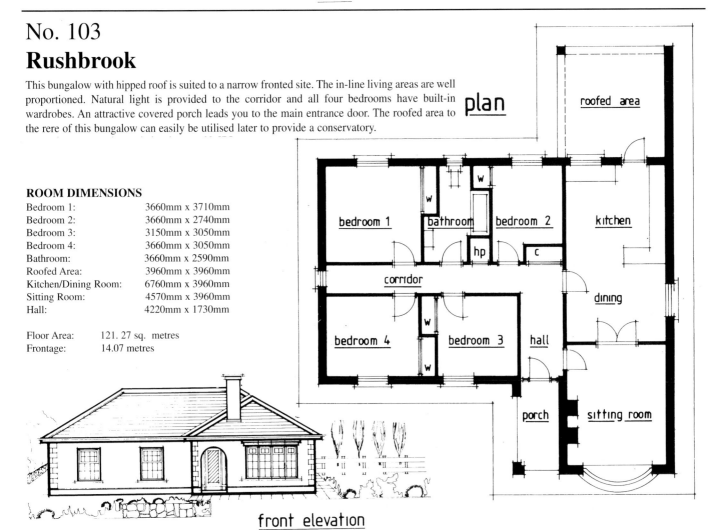

plan

front elevation

No. 104
Pampas

This bungalow has a beautiful granite trim on the front elevation, the granite being extended upwards to form the feature chimney stack. We have provided two open fireplaces and a solid fuel cooker and again, note the proximity of the hot press to the solid fuel cooker. Three of the four bedrooms have fitted wardrobes. The lounge and dining room interconnect by means of glazed doors. The straight roof is of medium pitch and covered with concrete tiles. View from the kitchen is to the side of the residence.

elevation

ROOM DIMENSIONS

Lounge:	5500mm x 3810mm
Dining Room:	4270mm x 3200mm
Kitchen:	4060mm x 3050mm
Utility Room:	1730mm x 1580mm
Bathroom:	2900mm x 2290mm
Bedroom 1:	3560mm x 3200mm
Bedroom 2:	3350mm x 2900mm
Bedroom 3:	2900mm x 2690mm
Bedroom 4:	2900mm x 2690mm
Floor Area:	122.29 sq. metres
Frontage:	16.86 metres

plan

front elevation

No. 105
Tyrone

An attractive four bedroomed bungalow with the sitting room located towards the back of the house. The large kitchen/dining room extends the full width of the house and two bedrooms have built-in wardrobes. The elevation is finished with brick and the roof is covered with concrete tiles.

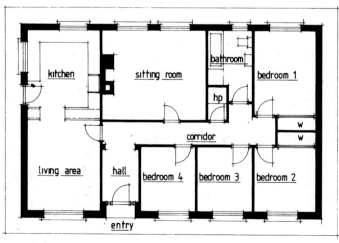

plan

ROOM DIMENSIONS

Kitchen:	4370mm x 3660mm
Living Area:	4220mm x 3660mm
Sitting Room:	5180mm x 4270mm
Bathroom:	3350mm x 2240mm
Bedroom 1:	4010mm x 2950mm
Bedroom 2:	3050mm x 2950mm
Bedroom 3:	3050mm x 2740mm
Bedroom 4:	3050mm x 2740mm
Hall:	2440mm x 1830mm
Floor Area:	123.23 sq. metres
Frontage:	14.94 metres

No. 106
Castlekelly

A bungalow with simple lines to the elevation and featuring a large kitchen/dining room with solid fuel cooker and adjacent hot press. The sitting room has an open fireplace. Three bedrooms have built in wardrobes. A shower is provided in Bedroom No. 2 en-suite. The building is L shaped and the roof is finished with concrete tiles.

front elevation

ROOM DIMENSIONS

Bedroom 1:	3050mm x 2740mm
Bedroom 2:	3810mm x 3050mm
Bedroom 3:	3860mm x 2600mm
Bedroom 4:	3510mm x 2740mm
Bathroom:	3050mm x 1730mm
Utility:	3050mm x 1220mm
Kitchen/Dining Room:	4880mm x 4570mm
Sitting Room:	4570mm x 4270mm
Hall:	2740mm x 1580mm
En Suite:	1520mm x 1220mm

Floor Area:	112.53 sq. metres
Frontage:	15.09 metres

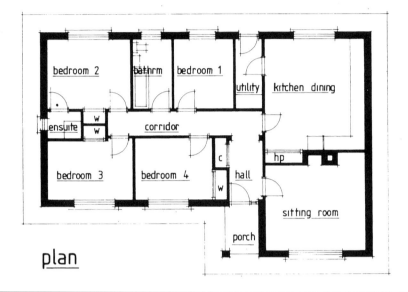

plan

elevation

No. 107
Brampton

This full sized four bedroom bungalow is suited to a site with restricted site frontage dimension and our design occupies only (7.92 metres). The roofed entrance porch leads to the main hall to meet the service corridor from which all main rooms open. An open fireplace is located in the lounge and the kitchen, towards the back of the residence, is fitted with a solid fuel cooker. All bedrooms have fitted wardrobes and we have located a fitted coats press in the entrance hall. The front elevation is pleasing with stone trim and the low pitch roof is covered with concrete tiles.

ROOM DIMENSIONS

Lounge:	5130mm x 3810mm
Kitchen/Dining Room:	5440mm x 3300mm
Utility Room:	1980mm x 1830mm
Bathroom:	3050mm x 2130mm
Bedroom 1:	3660mm x 3050mm
Bedroom 2:	3400mm x 3050mm
Bedroom 3:	3200mm x 3050mm
Bedroom 4:	3050mm x 2740mm

Floor Area:	114.48 sq. metres
Frontage:	7.92 metres

plan

No. 108
Drumcar

An economical four bedroomed bungalow with brick features on the front elevation. Three of the bedrooms have built-in wardrobes. Provision has been made for a solid fuel cooker in the kitchen and an open fireplace in the sitting room. We have indicated a recessed entrance and a built-in coats press in the hall.

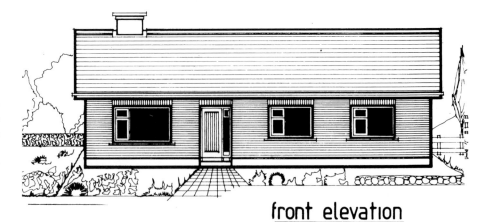

front elevation

ROOM DIMENSIONS

Kitchen/Dining Room:	5790mm x 3120mm
Bathroom:	3250mm x 2080mm
Bedroom 1:	4470mm x 3050mm
Bedroom 2:	3250mm x 2440mm
Bedroom 3:	3150mm x 2740mm
Bedroom 4:	4060mm x 2490mm
Hall:	1730mm wide
Sitting Room:	4240mm x 4170mm

Floor Area: 107.07 sq. metres
Frontage: 14.56 metres

plan

No. 109
Wagner

This fine four bedroomed home contains all up to date features. Integral fuel and pump room, solid fuel cooker, second toilet, two reception rooms, built-in wardrobes in three bedrooms. The front elevation features a recessed area with stone panels The Georgian style windows set off the total appearance. Feature arch in hall. Integral fuel store and boiler/pump room. Fully insulated walls, floors and roof. Good sized hot press and coats press opening off corridor.

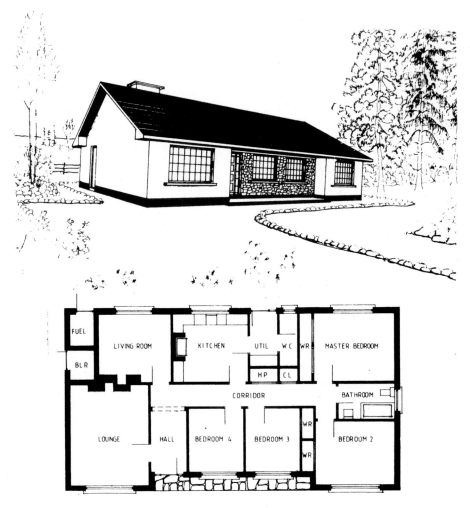

ROOM DIMENSIONS

Lounge:	4880mm x 3960mm
Living Room:	3960mm x 3300mm
Kitchen:	3810mm x 3300mm
Bedroom:	3960mm x 3050mm
Bedroom:	3660mm x 3050mm
Bedroom:	3050mm x 2740mm
Bedroom:	3050mm x 2740mm
Bathroom:	2820mm x 1730mm

Floor Area: 128.81 sq. metres
Frontage: 16.92 metres

No. 110
Hazelmere

A popular design with our clients featuring four good sized bedrooms and three living rooms. The master bedroom has a bathroom en-suite and a full wall wardrobe. The sitting room has two french windows. Provision has been made for a solid fuel cooker in the kitchen.

front elevation

ROOM DIMENSIONS

Living Room:	4220mm x 3330mm
Kitchen:	4370mm x 3050mm
Utility:	2360mm x 1520mm
Bathroom:	3050mm x 1930mm
En Suite:	3050mm x 914mm
Bedroom 1:	3450mm x 3050mm
Bedroom 2:	3910mm x 2900mm
Bedroom 3:	2740mm x 2590mm
Bedroom 4:	2740mm x 2670mm
Hall:	2740mm x 1830mm
Sitting Room:	4900mm x 3970mm

Floor area: 123.11sq.m.
Frontage dimension: 17.23m

plan

ELEVATION

LAYOUT

No. 111
Brackenfield

A no fuss practical home with sensible features. Four bedrooms, two having built in wardrobes. Two fireplaces and a solid fuel cooker, make this an easy to heat home. No fuss attractive exterior. We have included an integral garage as part of the design.

ROOM DIMENSIONS

Lounge:	4060mm x 3560mm
Living Room:	4370mm x 3560mm
Kitchen:	4370mm x 3810mm
Bedroom:	2900mm x 2950mm
Bedroom:	4060mm x 2640mm
Bedroom:	3020mm x 3810mm
Bedroom:	3020mm x 3100mm
Garage:	3200mm wide

Floor Area: 124.08 sq. metres
Frontage: 20.75 metres

No. 112
Mansfield

This four bedroom bungalow has an attractive stone feature on the projecting section of the front elevation. The roof is constructed so as to provide for later attic conversion and we have indicated a future stairs location. The floor plan is well laid out and two open fire places are provided. The exterior has a plaster finish and the roof is finished with concrete tiles.

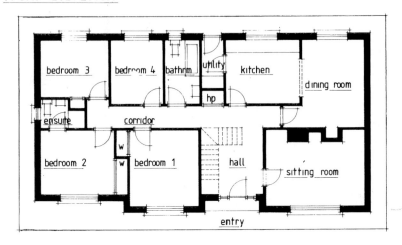

front elevation

ROOM DIMENSIONS

Bedroom 1:	3400mm x 3660mm
Bedroom 2:	3660mm x 3050mm
Bedroom 3:	3350mm x 2700mm
Bedroom 4:	3050mm x 2600mm
Hall:	3050mm x 3050mm
Sitting Room:	4880mm x 3660mm
Dining Room:	4220mm x 3050mm
Kitchen:	3660mm x 3050mm
Utility:	2290mm x 1070mm
Bathroom:	3050mm x 1730mm
En Suite:	2180mm x 1420mm
Floor Area:	127.15 sq. metres
Frontage:	16.47 metres

plan

elevation

No. 113
Norfolk

The **Norfolk** bungalow is a variation on our Elmwood design and features a well balanced front elevation with granite trim and recessed centre area. The residence offers four good sized bedrooms each with built-in wardrobes. The location of the solid fuel/oil fired cooker guarantees heat efficiency due to the proximity of the hot water cylinder and hot press. We have provided a fully fitted bathroom and a second toilet facility off the utility room. Access to the dining room is via the kitchen with a pair of glazed doors.

ROOM DIMENSIONS

Lounge:	4980mm x 3560mm
Dining Room:	3660mm x 3200mm
Kitchen:	4270mm x 3200mm
Utility Room:	2340mm x 1630mm
Entrance Hall:	1680mm wide
Bathroom:	3200mm x 1680mm
Bedroom:	3810mm x 3560mm
Bedroom:	3430mm x 3050mm
Bedroom:	3200mm x 2740mm
Bedroom:	3180mm x 2740mm
Floor Area:	124.24 sq. metres
Frontage:	15.80 metres

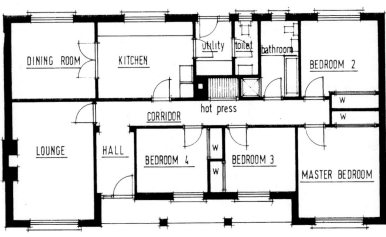

plan

82

No. 114
Seville

The layout of this fine four bedroomed home will suit a partially disabled person with its wide internal doors and main bathroom layout. We have provided a ramp to the rere entrance. The open plan lounge/dining room is a feature of the design with its central fire breast. Provision has been made for a solid fuel cooker in the kitchen. All bedrooms have fitted wardrobes and a fitted coats press is provided in the main access corridor. Direct connection is provided by means of a pair of glazed doors from the kitchen to the dining room. The front elevation is attractive with slated roof and stone trim.

ROOM DIMENSIONS

Lounge/Dining Room:	8080mm x 3960mm
Kitchen:	4270mm x 3150mm
Utility:	2290mm x 1630mm
Toilet:	2290mm x 970mm
Bathroom:	3150mm x 2130mm
Bedroom 1:	4470mm x 3050mm
Bedroom 2:	3560mm x 2900mm
Bedroom 3:	2900mm x 2740mm
Bedroom 4:	2900mm x 2590mm

Floor Area:	124.90 sq. metres
Frontage:	17.16 metres

No. 115
Kent

A fine four bedroomed gable facing bungalow with stone trim and arched recessed entrance. The roof pitch is medium and finished with concrete tiles. We have divided the living and sleeping accommodation on a left-right basis opening off a central corridor. Two open fireplaces are provided together with provision for a solid fuel cooker. The master bedroom has an en-suite shower. This bungalow will suit a site with restricted frontage dimensions. Our detailed plans include a design for a matching and adjoining garage.

ROOM DIMENSIONS

Lounge:	4120mm x 3860mm
Kitchen/Dining Room:	4120mm x 3430mm
Bathroom:	3200mm x 1880mm
Bedroom 1:	3760mm x 3510mm
Bedroom 2:	3510mm x 2490mm
Bedroom 3:	3510mm x 2490mm
Bedroom 4:	2740mm x 2670mm
Living Room:	4120mm x 3200mm
Utility:	3200mm x 2130mm
Shower Room:	2030mm x 1070mm

Floor Area:	118.83 sq. metres
Frontage:	9.42 metres

No. 116
Rosevale

This bungalow has many design features including an integral garage with side entry and cloistered style entrance. The three living rooms are well proportioned and two bedrooms have built-in wardrobes. The exterior is finished with white dash and the roof is finished with concrete tiles.

front elevation

ROOM DIMENSIONS

Kitchen:	4060mm x 3050mm
Bathroom:	3050mm x 2180mm
Bedroom 4:	3050mm x 2740mm
Bedroom 3:	3050mm x 2740mm
Master Bedroom:	4060mm x 3050mm
Bedroom 2:	3510mm x 2950mm
Garage:	5180mm x 3680mm
Sitting Room:	5180mm x 3660mm
Dining Room:	3660mm x 2950mm

Floor Area excl. Garage: 112.48 sq. metres
Frontage: 17.37metres

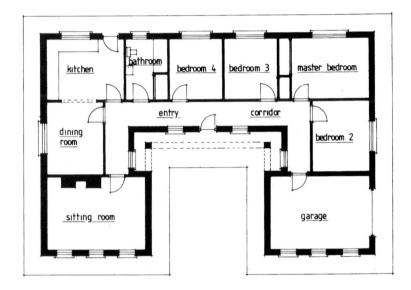

plan

elevation

plan

No. 117
Rochdale

The **Rochdale** home offers four good bedrooms, attractive insets to the front elevation and stone features. A sensible utility room opens off the Kitchen/dining room and provides access to the garage. For those who need only three bedrooms, then bedroom No. 4 is ideally located for use as a formal dining room. Fully insulated walls and roof. Stone features to the front elevation. Fire place in lounge. Solid fuel cooker in the kitchen, bathroom, hall with coats press. Walk-in hot press. Extra linen press. Full wall wardrobe space in bedroom No. 1. Suitable for most locations.

ROOM DIMENSIONS

Lounge:	4270mm x 4040mm
Kitchen:	4290mm x 3660mm
Utility Room:	3350mm x 2340mm
Garage:	4880mm x 3350mm
Bedroom:	3050mm x 3050mm
Bedroom:	4170mm x 3200mm
Bedroom:	4040mm x 3050mm
Bedroom:	3200mm x 2740mm

Floor Area incl. Garage: 133.27 sq. metres
Frontage: 17.15 metres

No. 118
Ashford

The projecting sitting room at the front of this fine family home, together with the attractive arched windows, offer you a very pleasant elevation. The layout has an open plan living area and four good sized bedrooms. Note the proximity of the cooker to the hot press. A fully fitted bathroom is located convenient to the bedrooms and a second toilet facility is located off the utility room.

ROOM DIMENSIONS

Bedroom:	3810mm x 3350mm
Bathroom:	3350mm x 2540mm
Bedroom 4:	3350mm x 3100mm
Toilet:	2640mm x 1070mm
Utility:	2640mm x 2440mm
Kitchen/Dining:	4880mm x 4520mm
Family Room:	4270mm x 3050mm
Sitting Room:	4900mm x 4120mm
Hall:	3050mm x 1830mm
Bedroom:	3050mm x 2900mm
Bedroom:	4220mm x 3350mm

Floor Area: 152.61 sq. metres
Frontage: 19.66 metres

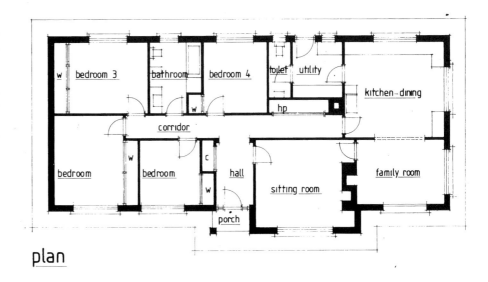

front elevation

plan

No. 119
Nashville

A full sized family home with four good bedrooms. The feature lounge cum dining room has patio doors to the rear. The large kitchen has provision for a solid fuel cooker. The entrance hall is well protected from the elements by means of a neat draught porch. The front elevation treatment is simple yet effective with its recessed stone feature. Three bedrooms have built-in wardrobes. The design drawings for this home incorporate a matching detached garage and boiler room.

ROOM DIMENSIONS

Lounge/Dining Room:	7750mm x 3960mm
Kitchen:	4120mm x 3350mm
Bedroom:	2900mm x 2740mm
Bedroom:	2900mm x 2740mm
Bedroom:	3960mm x 3200mm
Bedroom:	3860mm x 3020mm

Floor Area: 123.04 sq. metres
Frontage: 16.91 metres

front elevation

plan

No. 120
Kileen

An elegant four bedroomed bungalow with stone trim on the front elevation and a slated roof. The living rooms are of "inline" layout. Provision has been made for a solid fuel cooker in the family room. Three bedrooms have built in wardrobes and the master bedroom has a bathroom en-suite. The integral garage is suitable for later conversion to a living room.

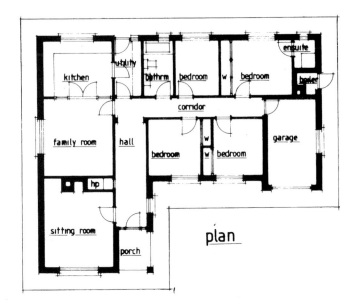

elevation

plan

ROOM DIMENSIONS

Sitting Room:	4780mm x 3860mm
Family Room:	4200mm x 3860mm
Kitchen:	3860mm x 2950mm
Utility Room:	2950mm x 1520mm
Bathroom:	2950mm x 1680mm
Hall:	1730mm wide
Bedroom:	2950mm x 2440mm
Bedroom:	3960mm x 2950mm
Bedroom:	3050mm x 2900mm
Bedroom:	3050mm x 2850mm
Garage:	4570mm x 2720mm

Floor Area incl.
Garage & porch: 142.66 sq. metres
Frontage: 16.91 metres

elevation

plan

No. 121
Arran

Another from our Classic stable, this version is a full sized rectangular bungalow with the familiar hipped roof, entrance portico and Georgian style windows. However take a look through the fine accommodation offered. The kitchen/dining room and lounge are capable of facilitating a large family. The lounge has an open fireplace and the kitchen is provided with a solid fuel cooker and adjacent hot press. The hall has a fitted coats press and each of the four fine bedrooms has a fitted wardrobe. We have recessed the front entrance door.

ROOM DIMENSIONS

Lounge:	4880mm x 3810mm
Dining Room:	4520mm x 3350mm
Kitchen:	5500mm x 3350mm
Utility Room:	2290mm x 1830mm
Bathroom:	3350mm x 2540mm
Bedroom 1:	4220mm x 3350mm
Bedroom 2:	4980mm x 3050mm
Bedroom 3:	3810mm x 3050mm
Bedroom 4:	3810mm x 3050mm
Entrance Hall:	2740mm x 1980mm

Floor Area: 150 sq. metres
Frontage: 18.43 metres

No. 122
Somerset

This fine four bedroomed home offers full family accommodation. The dining room and sitting room both have open fireplaces and provision has been made for a toilet facility opening off the utility room, and the walk-in hot press, are features of this design. An en-suite bathroom is located with the master bedroom. The roof is hipped and finished with slates.

ROOM DIMENSIONS

Sitting Room:	4880mm x 4470mm
Dining Room:	3760mm x 3660mm
Kitchen:	4930mm x 3760mm
Utility Room:	2540mm x 1830mm
Toilet:	2540mm x 1070mm
Bathroom:	3760mm x 2340mm
Bedroom/En Suite:	3810mm x 3300mm
Bedroom:	3400mm x 3050mm
Bedroom:	3300mm x 2740mm
Bedroom:	3300mm x 2900mm
Hall:	1980mm wide
Floor Area:	144.71 sq. metres
Frontage:	17.37 metres

elevation

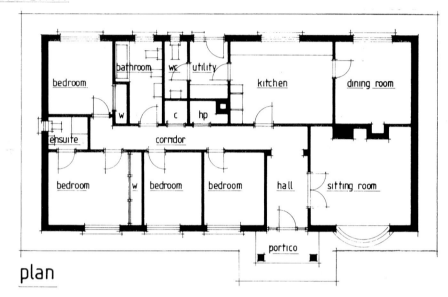

plan

No. 123
Canberra

Pleasant four bedroom L shaped bungalow with spacious accommodation. Stone feature to front elevation. Fully insulated slate or tiled roof. Hardwood joinery. Lounge fireplace and solid fuel cooker in kitchen.

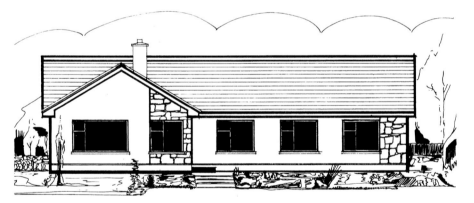

ROOM DIMENSIONS

Lounge:	4420mm x 5400mm
Dining Room:	3960mm x 3350mm
Kitchen:	4420mm x 3350mm
Utility Room:	1930mm x 2340mm
Bathroom:	3350mm x 1730mm
Bedroom:	2900mm x 2950mm
Bedroom:	2900mm x 2950mm
Bedroom:	3350mm x 3150mm
Bedroom:	4830mm x 3350mm

Floor Area:	138.57 sq. metres
Frontage:	17.83 metres

No. 124
Setanta

This elegant four bedroomed home has a floor area of approximately 139.50 sq. m. The central hall separates the living portion of the home from the sleeping areas. The master bedroom has an en-suite shower and hand basin. All bedrooms have built-in wardrobes. The walls are fully insulated, as is the roof space. Attractive front porch, supported by glass fibre columns in original style, coupled with Georgian style windows and hipped slated roof give the dwelling a distinctive elevation.

ROOM DIMENSIONS

Lounge:	4570mm x 3810mm
Kitchen/Dining Room:	7160mm x 3660mm
Utility Room:	2080mm x 2130mm
Bathroom:	2850mm x 2080mm
Hall:	1910mm wide
Bedroom:	3350mm x 3050mm
Bedroom:	3760mm x 3050mm
Bedroom:	3760mm x 2850mm
Bedroom:	3050mm x 2850mm
Floor Area:	138.05 sq. metres
Frontage:	19.93 metres

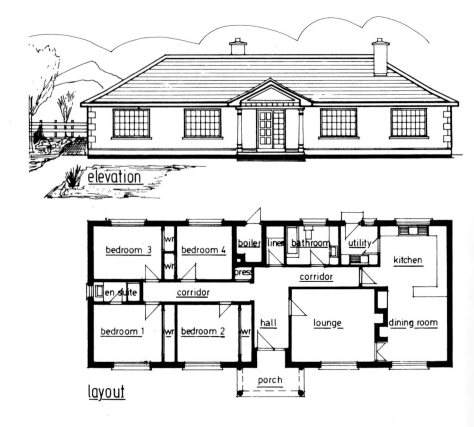

elevation

layout

No. 125
Pembroke

Behind this traditional elevation we have planned a fine family home with three living rooms and four good sized bedrooms. The main bathroom is fitted with a sauna. Note the unusual design around the master bedroom area, providing a dressing room and en-suite bathroom. The roof is finished with slates and the attractive bay windows balance the elevation.

ROOM DIMENSIONS

Bedroom 2:	3510mm x 3350mm
Bathroom:	3350mm x 3000mm
Utility:	2290mm x 1980mm
Kitchen:	5330mm x 3350mm
Dining Room:	3660mm x 3350mm
Lounge:	5130mm x 4120mm
Hall:	2130mm wide
Bedroom 4:	3960mm x 2900mm
Bedroom 3:	3960mm x 3050mm
Bedroom 1:	3960mm x 3350mm
Dressing Area:	2290mm x 1830mm
En Suite:	2440mm x 1070mm
Floor Area:	152.71 sq. metres
Frontage:	18.49 metres

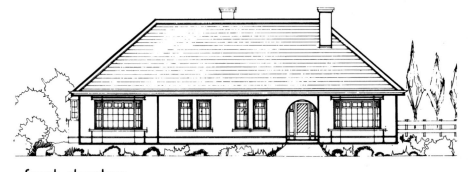

front elevation

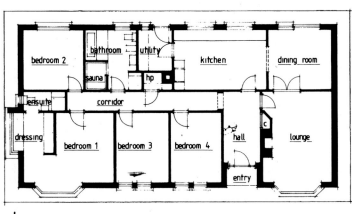

plan

No. 126
Ontario

The Ontario meets the demands of the family home. We feature front and rear draught porches to combat the winter weather. The kitchen has the facility of a solid fuel cooker. The front elevation is pleasing but not fussy. A tiled roof and napped plaster finish to the exterior gives a traditional appearance suited to all surroundings.

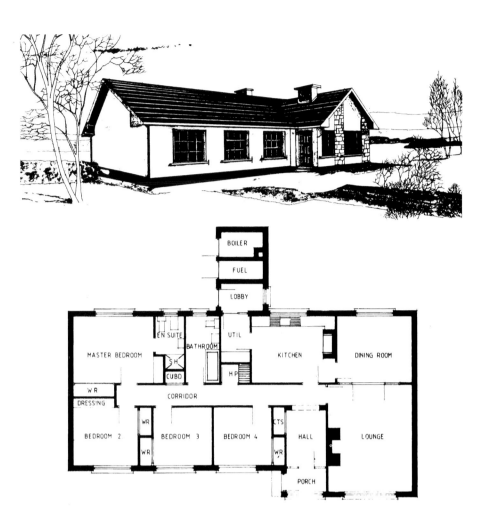

ROOM DIMENSIONS

Lounge:	5390mm x 4450mm
Dining Room:	3960mm x 3350mm
Kitchen:	4420mm x 3350mm
Hall:	2130mm wide
Master Bedroom:	4220mm x 3350mm
Bedroom:	3350mm x 3350mm
Bedroom:	3050mm x 2900mm
Bedroom:	3050mm x 2900mm
Bathroom:	3350mm x 1750mm
Floor Area:	151.29 sq. metres
Frontage:	18.27 metres

No. 127
Tunbridge

A brick fronted bungalow with full family accommodation. A matching garage is described on the plan. Provision has been made for a solid fuel cooker in the kitchen. A full wall wardrobe and vanity unit is described in Bedroom No. 1. The roof is finished with slates.

front elevation

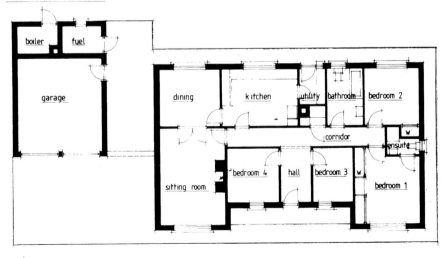

plan

ROOM DIMENSIONS

Dining Room:	3510mm x 3200mm
Kitchen:	4470mm x 3200mm
Utility:	2130mm x 1520mm
Bathroom:	3200mm x 2130mm
Bedroom 2:	3200mm x 3200mm
En Suite:	2030mm x 910mm
Bedroom 1:	3810mm x 3760mm
Bedroom 3:	3050mm x 2340mm
Hall:	3050mm x 2340mm
Bedroom 4:	3050mm x 3050mm
Sitting Room:	5440mm x 3810mm
Corridor:	1020mm wide

Floor Area:	170.28 sq. metres
Frontage:	15.85 metres
Floor Area (House only):	123.78 sq. metres

No. 128
Wicklow

A modern design with an attractive roofed terrace to the front of the house. The living areas are well laid out towards the front of the dwelling and provision is made for a solid fuel or oil fired cooker in the kitchen. The garage is connected to the dwelling by a roofed walkway. All bedrooms have built-in wardrobes. Note the generous dimensioned bathroom with corner bath.

front elevation

ROOM DIMENSIONS

Bathroom:	4170mm x 2640mm
Bedroom 2:	2900mm x 2790mm
Bedroom 3:	2850mm x 2790mm
Bedroom 4:	4170mm x 2540mm
Utility:	1730mm x 1630mm
Kitchen:	3660mm x 3050mm
Dining:	3960mm x 3050mm
Sitting Room:	4270mm x 3960mm
Hall:	1680mm wide
Bedroom:	3660mm x 3350mm
En Suite:	1830mm x 1520mm
Floor Area:	
124.62 sq. metres	
Frontage:	16.31 metres

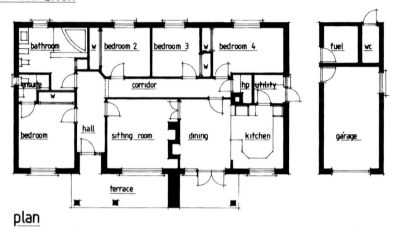

plan

No. 129
Classic

Almost 158.10 sq.m. of luxury. Four bedrooms, family kitchen, lounge, formal dining room, en-suite, large utility room, hipped and slated roof, porch, Georgian style windows. Indeed a mini-mansion with a frontage of 19.15 metres.

ROOM DIMENSIONS

Lounge:	3960mm x 4390mm
Dining Room:	4120mm x 3350mm
Kitchen:	5790mm x 4270mm
Utility Room:	3350mm x 2590mm
Bedroom:	4270mm x 3350mm
Bedroom:	3350mm x 2900mm
Bedroom:	3380mm x 3250mm
Bedroom:	4140mm x 3350mm
Floor Area:	158.10 sq. metres
Frontage:	19.15 metres

No. 130
Webster

The elevation features of this fine Ranch Style bungalow are the roofed entry detail, a self supporting bow window to the lounge area and a clean roof line. The main hall is divided from the main corridor by means of a segmental arch and the corridor itself takes in natural light from a feature window on the gable end wall. Note the proximity of the hot press to the solid fuel cooker in the kitchen. Two open fireplaces are provided and all four bedrooms have fitted wardrobes. The bathroom is fully fitted and includes a separate shower cabinet.

elevation

ROOM DIMENSIONS

Lounge:	4900mm x 4300mm
Living Room:	4600mm x 3800mm
Kitchen/Dining Room:	4900mm x 3400mm
Utility Room:	2100mm x 1900mm
Bathroom:	3400mm x 2100mm
Bedroom 1:	3900mm x 3400mm
Bedroom 2:	3400mm x 3200mm
Bedroom 3:	3400mm x 3200mm
Bedroom 4:	3400mm x 3200mm

Floor Area:	149.82 sq. metres
Frontage:	18.30 metres

plan

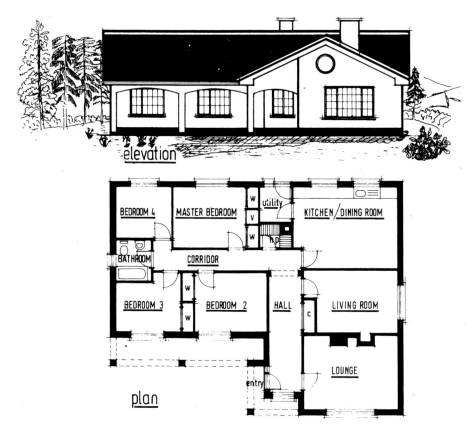

elevation

plan

No. 131
Washington

Although having a short frontage dimension this four bedroomed family home offers full family accommodation. The sleeping and living areas have been separated by design. The elevation detail is interesting with cloistered archways and projecting roof, finished with slates. The Georgian style windows set off the design. Three of the bedrooms have built-in wardrobes. A solid fuel cooker is provided in the kitchen with adjacent hot press. Two open fireplaces serve the living room and lounge.

ROOM DIMENSIONS

Lounge:	5180mm x 3960mm
Living Room:	4520mm x 3350mm
Kitchen/Dining Room:	5790mm x 4420mm
Utility Room:	1930mm x 1730mm
Master Bedroom:	3960mm x 3250mm
Bedroom 2:	3960mm x 3200mm
Bedroom 3:	3610mm x 2590mm
Bedroom 4:	3100mm x 2740mm
Bathroom:	2240mm x 1880mm

Floor Area:	149.73 sq. metres
Frontage:	16.15 metres

No. 132
Ashford

We have taken the kitchen dining room to the front of this well proportioned bungalow and located the sitting room to the rear of the house. Two of the bedrooms have built-in wardrobes and we have included a small study or fifth bedroom opening off the main hall. Natural light is provided in the corridor. The elevation is simple in detail and we have featured French windows on the front bedrooms. The roof is finished with concrete tiles.

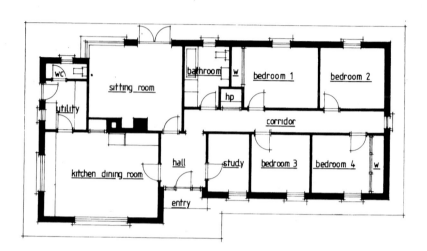

ROOM DIMENSIONS

Toilet:	2180mm x 760mm
Utility:	2440mm x 2180mm
Sitting Room:	4880mm x 4220mm
Bathroom:	3000mm x 2340mm
Bedroom 1:	3810mm x 3000mm
Bedroom 2:	3400mm x 3000mm
Bedroom 4:	3050mm x 2950mm
Bedroom 3:	3050mm x 2950mm
Study:	3050mm x 2130mm
Hall:	2390mm wide
Kitchen/Dining Room:	5990mm x 4270mm

Floor Area:	134.66 sq. metres
Frontage:	18.29 metres

No. 133
Meridian

An interesting four bedroomed bungalow with a brick face and a roof change over the entrance hall. This Bungalow is mean on site frontage occupying only 10.50 metres. The main hall has a fitted coats press and a toilet and basin discreetly located. The main service corridor continues from the main hall giving access to the living and sleeping accommodation. Three living rooms are laid out in-line with two open fireplaces and a chimney serving a Solid Fuel Cooker. All four bedrooms have fitted wardrobes.

elevation

plan

ROOM DIMENSIONS

Sitting Room:	4850mm x 4300mm
Living Room:	4850mm x 3350mm
Kitchen Dining Room:	4850mm x 3700mm
Utility Room:	3000mm x 2800mm
Bathroom:	3050mm x 2000mm
Shower Area:	2150mm x 1000mm
Main Hall:	2750mm x 3100mm
Toilet:	2200mm x 1100mm
Bedroom 1:	3600mm x 3200mm
Bedroom 2:	3600mm x 3000mm
Bedroom 3:	3600mm x 2750mm
Bedroom 4:	3600mm x 2750mm

Floor Area:	160.29 sq. metres
Frontage:	10.50 metres

No. 134
Canticle

FAMILY LUXURY. No other words can describe this magnificent bungalow. Huge kitchen dining room and lounge. Four double size bedrooms with cupboards and the master bedroom has its own full bathroom facility. Easy to heat features with solid fuel cooker and the boiler house is located adjoining the hot press. Fully fitted bathroom. Utility room with access to second Toilet. Walk-in linen press. Feature stone panels to front, together with bow windows to the kitchen and lounge

front elevation

ROOM DIMENSIONS

Kitchen/Dining Room:	6960mm x 4220mm
Lounge:	5790mm x 4220mm
Bedroom:	3660mm x 3350mm
Bedroom:	3350mm x 2900mm
Bedroom:	3860mm x 2820mm
Bedroom:	3050mm x 3120mm
Study:	2440mm x 2340mm

Floor Area:	159.77 sq. metres
Frontage:	19.38 metres

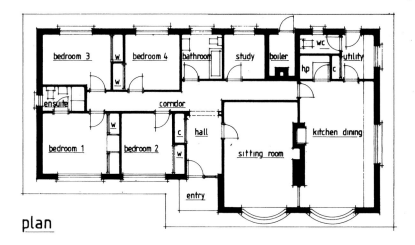

plan

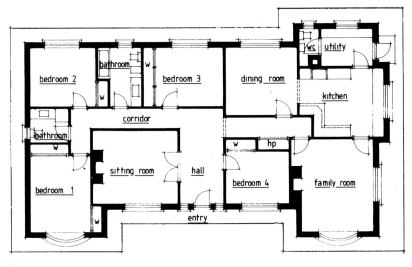

front elevation

plan

No. 135
Rodez

This well balanced family home has four bedrooms with built-in wardrobes. Two separate bathrooms are provided. The attractive living areas are laid out in up to the minute style and allow for complete ease of circulation. The sitting room opens off the front hall via double doors and bedroom No. 4 could well be used as a study. A second toilet facility is located opening off the utility room. The front elevation is finished with white dash and incorporates bow windows and a corbelled roof over the main entrance door.

ROOM DIMENSIONS

Bedroom 2:	3660mm x 3150mm
Bathroom:	3150mm x 2440mm
Bedroom 3:	3760mm x 3150mm
Dining Room:	4010mm x 3660mm
Utility:	2900mm x 1980mm
Toilet:	1980mm x 1070mm
Kitchen:	4780mm x 3660mm
Family Room:	4980mm x 4570mm
Bedroom 4:	3510mm x 2790mm
Hall:	5030mm x 2440mm
Sitting Room:	4720mm x 3960mm
Bedroom 1:	4120mm x 3350mm
Bathroom:	2180mm x 1830mm

Floor Area:	171.86 sq. metres
Frontage:	19.61 metres

No. 136
Concordia

A ranch style bungalow, with a long elevation that breaks with tradition in some way, has a sweeping roof line over the main entry. The two half dormer windows in the master bedroom provide an interesting detail internally and externally. The front bedroom window openings are trimmed with granite reveals and we have featured the entry area with brick, built in herringbone fashion. A feature of this design is the glazed solar trap to side part of the rere line. The accommodation is generous and suited to family living. The lounge is provided with an open fire and we have included a chimney in the family kitchen to cater for an inset fire, or solid fuel cooker.

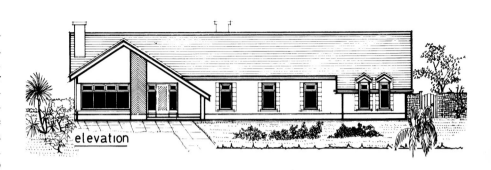

elevation

ROOM DIMENSIONS

Lounge:	5590mm x 4120mm
Dining Room:	3660mm x 3510mm
Family Kitchen:	6100mm x 3660mm
Utility Room:	3660mm x 1980mm
Toilet:	2260mm x 990mm
Bathroom:	3660mm x 2130mm
En Suite:	3660mm x 2690mm
Bedroom:	5590mm x 3660mm
Bedroom:	3660mm x 3050mm
Bedroom:	3050mm x 2900mm
Main Hall:	2440mm x 2440mm

Floor Area:	169.53 sq. metres
Frontage:	22.00 metres

plan

elevation

No. 137
Fenwick

A ranch style bungalow of generous proportions, this fine home has stone trim and low, long roof lines. We have divided the living and sleeping sections with the main hall and added 3 steps down to the sleeping areas. The central chimney stack in the living areas caters for two open fireplaces and a solid fuel cooker. A second toilet facility is located opening off the utility areas and we have provided an en-suite shower to cater for the master bedroom. Provision has been made for fitted wardrobes in three bedrooms.

PLAN

ROOM DIMENSIONS

Lounge:	7600mm x 4000mm
Dining Room:	4600mm x 3500mm
Kitchen:	4200mm x 4000mm
Utility Room:	2300mm x 1900mm
Toilet:	3000mm x 1100mm
Bathroom:	3000mm x 2500mm
En Suite:	2700mm x 1700mm
Bedroom 1:	4300mm x 3100mm
Bedroom 2:	4200mm x 3000mm
Bedroom 3:	3200mm x 3100mm
Bedroom 4:	3000mm x 2500mm
Boiler Room:	3100mm x 1650mm
Garage:	5800mm x 3100mm

Floor Area:	149.85 sq. metres
Frontage:	23.25 metres

No. 138
Bedford

This large and impressive home has everything to offer. Styled front with classic portico, large enough to use as a carport. Study, en-suite bathroom, formal dining room with fireplace etc.

FRONT ELEVATION

ROOM DIMENSIONS

Kitchen/Dining:	6000mm x 3650mm
Utility:	1750mm x 2350mm
Sitting Room:	4650mm x 5299mm
Dining Room:	3350mm x 3650mm
Hall:	1980mm wide
Bedroom:	3550mm x 3350mm
Bedroom:	3960mm x 3350mm
En-suite:	2059mm x 3000mm
Study:	4041mm x 3000mm
Boiler:	1388mm x 1850mm
Toilet:	1388mm x 1850mm
Bedroom:	4210mm x 3650mm
En-suite:	1071mm x 2804mm
Bathroom:	2409mm x 3650mm
Bedroom:	3650mm x 3549mm

Floor Area:	190.79 square metres
Frontage:	23.31 metres

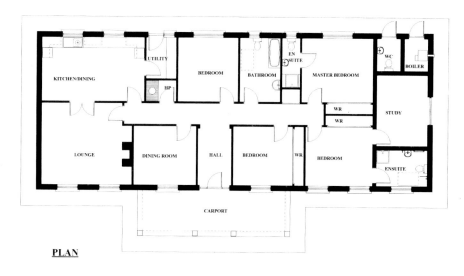

PLAN

elevation

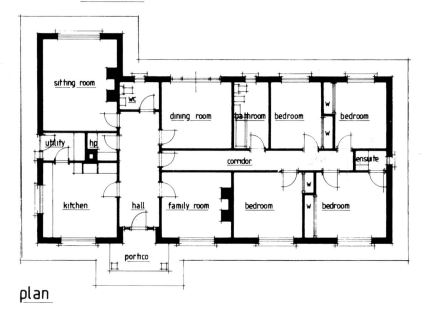

plan

No. 139
Moylough

This fine family home has the kitchen located to the front of the house. The three other living rooms are well proportioned and we have provided open fireplaces in the sitting room and family room. The kitchen is fitted with a solid fuel cooker. Front elevation features include curved top windows and an open portico. All bedrooms have fitted wardrobes. A second toilet facility opens off the main hall. The design is also available with a hipped roof.

ROOM DIMENSIONS

Kitchen:	4270mm x 4120mm
Utility:	2440mm x 1520mm
Sitting Room:	5030mm x 1520mm
Toilet:	2290mm x 1520mm
Family Room:	3960mm x 3560mm
Dining Room:	3960mm x 3660mm
Bathroom:	3660mm x 1980mm
Bedroom:	3960mm x 3560mm
Bedroom:	3910mm x 3560mm
Bedroom:	3660mm x 2900mm
Bedroom:	3660mm x 2900mm

Floor Area:	176.42 sq. metres
Frontage:	20.07 metres

No. 140
Brooklodge

This version of our Classic bungalow locates the dining room and lounge to the rere line of the home and will suit those whose site aspect demands living rooms in that location. The familiar lines of the front elevation are retained. The kitchen dining room provides the occupants with a view to the side and front of the house. We have provided a solid fuel cooker in the kitchen with adjacent hot press, and an open fireplace in the lounge. The four good size bedrooms each have fitted wardrobes. A second toilet facility is provided adjacent to the kitchen and the main bathroom is fully fitted.

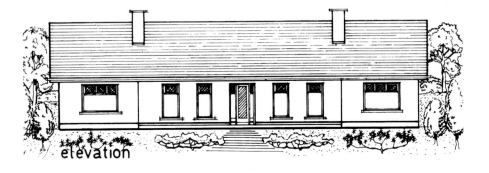

ELEVATION

ROOM DIMENSIONS

Kitchen:	4980mm x 3810mm
Dining Area:	3810mm x 3150mm
Formal Dining Room:	4470mm x 3660mm
Lounge:	4880mm x 3660mm
Utility Room:	2440mm x 2130mm
Toilet:	2130mm x 1270mm
Bathroom:	3660mm x 1880mm
Bedroom 1:	4270mm x 3150mm
Bedroom 2:	4980mm x 3050mm
Bedroom 3:	3660mm x 3150mm
Bedroom 4:	3510mm x 3150mm
Floor Area:	166.45 sq. metres
Frontage:	19.65 metres

PLAN

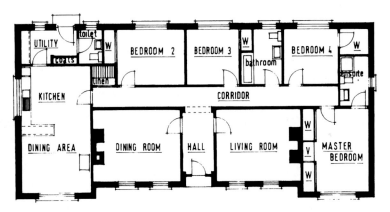

elevation

plan

No. 141
Lisdornan

An upmarket Ranch Style Bungalow. The elevation is properly balanced, the main entry being recessed and central to the design. Views from the kitchen dining room are offered to the side and front of the residence, and the two main reception rooms open directly from the main hall. We have included two open fireplaces and a solid fuel cooker in the layout. The main bathroom is fully fitted and a half bathroom services the master bedroom. All four bedrooms have fitted wardrobes. The clean roof line is emphasised by the slate covering and medium roof pitch.

ROOM DIMENSIONS

Kitchen Dining Room:	6900mm x 3900mm
Dining Room:	4800mm x 3900mm
Living Room:	4800mm x 3900mm
Utility Room:	3300mm x 1800mm
Toilet:	1800mm x 1300mm
Bathroom:	3000mm x 2300mm
En Suite:	2700mm x 1600mm
Bedroom 1:	4500mm x 3900mm
Bedroom 2:	3800mm x 3000mm
Bedroom 3:	3000mm x 3000mm
Bedroom 4:	3000mm x 3000mm
Floor Area:	179.50 sq. metres
Frontage:	20.11 metres

No. 142
Lissarda

A fine family home in our Classic style with four living rooms and four good sized bedrooms. The master bedroom has an en-suite bathroom and dressing area. All bedrooms have built-in wardrobes. Three open fireplaces are provided together with a solid fuel or oil fired cooker. Direct access is provided from kitchen to dining room via double doors.

elevation

ROOM DIMENSIONS

Toilet:	2130mm x 1370mm
Utility:	3100mm x 2130mm
Kitchen:	4570mm x 4270mm
Dining Room:	3810mm x 3610mm
Lounge:	6100mm x 4570mm
Hall:	2130mm wide
Bedroom 4:	3510mm x 3050mm
Bathroom:	3510mm x 2130mm
Bedroom 3:	3510mm x 3050mm
En Suite:	2130mm x 1780mm
Dressing:	2440mm x 2290mm
Master Bedroom:	4270mm x 3510mm
Bedroom 2:	3660mm x 3510mm
Family Room:	3660mm x 3510mm

Floor Area:	195.35 sq. metres
Frontage:	19.91 metres

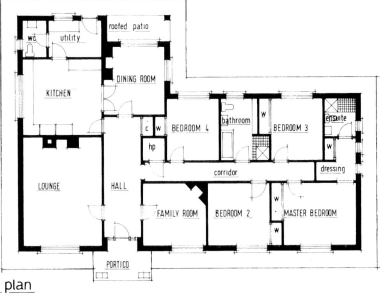

plan

No. 143
Killarney

This is a fine example of a customised design. The sleeping area is self contained and features four fine bedrooms each with a fitted wardrobe. The master bedroom has a bathroom ensuite. The living areas are well laid out and incorporate many design features. A separate toilet facility is provided, opening off the main hall. The elevation is distinctive and the plan creates an attractive courtyard around the entrance. Roof finish is of concrete tiles.

ROOM DIMENSIONS

Sitting Room:	6100mm x 4420mm
Dining Room:	4320mm x 3960mm
Kitchen:	3660mm x 3660mm
Utility Room:	2950mm x 2030mm
Family Dining Room:	4570mm x 3430mm
Toilet:	1980mm x 1370mm
Games Room:	5800mm x 4270mm
Bedroom/En Suite:	4010mm x 3400mm
Bedroom:	3050mm x 2900mm
Bedroom:	3890mm x 3660mm
Bedroom:	3660mm x 3120mm
Bathroom:	2520mm x 2390mm

Floor Area:	215.30 sq. metres
Frontage:	24.69 metres

No. 144
Gallow

This is an extended version of our design No. 125, incorporating an integral garage. A fine family home with four large bedrooms and well laid out living accommodation.

ROOM DIMENSIONS

Kitchen/Dining Room:	6600mm x 3350mm
Dining Room:	4470mm x 3350mm
Bathroom:	3350mm x 2740mm
Bedroom:	3510mm x 3050mm
Bedroom:	5280mm x 3960mm
Bedroom:	3960mm x 3050mm
Bedroom:	3960mm x 2900mm
Hall:	2130mm wide
Sitting Room:	5130mm x 4120mm
Garage:	5790mm x 3350mm
Utility Room:	3350mm x 2210mm

Floor Area:	179.42 sq. metres
Frontage:	21.79 metres

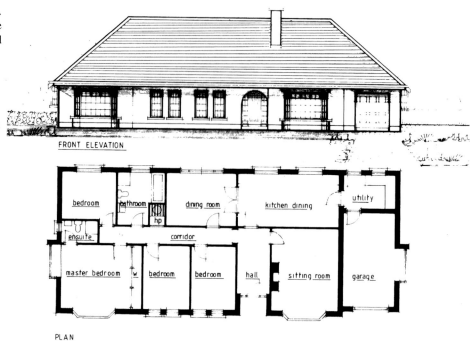

FRONT ELEVATION

PLAN

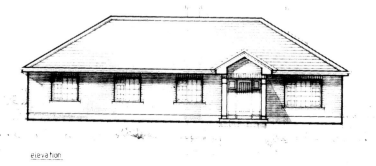

elevation

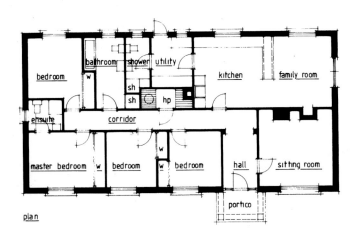

plan

No. 145
Danestown

This attractive brick bungalow features well laid out living and sleeping accommodation. The master bedroom has a bathroom ensuite. Provision is made for a boiler or cooker in the kitchen and open fireplaces in the family room and sitting room.

ROOM DIMENSIONS

Bedroom:	3810mm x 3050mm
Bedroom:	3050mm x 2900mm
Bedroom:	3050mm x 3200mm
Bedroom:	3150mm x 3300mm
Hall:	1980mm wide
Sitting Room:	4220mm x 4220mm
Dining Family Room:	3910mm x 3350mm
Kitchen Area:	4670mm x 3910mm
Utility Room:	2740mm x 2340mm
Toilet & Shower:	2740mm x 1420mm
Bathroom:	3910mm x 2340mm
En Suite Bathroom:	1980mm x 1680mm

Floor Area:	145.64 sq. metres
Frontage:	18.29 metres

No. 146
Kilnew

This design is an extended version of our popular design No. 103 and features additional bedrooms and ensuite bathroom. Suitable for a large family and could be used with five or six bedrooms. Additional bedroom space could be utilised as living area.

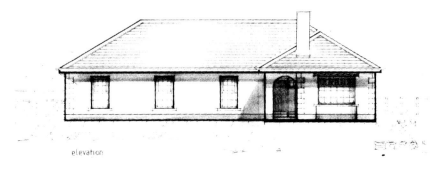
elevation

ROOM DIMENSIONS

Sitting Room:	4570mm x 3960mm
Kitchen/Dining Room:	6760mm x 3960mm
Hall:	3960mm x 1730mm
Bathroom:	3660mm x 2590mm
En Suite:	1980mm x 1370mm
Bedroom:	3660mm x 3710mm
Bedroom:	3660mm x 2740mm
Bedroom:	3150mm x 3050mm
Bedroom:	3660mm x 3050mm
Bedroom:	3660mm x 3120mm
Bedroom:	3120mm x 2790mm

Floor Area:	151.59 sq. metres
Frontage:	17.91 metres

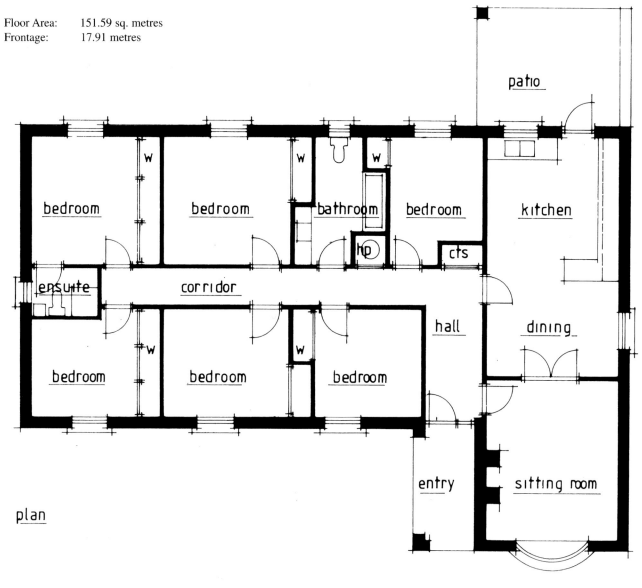
plan

No. 147
Douglas

An attractive four bedroomed home with the Kitchen located to the front of the house. This would particularly suit a south facing aspect. The layout incorporates four living rooms and four bedrooms. The master bedroom has a bathroom en-suite.

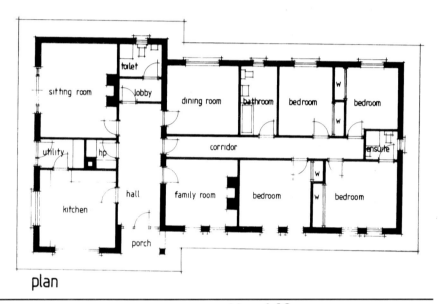

elevation

ROOM DIMENSIONS

Kitchen:	4270mm x 4120mm
Utility Room:	2440mm x 1520mm
Sitting Room:	5030mm x 4270mm
Hall:	2290mm wide
Toilet:	2290mm x 1730mm
Family Room:	3960mm x 3560mm
Dining Room:	3960mm x 3660mm
Bathroom:	3660mm x 1830mm
Bedroom:	3660mm x 2900mm
Bedroom:	3660mm x 2900mm
Bedroom:	3660mm x 2900mm
Bedroom:	3660mm x 3560mm
Bedroom:	3960mm x 3560mm
En Suite:	1730mm x 1520mm

Floor Area:	183.21 sq. metres
Frontage:	20.27 metres

plan

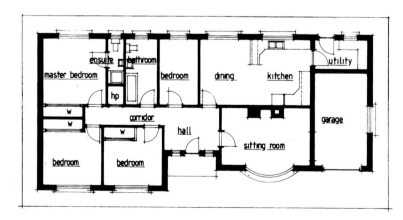

No. 148
Humber

Modern styling with brick features on the elevation and the integral garage makes this a very attractive design. The living and sleeping areas are well laid out. The roof is finished with concrete tiles.

ROOM DIMENSIONS

Sitting Room:	5300mm x 3200mm
Garage:	5050mm x 3000mm
Kitchen Dining:	6400mm x 3600mm
Hall:	3200mm x 2400mm
Utility Room:	3000mm x 1600mm
Bedroom:	3400mm x 3300mm
Bedroom:	3600mm x 3600mm
Bedroom:	3600mm x 3600mm
Bedroom:	3400mm x 3100mm
Bedroom:	3600mm x 2400mm
Bathroom:	3600mm x 1900mm
En Suite:	2500mm x 900mm

Floor Area:	138 sq. metres
Frontage:	19.45 metres

No. 149
Holbrook

Another of our designs with the living rooms facing front and suited to a southerly aspect. Four bedrooms are arranged in-line along the rere line of the house. The design features a particularly large Sitting Room. External finish is in white dash and the roof is finished with concrete tiles.

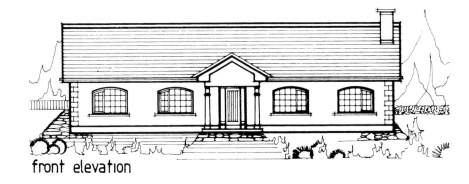

front elevation

ROOM DIMENSIONS

Kitchen:	3860mm x 3400mm
Family Room:	3660mm x 3560mm
Entrance Hall:	1830mm wide
Sitting Room:	7620mm x 4370mm
Utility Room/W.C.:	2590mm x 1830mm
Bedroom:	4270mm x 3400mm
Bedroom:	3200mm x 3050mm
Bedroom:	3200mm x 2590mm
Bedroom:	3200mm x 2590mm
Bathroom:	3560mm x 2130mm
En-Suite:	1980mm x 1520mm

Floor Area:	152.61 sq. metres
Frontage:	17.88 metres

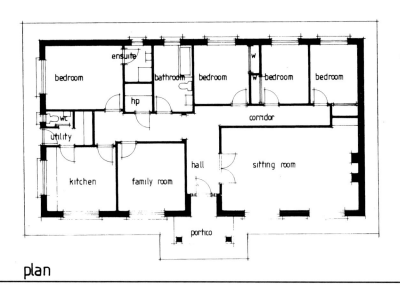

plan

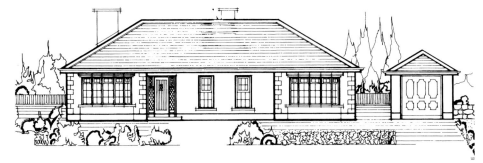

No. 150
Hadley

This is a four-bedroomed version of our design No. 62, featuring good living accommodation and a balanced elevation with bow window features. Two open fireplaces are provided and a chimney to cater for the central heating boiler. The detached garage is optional.

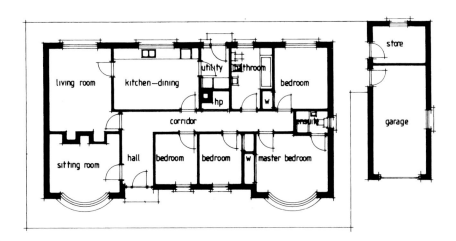

ROOM DIMENSIONS

Garage:	6000mm x 3400mm
Store:	3000mm x 2000mm
Sitting Room:	4100mm x 3400mm
Living Room:	4500mm x 3600mm
Kitchen Dining Room:	4900mm x 3400mm
Utility Room;	1600mm x 2400mm
Bathroom:	2300mm x 3400mm
En Suite:	2100mm x 2100mm
Bedroom;	4100mm x 3300mm
Bedroom:	3200mm x 3400mm
Bedroom:	2400mm x 2800mm
Bedroom:	2800mm x 2500mm

Floor Area:	125 sq. metres
Frontage:	16.60 metres

No. 151
Dauphin

This attractive four bedroomed bungalow has a simple elevation under a slated hipped roof. The accommodation is simply and effectively laid out. Provision is made for an oil-fired cooker or boiler in the kitchen, and two open fireplaces are provided. The bathroom is large and a bathroom is provided ensuite with the main bedroom. Built-in wardrobes are designed for two bedrooms. The fabric of the building is fully insulated.

front elevation

ROOM DIMENSIONS

Sitting Room:	4800mm x 4200mm
Family Room:	3600mm x 3300mm
Kitchen:	4100mm x 3300mm
Bathroom:	3300mm x 1900mm
En Suite:	3300mm x 1200mm
Bedroom:	3600mm x 3300mm
Bedroom:	3700mm x 3000mm
Bedroom:	3000mm x 3000mm
Bedroom:	3000mm x 2700mm
Hall:	1800mm wide

Floor Area:	124.60 sq. metres
Frontage:	17 metres

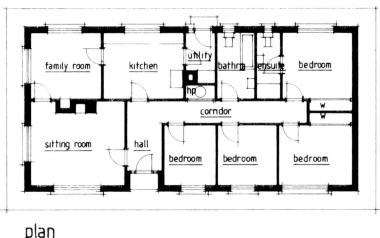

plan

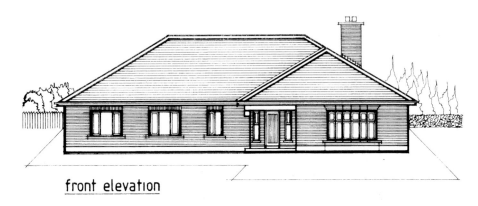

front elevation

No. 152
Dalgan

The attractive brick elevation is deceptive and fronts a large family home with four good sized bedrooms, a study, and large living areas. The master bedroom has a bathroom ensuite. A roofed terrace is provided at the rear of the kitchen/living room and this area can be glazed later to provide a conservatory. Two fireplaces are provided. The design drawings feature an adjoining garage, storage area and boiler room to complement the house design.

ROOM DIMENSIONS

Sitting Room:	6300mm x 5500mm
Kitchen Dining Room:	7600mm x 4000mm
Utility Room:	2500mm x 1900mm
Bathroom & Toilet:	3500mm x 2500mm
Hall:	3200mm wide
Bedroom:	3700mm x 3400mm
Bedroom:	3700mm x 3000mm
Bedroom:	5800mm x 3200mm
Bedroom:	5000mm x 4000mm
En Suite:	2500mm x 2400mm
Study:	3400mm x 2600mm

Floor Area:	199.09 sq. metres
Frontage:	21.20 metres

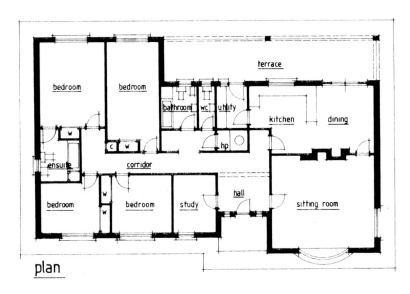

plan

No. 153
Abbeyland

A large family bungalow with hipped roof and front projecting areas with bow windows. Four bedrooms are designed, each with walk-in wardrobes. Two bedrooms have bathrooms en-suite. The dining room opens onto a patio area, which is roofed via French doors. The sleeping areas are self-contained. The utility area opens off a lobby. Open fireplaces are designed for the family room and sitting room. The hall and access corridor is of generous proportions.

ROOM DIMENSIONS

Utility Room:	2370mm x 3000mm
Toilet:	1800mm x 1200mm
Kitchen/Dining Room:	4270mm x 6710mm
Dining Room:	3700mm x 4348mm
Family Room:	4270mm x 6336mm
Sitting Room:	4570mm x 4270mm
Bathroom:	2690mm x 2768mm
Bedroom:	3470mm x 3934mm
Bedroom:	4270mm x 2917mm
En-suite:	2425mm x 1497mm
En-suite:	2425mm x 1500mm
Bedroom:	4270mm x 4153mm
Bedroom:	3470mm x 2085mm

Floor area: 227.31sq.m.
Frontage dimension: 20.50m

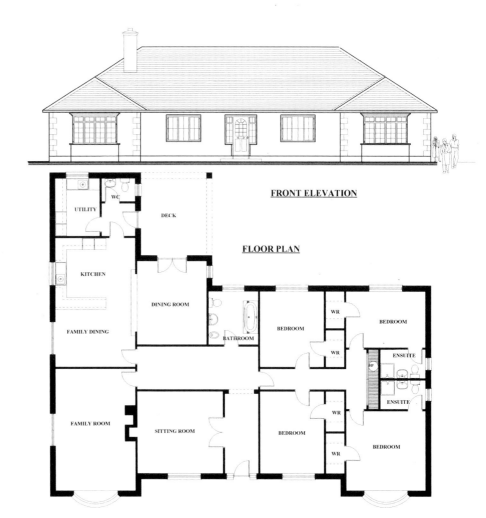

FRONT ELEVATION

FLOOR PLAN

front elevation

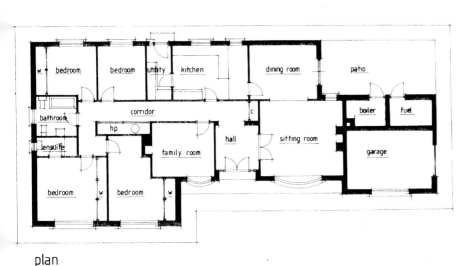

plan

No. 154
Stanbury

The four bedroomed bungalow with integral garage is suitable for a site with a wide frontage dimension. The accommodation is well laid out and the bedroom section is confined to one end of the house. All bedrooms are well dimensioned and three bedrooms have built-in wardrobes. The large sitting room leads directly, by steps, to the dining room. Open fireplaces are provided, one in the sitting room and one in the family room. The exterior is finished with napped plaster and the roof is covered with concrete tiles.

ROOM DIMENSIONS

Sitting Room:	5330mm x 4670mm
Dining Room:	4270mm x 3300mm
Kitchen:	4780mm x 3300mm
Family Room:	3960mm x 3350mm
Utility Room:	3300mm x 1520mm
Bedroom:	5280mm x 3660mm
Bedroom:	3960mm x 3810mm
Bedroom:	3200mm x 3000mm
Bedroom:	3300mm x 3050mm
Bathroom:	2590mm x 2440mm
En Suite:	2590mm x 1120mm
Garage:	5490mm x 3660mm
Boiler Room:	2520mm x 1700mm
Fuel Store:	2740mm x 1700mm
Hall:	2740mm wide

Floor Area: 207.39 sq. metres
Frontage: 25.98 metres

No. 155
Tredfort

This traditional four bedroomed bungalow offers well laid out accommodation in simple rectangular form for ease of construction. Two open fireplaces are provided. The bedrooms are generously dimensioned and two bedrooms have built-in wardrobes. All floors are suspended timber, the roof is covered with slates, and the exterior is finished with dry dash.

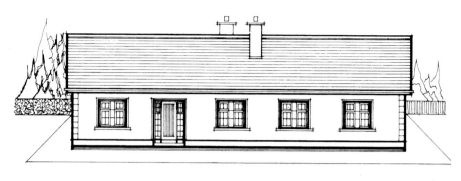

front elevation

ROOM DIMENSIONS

Kitchen:	4830mm x 3660mm
Dining Room:	3660mm x 3660mm
Sitting Room:	3660mm x 3660mm
Family Room:	3660mm x 3050mm
Utility Room:	2440mm x 1220mm
Bathroom:	3660mm x 2180mm
Bedroom:	3660mm x 3660mm
Bedroom:	3660mm x 3660mm
Bedroom:	3660mm x 3200mm
Bedroom:	3510mm x 3350mm
Floor Area:	147.59 sq. metres
Frontage:	17.77 metres

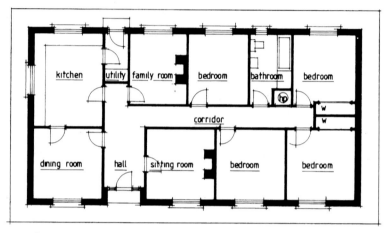

plan

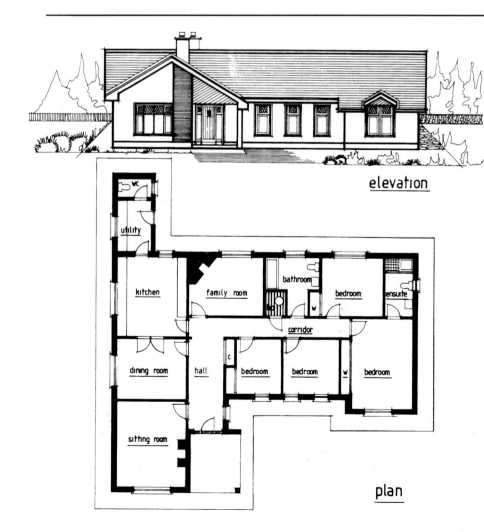

elevation

No. 156
Loxton

An unusual elevation and well laid out family accommodation features in this four bedroomed bungalow. The design has evolved from our design No. 136. Three bedrooms have built-in wardrobes, and the master bedroom has a bathroom ensuite. The sitting room and family room have open fireplaces and provision has been made for a cooker or boiler in the kitchen. The roof is finished with concrete tiles and the elevation has brick features.

ROOM DIMENSIONS

Sitting Room:	4880mm x 4170mm
Dining Room:	4170mm x 3510mm
Kitchen:	4570mm x 4170mm
Utility Room:	3000mm x 1980mm
Toilet:	1980mm x 1070mm
Family Room:	4470mm x 3350mm
Bathroom:	3350mm x 3300mm
En Suite:	3350mm x 1680mm
Bedroom:	5180mm x 3660mm
Bedroom:	3660mm x 3350mm
Bedroom:	3350mm x 3050mm
Bedroom:	3050mm x 2740mm
Floor Area:	175.11 sq. metres
Frontage:	18.28 metres

plan

No. 157
Tarnwood

A well laid out four bedroomed bungalow with hipped end roof, with a napped plaster finish externally, and a slated roof. All bedrooms have built-in wardrobes and the master bedroom has a bathroom ensuite. The living and sleeping areas are divided by the central hallway. Provision is made for open fireplaces in the sitting room and dining room. The kitchen may have an oil-fired cooker or boiler fitted. A walk-in hot press is located off the hallway

elevation

ROOM DIMENSIONS

Sitting Room:	4570mm x 3810mm
Dining Room:	3810mm x 3680mm
Kitchen:	4270mm x 3560mm
Utility Room:	2390mm x 1980mm
Bathroom:	2740mm x 2390mm
Bedroom:	3810mm x 3050mm
Bedroom:	3120mm x 3050mm
Bedroom:	3150mm x 3050mm
Bedroom:	3350mm x 3150mm
En Suite:	2130mm x 1070mm
Hall:	1980mm wide

Floor Area:	140.43 sq. metres
Frontage:	19.46 metres

plan

Send your order to:

Michael J. Allen. FASI. MRICS. FGIS. FCIOB.
Architect & Chartered Building Surveyor

BLUEPRINT HOME PLANS
Beechlawn, Kells, Co. Meath.
Telephone: (046) 9240349 Fax: (046) 9241638

2 Storey Dwellings

ELEVATION

No. 158 **Glendara**

This imposing two storey home has well laid out accommodation on both levels. The integral garage is approached from the side of the house and connects directly with the functional utility room. Direct access is provided from the dining area to the dining room and lounge. Four of the five bedrooms have built-in wardrobes and we have described two bathrooms on our plans.

Dining Room:	3510mm x 3350mm
Sitting Room:	4420mm x 4120mm
Hall:	2290mm wide
Family Room:	4420mm x 4120mm
Garage:	5500mm x 4570mm
Boiler Room:	1980mm x 1120mm
Toilet:	1980mm x 1070mm
Utility Room:	2900mm x 1980mm
Dining/Kitchen:	7110mm x 3350mm
Bedroom 1:	4060mm x 3350mm
En Suite:	2130mm x 1420mm
Bathroom:	2740mm x 2130mm
Bedroom 2:	3350mm x 2900mm
Bedroom 3:	4120mm x 3100mm
Bedroom 4:	2590mm x 2290mm
Bedroom 5:	4120mm x 3050mm

Floor Area: 175.77 sq. metres
Frontage: 17.12 metres

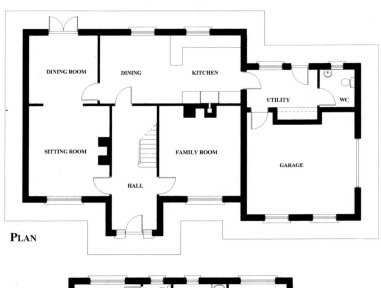

PLAN

UPPER FLOOR PLAN

106

No. 159
Meadowvale

This compact two storey home has a well balanced elevation with an attractive portico at the main entrance. A shower room is provided opening off the utility room. Open fireplaces are described in the sitting room and the family room and we have indicated a solid fuel cooker in the kitchen. All bedrooms have built-in wardrobes. The roof may be covered with slates or concrete tiles.

front elevation

ROOM DIMENSIONS

Kitchen/Dining:	5590mm x 2900mm
Utility Room:	2060mm x 1930mm
Toilet:	2060mm x 1370mm
Sitting Room:	4570mm x 3400mm
Hall:	2080mm wide
Family Room:	3730mm x 3400mm
Bedroom 2:	2900mm x 2900mm
Bathroom:	2290mm x 1700mm
Bedroom 1:	3350mm x 3050mm
Bedroom 4:	3400mm x 2620mm
Bedroom 3:	3400mm x 3120mm

Floor Area: 124.43
Frontage: 9.70 metres

ground floor plan

first floor plan

elevation

No. 160
Colebrook

A straightforward Georgian styled two storey residence with a medium pitch tiled roof, and a portico roof supported on glass fibre columns. The accommodation is generous on the ground floor and you will see that we have provided a half bathroom adjacent to the utility area. The four good sized bedrooms have fitted wardrobes and the bathroom is fully fitted with bath, toilet, wash basin and bidet. We have provided an open fireplace in the family room and lounge, the kitchen being provided with a separate flue to cater for a solid fuel cooker.

ground floor plan

first floor plan

ROOM DIMEMSIONS

Lounge:	4570mm x 3560mm
Family Room:	3660mm x 3560mm
Kitchen/Dining Room:	6350mm x 3180mm
Utility Room:	2260mm x 1630mm
Toilet:	2260mm x 1220mm
Bedroom 1:	3580mm x 3200mm
Bedroom 2:	3580mm x 3000mm
Bedroom 3:	3580mm x 2590mm
Bedroom 4:	3230mm x 2590mm
Bathroom:	2590mm x 2440mm

Floor Area: 133 sq. metres
Frontage: 10.00 metres

No. 161
Mountemple

A lovely brick two storey home. The sitting room extends the full width of the house and direct access is provided from the kitchen to the dining room via double doors. We have planned four bedrooms, a fully fitted bathroom and a walk-in hot press on the upper floor. The hipped roof is finished with slates.

front elevation

ROOM DIMENSIONS

Sitting Room:	6400mm x 3710mm
Kitchen:	5940mm x 3250mm
Dining Room:	3710mm x 3050mm
Hall:	2130mm wide
Bathroom:	2440mm x 2240mm
Bedroom 1:	3710mm x 3050mm
Bedroom 2:	3710mm x 3250mm
Bedroom 3:	2130mm x 2080mm
Bedroom 4:	3710mm x 3400mm
Floor Area:	124.99 sq. metres
Frontage:	10.36 metres

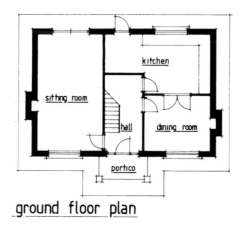

ground floor plan

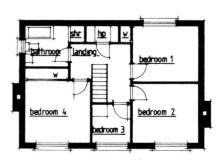

first floor plan

elevation

No. 162
Canterbury

This two storey home has a similar layout to our Virginia plan, but we have simplified the roof construction and given an alternative elevation with brick trim and Georgian styling. This very popular design offers full living and sleeping accommodation together with an integral garage suitable for future expansion of the living areas. The lounge and dining area are serviced with an open fireplace. All ground floors are of concrete fully insulated.

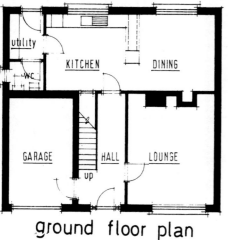

ground floor plan

first floor plan

ROOM DIMENSIONS

Lounge:	4880mm x 3960mm
Kitchen:	4220mm x 3350mm
Dining Area:	3530mm x 3350mm
Utility Room:	2030mm x 1520mm
Toilet:	1520mm x 1220mm
Garage:	4700mm x 2900mm
Bedroom 1:	3710mm x 2950mm
Bedroom 2:	3710mm x 3150mm
Bedroom 3:	3230mm x 2950mm
Bedroom 4:	3350mm x 3070mm
Bathroom:	2440mm x 2180mm
Floor Area:	124.00 sq. metres
Frontage:	9.93 metres

No. 163
Kilbeggan

This popular design has an attractive elevation and Georgian style windows. The three Living Rooms on the ground floor are adequately dimensioned. Open fireplaces are provided in the Sitting Room and Family Room and we have indicated a Solid Fuel Cooker in the Kitchen. Four good sized bedrooms and a fully fitted Bathroom are planned for the upper floor.

front elevation

ROOM DIMENSIONS

Sitting Room:	4270mm x 3300mm
Toilet:	2340mm x 910mm
Utility:	2340mm x 2290mm
Kitchen/Dining:	5740mm x 2950mm
Family Room:	3660mm x 3510mm
Hall:	2130mm wide
Bedroom 1:	3300mm x 3100mm
Bedroom 4:	2900mm x 2850mm
Bathroom:	2440mm x 1730mm
Bedroom 3:	2950mm x 2950mm
Bedroom 2:	3510mm x 3050mm

Floor Area:	124.31 sq. metres
Frontage:	9.73 metres

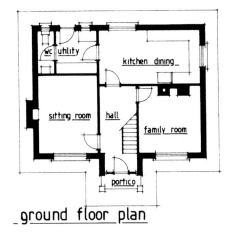

ground floor plan

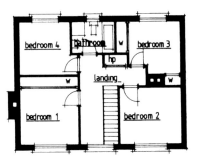

first floor plan

elevation

No. 164
Bailey

This gable facing Georgian style two storey has an attractive line to the front elevation with its offset at the study side and self supporting bow window in the Lounge. The Dining Room and Lounge both have open fireplaces. Construction is simple and the trussed Roof is finished with concrete tiles to a medium pitch. With three separate living Rooms and a Kitchen on the ground level and four good sized Bedrooms on the upper level, this compact home is,not surprisingly, a popular choice with our clients.

ground floor

first floor

ROOM DIMENSIONS

Lounge:	4060mm x 3660mm
Dining Room:	3660mm x 3350mm
Kitchen:	3300mm x 2740mm
Study:	3810mm x 2640mm
Utility Room:	2740mm x 1420mm
Bedroom 1:	3660mm x 3350mm
Bedroom 2:	3660mm x 2740mm
Bedroom 3:	3050mm x 2640mm
Bedroom 4:	2850mm x 2640mm
Bathroom:	2130mm x 1850mm

Floor Area:	124.99 metres
Frontage:	9.14 metres
Cost indicator:	€79,369-€95,617

No. 165
Moorefield

The Architect has packed amazing accommodation into a very compact floor area in this design. On the ground floor we provide three living rooms, a large utility room and a ground floor toilet. The boiler room is conveniently located to connect into the sitting room chimney stack. The upper floor comprises four bedrooms each with built-in wardrobes, a walk-in hot press and a fully fitted bathroom. The hipped roof is finished with slates and the front elevation features an attractive portico.

front elevation

ROOM DIMENSIONS

Kitchen/Dining:	5770mm x 3050mm
Utility:	3050mm x 1750mm
Toilet:	1730mm x 1070mm
Boiler:	1680mm x 1600mm
Sitting Room:	3660mm x 3580mm
Hall:	3660mm x 2080mm
Living Room:	3660mm x 3580mm
Bedroom 1:	3580mm x 3050mm
Bathroom:	2440mm x 1680mm
Bedroom 2:	3230mm x 3050mm
Bedroom 3:	3580mm x 3050mm
Bedroom 4:	3580mm x 2440mm

Floor Area:	124.90 sq. metres
Frontage:	10.06 metres

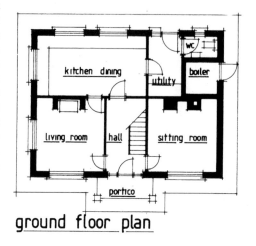

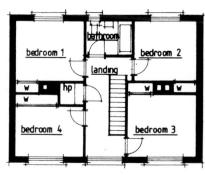

ground floor plan

first floor plan

elevation

No. 166
Rockwell

A sensible town house with brick features, a bow window to the dining area and Georgian style windows. The gable facing structure is imposing and the layout is serviceable. The ground floor provides a large kitchen dining area and utility room, with adjacent toilet facilities, a lounge of reasonable dimensions and an integral fuel room. The upper floor is laid out with four bedrooms, three of which are provided with built-in wardrobes, fitted bathroom and an en-suite shower. The kitchen dining area spans from front to rear thus giving a view towards the site frontage while working in the kitchen area.

ground floor plan.

first floor plan.

ROOM DIMENSIONS

Lounge:	4500mm x 3180mm
Kitchen:	3960mm x 3760mm
Dining Area:	3760mm x 3660mm
Utility Room:	3230mm x 2110mm
Hall:	2130mm wide
Toilet:	2110mm x 1070mm
Fuel Room:	1980mm x 1370mm
Bedroom:	3760mm x 3250mm
Bedroom:	3760mm x 2950mm
Bedroom:	3760mm x 3350mm
Bedroom:	3250mm x 3100mm
Bathroom:	2130mm x 2130mm

Floor Area:	143 sq. metres
Frontage:	10.46 metres

No. 167
Newport

A well balanced elevation with brick exterior open portico and hipped roof make this fine residence suited to any site, town or country. The sitting room extends the full width of the house. Direct access is provided between kitchen and family room. We have planned for a ground floor toilet and utility room. On the upper floor our plans provide for four generously dimensioned bedrooms each with built-in wardrobes, a fitted bathroom and a walk-in hot press.

front elevation

ROOM DIMENSIONS

Sitting Room:	7010mm x 3660mm
Toilet:	2590mm x 910mm
Utility:	2590mm x 1220mm
Kitchen:	3710mm x 3660mm
Family Room:	3660mm x 3200mm
Hall:	2240mm wide
Bedroom 1:	3660mm x 3350mm
Bathroom:	2540mm x 1730mm
Bedroom 2:	3350mm x 2900mm
Bedroom 3:	3660mm x 2790mm
Bedroom 4:	3660mm x 2900mm
Floor Area:	139.22 sq. metres
Frontage:	10.36 metres

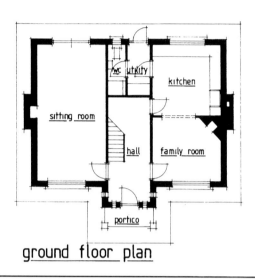

ground floor plan

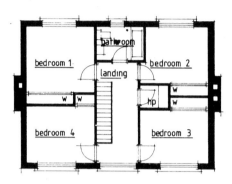

first floor plan

FRONT ELEVATION

No. 168
Virginia

The substantial two storey dwelling has a hipped roof with interesting profiles to the front elevation. A sun room is designed with access from the dining room via French doors. Provision is made for an oil fired cooker in the kitchen and three open fireplaces in the living areas. Four bedrooms are provided with bathroom ensuite in two bedrooms. Bedroom 1 has a walk-in wardrobe. Brick features are shown on the front elevation.

ROOM DIMENSIONS

Dining Room:	3040mm x 4310mm
Sitting Room:	4040mm x 5800mm
Kitchen/Dining Room:	6230mm x 3144mm
Study:	3100mm x 4876mm
Utility Room:	3640mm x 1700mm
WC:	3640mm x 1100mm
Bedroom:	2840mm x 3433mm
Master Bedroom:	4040mm x 4100mm
Bedroom:	3100mm x 3764mm
Bedroom:	3000mm x 3744mm
Bathroom:	2730mm x 2166mm
Floor Area:	185 sq. metres
Frontage Dimension: 9.87 metres	

No. 169
Kingfisher

A compact Georgian styled two storey home with four living rooms and five bedrooms all contained within a modest floor area. We have provided for three open fireplaces and a solid fuel cooker. Four bedrooms have built-in wardrobes. Bedroom No. 5 is suitable as a children's bedroom or study.

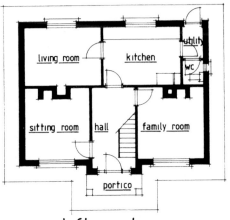

front elevation

ROOM DIMENSIONS

Living Room:	3960mm x 2900mm
Sitting Room:	3560mm x 3350mm
Hall:	2240mm wide
Family Room:	3560mm x 3350mm
Kitchen:	3910mm x 2900mm
Utility:	1580mm x 1070mm
Toilet:	1220mm x 1070mm
Bedroom 2:	3150mm x 2900mm
Bathroom:	2130mm x 1680mm
Bedroom 3:	3000mm x 2900mm
Bedroom 4:	3350mm x 3200mm
Bedroom 5:	2590mm x 2240mm
Bedroom 1:	3350mm x 2950mm

Floor Area:	124.71 sq. metres
Frontage:	9.75 metres

ground floor plan

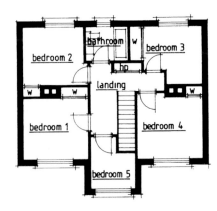

first floor plan

elevation

No. 170
Daytona

Two storey Georgian styled elegance is how this residence must be described, with its attractive portico, Georgian style windows and hipped slated roof. The ground floor caters for full family living and is serviced with three open fireplaces and a solid fuel cooker. The large utility room has a fitted sink unit and plumbing for washing machines. A ground floor toilet facility is provided. The upper floor provided four family sized bedrooms each with built-in wardrobes. A fully fitted bathroom with shower cabinet, bath, toilet, wash basin and bidet, completes the upper floor layout.

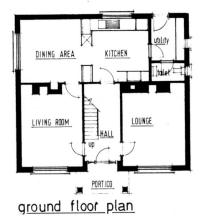

ground floor plan

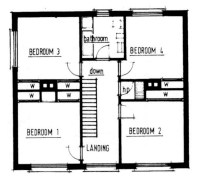

first floor plan

ROOM DIMENSIONS

Lounge:	4880mm x 3810mm
Living Room:	4880mm x 3810mm
Kitchen/Dining Room:	7930mm x 3710mm
Utility Room:	2540mm x 2080mm
Main Hall:	4270mm x 2290mm
Bedroom 1:	3810mm x 3710mm
Bedroom 2:	3710mm x 3510mm
Bedroom 3:	3810mm x 3610mm
Bedroom 4:	3810mm x 3610mm
Bathroom:	2590mm x 2520mm

Floor Area:	176.00 sq. metres
Frontage:	10.71 metres

No. 171
Kilkee

The integral garage in this fine residence is designed for later conversion to a living room. We have even provided a chimney for a future open fireplace. The large dining room opens onto a well appointed utility room. A sitting room with bow window and a good sized fuel room complete the ground floor accommodation. The first floor offers four well proportioned bedrooms each having a built-in wardrobe, a fully fitted bathroom, a walk-in hot press and an en-suite shower.

front elevation

ROOM DIMENSIONS

Fuel Room:	2130mm x 1220mm
Utility Room:	2290mm x 2130mm
Garage:	5330mm x 3710mm
Kitchen/Dining:	5940mm x 3560mm
Sitting Room:	4060mm x 3710mm
Hall:	2130mm wide
Bedroom 4:	3150mm x 2790mm
Bathroom:	2590mm x 2030mm
Bedroom 3:	3710mm x 3150mm
Bedroom 2:	3710mm x 3250mm
Landing:	2130mm wide
Bedroom 1:	3860mm x 3860mm

Floor Area:	154.66 sq. metres
Frontage:	10.52 metres

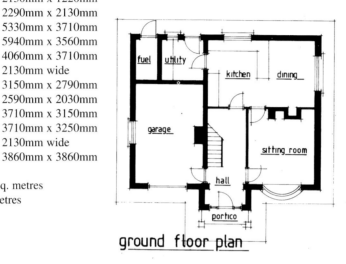

ground floor plan

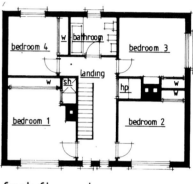

first floor plan

No. 172   Hawkfield

A very compact home with integral garage. The garage roof is wrapped around part of the front providing a covered entry porch. The exterior is finished with napped plaster and the windows are styled with Jacobean glazing. We have planned the kitchen dining room to extend the full width of the house. The upper floor has four good sized bedrooms, all with built-in wardrobes, and a fully fitted bathroom.

front elevation

ROOM DIMENSIONS

Garage:	6100mm x 4270mm	Bathroom:	3660mm x 1420mm
Boiler:	1980mm x 1420mm	Bedroom 3:	3350mm x 2740mm
Toilet:	1420mm x 1350mm	Bedroom 2:	3560mm x 2850mm
Sitting Room:	3660mm x 3560mm	Landing:	1420mm
Utility:	2500mm x 2340mm		
Hall:	2340mm wide	Floor Area excl.	
Kitchen/Dining:	6910mm x 3560mm	Garage & Boiler Room:	124.06 sq.m.
Bedroom 4:	3050mm x 2540mm	Frontage:	16.66 metres
Bedroom 1:	3660mm x 3560mm		

ground floor plan

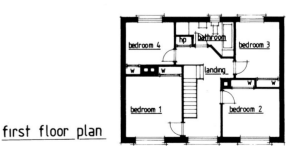

first floor plan

No. 173
Oldbridge

This is one of our most popular two storey homes. The integral garage is suited for later conversion to a bedroom or study. A ground floor toilet is provided opening off the utility room. We have indicated two open fireplaces. The upper floor has four fine bedrooms, three having built-in wardrobes, an en-suite shower and a fully fitted bathroom. Brick trim sets off the front elevation.

front elevation

ROOM DIMENSIONS

Dining Room:	4370mm x 3150mm
Sitting Room:	4370mm x 3660mm
Kitchen:	3860mm x 3200mm
Utility:	1880mm x 1630mm
Toilet:	1630mm x 1220mm
Garage:	5330mm x 2850mm
Hall:	1930mm wide
Bedroom 1:	3660mm x 3000mm
Bathroom:	2590mm x 1980mm
Bedroom 2:	3200mm x 3200mm
Bedroom 3:	3760mm x 2900mm
Bedroom 4:	2690mm x 2590mm
Landing:	1830mm wide
Shower Room:	1220mm x 1070mm

Floor Area excl. Garage: 124.62 sq. metres
Frontage: 9.45 metres

ground floor plan

first floor plan

front elevation

No. 174
Emyvale

This twin roofed residence offers full family accommodation. The ground floor features a large kitchen dining room with provision for a solid fuel cooker. The living room and sitting room each have an open fireplace. Note the large utility room. We have indicated a separate dining room and a ground floor bedroom on our plans. The upper floor is well laid out with three bedrooms, all having built-in wardrobes, two bathrooms and a walk-in hot press.

ROOM DIMENSIONS

Bedroom:	3960mm x 3510mm
Sitting Room:	4980mm x 3960mm
Toilet:	1680mm x 910mm
Utility:	3350mm x 2690mm
Dining Area:	3350mm x 3350mm
Kitchen:	4270mm x 4060mm
Living Room:	4420mm x 3960mm
Hall:	3100mm wide
Formal Dining:	3960mm x 3120mm
Bedroom:	4570mm x 3120mm
Bathroom:	2490mm x 2360mm
Bedroom:	3230mm x 3100mm
Bedroom:	3890mm x 3350mm
En Suite:	2130mm x 840mm

Floor Area: 183.95 sq. metres
Frontage: 16.31 metres

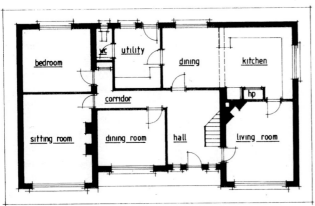

ground floor plan

first floor plan

No. 175
Brunswick

This magnificent home has four bedrooms and two bathrooms on the upper floor. The ground floor has a large sitting room extending the full width of the house, a compact family room and a well planned kitchen dining room. The single storey annex provides a garage, service rooms and utility area. We have indicated matching bay windows on the family room and sitting room.

front elevation

ROOM DIMENSIONS

Toilet:	1780mm x 1220mm
Boiler:	1780mm x 910mm
Utility:	2360mm x 1780mm
Garage:	4880mm x 3660mm
Kitchen/Dining Room:	6200mm x 3660mm
Family Room:	3660mm x 3660mm
Hall:	2440mm wide
Sitting Room:	7420mm x 3660mm
Bedroom 2:	3660mm x 2900mm
Bathroom:	2180mm x 2030mm
En Suite:	2180mm x 1220mm
Bedroom 1:	4270mm x 3510mm
Bedroom 4:	3660mm x 3050mm
Bedroom 3:	3660mm x 3050mm
Landing:	2440mm wide

Floor Area incl.
Garage: 174.06 sq. metres

Frontage: 14.48 metres

ground floor plan   first floor plan

front elevation

No. 176
Belmont

A two storey residence with simple styling, yet providing accommodation for full family living. The sitting room and family room each have open fireplaces and we have made provision or a solid fuel cooker in the kitchen. All four bedrooms have built-in wardrobes and we have provided a walk-in hot press on the landing. The bathroom is fully fitted.

ROOM DIMENSIONS

Sitting Room:	5500mm x 3910mm
Toilet:	1830mm x 1070mm
Utility:	2740mm x 1830mm
Dining/Kitchen:	6550mm x 3350mm
Family Room:	3960mm x 3910mm
Hall:	3960mm x 2540mm
Bedroom 2:	3910mm x 3350mm
Bathroom:	2080mm x 2540mm
Bedroom 1:	3910mm x 3350mm
Bedroom 4:	3910mm x 2740mm
Bedroom 3:	3910mm x 3350mm

Floor Area: 159.03 sq. metres
Frontage: 11.18 metres

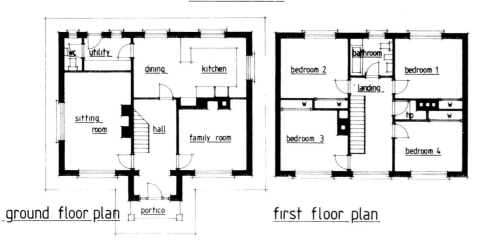
ground floor plan   first floor plan

No. 177
Garrybawn

This twin roofed dwelling offers many design features including an integral garage and roofed entry. A ground floor toilet facility is provided opening off the utility room. The upper floor has a fully fitted bathroom. All four bedrooms have built-in wardrobes. The exterior is finished with napped plaster.

front elevation

ROOM DIMENSIONS

Garage:	7620mm x 3810mm
Toilet:	2240mm x 1120mm
Utility:	2240mm x 2130mm
Sitting Room:	4270mm x 3350mm
Kitchen/Dining:	5790mm x 2900mm
Hall:	4620mm x 2130mm
Family Room:	3610mm x 3560mm
Bedroom 2:	3350mm x 2950mm
Bedroom 3:	2950mm x 2850mm
Bathroom:	2440mm x 1700mm
Bedroom 4:	2950mm x 2770mm
Bedroom 1:	3560mm x 3020mm

Floor Area excl. Garage: 124.25 sq. metres
Frontage: 13.89 metres

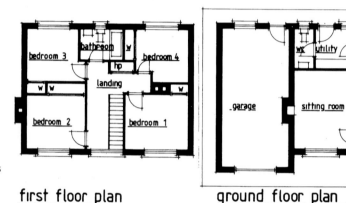

first floor plan

ground floor plan

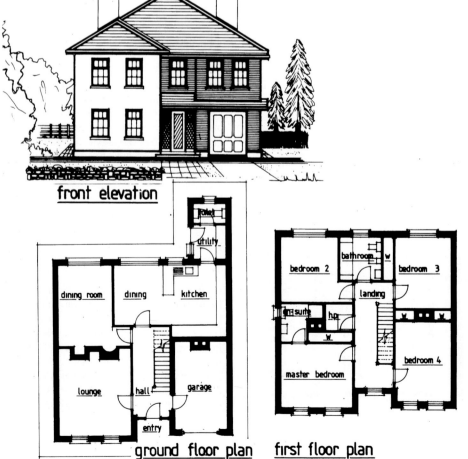

front elevation

ground floor plan

first floor plan

No. 178
Moyvore

We have packed numerous design features into this compact two storey residence. Under a hipped and slated roof we describe fine accommodation including an integral garage. The master bedroom has a bathroom en-suite. Provision has been made for a solid fuel cooker in the kitchen. The garage is suited for later conversion to a study or ground floor bedroom.

ROOM DIMENSIONS

Lounge:	4720mm x 4040mm
Dining Room:	4320mm x 3050mm
Kitchen/Dining:	6300mm x 3200mm
Utility:	1830mm x 1830mm
Toilet:	1830mm x 1070mm
Garage:	4720mm x 2950mm
Hall:	2130mm wide
Bedroom 2:	3480mm x 3230mm
Bathroom:	2290mm x 2290mm
Bedroom 3:	3810mm x 3070mm
Bedroom 4:	4240mm x 2950mm
Master Bedroom:	4040mm x 3450mm
En Suite:	2390mm x 2030mm

Floor Area: 171.93 sq. metres
Frontage: 10.03 metres

No. 179
Aisling

This unusual two storey residence provides up to the minute styling with its brick trim, long sloping roof and monopitch roofing detail. The fully utilised floor area provides generous living and sleeping accommodation, the main hall giving access to the living rooms and ground floor bedroom. The feature stairs rises to a landing with sloped ceiling and the upper floor contains three bedrooms, a bathroom, and an en-suite serving the master bedroom. A fully fitted kitchen opens on to the utility area. Provision has been made for a ground floor toilet and boiler room. The integral garage and carport complete the layout. The front elevation is trimmed with brick and the opening sashes on the front windows are fitted with Jacobean style glass. The sitting room and dining room both have open fireplaces.

ground floor plan

first floor plan

ROOM DIMENSIONS

Sitting Room:	5940mm x 3760mm
Dining Room:	4880mm x 3050mm
Main Hall:	3660mm x 2740mm
Kitchen:	4220mm x 4060mm
Bedroom 1:	3660mm x 3350mm
Carport:	3350mm x 3100mm
Garage:	4850mm x 3050mm
Utility Room:	2440mm x 2210mm
Boiler Room:	2520mm x 1220mm
Toilet:	2520mm x 1070mm
Bedroom 2:	3660mm x 3350mm
Bedroom 3:	3150mm x 2740mm
Bedroom 4:	3050mm x 3050mm
Bathroom:	2130mm x 2030mm
En Suite:	3050mm x 1370mm

Floor Area (incl. Garage and incl. Carport):	175.70 sq. metres
Frontage:	18.60 metres

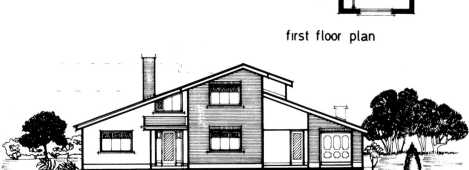

elevation

No. 180
Kilcormack

This twin roofed two storey residence is a firm favourite with our clients providing generous living accomodation, an integral garage and service rooms and four good bedrooms, one located on the ground floor level. The imposing elevation is clean lined with brick trim surrounding the entrance door. The lounge has a featured angle window to the front. We have located the stairs away from the front entrance hall for privacy reasons. The roofs are of low pitch and finished with concrete tiles.

elevation

ROOM DIMENSIONS

Lounge:	5890mm x 4880mm
Formal Dining Room:	3960mm x 3350mm
Kitchen Dining Room:	7870mm x 3350mm
Lobby:	3660mm x 1730mm
Utility:	2340mm x 1830mm
Garage:	5490mm x 3660mm
Bedroom:	3960mm x 3050mm
Toilet:	2900mm x 1370mm
Main Hall:	2540mm wide
Bedroom:	3350mm x 3150mm
Bedroom:	3610mm x 2900mm
Bedroom:	4830mm x 3450mm
Bathroom:	3350mm x 2240mm

Floor Area:	179.49 sq. metres
Frontage:	17.52 metres

ground floor plan

first floor plan

No. 181
Mondego

A fine two storey residence with sweeping roof line and distinctive detailing around the front elevation. This residence is suited to a town site or a country plot with restricted frontage dimension. The design provides sensible living accommodation, four good bedrooms and an integral garage. Both lounge and dining room, have open fireplaces and the kitchen is provided with a solid fuel cooker. We have included a ground floor toilet facility. Three of the bedrooms have fitted wardrobes and the bathroom is fully fitted and has a separate shower cabinet.

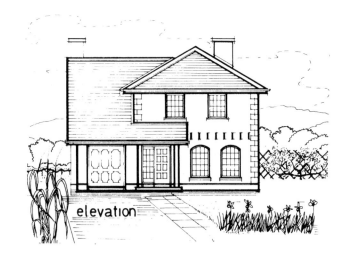
elevation

ROOM DIMENSIONS

Lounge:	5230mm x 4420mm
Kitchen:	4830mm x 3350mm
Dining Room:	4520mm x 3070mm
Garage:	5180mm x 2900mm
Utility Room:	2030mm x 1730mm
Toilet:	1730mm x 1220mm
Bedroom:	3910mm x 3450mm
Bedroom:	3450mm x 3350mm
Bedroom:	4520mm x 3070mm
Bedroom:	3910mm x 3100mm
Bathroom:	2440mm x 2235mm

Floor Area (excl. Garage):144.24 sq. metres
Frontage: 10.38 metres

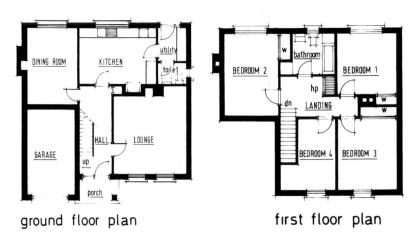
ground floor plan   first floor plan

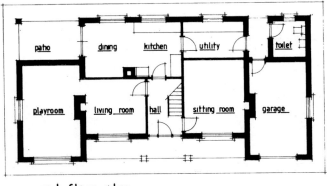
front elevation

ground floor plan

No. 182
Pinewood

Many design features are on offer in this attractive two storey home. The roofed entrance is a nice idea. Note the living room/playroom area allowing supervision and still affording privacy. The kitchen dining room opens onto a roofed patio. The large utility room leads you through to a toilet facility and the garage. The upper floor has a well lighted landing, four bedrooms, three having built-in wardrobes, and a fully fitted bathroom.

ROOM DIMENSIONS

Playroom:	5330mm x 3510mm	Bedroom 4:	3660mm x 2690mm
Living Room:	3660mm x 3200mm	Bathroom:	3610mm x2790mm
Dining/Kitchen:	5890mm x 3200mm	Bedroom 2:	3350mm x 2790mm
Utility:	3660mm x 2130mm	Bedroom 1:	3660mm x 3050mm
Sitting Room:	4270mm x 3660mm		
Hall:	3200mm x 2130mm		
Toilet:	2130mm x 2060mm	Floor Area (incl. Garage	
Garage:	4500mm x 3510mm	& Patio area):	180.98 sq. metres
Bedroom 3:	3050mm x 3050mm	Frontage:	17.88 metres

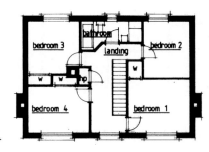
first floor plan

No. 183
Aylesbury

A fine country home with traditional styling. The hipped roof is finished with slates or concrete tiles. A ground floor toilet opens off the utility room. The upper floor comprises four well proportioned bedrooms with wardrobe spaces, a walk-in hot press, and two bathrooms, one of which is en-suite with the master bedroom.

front elevation

ROOM DIMENSIONS

Lounge/Dining:	7930mm x 3860mm
Toilet:	1830mm x 1020mm
Utility:	2740mm x 2290mm
Hall:	2740mm wide
Kitchen:	4170mm x 3860mm
Family Room:	3860mm x 3660mm
Bedroom 1:	4170mm x 3860mm
En Suite:	2080mm x 1220mm
Bathroom:	2440mm x 2080mm
Bedroom 2:	4170mm x 2850mm
Bedroom 3:	3860mm x 3050mm
Bedroom 4:	3860mm x 3660mm
Landing:	2740mm wide

Floor Area:	172.40 sq. metres
Frontage:	11.26 metres

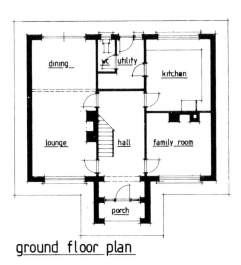

ground floor plan

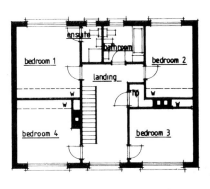

first floor plan

first floor plan

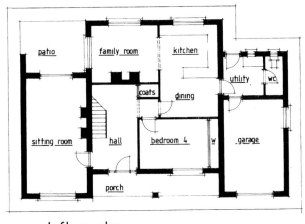

ground floor plan

front elevation

No. 184
Avignon

This popular design concept offers not only an attractive elevation but well designed accomodation on ground and upper floors. We have provided an integral garage and a ground floor bedroom. The upper floor is planned for three well proportioned bedrooms with built-in wardrobes, two bathrooms and a walk-in hot press.

ROOM DIMENSIONS

Sitting Room:	6710mm x 3660mm
Family Room:	4010mm x 3350mm
Kitchen/Dining Room:	5440mm x 3510mm
Bedroom 4:	4120mm x 2900mm
Hall:	2740mm wide
Utility:	2490mm x 2130mm
Toilet:	2130mm x 1070mm
Garage:	5490mm x 3660mm
Bedroom 1:	3350mm x 3960mm
En Suite:	2130mm x 1520mm
Bathroom:	3350mm x 1930mm
Bedroom 2:	3660mm x 3450mm
Bedroom 3:	3400mm x 3350mm
Landing:	1520mm

Floor Area:	181.07
Frontage:	16.15 metres

No. 185
Frumpton

A compact three bedroomed house suited to town or suburban sites. The Carport is an attractive feature. A ground floor toilet is provided opening off the hall. Open fire-places are indicated in the dining room and sitting room. The upper floor has three good sized bedrooms, two having built-in wardrobes, a fully fitted bathroom and a walk-in hot press.

front elevation

ROOM DIMENSIONS

Utility:	3200mm x 1520mm
Kitchen:	3810mm x 3200mm
Dining Room:	4270mm x 3350mm
Sitting Room:	4570mm x 3350mm
Hall:	2440mm wide
Bathroom:	2290mm x 2080mm
Bedroom 1:	3710mm x 3560mm
Bedroom 2:	3960mm x 3050mm
Bedroom 3:	2740mm x 2740mm

Floor Area (excl. garage): 114.76 sq. metres
Frontage: 9.50 metres

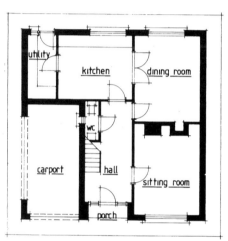

ground floor plan

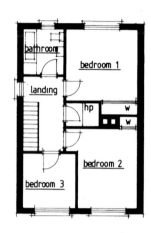

first floor plan

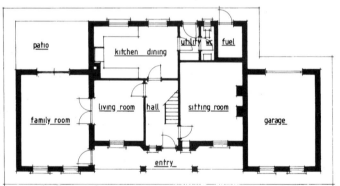

ground floor plan

No. 186
Limerick

This twin roofed residence has a very attractive styling and well planned accommodation on both floors. We have provided four generously dimen-sioned living rooms, service areas and an integral garage on the ground floor. The upper floor has four bedrooms all with built-in wardrobes, a fully fitted bathroom and a walk-in hot press.

ROOM DIMENSIONS

Family Room:	5490mm x 4270mm
Living Room:	3660mm x 3100mm
Kitchen/Dining Room:	5230mm x 3100mm
Utility:	1910mm x 1220mm
Toilet:	1910mm x 810mm
Fuel:	1910mm x 1600mm
Hall:	2030mm wide
Sitting Room:	4720mm x 3960mm
Garage:	5490mm x 4270mm
Bedroom 3:	3100mm x 3050mm
Hot Press:	1550mm x 970mm
Bathroom:	2390mm x 1550mm
Bedroom 4:	2670mm x 2540mm
Bedroom 1:	3960mm x 3430mm
Bedroom 2:	3100mm x 3050mm

Floor Area: 151.96 sq. metres
Frontage: 19.05 metres

first floor plan

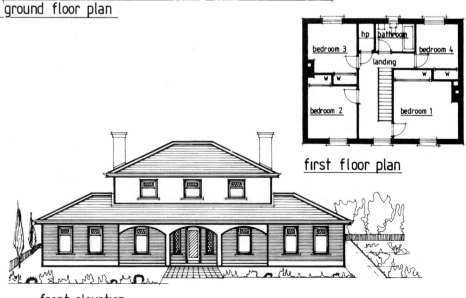

front elevation

No. 187
Hamwood

This house has a traditional appearance with hipped roof and two bay windows. We have arranged the floor plan to include one bedroom at ground floor level and three bedrooms on the upper floor. The large kitchen dining room is front facing with a bay window. Bedroom no. 2 has a bathroom en-suite.

FRONT ELEVATION

ROOM DIMENSIONS

Bedroom 1:	3650mm x 3040mm
Living Room:	3650mm x 3350mm
Utility Room:	4142mm x 1200mm
Toilet:	838mm wide
Kitchen:	3650mm x 4516mm
Bedroom 4:	3650mm x 3040mm
Bedroom 3:	3650mm x 3350mm
Bathroom:	3650mm x 2100mm
Bedroom 2:	3650mm x 3352mm

Floor Area: 122.40 square metres
Frontage: 10.03 metres

GROUND FLOOR PLAN

FIRST FLOOR PLAN

No. 188
Ashpark

This elegant house has five bedrooms all with built-in wardrobes. The master bedroom has a bathroom en-suite and a walk-in wardrobe. The main bathroom is fully fitted with bath, shower, bidet, wc and wash basin. On the ground floor level the utility room is self-contained and provision is made for a visitable disabled toilet. All the living rooms have generous dimensions and an attractive sun room opens directly off the dining room.

FRONT ELEVATION

ROOM DIMENSIONS

Conservatory:	3500mm x 3800mm
Kitchen/Dining:	7300mm x 4000mm
Family Room:	4800mm x 4200mm
Study:	4800mm x 3000mm
Utility Room:	3200mm x 3600mm
Bathroom:	3200mm x 1700mm
Sitting Room:	4600mm x 4500mm
Hall:	2400mm wide
Bedroom:	4150mm x 3063mm
Bedroom:	4150mm x 3063mm
Bedroom:	4800mm x 3200mm
Bedroom:	4600mm x 3925mm
En-suite:	1800mm x 1800mm
Master Bedroom:	4600mm x 3500mm
Bathroom:	2377mm x 2600mm

Floor area: 269sq.m.
Frontage dimension: 12.60m

GROUND FLOOR PLAN

FIRST FLOOR PLAN

No. 189
Newbury

Note the unusual roof lines on this fine two storey dwelling. The family room has a feature bow window and an open fireplace. The integral garage with side entry is suitable for later conversion to a living room. Provision has been made for a solid fuel or oil fired cooker in the kitchen. The upper floor features four bedrooms with built-in wardrobes and a study/bedroom. We have described two bathrooms, one en-suite with the master bedroom. The elevation has brick features and the roof is covered with concrete tiles.

front elevation

ROOM DIMENSIONS

Formal Dining:	3250mm x 3050mm
Sitting Room:	4320mm x 3710mm
Dining/Kitchen:	6600mm x 3250mm
Utility:	2740mm x 1980mm
Toilet:	1980mm x 1020mm
Boiler:	1980mm x 1070mm
Garage:	5180mm x 4420mm
Family Room:	4320mm x 3710mm
Hall:	5080mm x 2130mm
Bedroom 1:	3960mm x 3300mm
En Suite:	2030mm x 1120mm
Bathroom:	2440mm x 2030mm
Bedroom 4:	3250mm x 2590mm
Bedroom 3:	3710mm x 3660mm
Study:	2740mm x 2130mm
Bedroom 2:	3710mm x 2950mm

Floor Area:	194.18 sq. metres
Frontage:	15.85 metres

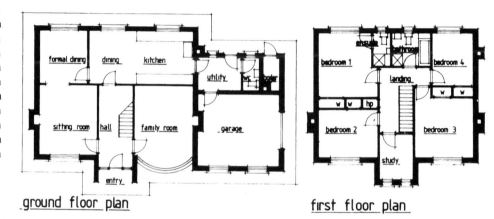

ground floor plan

first floor plan

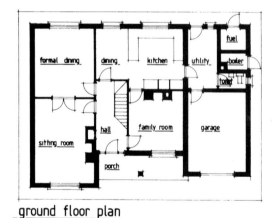

ground floor plan

No. 190
Carlton

A magnificent two storey dwelling with integral garage. Four living rooms and service rooms on the ground floor, and four generously dimensioned Bedrooms on the upper floor are all suited to family living. A bathroom is provided en-suite with the master bedroom and we feature a walk-in hot press on the landing.

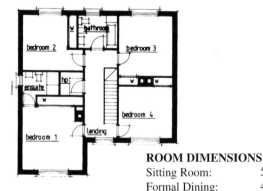

first floor plan

ROOM DIMENSIONS

Sitting Room:	5490mm x 4060mm
Formal Dining:	4470mm x 4060mm
Dining/Kitchen:	5890mm x 3910mm
Utility:	3960mm x 1980mm
Fuel Room:	1750mm x 1370mm
Boiler Room:	1750mm x 1070mm
Toilet:	1850mm x 1120mm
Garage:	5180mm x 3960mm
Family Room:	3960mm x 3660mm
Hall:	2130mm wide
Bedroom 2:	3610mm x 2950mm
Bathroom:	2590mm x 2130mm
Bedroom 3:	3910mm x 3660mm
Bedroom 4:	3660mm x 3350mm
Bedroom 1:	4060mm x 4060mm
En Suite:	2440mm x 1520mm

Floor Area: 214.37 sq. metres
Frontage: 14.94 metres

front elevation

No. 191
Vermont

This twin roof two storey offers ease of construction and yet gives a very attractive elevation with a covered entrance porch and bow windows. The central hall with turned stairs opens on to generously dimensioned living accomodation on the ground floor and well laid out bedrooms and bathroom on the first floor. Full family living has been catered for throughout and this is particularly reflected in the ground floor layout. A ground floor toilet is located opening off the utility room. The double garage has a service entrance to the utility area.

elevation

ROOM DIMENSIONS

Lounge/Formal Dining:	7930mm x 4120mm
Kitchen Dining Room:	6200mm x 3960mm
Family Room:	3860mm x 3450mm
Hall:	4470mm x 2640mm
Garage:	6350mm x 4120mm
Utility Room:	3050mm x 2290mm
Bedroom:	4120mm x 3660mm
Bedroom:	3510mm x 3450mm
Bedroom:	3510mm x 2790mm
Bedroom:	3450mm x 2640mm
Bathroom:	2640mm x 2290mm
Floor Area:	205 sq. metres
Frontage:	15.39 metres

first floor plan

ground floor plan

No. 192
Thornwood

A magnificent family home of generous dimension, this two storey residence provides for full family living. Provision has been made for a solid fuel or oil fired cooker in the kitchen and the study, lounge and living room are provided with an open fireplace. Dual access is offered to the formal dining room, and there is a connecting door between the kitchen and living room. A ground floor toilet is located off the utility room. The upper floor provides four well proportioned bedrooms all with built-in wardrobes. An en-suite bathroom is provided with the master bedroom. A fully fitted bathroom and walk-in hot press complete the upper floor. Although traditional in appearance, the front elevation is impressive with its portico, feature entrance windows and hipped roof.

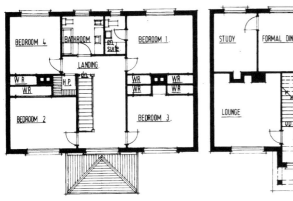

elevation

first floor plan

ground floor plan

ROOM DIMENSIONS

Living Room:	4570mm x 4270mm
Entrance Hall:	3150mm wide
Lounge:	4570mm x 4270mm
Study:	3660mm x 2740mm
Formal Dining:	3660mm x 3510mm
Kitchen:	5180mm x 3660mm
Utility:	2740mm x 2290mm
Garage:	6350mm x 3660mm
Bedroom:	4270mm x 3660mm
Bedroom:	4270mm x 3250mm
Bedroom:	4270mm x 3250mm
Bedroom:	3660mm x 3280mm
Bathroom:	2670mm x 2440mm
En Suite:	2440mm x 1370mm
Floor Area:	198 sq. metres
Frontage:	16.37 metres

No. 193
Arizona

A residence of distinction with sweeping roof lines and brick trim. The ground floor layout provides full family accommodation, a utility room, ground floor toilet facility and an integral two car garage. A boiler room is located to the rear of the garage. We have provided an extra flue to cater for a solid fuel cooker and the family room and lounge both have open fireplaces. The main hall is separated from the exterior by means of a draught porch. On the upper floor, we have provided five full sized bedrooms, a fitted bathroom, an en-suite servicing the master bedroom and a walk-in linen room.

elevation

ROOM DIMENSIONS

Lounge:	5640mm x 4060mm
Formal Dining Room:	4520mm x 3450mm
Kitchen Dining Room:	6200mm x 3350mm
Family Room:	4570mm x 3350mm
Utility Room:	2290mm x 1830mm
Toilet:	1830mm x 1070mm
Boiler Room:	1830mm x 1500mm
Outer Hall:	2440mm x 1930mm
Main Hall:	4570mm x 2130mm
Bedroom:	4170mm x 3500mm
Bedroom:	3860mm x 3610mm
Bedroom:	3990mm x 3350mm
Bedroom:	3350mm x 3350mm
Bedroom:	3050mm x 3020mm
Bathroom:	2590mm x 2130mm

Floor Area:	194.37 sq. metres
Frontage:	15.85 metres

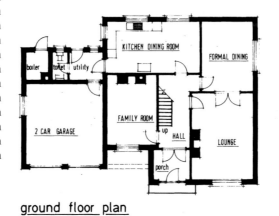

ground floor plan

first floor plan

No. 194
Kilsharvin

This well designed two storey house has four good sized bedrooms, one with bathroom en-suite. A walk-in hot press is located at the landing level. The ground floor has a large kitchen/dining room, a formal dining room and a sitting room with an open fireplace. A study is provided to open off the entrance hall. The elevation is finished with a half-brick front and features an unusually angled bay window detail, extending to the upper floor.

FRONT ELEVATION

ROOM DIMENSIONS

Dining Room:	4200mm x 3800mm
Kitchen/Dining:	6480mm x 3800mm
Utility Room:	2150mm x 2400mm
Bathroom:	1400mm x 2400mm
Study:	3650mm x 4000mm
Hall:	2030mm wide
Sitting Room:	4700mm x 5400mm
Bedroom:	4186mm x 2634mm
Bedroom:	2544mm x 2634mm
Bedroom:	2715mm x 2700mm
Bedroom:	4015mm x 3616mm
En-suite:	3001mm x 1250mm
Bathroom:	3001mm x 1600mm

Floor Area:	168.25 sq. metres
Frontage:	11.38 metres

GROUND FLOOR PLAN

FIRST FLOOR PLAN

No. 195
Garfield

A distinctive family home with a brick exterior and featuring a semi-circular portico and balcony. The integral garage has access to the utility area. Open fireplaces are provided in the family room, sitting room and study. The four fine bedrooms have built-in wardrobes. A bathroom is provided en-suite with the master bedroom. Access to the balcony is from the landing.

ROOM DIMENSIONS

Hall:	4500mm x 2900mm
Sitting Room:	4500mm x 4500mm
Study:	3700mm x 3100mm
Family Room:	4300mm x 3000mm
Kitchen:	4500mm x 3700mm
Utility:	2800mm x 1700mm
Toilet:	2800mm x 1000mm
Garage:	4900mm x 4900mm
Dining Room:	4500mm x 4500mm
Bedroom 3:	3700mm x 3600mm
Bedroom 2:	4500mm x 3300mm
Bedroom 1:	3900mm x 3800mm
En Suite:	1800mm x 1700mm
Bathroom:	3100mm x 2500mm
Bedroom 4:	3700mm x 3000mm

Floor Area: 232.71 sq. metres
Frontage: 17.90 metres

front elevation

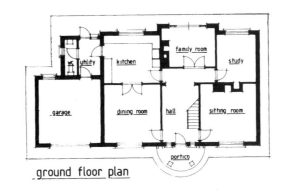

ground floor plan

first floor plan

No. 196
Waldorf

One of the most imposing designs in our book, this fine residence offers excellent family accommodation and a particularly striking elevation. The roof lines, roofed porch and bay windows help consolidate a very attractive house shape. The integral garage is approached from the side. Four living rooms of generous dimension together with service rooms and conservatory, make up the ground floor. The upper floor gives you five bedrooms, two bathrooms and a walk-in hot press.

ROOM DIMENSIONS

Dining Room:	4880mm x 3660mm
Sitting Room:	5490mm x 4570mm
Conservatory:	3660mm x 2740mm
Toilet:	1830mm x 810mm
Utility:	2440mm x 1980mm
Dining/Kitchen:	7260mm x 3710mm
Family Room:	4270mm x 3660mm
Hall:	2590mm wide
Garage:	5180mm x 3660mm
Bedroom 2:	3810mm x 3660mm
Bathroom:	2850mm x 2290mm
Bedroom 3:	4320mm x 3660mm
Bedroom 4:	3660mm x 3660mm
Bedroom 5:	2590mm x 2130mm
Bedroom 1:	4780mm x 3960mm
En Suite:	2440mm x 1680mm

Floor Area: 221.81 sq. metres
Frontage: 17.11 metres

front elevation

first floor plan

ground floor plan

No. 197
Southford

This luxury two storey home has full family accommodation with its five living rooms and service areas on the lower level and four full sized bedrooms on the upper floor. The impressive roofed portico and granite trim around the entrance door leads you into the main hall. The two main reception rooms are balanced in dimension and have open fireplaces. Our kitchen dining room and family room adjoin, the kitchen having a solid fuel or oil fired cooker and the family room having an open fireplace. The utility wing creates a sheltered area for the patio. On the upper floor the main bathroom is fully equipped and we have included an ensuite half bathroom opening from the master bedroom. All bedrooms have fitted wardrobes.

ROOM DIMENSIONS

Lounge:	4570mm x 4570mm
Dining Room:	4570mm x 4570mm
Study:	3660mm x 3200mm
Family Room:	4270mm x 3050mm
Kitchen:	4570mm x 3660mm
Utility Room:	2180mm x 2130mm
Shower Room:	2180mm x 1520mm
Boiler Room:	2180mm x 1520mm
Main Hall:	4570mm x 2900mm
Bedroom 1:	4570mm x 4010mm
Bedroom 2:	3560mm x 3050mm
Bedroom 3:	4570mm x 3660mm
Bedroom 4:	4570mm x 3250mm
Bathroom:	3250mm x 2490mm
En Suite:	2080mm x 1680mm

Floor Area:	225 sq. metres
Frontage:	12.90 metres

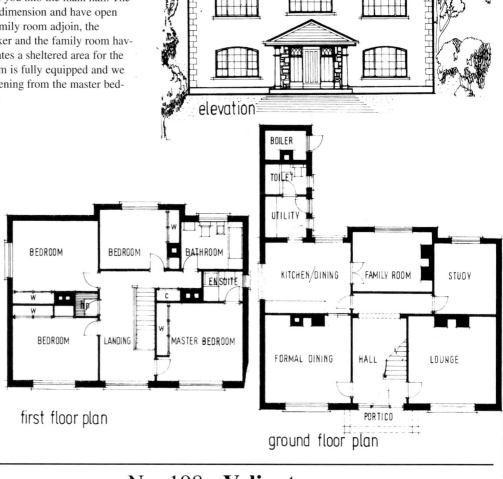

elevation

first floor plan

ground floor plan

No. 198   Valiant

This family home of circa 279 sq. m.. offers first class accommodation. Sturdy construction. Georgian styled windows and fully insulated fabric. Adequate provision for fireplaces and solid fuel cooker. Four good bedrooms all with built-in cupboards. Utility room and ground floor toilet. Slated roof. Feature bathroom. Shower room and linen room.

ROOM DIMENSIONS

Lounge:	5130mm x 5180mm
Main Hall:	3660mm wide
Study:	5180mm x 3050mm
Formal Dining Room:	4880mm x 3660mm
Living Room:	3660mm x 3660mm
Kitchen Dining Room:	4470mm x 4270mm
Bedroom:	5180mm x 3890mm
Bedroom:	4470mm x 3710mm
Bedroom:	4470mm x3050mm
Bedroom:	4880mm x 3250mm
Bathroom:	3660mm x 3200mm
Floor Area	279 sq. metres
Frontage:	14.99 metres

GROUND FLOOR PLAN

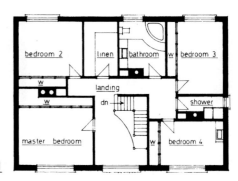

FIRST FLOOR PLAN

126

No. 199
Knockbride

A fine four bedroomed two storey home,
Featuring well laid out living rooms and four
fine bedrooms. Bathroom facilities include a
ground floor toilet, main bathroom and en-
suite bathroom. The external finish is in
napped plaster or white dash and the roof is
finished in slates or tiles.

ELEVATION

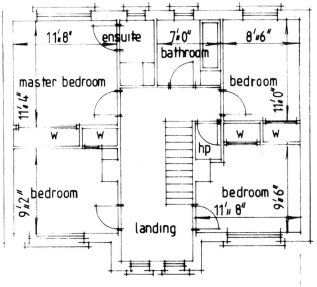

FIRST FLOOR

ROOM DIMENSIONS

Hall: 2440mm wide
Sitting Room: 4880mm x 3560mm
Kitchen/Dining: 7010mm x 3560mm
Bedroom: 2790mm x 3560mm
Master Bedroom: 3450mm x 3560mm
Bedroom: 3350mm x 2590mm
Bedroom: 2900mm x 3560mm

Floor Area: 141.36 sq. metres
Frontage: 10.36 metres

GROUND FLOOR

No. 200
Morrell

An expanded version of our No. 178 with provision for a separate dining room and integral garage block. Brick features are incorporated on the front elevation and the attractive details on the roofs are finished with slates.

ELEVATION

ROOM DIMENSIONS

Sitting Room:	4720mm x 4040mm
Family Room:	4320mm x 3050mm
Kitchen:	6300mm x 3200mm
Dining Room:	4850mm x 3070mm
Hall:	2130mm wide
Garage:	6400mm x 3350mm
Utility Room:	2180mm x 2130mm
Toilet:	1830mm x 1070mm
Boiler Room:	1420mm x 940mm
Master Bedroom:	4040mm x 3450mm
En Suite:	2390mm x 2030mm
Bedroom:	3960mm x 3450mm
Bathroom:	2210mm x 3450mm
Bedroom:	3070mm x 3660mm
Bedroom:	3070mm x 4340mm

Floor Area:	198.30 sq. metres
Frontage:	13.65 metres

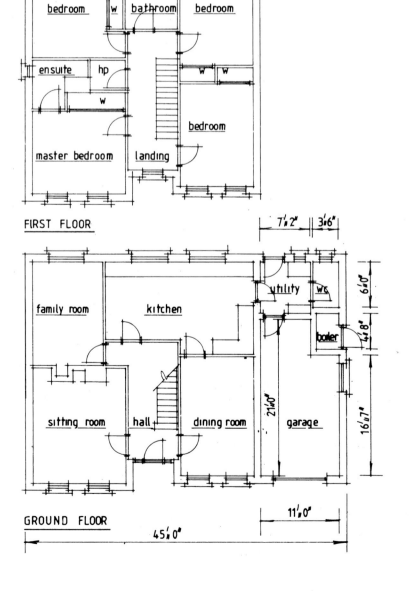

FIRST FLOOR

GROUND FLOOR

No. 201
Moyfin

This compact three bedroomed two storey dwelling has brick features on the front elevation and a tiled roof. The living accommodation is well laid out and the room sizes are generous. Built-in wardrobes are provided in two bedrooms.

ROOM DIMENSIONS

Sitting Room:	4570mm x 3350mm
Dining Room:	4270mm x 3350mm
Hall:	2440mm wide
Bathroom:	2290mm x 2080mm
Kitchen:	3200mm x 3810mm
Bedroom:	3510mm x 3350mm
Bedroom:	4010mm x 3050mm
Bedroom:	2740mm x 2740mm
Utility Room:	3050mm x 1070mm

Floor Area:	113.27 sq. metres
Frontage:	9.04 metres

elevation

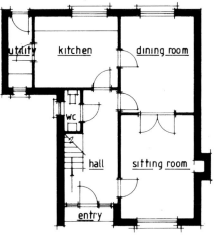

ground floor

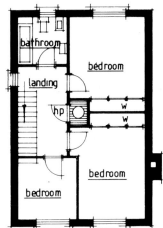

first floor

No. 202
Fassaroe

Similar in style to our design No. 182, this two storey home has extensive living areas and four good bedrooms, all with built-in wardrobes. We have located a large shower room off the utility area. The external finish on this house comprises white dash and the roof is covered with tiles.

ELEVATION

GROUND FLOOR

FIRST FLOOR

ROOM DIMENSIONS

Playroom:	4420mm x 3510mm
Family Room:	3660mm x 3200mm
Hall:	2130mm wide
Sitting Room:	4270mm x 3660mm
Garage:	7720mm x 3510mm
Shower Room:	2130mm x 2130mm
Utility Room:	3660mm x 2130mm
Dining Room:	3510mm x 3200mm
Kitchen:	3660mm x 3200mm
Bedroom:	3660mm x 3050mm
Bedroom:	3660mm x 3050mm
Bedroom:	2900mm x 2740mm
Bedroom:	3660mm x 2850mm
Bedroom:	3050mm x 3050mm
Bathroom:	3510mm x 1930mm

Floor Area:	180.98 sq. metres
Frontage:	17.83 metres

No. 203
Caranbrook

A fine family two storey dwelling with three good sized bedrooms. The master bedroom has a bathroom en-suite. The living accommodation is well laid out and features a separate dining room.

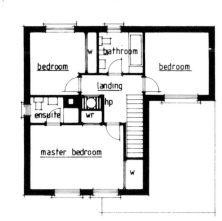

elevation

ROOM DIMENSIONS

Hall:	2130mm wide
Sitting Room:	4880mm x 3960mm
Kitchen:	5870mm x 3350mm
Utility Room:	2130mm x 1830mm
Bathroom:	2130mm x 1420mm
Boiler Room:	1520mm x 1070mm
Dining Room:	4670mm x 3350mm
Master Bedroom:	4880mm x 3450mm
Bedroom:	3560mm x 3350mm
Bedroom:	3350mm x 3050mm
Bathroom:	2440mm x 2130mm
Floor Area:	145.82 sq. metres
Frontage:	10.47 metres

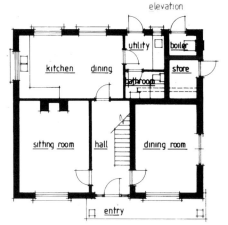

ground floor

first floor

elevation

No. 204
Vernon

This two storey home features the now popular bay windows in the sitting room and in the front bedrooms. Attractive brick features on the elevation and a traditional tiled roof make this a very attractive design. Three good bedrooms are provided and the master bedroom has a bathroom en-suite.

ground floor

first floor

ROOM DIMENSIONS

Kitchen:	3810mm x 3200mm
Dining Room:	4270mm x 3350mm
Sitting Room:	4570mm x 3350mm
Utility Room:	3200mm x 1520mm
Bathroom:	2290mm x 1830mm
Bedroom:	3710mm x 3560mm
Bedroom:	3960mm x 3050mm
Bedroom:	2740mm x 2740mm
Floor Area:	114.76 sq metres
Frontage:	9.50 metres

gloucester

No. 205
Hermitage

This two storey dwelling house has a farm-house style elevation and roof line. The windows are traditional in design, and this type of elevational treatment is favoured by some Local Authorities where building takes place in sensitive areas. The accommodation is well laid out and fireplaces are provided in the sitting room and family room. The large utility room can accommodate laundry equipment. Three of the four bedrooms have built-in wardrobes, and the master bedroom has a bathroom ensuite. External finish is in dry dash and the roof is finished with slates.

front elevation

ROOM DIMENSIONS

Sitting Room:	4880mm x 3660mm
Family Room:	3810mm x 3660mm
Kitchen/Dining Room:	6400mm x 3810mm
Utility Room:	2740mm x 1930mm
Toilet:	2740mm x 1070mm
Bedroom:	3660mm x 3200mm
Bedroom:	3660mm x 3200mm
Bedroom:	3660mm x 3100mm
Bedroom:	3450mm x 3100mm
Bathroom:	3100mm x 2290mm
Hall and Landing:	2080mm wide

Floor Area:	168.65 sq. metres
Frontage:	10.18 metres

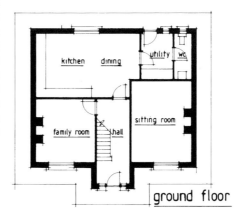

ground floor

first floor

front elevation

No. 206
Tailtean

This attractive two storey dwelling-house has an old world collar roof and elegant elevation details. External finish is in napped plaster, with brick details over the front windows. The accommodation is well laid out, giving good room dimensions within a reasonable floor area. Three bedrooms have built-in wardrobes. The upper floor rooms at the rear of the house are provided with Velux roof windows. All floors are in concrete.

ROOM DIMENSIONS

Sitting Room:	4670mm x 4170mm
Dining Room:	4060mm x 3150mm
Kitchen/Dining Room:	5180mm x 3050mm
Utility Room:	2740mm x 1520mm
Toilet:	1520mm x 1220mm
Study:	3050mm x 2440mm
Hall:	2130mm
Bedroom:	4670mm x 3560mm
Bedroom:	3760mm x 2740mm
Bedroom:	2900mm x 2740mm
Bedroom:	3050mm x 2740mm
Bathroom:	2590mm x 2740mm
En Suite:	2540mm x 1830mm

Floor Area:	153.89 sq. metres
Frontage:	10.64 metres

ground floor

first floor

No. 207
Trimton

This fine family two storey home has an integral garage and well laid out accommodation. The ground floor features a large kitchen/dining room, formal dining room and two further living rooms. The utility room is self-contained and there is a ground floor bathroom adjoining. Four bedrooms and two bathrooms are located on the upper floor. A walk-in hot press opens off the landing. The front elevation is finished with dry dash. All ground floors are concrete, and the roof is finished with slates.

front elevation

ROOM DIMENSIONS

Sitting Room:	4620mm x 4170mm
Dining Room:	4170mm x 3710mm
Kitchen/Dining:	6250mm x 3710mm
Family Room:	3960mm x 3760mm
Hall:	2180mm wide
Utility Room:	2340mm x 1830mm
Toilet:	2340mm x 1070mm
Garage:	5210mm x 3660mm
Bedroom:	4170mm x 3810mm
Bedroom:	4170mm x 3100mm
Bedroom:	3100mm x 2790mm
Bedroom:	3960mm x 2950mm
Bathroom:	3350mm x 1960mm
En Suite:	2540mm x 1320mm

Floor Area:	198.78 sq. metres
Frontage:	15.05 sq. metres

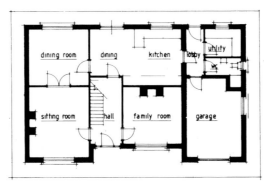

first floor

No. 208
Kilkerly

This fine two storey dwelling has a brick exterior and a slated roof. The accommodation is well laid out and features four family rooms on the ground floor, a self-contained utility room, and a ground floor toilet. The bedrooms are well dimensioned and the master bedroom has a bathroom en-suite.

ROOM DIMENSIONS

Sitting Room:	5230mm x 3810mm
Family Room:	4270mm x 3810mm
Dining Room:	3400mm x 3250mm
Kitchen/Dining Room:	6400mm x 3250mm
Utility & Toilet:	3000mm x 2440mm
Hall:	2080mm wide
Bedroom:	3810mm x 3810mm
Bedroom:	3350mm x 2690mm
Bedroom:	3610mm x 3250mm
Bedroom:	3810mm x 3610mm
Bathroom:	2240mm x 2080mm
En Suite:	2240mm x 1220mm

Floor Area:	170.36 sq. metres
Frontage:	10.50m

front elevation

ground floor

first floor

132

Dormer Homes

NEW DESIGN!

FRONT ELEVATION

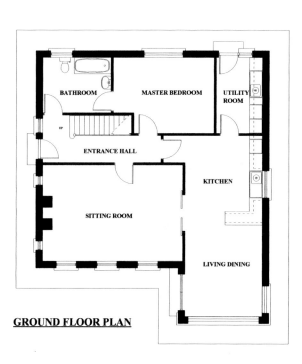

GROUND FLOOR PLAN

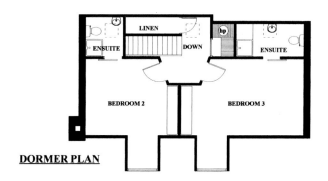

DORMER PLAN

No. 209
Winsford

A dormer house with attractive features on the front elevation and unusual floor plan. The main entrance is located at the side of the dwelling. The roof is finished with Dutch gables. We have located the master bedroom with bathroom access on the ground floor. Two bedrooms are located on the dormer floor, both with bathrooms en-suite. A mix of natural stone and brick are featured on the front elevation.

ROOM DIMENSIONS

Bathroom:	3129mm x 2450mm
Hall:	2100mm wide
Sitting Room:	6400mm x 4250mm
Dining Area:	3200mm x 4050mm
Kitchen:	3200mm x 3950mm
Utility Room:	2100mm x 3350mm
Master Bedroom:	4571mm x 3350mm
En-suite:	1690mm x 1746mm
Bedroom 2:	4220mm x 3378mm
Bedroom 3:	5655mm x 3378mm
En-suite:	3100mm x 1446mm

Floor Area: 153.54 sq. metres
Frontage Dimension: 10.60 metres

No. 210
Cashel

The layout of this dormer house features a living room to the rear of the dwelling. The kitchen and living room have a curved wall detail and the dining area opening off the kitchen is in fact, a sun room. One ground floor bedroom and an adjoining bathroom are provided. The ground floor bedroom may be utilised as a study. Three good sized bedrooms are designed on the dormer floor, together with a half-bathroom and a walk-in hot press.

ROOM DIMENSIONS

Living Room:	5220mm x 4630mm
Bathroom:	2550mm x 2000mm
Bedroom:	3650mm x 3650mm
Kitchen:	3650mm x 3880mm
Utility:	2600mm x 1800mm
Bedroom:	4075mm x 2800mm
Bedroom:	2909mm x 3265mm
Bedroom:	2909mm x 3265mm
Bathroom:	1095mm x 2799mm

Floor Area:	133.38 square metres
Frontage:	8.52 metres

GROUND FLOOR PLAN

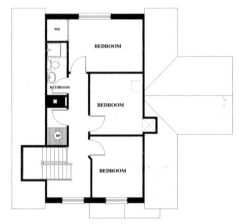

DORMER FLOOR PLAN

No. 211
Ballincar

A compact dormer house suited to a narrow fronted site. The ground floor offers a sitting room, kitchen, utility room, two bedrooms and a bathroom. On the upper floor we have provided two further bedrooms and a half bathroom. The exterior has a napped plaster finish and the roof is covered with slates.

front elevation

ROOM DIMENSIONS

Bedroom:	3660mm x 3350mm
Bathroom:	3350mm x 1630mm
Bedroom:	3660mm x 3350mm
Utility:	2080mm x 1780mm
Kitchen/Dining:	3660mm x 3510mm
Sitting Room:	4270mm x 3510mm
Bedroom:	3350mm x 2590mm
Bedroom:	3910mm x 2440mm
Bathroom:	3530mm x 2440mm
Void:	3530mm x 2540mm

Floor Area:	114.86 sq. metres
Frontage:	9.75 metres

ground floor plan

dormer plan

No. 212
Monroe

This extendible dormer home provides initially, three good bedrooms, and later can accommodate at least two further bedrooms and a second bathroom on the upper level. The elevation is attractive, gable facing and trimmed with brick. We can provide this design roofed the other way if preferred. Our designers have allowed adequate dimension to cater for a future stairs to the upper level. All bedrooms have fitted wardrobes. The lounge has an open fireplace and provision has been made in the living room for a solid fire cooker. Our bathroom layout features a separate shower cabinet.

plan

ROOM DIMENSIONS

Lounge:	4420mm x 3960mm
Living Dining Room:	5740mm x 3510mm
Kitchen:	3960mm x 3250mm
Utility Room:	2130mm x 1370mm
Bathroom:	2290mm x 1930mm
Bedroom 1:	4010mm x 3250mm
Bedroom 2:	3510mm x 3250mm
Bedroom 3:	3510mm x 3050mm
Floor Area:	122.85 sq. metres
Frontage:	14.42 metres

elevation

ground floor plan

No. 213
Ballykilty

The well balanced elevation of this dwelling is finished with napped plaster and the roof is covered with concrete tiles. The ground floor accommodation is well laid out to cater for family occupation, and you will note that the kitchen dining room extends the full width of the house. Provision is made for a solid fuel cooker in the kitchen and the sitting room has an open fireplace. Three bedrooms and two bathrooms together with a generously dimensioned utility room complete the ground floor layout. Initial development of the upper floor describes one further bedroom and a storage area. A fifth bedroom can be accommodated at a later date.

ROOM DIMENSIONS

Kitchen/Dining:	7980mm x 4570mm	Sitting Room:	4880mm x 4720mm
Utility:	3350mm x 3300mm	Hall:	2740mm wide
Bathroom:	3300mm x 2240mm	Bedroom:	4570mm x 3350mm
Bedroom:	3300mm x 2740mm		
Bedroom:	3300mm x 2950mm		
En Suite:	1780mm x 1070mm	Floor Area:	146.66 sq. metres
Bedroom:	3910mm x 3350mm	Frontage:	17.53 metres

front elevation

dormer plan

135

No. 214
Dungloe

Versatile dormer bungalow that can be developed in a number of stages to suit the client's financial resources. The frontage is less than fifty feet so the **DUNGLOE** is suited to most sites including town sites. This design allows for full insulation. Hall with stairs, bathroom, utility room and garage. Second bathroom on first floor.

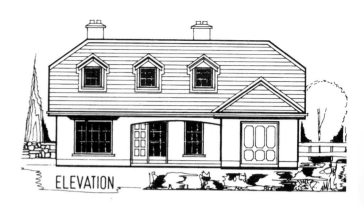

ELEVATION

ROOM DIMENSIONS

Kitchen:	3510mm x 3350mm
Lounge:	5500mm x 3660mm
Bedroom:	4040mm x 2920mm
Bedroom:	3660mm x 3250mm
Living Dining Room:	3960mm x 3660mm
Bedroom:	3660mm x 3350mm
Bedroom:	4420mm x 3250mm

Floor Area:	186.47 sq. metres
Frontage:	13.36 metres

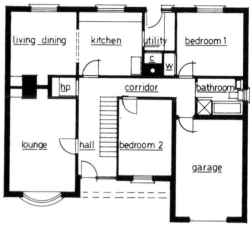

GROUND FLOOR LAYOUT

FRONT ELEVATION

NEW DESIGN!

No. 215
Balrenny

This attractive dormer house is designed for a site with modest frontage and does not overlook adjoining properties. The accommodation is well laid out with one bedroom on ground floor level and two further bedrooms on the upper floor. A large utility room and kitchen dining room are provided. French doors lead from the dining area to the rear garden. Double doors lead from the dining area to the large sitting room.

ROOM DIMENSIONS

Utility Room:	2530mm x 2742mm
Kitchen Dining Room:	6170mm x 3810mm
Sitting Room:	3600mm x 6000mm
Hall:	1960mm wide
Bedroom 3:	3000mm x 3040mm
Bathroom:	2530mm x 2134mm
Bedroom 1:	3600mm x 4164mm
Bedroom 2:	4100mm x 2564mm

Floor Area:	116 square metres
Frontage:	9.40 metres

GROUND FLOOR PLAN

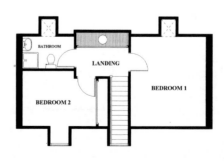

DORMER PLAN

No. 216
Sobrando

A beautiful lodge style dormer home of modest proportions with pleasant surprises in the layout. The master bedroom and en-suite are located on the ground floor, as is the main bathroom. Our kitchen, dining room and lounge are of good dimension and we have provided two open fireplaces. Access to the upper floor is by spiral stairs leading onto two fine bedrooms. The elevation is well balanced with its hipped and slated roof. The portico roof is supported on glass fibre columns. This home is suited to both town and country sites.

ROOM DIMENSIONS

Lounge:	4600mm x 4400mm
Master Bedroom:	3900mm x 3200mm
En Suite:	2100mm x 1900mm
Bathroom:	3500mm x 1700mm
Kitchen:	3200mm x 3000mm
Dining Room:	3200mm x 2800mm
Utility Room:	1700mm x 1500mm
Bedroom 2:	4600mm x 2400mm
Bedroom 3:	2000mm x 3000mm

Floor Area:	119 sq. metres
Frontage:	11.90 metres

ground floor plan

elevation

front elevation

No. 217
Carlingford

A compact dormer home with simple styling to the front elevation. The ground floor comprises a large kitchen/dining room, sitting room with open fireplace and two bedrooms with built-in wardrobes. On the upper floor we have planned for two bedrooms, a bathroom and a shower en-suite. Note the large walk-in hot press. The roof of the Carlingford home is finished with slates.

ROOM DIMEMSIONS

Bedroom:	3960mm x 2950mm
Bedroom:	3710mm x 2950mm
Dining/Kitchen:	5990mm x 3960mm
Sitting Room:	4570mm x 3710mm
Hall:	1980mm wide
Bedroom:	3960mm x 2950mm
Bathroom:	2130mm x 1780mm
Shower:	1780mm x 810mm
Bedroom:	3510mm x 3300mm

Floor Area:	116.35 sq. metres
Frontage:	10.29 metres

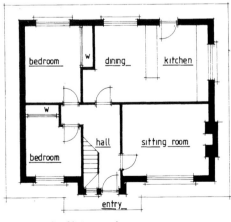

ground floor plan

dormer plan

FRONT ELEVATION

No. 218
Chesire

The ground floor plan of this dwelling is similar to our Design No. 1. This design has a dormer floor with two bedrooms and a bathroom en-suite. On the ground floor, the dwelling is suitable for further extension on the bedroom side. The front elevation has a natural stone feature. The modest floor area renders this house suitable as a starter home.

GROUND FLOOR PLAN

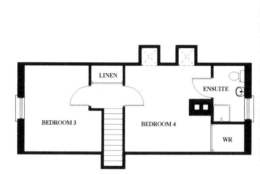

DORMER PLAN

ROOM DIMENSIONS

Bedroom 1:	3410mm x 2750mm
Hall:	1450mm wide
Sitting Room:	3800mm x 3616mm
Kitchen/	
Dining Room:	4084mm x 3200mm
Bathroom:	1800mm x 3200mm
Bedroom 3:	3410mm x 3700mm
Bedroom 4:	3775mm x 3700mm
Ensuite:	2407mm x 1375mm
Floor Area:	105.81 sq. metres
Frontage:	10.30 metres

No. 219
Chester

A modern dormer home with integral garage, this design is totally balanced, the front elevation featuring the main entrance. The living rooms open off the main hall, which is large enough to furnish and contains a hardwood stairs. We have provided a ground floor shower and toilet opening off the utility room. The kitchen/dining room and living room are serviced by open fireplaces. The upper floor contains three good bedrooms, two of which have fitted wardrobes. The bathroom on the upper floor is fully fitted.

elevation

dormer plan

ground floor plan

ROOM DIMENSIONS

Kitchen Dining Room:	5200mm x 3900mm
Main Hall:	4100mm x 3500mm
Living Room:	4000mm x 3900mm
Utility Room:	3900mm x 1500mm
Shower Room:	2800mm x 1200mm
Garage:	8000mm x 3900mm
Bedroom 1:	4600mm x 4050mm
Bedroom 2:	3900mm x 2700mm
Bedroom 3:	3900mm x 2700mm
Bathroom:	2550mm x 1800mm
Floor Area:	159.80 sq. metres
Frontage:	12.90 metres

No. 220
Ballybrew

The architect has employed modern styling for this attractive dormer home. Open fireplaces are provided in the dining room and sitting room and provision has been made for a solid fuel cooker in the kitchen. Three bedrooms, two bathrooms, a fine utility room and an integral garage complete the ground floor. On the dormer plan we have provided two further bedrooms, a bathroom and an en-suite. The clean lines of the elevation incorporate a roofed entry and an attractive bay window in the sitting room.

front elevation

ROOM DIMENSIONS

Bedroom:	3200mm x 2900mm
Bedroom:	2900mm x 2540mm
Bathroom:	3660mm x 2850mm
En Suite:	2290mm x 1220mm
Bedroom:	3660mm x 3200mm
Hall:	1630mm wide
Sitting Room:	4570mm x 3660mm
Garage:	5330mm x 3350mm
Kitchen/Dining Room:	6200mm x 4220mm
Utility:	3350mm x 2440mm
Bathroom:	2440mm x 2030mm
Storage:	3150mm x 1830mm
Bedroom:	3150mm x 2850mm
En Suite:	3150mm x 2850mm
Bedroom:	5280mm x 4270mm
Landing:	2030mm wide

Floor Area:	173.35 sq. metres
Frontage:	13.41 metres

dormer plan   ground floor plan

No. 221
Saxony

An attractive dormer home suited to stage development. The ground floor alone provides adequate accommodation as a starter home and the upper floor may be developed later. The large kitchen/dining area is provided with a solid fuel or oil fired cooker and opens onto a utility room. The ground floor bathroom offers a shower cabinet, toilet and wash basin. Two further bedrooms are provided on the upper floor, together with a fully fitted bathroom. The front elevation is finished with brick trim.

elevation

ROOM DIMENSIONS

Sitting Room:	4570mm x 3350mm
Kitchen/Dining Room:	5690mm x 3350mm
Utility Room:	2740mm x 1370mm
Bedroom 1:	3560mm x 2740mm
Bedroom 2:	3050mm x 2440mm
Bathroom:	2290mm x 1680mm
Garage:	5030mm x 2620mm
Entrance Hall:	1980mm wide
Bedroom 3:	4270mm x 3050mm
Bedroom 4:	2740mm x 2570mm
Bathroom:	3350mm x 2030mm

Floor Area:	119.69 sq. metres
Frontage:	11.43 metres

ground floor plan.

first floor plan.

No. 222
Ashbrook

The modern elevation of this design conceals practical accommodation. Two bedrooms are provided on the ground floor together with a large kitchen/dining room, a sitting room, utility room and integral garage. The upper floor has two bedrooms, a bathroom and a half bathroom en-suite.

ROOM DIMENSIONS

Bedroom:	3960mm x 2950mm
Toilet:	1780mm x 1020mm
Bedroom:	2950mm x 2590mm
Sitting Room:	4570mm x 3710mm
Garage:	5640mm x 2900mm
Utility:	2900mm x 1450mm
Kitchen/Dining:	5990mm x 3960mm
Bedroom:	4270mm x 2950mm
Bathroom:	1980mm x 1830mm
En Suite:	1980mm x 1120mm
Bedroom:	4270mm x 3510mm

Floor Area:	138.20 sq. metres
Frontage:	10.31 metres

front elevation

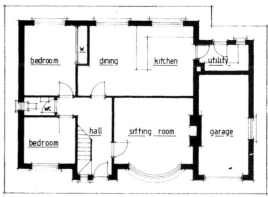

ground floor plan

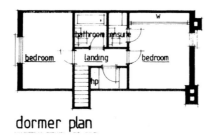

dormer plan

elevation

No. 223
Preston

An exceptional dormer home with five bedrooms, two of which are located on the ground floor. Georgian style windows and arched entry provide a pleasing elevation. The roof is covered with asbestos slates. The ground floor layout provides three full sized living rooms and we have included two open fireplaces. A fully fitted bathroom is include and a second toilet facility opening off the rere lobby. The upper floor has three fine bedrooms and a half bathroom. Three colas centre pivoting roof windows light the landing corridor and upper floor bathroom.

ROOM DIMENSIONS

Lounge:	4570mm x 4170mm
Family Room:	3510mm x 3250mm
Kitchen/Dining Room:	4620mm x 3200mm
Bedroom 5:	3150mm x 3050mm
Bedroom 4:	3510mm x 3150mm
Bathroom:	3200mm x 1730mm
Toilet:	2440mm x 810mm
Lobby:	2440mm x 910mm
Boiler Room:	1980mm x 910mm
Bedroom 1:	3960mm x 3660mm
Bedroom 2:	3910mm x 2740mm
Bedroom 3:	4170mm x 2740mm
Half Bathroom:	2540mm x 1880mm

Floor Area:	153 sq. metres
Frontage:	13.61 metres

ground floor plan

dormer plan

No. 224
Afton

A well proportioned design with four living rooms and two bedrooms on the ground floor. We have planned for a fully fitted bathroom on the ground floor also. The sitting room has an open fireplace and a bow window. French doors lead off the family room. On the upper floor we have planned for two bedrooms, one with bathroom en-suite, a toilet opening off the landing and a remaining dormer area for future development.

ROOM DIMENSIONS

Utility:	3050mm x 2490mm	Bedroom:	3250mm x 2590mm
Bathroom:	3050mm x 2790mm	Bedroom:	4270mm x 3760mm
Bedroom:	3660mm x 3350mm	En Suite:	2290mm x 1520mm
Bedroom:	3660mm x 2740mm	Toilet:	1630mm x 1220mm
Hall:	2390mm wide		
Sitting Room:	4830mm x 4270mm		
Family Room:	4220mm x 3660mm	Floor Area:	166.01 sq. metres
Kitchen/Dining:	6810mm x 4220mm	Frontage:	14.33 metres

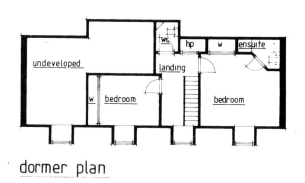

dormer plan

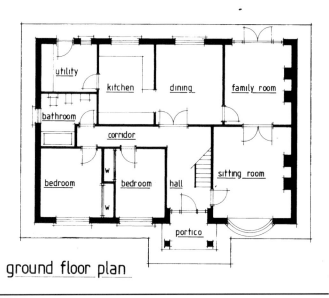

ground floor plan

FRONT ELEVATION

NEW DESIGN

No. 225
Broadfort

This attractive dormer home is cruciform shape and the exterior is finished with natural stone on the front elevation. The sitting room has a bay window to the side. All rooms are well proportioned and a fireplace is included in the sitting room and the family room. The dormer floor has three good sized bedrooms, a full sized bathroom and a bathroom en-suite.

ROOM DIMENSIONS

Sitting Room:	4400mm x 6100mm
Kitchen/	6100mm x 6452mm
Dining Room:	4400mm x 6100mm
Family Room:	6101mm x 3308mm
Entrance Hall:	1639mm x 1700mm
Toilet:	4400mm x 3069mm
Bedroom:	3069mm x 5176mm
Bedroom:	5916mm x 3069mm
Mater Bedroom:	3069mm x 1976mm
Bathroom:	
Floor Area:	207.73 sq. metres
Frontage:	15.70 metres

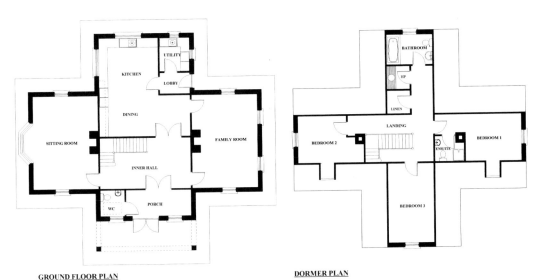

GROUND FLOOR PLAN

DORMER PLAN

No. 226 Kilmoon

The sitting room in this fine dormer home extends to the full width of the house. We have attached a garage and boiler room. The large kitchen/dining room has provision for a solid fuel cooker. Note the recessed entrance and attractive staircase. The upper floor is well laid out with three bedrooms, a bathroom and a walk in hot press. We have finished the elevation of this dwelling with brick.

ROOM DIMENSIONS

Boiler Room:	3000mm x 1400mm
Garage:	6350mm x 3000mm
Sitting Room:	8000mm x 4050mm
Toilet:	2800mm x 1200mm
Utility:	3900mm x 1500mm
Hall:	4100mm x 3500mm
Family Room:	4000mm x 3900mm
Kitchen/Dining:	5200mm x 3900mm
Bedroom:	4600mm x 4050mm
Bathroom:	2550mm x 1750mm
Bedroom:	3900mm x 2700mm
Bedroom:	3900mm x 2700mm

Floor Area: 158.17 sq. metres
Frontage: 13.10 metres

front elevation

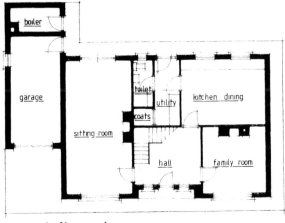

ground floor plan

dormer plan

No. 227

Domingo

An unusual exterior yet the accommodation is both practical and well laid out. On the ground floor we have provided three living rooms, a utility room, study and integral garage. The upper floor has three bedrooms and two bathrooms, one of which is en-suite. The roof is covered with slates and the elevation has black trim.

front elevation

ground floor plan

dormer plan

ROOM DIMENSIONS

Fuel Room:	3280mm x 1090mm
Garage:	4400mm x 3350mm
Utility:	2290mm x 1680mm
Study:	3710mm x 3350mm
Kitchen:	3760mm x 3710mm
Living Room:	4270mm x 3710mm
Sitting Room:	6170mm x 4880mm
Bedroom:	4040mm x 3960mm
En Suite:	2160mm x 2060mm
Bathroom:	2970mm x 2060mm
Bedroom:	3180mm x 3050mm
Bedroom:	3200mm x 3050mm

Floor Area: 141.27 sq. metres
Frontage: 11.58 metres

No. 228
Northville

This energy efficient dormer home offers full family accommodation on both levels, the lower level rooms are of fine dimension and interesting in shape. The central chimney stack provides for an open fire in both Sitting and dining rooms and a separate flue to cater for the solid fuel cooker in the kitchen. A roofed entry and shaped conservatory provide an unusual detail towards the southerly aspect. Opening off the main hall we have located a half bathroom and a small library. The upper level accommodation has four bedrooms, a fully fitted bathroom and a full bathroom to service the master bedroom. Our hot press gives adequate area for ironing.

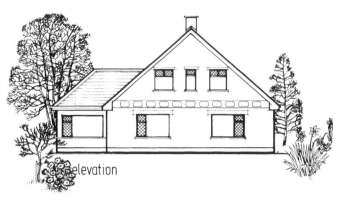
elevation

ROOM DIMENSIONS

Sitting Room:	5500mm x 4720mm
Dining Room:	4880mm x 4120mm
Kitchen (L-shape)	16.37 sq. metres
Utility Room:	2340mm x 1830mm
Library:	2440mm x 1830mm
Half Bathroom:	1830mm x 1220mm
Conservatory/Entry:	4010mm x 3050mm
Bedroom 1:	4060mm x 3150mm
Bedroom 2:	3050mm x 2500mm
Bedroom 3:	2740mm x 2440mm
Bedroom 4:	2790mm x 2390mm
Floor Area:	161.72 sq. metres
Frontage:	11.07 metres

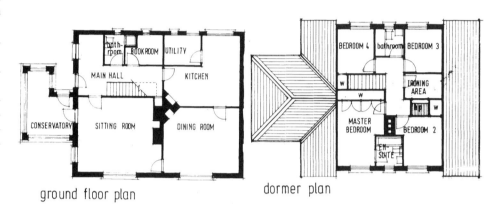

ground floor plan   dormer plan

elevation

Provincial

VARIATIONS ON A THEME

In our previous edition we featured our Classic design, now a household title with hundreds of our clients. This time we feature the Provincial style Dormer home. On the following pages we feature eight plan styles suitable to two stylish elevations. The choice is yours!

No. 229
Provincial

This dormer home has a well balanced elevation trimmed in brick. The roof window and hipped roof create an air of luxury, with the roof extensions on the bedroom and lounge ends providing a formal garden and entrance patio to the space in between. The main hall features the stairs and study door and a segmental arch leads you into the main service corridor. The ground floor alone provides full accommodation, and the upper floor may be developed later. In total this home has four good bedrooms, three of which have fitted wardrobes. The kitchen dining room is serviced with a solid fuel cooker and the lounge has an open fireplace. Glazed doors connect the dining room with the lounge.

elevation

ROOM DIMENSIONS

Lounge:	5900mm x 3960mm
Dining Room:	3560mm x 3350mm
Kitchen:	4420mm x 3350mm
Utility:	3350mm x 1520mm
Bathroom:	3350mm x 1930mm
Bedroom 1:	4720mm x 3250mm
Bedroom 2:	3350mm x 3350mm
Study:	3050mm x 2740mm
Main Hall:	4220mm x 3050mm
Bedroom 3:	4570mm x 3120mm
Bedroom 4:	3910mm x 3050mm
Hot Press:	1580mm x 1220mm
Dormer Bathroom:	2390mm x 1580mm

Floor Area: 188.31 sq. metres
Frontage: 15.77 metres

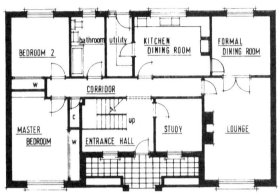

ground floor plan

dormer plan

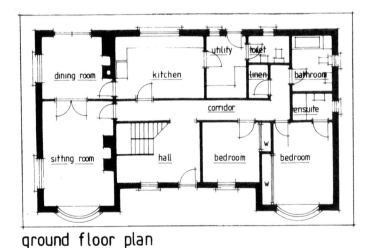

ground floor plan

dormer plan

No. 230
Provincial

The elevation is similar to our design No. 226, but the accommodation is laid out in a different manner. Sitting room and dining room have open fireplaces and provision has been made for a solid fuel cooker in the kitchen. A toilet opens off the large utility room. We have located two bedrooms and bathroom facilities on the ground floor. The upper floor is well laid out with two further bedrooms, a half bathroom and a walk-in hot press.

ROOM DIMENSIONS

Dining Room:	3810mm x 3200mm
Kitchen:	4720mm x 3200mm
Utility Room:	3200mm x 2130mm
Toilet:	2180mm x 1370mm
Bathroom:	2850mm x 2130mm
En Suite:	2130mm x 1370mm
Bedroom:	4320mm x 3810mm
Bedroom:	3050mm x 3050mm
Hall:	4420mm x 3050mm
Sitting Room:	5440mm x 3810mm
Bedroom:	3710mm x 3610mm
Bathroom:	2240mm x 1370mm
Bedroom:	3710mm x 3510mm

Floor Area: 171.40 sq. metres
Frontage: 16.00 metres

No. 231
Provincial

Another fine home with an elevation similar to our design No. 229. The sitting room and the formal dining area extend the full width of the house. The large kitchen dining room has an open fireplace. We have provided a half bathroom opening off the utility room. The master bedroom and bathroom en suite complete the ground floor layout. On the upper floor we have planned for two further bedrooms and a bathroom.

ROOM DIMENSIONS

Bedroom:	3960mm x 3050mm
Bathroom:	2850mm x 1830mm
Bedroom:	4420mm x 3300mm
Dining Room:	3960mm x 3350mm
Sitting Room:	5890mm x 3960mm
Bedroom:	3810mm x 3350mm
En Suite:	2690mm x 1070mm
Utility:	3350mm x 2540mm
Shower Room:	2790mm x 1520mm
Kitchen:	3710mm x 2900mm
Family Room:	4720mm x 3960mm
Study:	3050mm x 2900mm
Hall:	4120mm x 3050mm

Floor Area:	179.58 sq. metres
Frontage:	15.85 metres

dormer plan

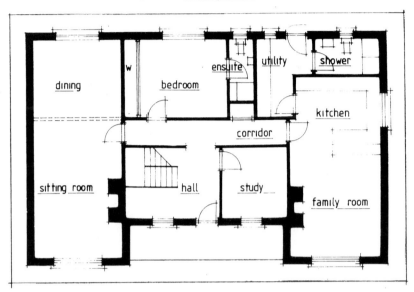

ground floor plan

No. 232
Provincial

Many of our clients prefer to complete the Provincial design in two stages and here we indicate how you can achieve adequate accommodation at ground floor level initially. We have planned for three fine living rooms, bathroom, utility room and three bedrooms, one having a shower en-suite. The compact study provides the location for the stairs at second stage development. The detail plans for this design incorporate the garage as shown in the sketch.

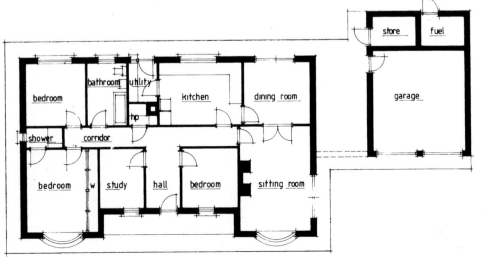

ground floor plan

ROOM DIMENSIONS

Bedroom:	3200mm x 3200mm
Bathroom:	3200mm x 2130mm
Utility:	2030mm x 1520mm
Kitchen:	4470mm x 3200mm
Dining Room:	3510mm x 3200mm
Sitting Room:	5440mm x 3810mm
Bedroom:	3050mm x 3050mm
Hall:	3050mm x 1830mm
Study:	3050mm x 2340mm
Bedroom:	4320mm x 3810mm
Shower Room:	1980mm x 1020mm
Garage:	5180mm x 4880mm
Store:	2340mm x 1520mm
Fuel:	
Floor Area:	123.74 sq. metres
Frontage:	15.81 metres

No. 233
Provincial

An elevation similar to design No. 229, this is a stretched version with the addition of a third dormer window and a recessed entrance detail. This fine family home provides a granny bedroom and half bathroom en-suite on the ground floor level. We have provided a compact office which could also be utilised as a playroom. The upper floor incorporates two bedrooms and a bathroom.

dormer plan

ROOM DIMENSIONS

Dining Room/ Kitchen: 6250mm x 3510mm
Utility: 3510mm x 1470mm
Bathroom: 3510mm x 1730mm
Bedroom: 3510mm x 3100mm
Office: 3510mm x 2440mm
Lobby: 1980mm x 1730mm
Toilet: 1730mm x 1070mm
En Suite: 2130mm x 1220mm
Granny Bedroom: 4270mm x 3300mm
Bedroom: 3050mm x 3050mm
Hall: 3960mm x 2590mm
Family Room: 3050mm x 3050mm
Sitting Room: 5590mm x 3960mm
Bedroom: 4270mm x 3350mm
Bedroom: 5280mm x 4270mm
Hot Press: 1830mm x 1220mm
Bathroom: 1980mm x 1830mm
Storage: 4270mm x 2130mm

Floor Area: 214.11 sq. metres
Frontage: 18.88 metres

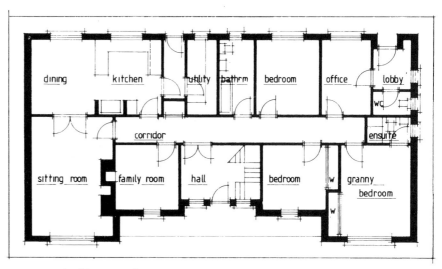

ground floor plan

ground floor plan

No. 234
Provincial

This design shows our second elevation for the Provincial theme. Note the architect's detail in the hall and dining room featuring spiral stairs and the angular fireplace. Direct access is provided from the integral garage through to the lobby and kitchen. A bedroom, bathroom and a compact study completes the ground floor accommodation. On the upper floor we have planned for three bedrooms, bathroom, and a walk-in hot press.

ROOM DIMENSIONS

Garage:	4950mm x 3380mm	Bathroom:	2640mm x 2490mm
Lobby:	2850mm x 1470mm	Bedroom:	3450mm x 2900mm
Kitchen:	4270mm x 3510mm	Bedroom:	2900mm x 2440mm
Dining Room:	3510mm x 3510mm	Bedroom:	4120mm x 3350mm
Sitting Room:	5790mm x 3860mm	Bathroom:	2440mm x 1220mm
Study:	3100mm x 2640mm		
Hall:	3300mm x 3100mm	Floor Area:	172.33 sq. metres
Bedroom:	3860mm x 3200mm	Frontage:	15.24 metres

front elevation

dormer plan

No. 235
Provincial

This fine home has an elevation similar to our design No. 234. The accommodation is well laid out on both floor levels and open fireplaces are provided in the sitting room and living room. The ground floor also has two bedrooms and two bathrooms, one of which is en-suite. The upper floor has two further bedrooms, a walk-in hot press and a fully fitted bathroom.

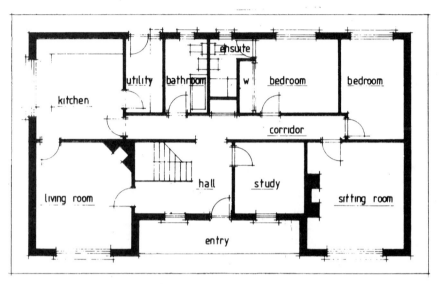

dormer plan

ROOM DIMENSIONS

Kitchen:	4370mm x 3860mm
Utility Room:	3200mm x 1630mm
Bathroom:	3200mm x 1830mm
En Suite:	2440mm x 1220mm
Bedroom:	3660mm x 3200mm
Bedroom:	4370mm x 2790mm
Sitting Room:	4570mm x 4270mm
Study:	3050mm x 3050mm
Hall:	4270mm x 3050mm
Living Room:	4570mm x 4270mm
Bedroom:	3810mm x 3350mm
Bathroom:	2440mm x 1680mm
Bedroom:	4320mm x 3810mm

Floor Area:	190.17 sq. metres
Frontage:	16.72 metres

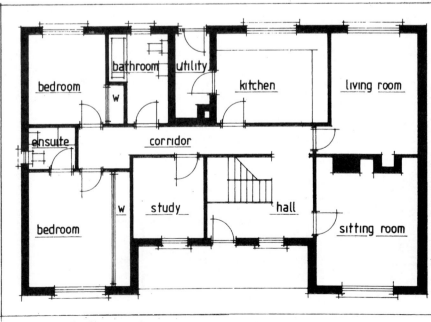

ground floor plan

dormer plan

No. 236
Provincial

Completing our range of Provincial homes, this well designed house has an elevation similar to our design No. 234. The ground floor offers three living rooms, a study, two bedrooms, main bathroom and a half bathroom en-suite. The utility room has a chimney to cater for an internal central heating boiler. On the upper floor we have planned for two bedrooms, a walk-in hot press and a half bathroom.

ROOM DIMENSIONS

Bedroom:	4300mm x 4000mm
Shower:	1600mm x 1600mm
Bedroom:	4000mm x 2700mm
Bedroom:	3400mm x 3000mm
Bathroom:	3400mm x 2350mm
Utility Room:	3400mm x 1500mm
Kitchen:	4400mm x 3400mm
Living Room:	4600mm x 3400mm
Sitting Room:	4850mm x 4000mm
Hall:	4200mm x 3000mm
Study:	3000mm x 2800mm
Bedroom:	4350mm x 3300mm
En Suite:	1850mm x 1600mm

Floor Area:	179.00 sq. metres
Frontage:	15.90 metres

ground floor plan

No. 237
Dorset

This well designed dormer home has one bedroom on the ground floor and three bedrooms on the upper floor. A bathroom is provided on both levels. The large kitchen/dining room and the sitting room have open fireplaces. Front elevation details include feature archways and a slated roof. Ground floors are of concrete, insulated, and upper floors comprise timber boarding on joists. The fabric of the house is fully insulated. All windows are double glazed.

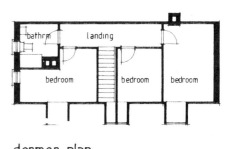

front elevation

ROOM DIMENSIONS

Sitting Room:	4420mm x 4270mm
Kitchen/Dining Room:	6170mm x 3810mm
Utility Room:	2440mm x 1680mm
Bathroom:	3200mm x 1880mm
Bedroom:	3760mm x 3050mm
Hall:	2130mm wide
Bedroom:	4420mm x 2900mm
Bedroom:	2900mm x 2590mm
Bedroom:	4270mm x 2850mm
Bathroom:	2440mm x 2180mm

Floor Area:	136.54 sq. metres
Frontage:	11.73 metres

ground floor plan

dormer plan

front elevation

No. 238
Kimberlin

An exciting dormer design with three bedrooms on the ground floor level and provision for two further bedrooms and a bathroom on the dormer floor level. The large kitchen/dining room has an open fireplace and patio doors to the side. The utility room is self-contained and a toilet is located nearby. All bedrooms are adequate in size, and the master bedroom incorporates a dressing area, which could become an ensuite bathroom. Front elevation treatment is in brick and slate cladding, and the variety of roof lines make this a very attractive dwellinghouse.

ground floor plan

ROOM DIMENSIONS

Sitting Room:	5180mm x 4270mm
Kitchen:	6400mm x 3350mm
Dining Area:	4270mm x 3050mm
Utility Room:	2590mm x 2130mm
Lobby:	1220mm wide
Toilet:	2130mm x 910mm
Hall:	1830mm wide
Bedroom:	3350mm x 2740mm
Bedroom:	4270mm x 3350mm
Dressing Area:	2130mm x 1830mm
Bedroom:	3560mm x 3350mm
Bathroom:	3510mm x 2130mm
Bedroom:	3810mm x 3350mm
Bedroom:	3660mm x 3350mm
Bathroom:	2130mm x 1830mm

Floor Area:	209.34 sq. metres
Frontage:	17.47 metres

No. 239
Yeovil

The simple elevation on this dormer bungalow conceals a full-sized family home.
Ground floor accommodation is well laid
out and provides three good sized bedrooms.
The kitchen dining room faces the front of
the house, and provision is made in the
kitchen for an oil-fired cooker. A large utility room will accommodate all laundry
equipment. The dormer floor can accommodate three bedrooms and a half bathroom.
The roof is covered with slates, and the
external finish is in napped plaster.

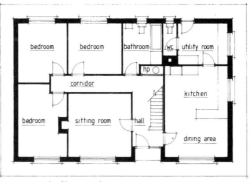

front elevation

ROOM DIMENSIONS

Kitchen Dining Room:	6020mm x 4270mm
Sitting Room:	4270mm x 4240mm
Utility Room:	3350mm x 2740mm
Toilet:	2130mm x 910mm
Bathroom:	3350mm x 2640mm
Bedroom:	3660mm x 3350mm
Bedroom:	3910mm x 3350mm
Bedroom:	4850mm x 3350mm
Bedroom:	4720mm x 4270mm
Bedroom:	5500mm x 3200mm
Bedroom:	3350mm x 2900mm
Bathroom:	2130mm x 1830mm

Floor Area:	194.83 sq. metres
Frontage:	14.93 metres

ground floor plan

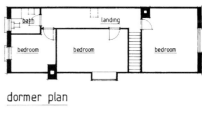

dormer plan

No. 240
Clayton

This design is a mirror image of our
Provincial design No. 234, with revisions on
the ground floor. The large sitting room and
the dining room have open fireplaces, and
provision is made in the kitchen for an oil-
fired cooker or boiler. The layout of the master bedroom is attractive, and provides a
dressing area and ensuite. A ground floor toilet opens off the entrance hall. The dormer
floor has two good bedrooms, a storage
room (or study) and a bathroom. Exterior
finish is in napped plaster and the roof is finished with slates.

ROOM DIMENSIONS

Sitting Room:	5790mm x 3860mm
Dining Room:	3510mm x 3510mm
Kitchen:	4270mm x 3510mm
Utility Room:	2180mm x 1520mm
Garage:	4900mm x 3380mm
Study:	3100mm x 2690mm
Hall:	3050mm wide
Master Bedroom:	3860mm x 3350mm
En Suite:	2340mm x 2340mm
Bedroom:	4270mm x 3350mm
Bedroom:	4270mm x 2900mm
Storage Room:	3100mm x 2440mm
Bathroom:	2440mm x 1220mm

Floor Area:	175.86 sq. metres
Frontage:	15.23 metres

front elevation

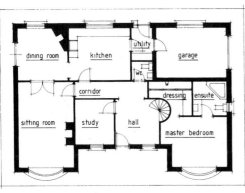

ground floor plan

dormer plan

No. 241
Kelton

A mirror image, with variations, on our design no. 216, this three bedroomed compact dormer home offers well laid out accommodation. The front elevation features two bow windows and a portico. An open fireplace is provided in the sitting room and dining area. Dual access is provided to the ground floor bathroom. Two good sized bedrooms and a bathroom are provided on the dormer floor. External finish is in napped plaster and the floor is covered with slates.

front elevation

ROOM DIMENSIONS

Sitting Room:	4600mm x 4400mm
Kitchen/Dining Room:	6000mm x 3200mm
Master Bedroom:	4600mm x 3200mm
Bathroom:	2600mm x 2300mm
Utility Room:	3500mm x 1700mm
Lobby:	1700mm x 1600mm
Hall:	2000mm wide
Bedroom:	4100mm x 2500mm
Bedroom:	4100mm x 2600mm
Bathroom:	2000mm x 1600mm

Floor Area:	123.46 sq. metres
Frontage:	12.00 metres

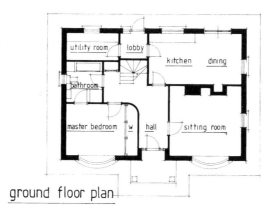

ground floor plan

dormer plan

elevation

No. 242
Crusade

This attractive dormer home has three good sized bedrooms, one located on the ground floor level. Two bathrooms are provided. A large kitchen dining room and a well-proportioned sitting room both have open fireplaces. The roof is finished with tiles, and an attractive stone feature sets off the front elevation.

ROOM DIMENSIONS

Kitchen:	4270mm x 3050mm
Dining Room:	4270mm x 3050mm
Sitting Room:	4270mm x 3960mm
Bathroom:	3350mm x 3050mm
Bedroom:	3350mm x 3250mm
Utility Room:	2340mm x 1520mm
Hall:	1520mm wide
Bedroom:	3960mm x 3350mm
Bedroom:	3350mm x 3050mm
Bathroom:	2130mm x 1680mm

Floor Area:	125.09 sq. metres
Frontage:	9.96 metres

ground floor plan

dormer plan

No. 243
Rathcoon

A substantial dormer house with three bedrooms in the dormer area and one bedroom on the ground floor level. The dwelling has a bathroom on the dormer floor and a bathroom en-suite with the master bedroom. The elevation is finished with a stone finished projecting porch and two bay windows. The kitchen/living room extends the full depth of the building.

FRONT ELEVATION

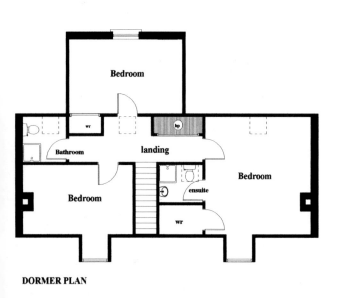

DORMER PLAN

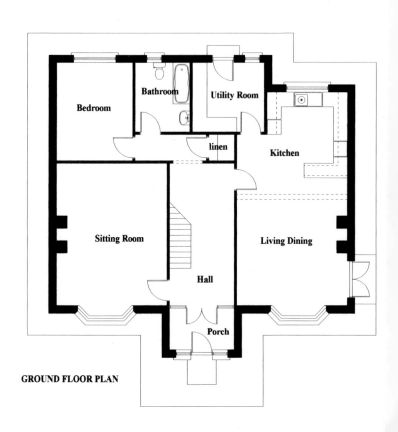

GROUND FLOOR PLAN

ROOM DIMENSIONS

Kitchen/Living Room:	8700mm x 4650mm
Sitting Room:	5800mm x 4650mm
Utility Room:	3000mm x 2834mm
Bathroom:	2834mm x 2300mm
Hall & Stairs:	2700mm wide
Ground Floor Bedroom:	4000 x 3200mm
Master Bedroom:	4788mm x 4500mm
En-suite:	1541mm x 1850mm
Bedroom:	4650mm x 2835mm
Bedroom:	4788mm x 3036mm
Half Bathroom:	1836mm x 1853mm
Floor area:	190sq.m.
Frontage dimension:	12.82m

FRONT ELEVATION

No. 244
Stonefield

This dormer house is designed as a two bedroom unit initially. The accommodation is well laid out and features a large kitchen dining room, extending the full depth of the house. Box windows are provided off the kitchen dining room and off the living room. An open fireplace is located in the living room. Later development on the upper floor will provide two further bedrooms and a bathroom. Initially the attic space would be floored out. The front elevation is finished with features of natural stone and brick.

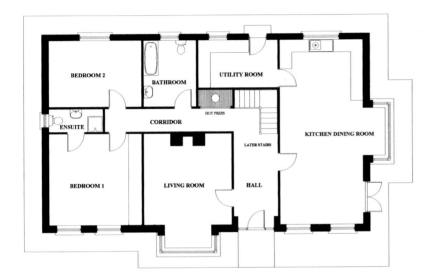

PLAN

ROOM DIMENSIONS

Kitchen/Dining:	4100mm x 8900mm
Hall:	2200mm wide
Utility:	3950mm x 2300mm
Bathroom:	2600mm x 3200mm
Bedroom:	4600mm x 3200mm
En-suite:	1100mm x 2683mm
Bedroom:	4600mm x 4400mm
Lounge:	4350mm x 4400mm

Floor Area: 143.46 square metres
Frontage Dimension: 16.25 metres

No. 245
Newtown

A full sized family home having three bedrooms on ground floor and two bedrooms on the dormer floor level. Four bedrooms have bathrooms en-suite. A walk-in hot press is located on the landing. The large kitchen dining room and sitting room are inter-connected with glazed doors. Fireplaces are provided in the sitting room and compact size family room. Two bay windows provide detail on the front elevation and the roof is of hipped style.

ROOM DIMENSIONS

Dining Area:	2640mm x 3500mm
Kitchen:	3600mm x 3500mm
Utility:	2200mm x 3500mm
Bathroom:	2132mm x 3500mm
Bedroom:	5164mm x 3500mm
En-suite:	2144mm x 2600mm
En-suite:	2144mm x 2100mm
Bedroom:	3960mm x 4280mm
Bedroom:	3000mm x 3000mm
Hall:	3960mm wide
Family Room:	3000mm x 3000mm
Sitting Room:	3960mm x 5580mm
Corridor:	1200mm wide
Dormer Bedroom:	4455mm x 4200mm
Dormer Bedroom:	5210mm x 4200mm

Floor Area: 214.11 square m.
Frontage: 18.90 metres

FRONT ELEVATION

GROUND FLOOR PLAN

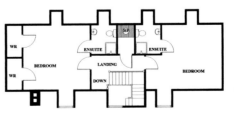

DORMER PLAN

FRONT ELEVATION

No. 246
Wexford

This dormer house has a traditional elevation with clean roof lines and vertical emphasis windows. The accommodation is well laid out and provides two bedrooms on the ground floor and two bedrooms on the dormer floor level. Bathrooms are located on both levels. The elevation features an enclosed porch, and the roof is finished with slates. French doors lead from the kitchen dining room to the exterior.

ROOM DIMENSIONS

Kitchen/		Bedroom:	4150mm x 3500mm
Dining Room:	4576mm x 3400mm	Bedroom:	3000mm x 4020mm
Sitting Room	4150mm x 4200mm	Bedroom:	2325mm x 2670mm
Porch:	2000mm wide	Bathroom:	2950mm x 1960mm
Hall:	2200mm wide	Linen Room:	2950mm x 1940mm
Lobby:	1066mm x 2234mm		
Bathroom	2250mm x 2234mm	Floor Area:	129.91 metres
Bedroom:	2500mm x 4100mm	Frontage:	11.30 metres

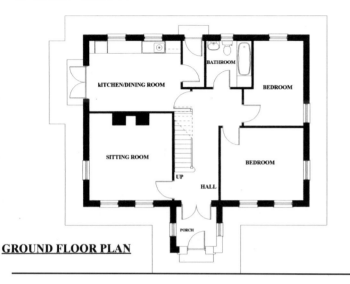

GROUND FLOOR PLAN

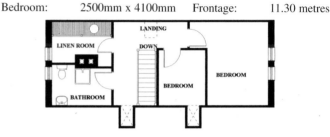

DORMER FLOOR PLAN

No. 247
Lisclougher

This large dormer house offers extensi accommodation on both floor levels. O guest bedroom with bathroom en-suite located on the ground floor level and fo bedrooms are located on the dormer lev A variety of well laid out living acco modation is provided and includes a s contained utility room and an integ garage. The upper floor has a walk linen room. The main bedroom on upper floor has a bathroom en-suite an walk-in wardrobe. The front elevation balanced with two projecting wings wh are finished in natural stone.

ROOM DIMENSIONS

Master Bedroom:	4200mm x 5286
En-suite:	1800mm x 2593
Bathroom:	3700mm x 2593
Bedroom:	5286mm x 4185
Bedroom:	4925mm x 2593
Bedroom:	4925mm x 2593
Bedroom:	5000mm x 4260
Sitting Room:	5000mm x 5500
Study:	3000mm x 3000
Bathroom:	2874mm x 3094
Playroom:	2700mm x 3094
Dining Room:	3650mm x 4166
Living Room:	5000mm x 5500
Dining/Kitchen:	8526mm x 6060
Utility Room:	2430mm x 2430
Toilet:	1200mm x 2430
Garage:	5500mm x 4500

Floor Area:	367.67 square metres
Frontage:	20.00 metres

FRONT ELEVATION

DORMER FLOOR PLAN

GROUND FLOOR PLAN

FRONT ELEVATION

NO. 248

Lislea

This attractive dormer house has well laid out accommodation and has the master bedroom located on the ground floor level. A bathroom and dressing area are designed for the master bedroom. Access through from the kitchen to the dining room and sitting room is provided via glazed double doors. The hall features a spiral stairs leading to the dormer floor. Two further bedrooms are provided on the dormer floor, one having bathroom en-suite. The elevation is finished in plaster.

ROOM DIMENSIONS

Dining Room:	3960mm x 3650mm	Utility:	2130mm x 3650mm
Sitting Room:	3650mm x 5500mm	Kitchen:	4260mm x 3650mm
Study:	3200mm x 3000mm	Bedroom:	3404mm x 2674mm
Hall:	4263mm wide	Bathroom:	3000mm x 2674mm
Master		Bedroom:	3760mm x 3124mm
Bedroom:	3650mm x 6700mm	En-suite:	1500mm x 1824mm
En-suite:	1520mm x 2450mm		
Dressing:	1500mm x 2450mm	Floor Area: 187.11 sq. metres	
Toilet:	1520mm x 3650mm	Frontage: 16.64 metres	

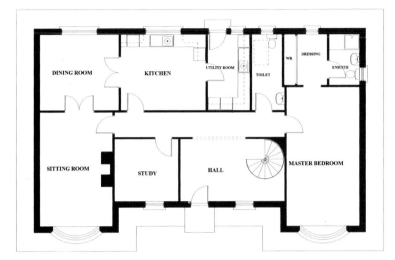

GROUND FLOOR PLAN

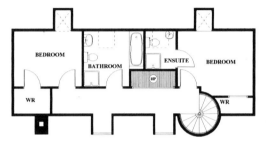

DORMER PLAN

No.249

Kilfannan

This large dormer house has six bedrooms, three of which feature a bathroom en-suite. The large entrance hall has a feature stairs, built in coats press and minimum corridor access. The kitchen/dining room is well laid out and French doors open off the dining area. The utility room is fully fitted. Two bay windows feature on the front elevation.

ROOM DIMENSIONS

Kitchen / Dining	6240mm x 5720mm
Utility:	2200mm x 3920mm
Bathroom:	2480mm x 3920mm
Bedroom 1:	4816mm x 4360mm
En-suite:	2144mm x 2130mm
En-suite:	2144mm x 2130mm
Bedroom 2:	3960mm x 5640mm
Bedroom 3:	3000mm x 4360mm
Family Room:	3000mm x 3000mm
Sitting Room:	3960mm x 5580mm
Bedroom 4:	3385mm x 4200mm
Bedroom 5:	3230mm x 2500mm
Bathroom:	3230mm x 2500mm
En-suite:	1803mm x 2500mm
Bedroom 6:	3308mm x 4200mm

Floor Area:	270.15 square metres
Frontage:	18.88 metres

FRONT ELEVATION

GROUND FLOOR PLAN

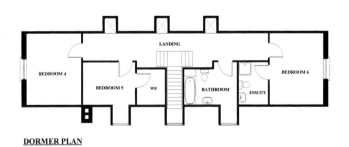

DORMER PLAN

No. 250
Whitewood

FRONT ELEVATION

This house is similar to our design no. 241 on the ground floor. The roof is altered to provide additional accommodation and features Dutch gables. The accommodation is well laid out and incorporates attractive features. As in all our designs, the layout complies with the visitable disabled regulations. External finish is in napped plaster or dry dash.

ROOM DIMENSIONS

Utility Room:	3500mm x 1700mm
Lobby:	1700mm x 1600mm
Kitchen / Dining:	6000mm x 3500mm
Sitting Room:	4600mm x 4400mm
Hall:	2000mm wide
Bedroom:	4600mm x 3500mm
Bathroom:	2300mm x 2600mm
Bedroom:	3500mm x 4100mm
Bathroom:	1600mm x 1600mm

Floor area: 150.18sq.m.
Frontage dimension: 12m

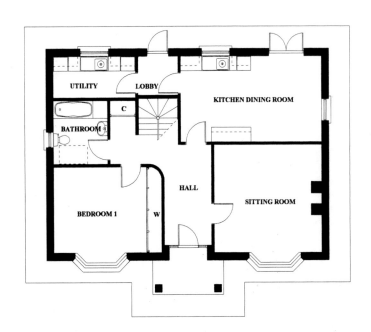

GROUND FLOOR PLAN

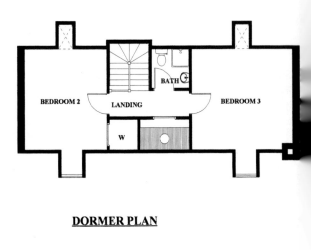

DORMER PLAN

Garage Designs

The sketches show a representative selection of our stock garage designs.
Special drawings can be prepared on request

GARAGE DESIGN NO.1

FRONT ELEVATION

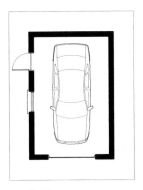

PLAN

arage: 5200mm x 3400mm
stimated Cost: €10,700

GARAGE DESIGN NO.2

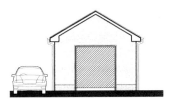

FRONT ELEVATION

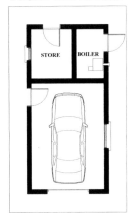

PLAN

Garage: 5200mm x 3650mm
Store: 2430mm x 2025mm
Boiler: 2430mm x 1400mm
Estimated Cost: €17,200

GARAGE DESIGN NO.3

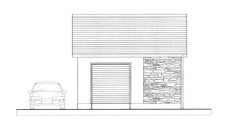

FRONT ELEVATION

PLAN

Garage: 6100mm x 3100mm
Store: 2938mm x 1800mm
Boiler: 2958mm x 1800mm
Estimated Cost: €18,750

GARAGE DESIGN NO.4

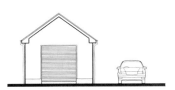

FRONT ELEVATION

PLAN

arage: 5500mm x 3650mm
ilet: 1800mm x 1100mm
ore: 1750mm x 1100mm
timated Cost: €14,600

GARAGE DESIGN NO.5

FRONT ELEVATION

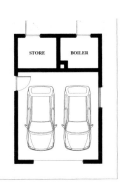

PLAN

Garage: 4870mm x 5180mm
Store: 2323mm x 1800mm
Boiler: 2323mm x 1800mm
Estimated Cost: €21,000

GARAGE DESIGN NO.6

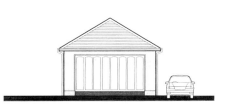

FRONT ELEVATION

PLAN

Garage: 5480mm x 5180mm
Store: 2478mm x 1800mm
Boiler: 2478mm x 1800mm
Estimated Cost: €23,000

GARAGE DESIGN NO.7

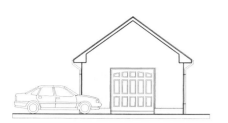

FRONT ELEVATION

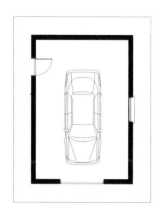

PLAN

Garage: 6850mm x 4720mm
Estimated Cost: €19,300

GARAGE DESIGN NO.8

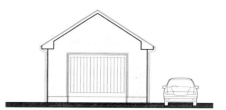

FRONT ELEVATION

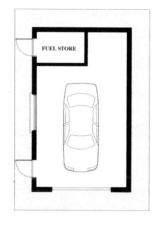

PLAN

Garage: 7620mm x 4570mm
Fuel Store: 2430mm x 1520mm
Estimated Cost: €20,700

GARAGE DESIGN NO.9

FRONT ELEVATION

PLAN

Garage
(including Boiler Room): 6500mm x 5075r
Boiler Room: 3138mm x 1500r
Estimated Cost: €19,700

GARAGE DESIGN NO.10

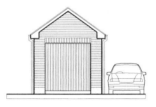

FRONT ELEVATION

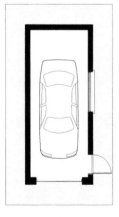

PLAN

Garage: 6500mm x 2650mm
Estimated Cost: €10,300

GARAGE DESIGN NO.11

FRONT ELEVATION

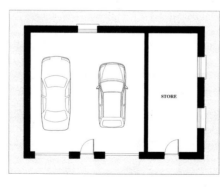

PLAN

Garage: 7000mm x 7000mm
Store: 7000mm x 3000mm
Estimated Cost: €42,500

GARAGE/STABLES DESIGN NO.12

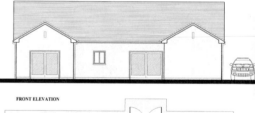

FRONT ELEVATION

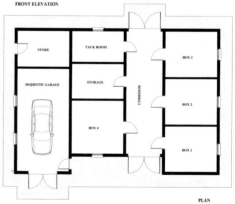

PLAN

This is an example of a stable block with a domestic garage included. Our designs can incorporate stables only and/or a garage with a number of boxes as required. All details for stables comply with the appropriate Department of Agriculture regulations.

Domestic garage:	8225mm x 4260mm
Store, with garage:	4260mm x 2875mm
Tack room:	2460mm x 2465mm
Storage room:	4260mm x 2800mm
Box 4:	4260mm x 4260mm
Box 3,2,1:	4260mm x 3650mm
Corridor:	3000mm wide

Estimated cost: €112,000

THIS IS AN EXAMPLE OF A DESIGN FOR HOUSING DEVELOPMENT WITH BOTH SEMI-DETACHED AND DETACHED HOMES. THE FLOOR AREA OF THIS HOUSE IS IN THE REGION OF 116 SQ.M.

SEMI DETACHED HOUSE

DETACHED HOUSE

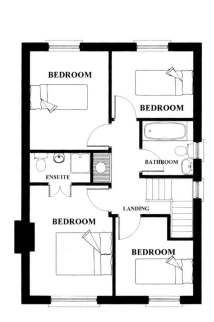

FIRST FLOOR PLAN

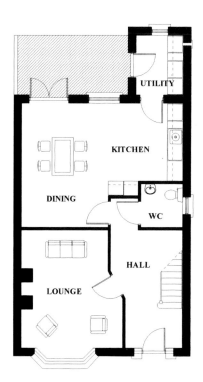

GROUND FLOOR PLAN

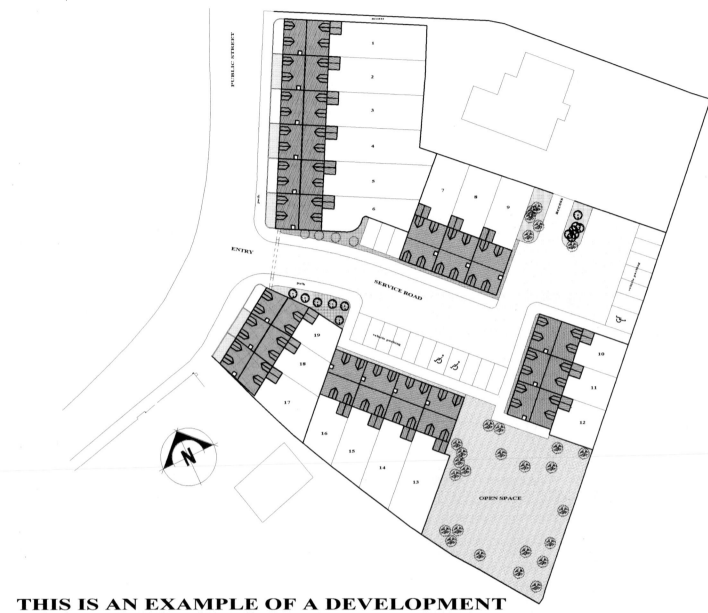

THIS IS AN EXAMPLE OF A DEVELOPMENT
OF TOWN HOUSES ON AN URBAN SITE
UTILISING STREET FRONTAGE AND BACKLANDS

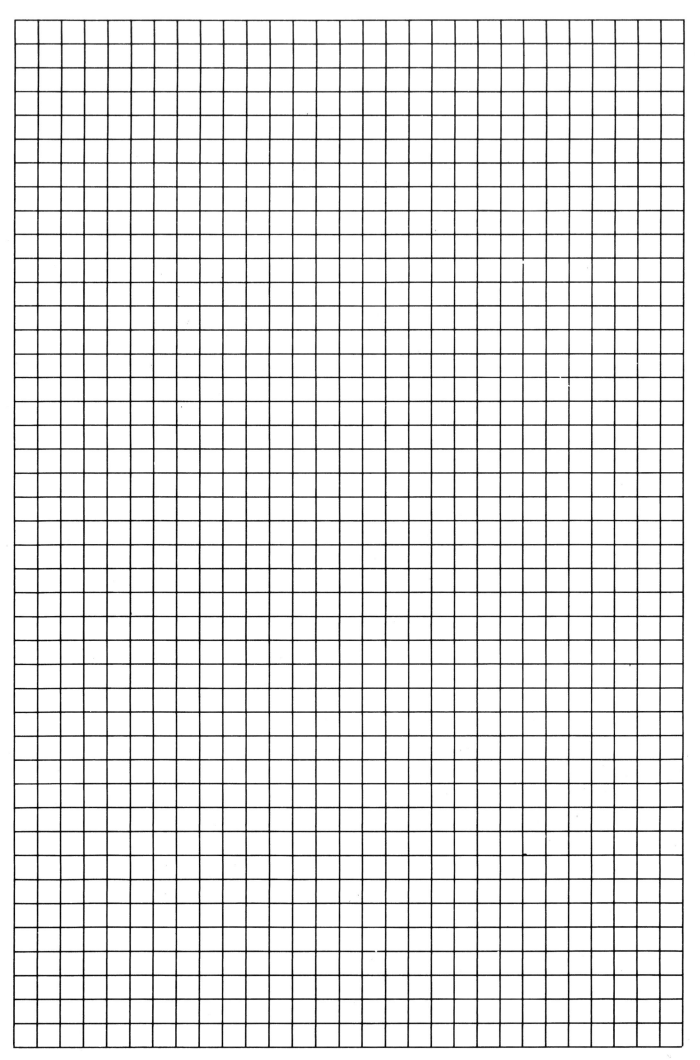

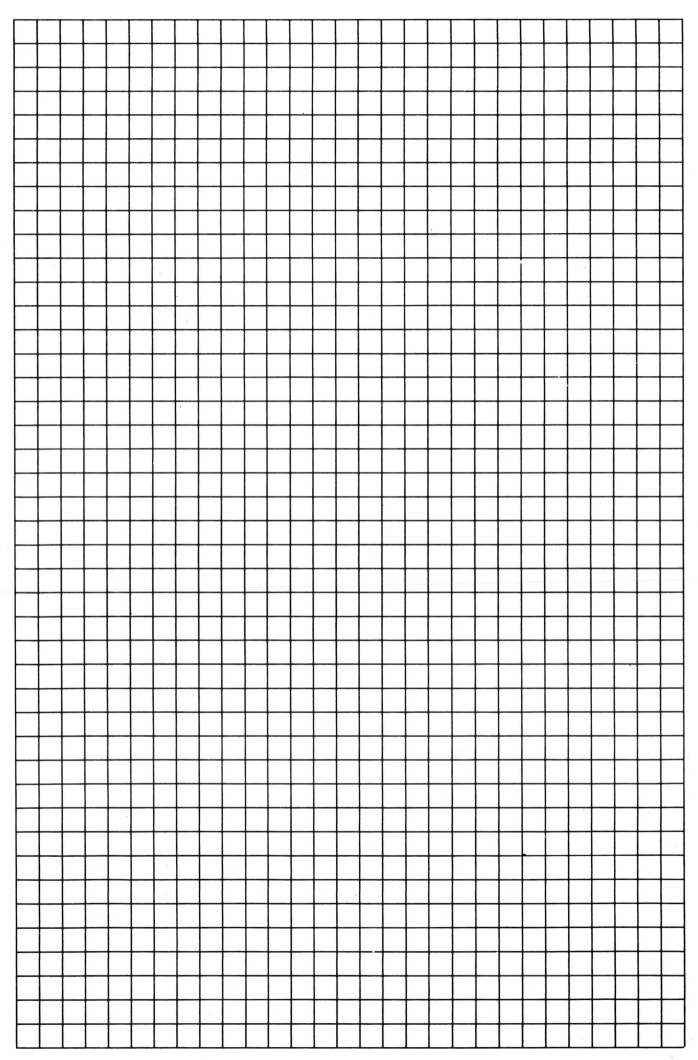

FEET & INCHES TO METRES

FEET \ INCHES	0	1	2	3	4	5	6	7	8	9	10	11
0	METRES	0.0254	0.0508	0.0762	0.1016	0.1270	0.1524	0.1778	0.2032	0.2286	0.2540	0.2794
1	0.3048	0.3302	0.3554	0.3810	0.4064	0.4318	0.4572	0.4826	0.5080	0.5334	0.5588	0.5842
2	0.6096	0.6350	0.6604	0.6858	0.7112	0.7366	0.7620	0.7874	0.8128	0.8382	0.8636	0.8890
3	0.9144	0.9398	0.9652	0.9906	1.0160	1.0414	1.0668	1.0922	1.1176	1.1430	1.1684	1.1938
4	1.2192	1.2446	1.2700	1.2954	1.3208	1.3462	1.3716	1.3970	1.4224	1.4478	1.4732	1.4986
5	1.5240	1.5494	1.5748	1.6002	1.6256	1.6510	1.6764	1.7018	1.7272	1.7526	1.7780	1.8034
6	1.8288	1.8542	1.8796	1.9050	1.9304	1.9558	1.9812	2.0066	2.0320	2.0574	2.0828	2.1082
7	2.1336	2.1590	2.1844	2.2098	2.2352	2.2606	2.2860	2.3114	2.3368	2.3622	2.3876	2.4130
8	2.4384	2.4638	2.4892	2.5146	2.5400	2.5654	2.5908	2.6162	2.6416	2.6670	2.6924	2.7178
9	2.7432	2.7686	2.7940	2.8194	2.8448	2.8702	2.8956	2.9210	2.9464	2.9718	2.9972	3.0226
10	3.0480	3.0734	3.0988	3.1242	3.1496	3.1750	3.2004	3.2258	3.2512	3.2766	3.3020	3.3274
11	3.3528	3.3782	3.4036	3.4290	3.4544	3.4798	3.5052	3.5306	3.5560	3.5814	3.6068	3.6322
12	3.6576	3.6830	3.7084	3.7338	3.7592	3.7846	3.8100	3.8354	3.8608	3.8862	3.9116	3.9370
13	3.9624	3.9878	4.0132	4.0386	4.0640	4.0894	4.1148	4.1402	4.1656	4.1910	4.2164	4.2418
14	4.2672	4.2926	4.3180	4.3434	4.3688	4.3942	4.4196	4.4450	4.4704	4.4958	4.5212	4.5466
15	4.5720	4.5974	4.6228	4.6482	4.6736	4.6990	4.7244	4.7498	4.7752	4.8006	4.8260	4.8514
16	4.8768	4.9022	4.9276	4.9530	4.9784	5.0038	5.0292	5.0546	5.0800	5.1054	5.1308	5.1562
17	5.1816	5.2070	5.2324	5.2578	5.2802	5.3086	5.3340	5.3594	5.3848	5.4102	5.4356	5.4610
18	5.4864	5.5118	5.5372	5.5626	5.5880	5.6134	5.6388	5.6642	5.6896	5.7150	5.7404	5.7658
19	5.7912	5.8166	5.8420	5.8674	5.8928	5.9182	5.9436	5.9690	5.9944	6.0198	6.0452	6.0706
20	6.0960	6.1214	6.1468	6.1725	6.1976	6.2230	6.2484	6.2738	6.2992	6.3246	6.3500	6.3754

1 inch = 25.4mm

FEET & INCHES TO METRES

FEET	INCHES 0	1	2	3	4	5	6	7	8	9	10	11
	METRES											
21	6.4008	6.4262	6.4516	6.4770	6.5024	6.5278	6.5532	6.5786	6.6040	6.6294	6.6548	6.6802
22	6.7056	6.7310	6.7564	6.7818	6.8072	6.8326	6.8580	6.8834	6.9088	6.9342	6.9596	6.9850
23	7.0104	7.0358	7.0612	7.0866	7.1120	7.1374	7.1628	7.1882	7.2136	7.2390	7.2644	7.2898
24	7.3152	7.3406	7.3660	7.3914	7.4168	7.4422	7.4676	7.4930	7.5184	7.5438	7.5692	7.5946
25	7.6200	7.6454	7.6708	7.6962	7.7216	7.7470	7.7724	7.7978	7.8232	7.8486	7.8740	7.8994
26	7.9248	7.9502	7.9756	8.0010	8.0264	8.0518	8.0772	8.1026	8.1280	8.1534	8.1788	8.2042
27	8.2296	8.2550	8.2804	8.3058	8.3312	8.3566	8.3820	8.4074	8.4328	8.4582	8.4836	8.5090
28	8.5344	8.5598	8.5852	8.6106	8.6360	8.6614	8.6868	8.7122	8.7376	8.7630	8.7884	8.8138
29	8.8392	8.8646	8.8900	8.9154	8.9408	8.9662	8.9916	9.0170	9.0424	9.0678	9.0932	9.1186
30	9.1440	9.1694	9.1948	9.2202	9.2456	9.2710	9.2964	9.3218	9.3472	9.3726	9.3980	9.4234
31	9.4488	9.4742	9.4996	9.5250	9.5504	9.5758	9.6012	9.6266	9.6520	9.6774	9.7028	9.7282
32	9.7536	9.7790	9.8044	9.8298	9.8552	9.8806	9.9060	9.9314	9.9568	9.9822	10.0076	10.0330
33	10.0584	10.0838	10.1092	10.1346	10.1600	10.1854	10.2108	10.2362	10.2616	10.2870	10.3124	10.3378
34	10.3632	10.3886	10.4140	10.4394	10.4648	10.4902	10.5156	10.5410	10.5664	10.5918	10.6172	10.6426
35	10.6680	10.6934	10.7188	10.7442	10.7696	10.7950	10.8204	10.8458	10.8712	10.8966	10.9220	10.9474
36	10.9728	10.9982	11.0236	11.0490	11.0744	11.0998	11.1252	11.1506	11.1760	11.2014	11.2268	11.2522
37	11.2776	11.3030	11.3284	11.3538	11.3792	11.4046	11.4300	11.4554	11.4808	11.5062	11.5316	11.5570
38	11.5824	11.6078	11.6332	11.6586	11.6840	11.7094	11.7348	11.7602	11.7856	11.8110	11.8364	11.8618
39	11.8872	11.9126	11.9380	11.9634	11.9888	12.0142	12.0396	12.0650	12.0904	12.1158	12.1412	12.1666
40	12.1920	12.2174	12.2428	12.2682	12.2936	12.3190	12.3444	12.3698	12.3952	12.4206	12.4460	12.4714

1 inch = 25.4mm

The Donabate and Portrane peninsula is no longer a hidden jewel in the crown of Fingal, thanks to the input and representations of the Chamber of Commerce. Our initiatives over the past 10 years include the village marking stones, the restoration of the John Tayleur anchor and its siting at Portrane,

involvement in the selection of a new sculpture for Donabate ("**The Gate of the Swans**", maquette pictured above), the local business directories and the Donabate and Portrane website. Christmas is heralded each year by the Christmas lighting display. Members of the Chamber participate in numerous committees including the Chamber of Commerce of Fingal, Fingal County Council Strategic Planning Committee for Parks and the Environment, Secondary School Steering Committee, PLATO, Women in Enterprise, Edge Cities to mention a few.

Dates for your diary

Tuesday 4th May, 8pm
Chamber AGM, Unit 12, Donabate Town Center.
Thursday 13th May, 8pm
Fund raising Quiz Night, Keeling's Dome Lounge.
Summer 2004 (date to be confirmed)
Official Unveiling of Donabate Village Sculpture, Donabate Town Centre.
Saturday 4th December
Official Christmas Lights Ceremony, Donabate Town Center.

John Tayleur remembered

Last month marked the 150th anniversary of the sinking o the John Tayleur at Lambay Island with the loss of over 3C lives. There has been keen interest shown at the many talk given in Rush Y.C., Malahide Y.C. and the Donabate and Portrane Community Centre. The Donabate and Portrane Chamber of Commerce encourage you to view the Bower Anchor monument in Portrane erected by the Chamber in conjunction with Fingal County Council in 1998. This A⸱ chor was donated by dive leader **John Finucane** *"as a me morial to those that lost their lives on that terrible night and also as a reminder to the living of our own mortality"*

Donabate & Portrane Chamber of Commerce Newsletter

Donabate and Portrane Chamber of Commerce. Unit 12, Donabate Town Centre, Donabate, Co. Dublin

Celebrating 10 Years

2004 marks our tenth year repre-senting the business community of our peninsula, facilitating network-ing between members, and business to business contacts which over the years have developed into firm friendships. As our community grows through a population level of 10,000 and gains town status the rel-vance of our local Chamber of Commerce cannot be un-restimated. Whether you are a resident business executive, a business owner or aspiring entrepreneur we welcome your input in our local chamber.

arl Harte President

rightening up those winter nights

onabate and Portrane Chamber of Commerce are proud to ave supplied the Christmas Lighting on the peninsula for the st ten years. From our humble beginings, consisting of a sin-e Christmas tree with approximately 120 bulbs located where e shopping centre is now, we now have a new multi-location ghting extravaganza comprising 2,400 light bulbs, 6 coloured oving features and three illuminated Christmas trees, consum-g in excess of 30 kWatts per hour.

Velcome to our new members

warm welcome to all our new members of the Donabate and ortrane Chamber of Commerce. We would like to thank our isting members for their continued support, assistance and en-usiasm in the past year. We would like to encourage our ever-xpanding community in Donabate and Portrane to continue to pport our local businesses.

Support our Quiz Night in aid of annual Christmas Lighting

13th May, Keeling's Pub at 8pm.

DonabatePortrane.com

- Interested in the latest news about our peninsula?
- Looking for information about local services, clubs and societies?
- Or maybe you want to keep up with the burning issues in Donabate and Portrane, and to share your point of view with other residents?

Donabate and Portrane Chamber of Commerce is proud to have a com-munity web site that reflects all the diversity of life in and around our two villages.

The website, **www.donabateportrane.com** brings together pages for local businesses and voluntary groups, which they are able to maintain themselves, as well as an on-line dis-cussion forum where anyone can have their say about topics of local interest. Recent discussions include planning is-sues, train services, local sports, and child care. The site has been a resounding success, clocking up over 7,000 page views per month, and is continuing to build on this extraor-dinary popularity.

So why not add www.donabateportrane.com to your Favourites today?

HOW TO ORDER YOUR PLANS & SPECIFICATIONS

Only one dwelling house may be constructed from a set of BLUEPRINT HOME PLANS. Where a client intends to construct more than one building from the design drawings supplied, special arrangements may be made and additional copies of documents will be furnished.

The designs are copyright of the architect and may not be reproduced without written consent, otherwise infringement of copyright will occur. Design drawings of the book are for illustration only and are not to specific scale. Detailed drawings may indicate minor revisions in dimensions, layout and gross floor area, to satisfy design standards and regulations pertaining at the time of issue, over those drawings published in the book. No responsibility or liability will be held by the Publisher or Designers in respect of such revisions or alterations. The right to revise, amend or remove any design within the book is reserved.

Mirror Images

Mirror images or reversed image plans will be supplied at standard fees, only where the specific design drawings have already been prepared. Where the design drawings have not been prepared, an additional fee will be charged.

Order Form

Complete the order form, using BLOCK CAPITALS for your name and address and forward to the address shown, together with the appropriate remittance.

Personalised Designs

If you require a personalised design or wish to have alterations carried out to one of our standard designs, forward a rough sketch of your requirements for a quote and further advice. Revisions to our standard designs attract a reasonable extra fee. In some cases, the revisions required may have been previously completed and where this is the case, no extra fee will be required.

The Architect will prepare personalised or special house designs and on completion of the design work will supply the master drawings in electronic format. The fees to prepare a special design, excluding the preparation of site plans and maps are based on a fee scale of €10.00 per square metre of floor area, excluding outlay and by agreement prior to commencing final design work. This fee includes initial consultation, a preliminary design drawing, a second consultation if required and completion of final design drawings and specifications. The fee does not include site surveys and investigations and we will rely on the information and maps supplied by the client for the preparation of site location maps and site layout plans if required.

We supply seven copies of our design drawings and specifications drawn to a scale of 1:50 and 1:100 where appropriate. Six copies of the drawings are required by the Local Authority for the purpose of making a planning application.

Fee Schedule

€305.00	TWO BEDROOM HOUSE DESIGNS
€355.00	THREE AND FOUR BEDROOM HOUSE DESIGNS
€375.00	TWO STOREY & DORMER DESIGNS
€50.00	EXTRA COPIES OF PLANS & SPECIFICATIONS
€95.00	GARAGE DESIGNS
€105.00	SITE LOCATION MAPS FROM INFORMATION SUPPLIED
€105.00	SITE LAYOUT PLANS FROM INFORMATION SUPPLIED
€20.00	ADMINISTRATION FEE

If your require as additional, the design drawings in electronic format, we will supply the drawings in ACAD format on a zip disk for a fee of €80. This covers only the cost of the zip disk and the download time.

ORDER FORM

Design Name and Design Number required. (PLEASE USE BLOCK CAPITALS)

Design No. [| |]   **Design Name:** [| | | | | | | | | | | | | | | | | | |]

Blueprint Home Plans with copies of plans and specifications .... € ——

Extra copies of plans and specifications .... € ——

Prepare 1:2500 site maps and I enclose map and details .... € ——

Supply copies of garage and design number _____ € ——

Administration, postage and packing .... € 20.00

Refund cost of Book _____ € 15.00

Total amount enclosed with order form .... €____

SEND YOUR ORDER TO:

Michael J. Allen, FASI. MRICS. FGIS. FCIOB.
Architect & Chartered Building Surveyor
Blueprint Home Plans,
Beechlawns, Kells, Co. Meath.

Telephone: (046) 9240349
Fax: (046) 9241638
Email: allenarchitect@eircom.net

Please forward to:

Name: _____

Address: _____

_____

_____

Telephone no. _____

Please allow fourteen days for
receipt of plans and specifications.

ORDER FORM

Design Name and Design Number required. (PLEASE USE BLOCK CAPITALS)

Design No. [| |]   **Design Name:** [| | | | | | | | | | | | | | | | | | |]

Blueprint Home Plans with copies of plans and specifications .... € ——

Extra copies of plans and specifications .... € ——

Prepare 1:2500 site maps and I enclose map and details .... € ——

Supply copies of garage and design number _____ € ——

Administration, postage and packing .... € 20.00

Refund cost of Book _____ € 15.00

Total amount enclosed with order form .... €____

SEND YOUR ORDER TO:

Michael J. Allen, FASI. MRICS. FGIS. FCIOB.
Architect & Chartered Building Surveyor
Blueprint Home Plans,
Beechlawns, Kells, Co. Meath.

Telephone: (046) 9240349
Fax: (046) 9241638
Email: allenarchitect@eircom.net

Please forward to:

Name: _____

Address: _____

_____

_____

Telephone no. _____

Please allow fourteen days for
receipt of plans and specifications.